MAKING SALES

RECENT VOLUMES IN . . .
SAGE LIBRARY OF SOCIAL RESEARCH

MAKING SALES
Influence as Interpersonal Accomplishment

Robert C. Prus

Volume 172
SAGE LIBRARY OF
SOCIAL RESEARCH

SAGE PUBLICATIONS
The Publishers of Professional Social Science
Newbury Park   London   New Delhi

Copyright © 1989 by Sage Publications, Inc.

For information address:

SAGE Publications, Inc.
2111 West Hillcrest Drive
Newbury Park, California 91320

SAGE Publications Ltd.
28 Banner Street
London EC1Y 8QE
England

SAGE Publications India Pvt. Ltd.
M-32 Market
Greater Kailash I
New Delhi 110 048 India

Printed in the United States of America

Library of Congress Cataloging-in-Publication Data

Prus, Robert C.
    Making sales : influence as interpersonal accomplishment / by
Robert C. Prus.
        p.   cm. — (Sage library of social research ; v. 172)
    Bibliography: p.
    ISBN 0-8039-3409-2.   ISBN 0-8039-3410-6 (pbk.)
    1. Selling.   I. Title.   II. Series.
    HF5438.25.P78 1989
    658.8′5—dc19   88-27621
                                                             CIP

FIRST PRINTING 1989

CONTENTS

DEDICATION

To my daughter, Angela Robin, who always makes the sun shine. . . .

And in memory of Herbert Blumer, who for over 50 years championed a social science focused on the study of social action and grounded in people's lived experiences.

FOREWORD

Pioneering in his subject matter, novel in his approach, Robert Prus has broken new ground with this two-volume study of marketing behavior. In his previous books, *Road Hustlers* and *Hookers, Rounders, and Desk Clerks,* Professor Prus has provided us with an insider's portrait of the worlds of traveling rings of professional card and dice cheaters, and the colorful underside of deviant roles in the rougher hotel scene. Now he brings life to the activities of buyers, sellers, and merchandisers in the respectable community of the marketplace.

In many ways, this project represents a more difficult undertaking. We are all consumers, customers, clients, patients, and buyers, and for that reason, the scenes Prus describes here are ones that we find familiar. While describing the exotic may sometimes be inherently more interesting, to provide a sociological understanding of a mundane arena of everyday life requires a different and more sensitive type of "sociological optic." In these two volumes, we see how sellers (retailers, wholesalers, manufacturers, and promoters) do their business, develop clients, purchase and price products, and generally negotiate the world of mercantile exchange.

In focusing on mercantile exchange, Prus pursues a thread that has run constant throughout his work. His occupational studies, whether of professional criminals, the boundary between the deviant and the respectable, or of legitimate business, are all marked by descriptions of people making human responses to the structural features of their scenes. As such, they tell us about how people go about solving the same problems under very different circumstances. They also all involve, at their base, a pervasive human concern: money. The most symbolic of

15

human media, money provides a key for the insightful and detailed observer of human life to grasp both bold and subtle nuances of human relations, motivations, actions, organization, and, ultimately, social structure. Like Simmel, Prus has chosen to look into the social forms and social relations surrounding money to learn about human behavior generally. By diversifying the focus of his work between legitimate and illegitimate marketplaces, Prus has further created a foundation of knowledge and insights from which to make comparative analysis.

Through his cumulative life's work, and with this set of books in particular, Prus has made a significant and lasting contribution to the vastly underaddressed field of *social economy*. Falling on the cusp between sociology and economics, this area of inquiry has been largely neglected. Those who have looked at human economic behavior have focused mostly on macro dimensions of the economy, or on micro aspects of the psychology of human finance. Both of these have been extremely rationalistic in their approach, and little attention has been focused on the way humans, in groups, or as individuals within groups, make economic decisions. This particularly sociological problem is taken up by Prus in these volumes. In them, he extends our knowledge of human behavior, from the interactionist perspective, to show how people reach for, draw upon, and manipulate human communication, symbolic meanings, relationships, and the norms of the moral order, to accomplish their goals.

In so doing, he also adds to our understanding of symbolic inter-actionist theory and shows its major advantages over other social psychological theories. His depiction of human group life as socially constructed, perspectival, reflective, negotiable, relational, and pro-cessual, combines all of the major tenets of interactionism, and illus-trates for the reader its appropriateness for analyzing any kind of setting, behavior, or interaction. Not only are we provided with a view of buyers and sellers, but of organizations, interactions, stratification, relationships, and social psychological processes.

These volumes are also especially welcome because of the paucity of ethnographic work in this arena. Prus goes into fascinating detail about the world of "marketing and sales." It is ironic that, despite its omnipresence in our lives, this area has received short shrift in the sociological literature. Although a number of books exist that tell us the "hows" of marketing, few exist that phenomenologically describe and explain the subtle nuances, the behind-the-scenes dramas, and the interactional dimensions of selling behavior. To social scientists, the everyday marketplace has remained a rather conspicuous, but understudied, phenomenon. Perhaps too afraid to enter into worlds so close to home, most social scientists have apparently considered the interactional dynamics of marketplace behavior unworthy of study. Prus's penetration beyond the fronts, deceptions, schemes, sales pitches, and dramaturgical presentations that are so characteristic of these scenes has yielded a plethora of consumer commerce. After reading these books, sociological understanding of the marketplace will advance well beyond the mostly formulaic laws laid down by economists, or the attempts at understanding the psyche of the buyer that is so evident in pop psychological treatments of this area, to the inner fabric and underlying, dynamic processes that occur between buyer and seller.

Prus could not have provided such a picture without employing a methodology that remained true to the everyday world he studied. Shunning the standard methods often employed in (largely market research) studies of selling behavior, these books reveal an ethnographic approach that accentuates the richly diverse and contoured reality of marketplace behavior. Prus is searching for generic concepts and features that characterize all selling behavior, drawn from a variety of settings and participants, to provide the reader with a theory that will go beyond the particularistic features of a single type of marketing. He is not satisfied by merely describing the activities, but wants to take us beyond them to show how they sociologically represent a range of interactional procedures. The marketplace, in many ways, is for Prus a metaphor for the daily exchanges we enter into in all walks of life. We, the readers, get the benefits of a wide sampling of sellers, hear them tell us, in their own words, how they do their business, and we are then permitted, along with Prus, to step back and assess these in light of sociological theory and research.

Two volumes may seem a lot to devote to a single work, but with the paucity of information we have had on this behavior, and the relevance it holds to us on a daily basis, the following pages will touch a sensitive nerve in all. These descriptions ring true to our understanding of these scenes. After reading these books, we will obtain a new perspective, the fresh look and unique viewpoint that only a sociological grounding can provide. Dive in, enjoy, learn, and react, for reading these books, like

the scenes they describe, should be an interactional process, where
reader and author, like buyer and seller, negotiate their ways together
and build on the knowledge that we all have as participants in the
mercantile exchanges of human behavior.

Patricia A. Adler
University of Colorado

Peter Adler
University of Denver

ACKNOWLEDGMENTS

During the eight years that I've been studying the marketplace, I've been fortunate in having had the opportunity to discuss this project with a great many people in North America and to a lesser extent scholars around the world. Accordingly, my acknowledgments take several forms.

First and foremost, I would like to thank all of the people in marketing and sales who have so generously shared their life experiences with us. I undertook the task of gathering and assembling this material and trying to present it in a manner that accurately portrays their activities, dilemmas, and adjustments, but their contributions were vital and this book is very much their product. They remain anonymous, but they are most heartily thanked for their input and the education that they have collectively provided for us.

My second set of acknowledgments go to a rather extensive set of colleagues and other benefactors. I am very much indebted to all those who provided assistance and encouragement in the process of developing this material. I know that any listing I might assemble will inevitably miss some to whom I am grateful, so I offer my apologies in advance. With that caveat in mind, allow me to extend my thanks to: Cheryl and Dan Albas, Paul Anderson, Eleen Baumann, Russ Belk, Herbert Blumer, David Booth, Craig Boydell, Dick Brymer, Janet Burns, Diane Clark, Dorothy Counts, Carl Couch, Jim Curtis, Donna Darden, Julie Dembski, Mary Lou Dietz, Robert Emerson, Frank Fasick, Augie Fleras, Wendy Frisby, Mary Gallant, Julie Gigante, Scott Grills, Ed Gross, Gerhard Gruetzmacher, Jack Haas, Ian Hall, Nancy Herman, John Johnson, Ron Lambert, Ed Lemert, Jean Langdon, John Lofland, Stan Lyman, Nancy Mandell, Jim Marks, Barbara McKenzie, Ken Menzies, Sonia Miller, Barabara Ann Mitchell, Rich Mitchell, Tom

Morrione, Frank Nutch, Al Olmstead, Ursula Ortmann, Andrea Pag-
nutty, Trevor Pinch, Howard Robboy, Julius Roth, Ron Roznaczuk,
Susie Russell, Clint Sanders, Marvin Scott, Bill Shaffir, John Sherry,
Charlie Smith, Bob Stebbins, Anselm Strauss, John Swan, Bev Taylor,
Graham Tomlinson, Melanie Wallendorf, Bob Whitehurst, Audry Wip-
per, and Lou Zurcher.

I have also benefited from opportunities to use earlier drafts of this
statement in a course on the sociology of marketing and sales. We've
run the course seven times now, and with enrollments comparable to
those in our deviance and social psychology courses. Not all of these
classes were equally stimulating, but the forums and feedback they
generated were helpful in developing this material into its present form.

I would also like to thank Mitch Allen of Sage for his willingness to
brave new frontiers and for his recognition of the necessity of building
a social science on the lived experiences of people. Finally, I would like
to express my gratitude to Peter and Patti Adler for writing a foreword
to these volumes. I have been immensely impressed with both their
written work and the depth they possess vis-à-vis the interpretive social
sciences. I also value the interest that they have taken in my work over
the years and very much appreciate the time they have taken from their
own highly demanding schedules to share their insights with us.

                                                    —Robert C. Prus

Chapter 1
DOING INFLUENCE WORK

I think that no matter what you do, no matter what your job is, you have to be able to sell, whether it's yourself or your merchandise, whatever [jewelry].

This book has two central objectives. The first and more obvious task is that of providing a fine-grained, ethnographic inquiry into the day-to-day practices of those involved in sales activities. It is an attempt to portray sales work as it is experienced and worked out by the people involved. Using interview, observation, and participant observation materials, the emphasis is on providing a careful, thorough analysis of the ways in which those involved in sales pursue their tasks at hand. The material on sales has been organized around the "doing of activities" or the "ongoing social production of action." And, through the extensive use of quotations, the participants provide much insight into the ways in which they accomplish their activities by directly speaking about their lived experiences. Thus, rather than attempt to provide "magic formulae for success" or advice on "how to sell a million," this monograph depicts the dilemmas, strategies, practical limitations, frustrations, and excitement experienced by vendors in their dealings with the customers they encounter.

The second, and theoretically more consequential objective is that of providing an empirically "grounded" (Glaser and Strauss, 1967) conceptual statement on "influence as interpersonal accomplishment." Insofar as people may attempt to influence (and resist) one another in all realms of group life, a study of persuasion practices can be seen as generating concepts applicable to human relations regardless of context. Focusing on the processes by which people endeavor to "get their own ways" in their dealings with others, the material developed herein is exceedingly fundamental to questions of the sort following. How do people influence one another? How do they pursue their interests in their dealings with others? What sorts of resistances do they encounter? How do they endeavor to neutralize these obstacles? How do people obtain commitments from others? How do they develop long-term bonds and lines of influence? What dilemmas do they face? How do people sustain enthusiasm in the face of possible rejection? This volume cannot provide complete answers to these questions, but a detailed examination of sales activities generates considerable insight into the ways in which influence work is accomplished in everyday life.

Given these dual tasks, generating a detailed, ethnographic account of the selling process and developing a grounded (Glaser and Strauss, 1967) statement on the influence process, it is hoped that all readers will develop a fuller appreciation of the dynamics of marketplace exchanges and the wide-sweeping significance of examining influence as interpersonal accomplishment. With a focus on the "social fabric of marketplace exchanges," this book details the processes by which salespeople encourage prospective customers to purchase their products on both an immediate (or situated) and a sustained (or ongoing) basis. Considering the ways in which people attempt to shape the interests, pursuits, and commitments of others, it is most fundamentally an examination of the social production of action.

In contrast to those who envision customers as the passive targets of vendor enterprise, this statement explicitly acknowledges customers' abilities not only to resist vendor efforts (i.e., as elusive targets), but also their abilities to shape the eventual directions and outcomes of their interchanges with salespeople. Hence, while this project is very much vendor based, the emphasis throughout is on an interactive model of persuasion. Vendors are also customers in their other dealings in the marketplace,[1] but much more important for our immediate purposes is the recognition that vendors are ultimately dependent on buyer interpretations and cooperation. Vendors may engage in extensive preparations in their attempts to anticipate and direct customer encounters.[2] However, each and every encounter remains to be worked out by the parties involved. And, although we typically envision buyers as the targets of salespeople's enterprises, we should recognize that vendors may serve as targets in the pursuits of prospective buyers. Prospects can shop around and may "work" vendors for deals of various sorts as well as pursue warranties and other terms of sale (e.g., return policies, matching prices) with considerable intensity.

Attending to Activity

While much overlooked as an arena of study by social scientists,[3] the marketplace represents a setting rich in human dynamics (and contrasts). Marketplaces are often envisioned in terms of locations, structures, decor, and displays, and these elements are important in denoting "shells" of sorts or focal points around which a considerable amount of trade may take place. But it is not the location, the structure, the decor, or the displays that define the marketplace. It is through the preparations, the reflective deliberations, the interchanges, and the adjustments that people make that the essence of marketplace is realized. Particular locations may offer vendors and buyers certain conveniences, as may structures of various sorts, or various props and signs, but these elements are important only to the extent that people incorporate them into their selling and purchasing routines. Vendors may very well attempt to foster trade by defining the settings in which they plan to conduct trade (and this "forging of action" then becomes important for our purposes). However, it is vital that we view the marketplace not as a shell but as a setting defined by human association and all implied therein. The marketplace is thoroughly and fundamentally social in its constitution. It involves preparation and adjustment, planning and uncertainty, persuasion and resistance, trust and skepticism, commitment and reservation, dreams and disappointments, frustration and excitement, as well as friendship and animosity. Marketplace activity reflects people's past experiences and their anticipations of the future, but it takes its shape in the here and now as people work out aspects of their lives in conjunction with the other people whose lives intersect with their own.

A WORLD OF IMAGES

Like other realms of human endeavor, the marketplace is a setting fundamentally steeped in images. Despite the physical qualities that people may associate with particular products (or mediums of exchange), exchanges are symbolic in their essence. In purchasing products, people are not only buying all of the images (e.g., comfort, style, prestige, performance, reliability, savings, "newness," and the like) that they associate with particular products, but also all of the images that they have of vendors (stores, manufacturers, salespeople) involved. Similarly, as the recipients of the goods the buyers offer in exchange (e.g., money, livestock, produce), sellers work with images of what these items mean to them. Influence work thus becomes a matter of "image work." It is first and foremost symbolic activity. These images overlap and exist in a very precarious manner, one to another, but they are all dependent on people's ongoing associations with others for their essence and existence. While people may take certain aspects of the setting for granted as they concentrate on acquiring particular objects, it is in the (social) production of action that people see the very world (of images) unfolding before their eyes.

AN INTERACTIVE THEATRE

Viewed in terms of influence and images, the marketplace becomes a dynamic, interactive theater. People's existing "stocks of knowledge" (Schutz, 1971) may be seen to provide them with generalized "scripts" with which to approach their respective roles as buyers and sellers.[4] But since each exchange has to be enacted anew and the participants may have a great many concerns other than merely maintaining particular (and not necessarily important) notions of marketplace association, these generalized anticipations often fade into the backgrounds as the participants endeavor to work out their interests in conjunction with the others whose lives intersect with their own.

Both parties are able to plan, and both may try to anticipate the positions of the other. Likewise, as Goffman (1959) would emphasize, both parties can selectively project (accentuate, conceal, and misrepresent) images of self, other, and other objects, using a variety of props and ploys. As a result, their encounters assume a problematic and emergent quality. Not only may each have considerable difficulty ascertaining the positions and strategies of the other, but both parties may find that their definitions of objects, their interests, and their strategies for interaction undergo change (sometimes quite dramatically) as they attempt to adjust to encounters that are effectively being constituted as they interact with one another.

GENERIC IMPLICATIONS

Working with these understandings, we ask not why someone bought or sold this or that item, or what caused (or made) someone to do this or that, but rather we ask how human interchange is accomplished. We focus on the ways in which encounters, "successful" or otherwise, are worked out by the people involved. And while this material is empirically grounded in the marketplace experiences of those engaged in sales, by no means do its implications end here.

To the contrary, the emphasis on activities (and the processes by which activities are constituted) provides us with conceptual material seemingly applicable to all human associations. As a result, the investigation of interpersonal accomplishment in this setting enables us to extend our knowledge of human relations (social psychology et al.) as this pertains to the ways in which people attempt to (1) promote interest in objects (ideas, beliefs, life-styles, people, and so on) on the part of others, (2) generate trust (i.e., a sense of confidence, credibility, reliability, performance) on the part of others (3) neutralize any reservations or resistances they may encounter in their dealings with others, (4) pursue and obtain any manner of commitments from others, (5) define and manage disruptions involving other people, (6) foster long-term relationships with other people, and (7) maintain enthusiasm in their pursuits in both immediate and long-term respects.[5] The marketplace provides us with much rich material with which to examine the promotion of generalized viewpoints as well as more specific images of objects, the development of personal and group-focused identities, the initiation, stabilization, and dissipation of relationships, and the actualities of negotiation via persuasion, resistance, commitments, and evasions.

While substantively situated in the marketplace, the transsituational or "generic" social processes (Prus, 1987) outlined herein have immense implications for our understanding of group life. Providing much heretofore unexplored mapping into very basic features of human association, *Making Sales* should be of interest to anyone interested in the dynamics of "people work" or the study of human behavior. Thus, although people involved in the marketplace as buyers or sellers may find much material of particular substantive relevance, people interested in the ways in which identities, persuasion, negotiation, and relationships are accomplished in other settings are also likely to find much that they can glean conceptually from this statement. For instance, people focusing on peer relations or friendship, or those involved in dating, marital, or family relationships could readily apply many of the concepts developed herein to those settings. Similarly, those attending to professional services, such as those involving doctors, dentists, stock brokers, or bankers and their relationships with their clientele will find much material of significance in understanding these situations. Likewise, those interested in the clergy and their congregations, artists or entertainers and their audiences, or politicians and their publics would encounter a great many conceptual parallels of consequence, as would those who wish to consider interchanges among managers and their staffs, union leaders and their members, coaches and their players, teachers and their students, or agency workers and their clients.

The conceptual scheme developed herein is relevant to all these settings, and others wherein people attempt to work out their interests in conjunction with others. The marketplace represents only one setting in which to explore the ways in which human behavior is accomplished. However, by examining the manners in which vendors assemble their activities in their dealings with others, we arrive at a better understanding of the processes by which group life is constituted more generally.

For readers well acquainted with the contents of *Pursuing Customers* (Prus, 1989), the next several sections of this chapter (vendor activities in context, the literature, basic premises, buyer behavior, and the data base) will appear largely redundant. For those not familiar with that volume, however, this material is exceedingly central in establishing the contextual and conceptual core of the present volume (and the larger project from which this statement was derived). The last section of this chapter provides a summary overview of the topics covered in this volume.

Vendor Activities in Context

Selling is moving a product, anything that you are doing to convince people to make the purchase, the benefits. . . . Selling is doing all the things that it takes to get the order, to make the sale. So selling is providing a service, and setting up the displays, and talking to the people, selling is fitting things into their stores, selling is the travel, the order taking and the collecting, all those things, and more [wholesale—giftware].

As will become apparent as the material unfolds, marketing (and sales) consists of a plurality of activities,[6] each of which is dependent on the others for overall effect.[7] Thus how one structures one's business will have implications for styles of management, buying supplies, pricing, recruiting customers, presenting products, developing loyal customers, and vice versa. The same is true in reference to the other activities. How one buys can affect the prices one charges, the ways customers are recruited, how products are presented, and so on. Changes in any aspect of one's marketing procedure can affect the significance of each of the other components. The effect of any marketing program is not, however, a direct function of the ways in which vendors define their activities. Since sales are contingent on the cooperation of the buyers, any changes in the prospective buyers' interests or options can dramatically affect the effectiveness of any and all of these activities.

From the material collected (in the larger project from which this volume is derived), 15 areas of activity have emerged as central to understanding marketing and sales. These 15 activities subsequently have been organized around two more basic themes, reflecting vendor preparations (in pursuit of customer contact) and interpersonal sales processes. While the present volume, *Making Sales,* has focused primarily on influence processes in interpersonal settings, it is most important that the material be presented here be contextualized relative to those activities in which vendors engage in preparation for, and in anticipation of, these interpersonal encounters.

A companion volume, *Pursuing Customers,* addresses the preparations that vendors make in anticipation of customer encounters. These stage-setting activities not only reflect vendor anticipations of the behaviors of both the competitors they envision on the horizon and the customers with whom they expect to deal in the future, but these preparations also reflect ongoing vendor adjustments to both the customers with whom they have previously dealt and their appraisals of their competitors' activities to date. Thus these adjustments assume a dialectic, processual quality. While vendors act in the present, they are acting in reference to their assessments of their past experiences and the (rather unpredictable) future. Further, they live in an interactive world, a world in which their outcomes reflect not only their own enterprises, but are also shaped by the activities of all of those whose lives intersect with those of the vendors. Accordingly, *Pursuing Customers* is very much a study of the anticipation of "the generalized other" (Mead, 1934). Most people (as consumers) seem much more sensitive to the drama (i.e., their dilemmas, sacrifices, risks) entailed in direct interpersonal encounters with vendors, but vendors most acutely experience their dilemmas, investments, and gambles in setting the stage for their encounters with the generalized other. This is not to imply that vendors do not experience pressure and tactical dilemmas in dealing with the specific people they encounter in the course of doing business or that these individual encounters are not consequential to the overall success of that business. However, it is in the activities involved in preparing for these (necessarily ambiguous) encounters that vendors are most cognizant of the dramatic nature of their undertakings.

The present text, *Making Sales,* builds on these ongoing background preparations and adjustments, but primarily focuses on vendors' direct encounters with prospective buyers. The emphasis is on what is sometimes termed, "eye-to-eye, belly-to-belly selling." It is an examination of "people work" as evidenced by the social production of interest and trust, the neutralization of skepticism and the pursuit of commitment, the management of trouble, the development of more enduring relationships, the promotion and the drawbacks of creating action, and the problematics of sustaining enthusiasm. It is a study of the ways in which interpersonal encounters are constituted. The tactics vendors invoke in pursuing buyer cooperation are considered, but so are their dilemmas and hesitations, their concerns with immediate and long-term buyer relations, and the difficulties they face in trying to accomplish their objectives while dealing with buyers who are also tacticians in their own right.

The material following provides an overview of these activities relative to the emphases of these two volumes

Pursuing Customers
  Setting Up Business
  (options, formats, ownership dilemmas)
  Doing Management
  (responsibilities, staffing, performance)
  Purchasing Products
  (concerns, gaming, relationships)
  Setting prices
  (price, value, profit)
  Using the Media
  (tasks, formats, dilemmas)
  Working the Field
  (prospecting, calls, pressures)
  Exhibiting Products
  (location, displays, assessments)

Making Sales
   Presenting Products
   (approach, qualification, interest)
   Generating Trust
   (integrity, quality, obligations)
   Neutralizing Resistance
   (skepticism, price, loyalties)
   Obtaining Commitments
   (closings, groups, dilemmas)
   Encountering Troublesome Customers
   (carelessness, rudeness, returns)
   Developing Loyalty
   (service, signification, contact)
   Holding "Sales"
   ("bargains," action, dilemmas)
   Maintaining Enthusiasm
   (pressures, slumps, support)

The Literature

To locate better the present statement within a broader context, it seems advisable to consider the efforts to date of other researchers in marketing and sociology (as a representative of the social sciences).[8]

THE MARKETING TRADITION

There is a very large marketing and sales literature. This literature is also quite diverse. It ranges from "quick and slick ways to sell a million" and popular applied business, characterized by practical advice on all sorts of business matters, to "scientific" attempts to better predict and control the business world, generally by using experimental and survey data. Mixed between and variously reflecting these emphases is a wide selection of textbooks presenting elementary and advanced statements on the "art and science" of marketing. While these texts generally have a chapter or two on the social sciences, this material is very limited. The desirability of incorporating sociology and psychology into marketing schemes is often emphasized, with general references to Maslow's (1954) vague statement on the "hierarchy of needs,"[9] Hyman's (1960, generally uncited) concept of "reference groups," Festinger's (1957) theory of "cognitive dissonance," Warner and Lunt's (1941) and Warner et al.'s (1949) analysis of "social class." In large part, this material seems intended to provide insight into customer motivations. These themes are sometimes supplemented with material indicating the desirability of conducting demographic (e.g., age, class, gender, ethnic compositions) analyses of prospective populations of customers; the implication is that certain categories of persons would be more apt to have certain interests in making purchasing decisions. This material, which largely focuses on consumers, is then left behind as marketing and sales procedures are discussed. In discussing the role of the vendor, the emphasis is extensively on definitions and technical prescriptions with the seeming inference that good technicians would do the proper thing at the right time in the appropriate degree. Scant attention is paid to vendors as persons in situations that remain to be worked out with others (prospective customers). As Bagozzi (1979), Enis (1979), and Lutz (1979) so aptly note, marketers have spent a great deal of time developing models and giving advice, but have given minimal consideration to the actualities of marketplace activities, interactions, and the relationships emerging therein.[10] Unfortunately, their observations have not been heeded by most academic practitioners. Long-standing traditions and (the related) gatekeepers of the major journals in this area have largely disregarded these notions. This is even more ironic in light of the practitioner backgrounds of many of those in marketing schools. Insofar as they, themselves, have run businesses, engaged in saleswork, tried management, and the like, one would expect to see more evidence of their own lived experiences in their depictions of the marketplace. Instead, it is as though they operate with two largely nonintegrated sets of knowledge—their own lived experiences and what might be termed *academic positivism.*[11]

The American Marketing Association recently defined *marketing* in the following manner:

Marketing is the process of planning and executing the conception, pricing, promotion, and distribution of ideas, goods, and services to create exchanges that satisfy individual and organizational objectives. [*Marketing News:* March 1, 1985).

This view of marketing as a "process," subject to planning and implementation, is very consistent with the material presented in this text and its companion volume, *Pursuing Customers.* However, in contrast to the more traditional marketing literature, the material contained in these two volumes focuses more directly on the manner in which these activities are actually accomplished.

SOCIOLOGY ET AL.

For their part, the social sciences have given very little attention to the study of marketing and sales. This is not to say that there is no theory that could be applied to this activity, only that there has been little work done in this area by social scientists. Most applications of social science concepts to this realm reflect the initiatives of marketing people. They recognize that marketing involves people, but are not familiar with much that the social sciences could offer. Without going into much detail, the work in sociology seems typical of the social sciences more generally.[12]

Despite the centrality of marketing and sales for industry and general consumption, one finds relatively few sociological studies of this phenomenon. While purporting interest in all facets of society, this very significant aspect of group life has been largely neglected by sociologists.[13] The bases of this oversight are unclear, but may reflect some combination of the following: (1) the stigma attached to "crass and commercial" activities by social scientists,[14] (2) a tendency to see business as consisting of mundane exchanges,[15] (3) a perception that business people (and/or economists) have already done this or are more adequately equipped to study marketing activity, (4) minimal personal contact and/or familiarity with this setting, (5) an anticipation of resistance to sociological inquiry on the part of business people, (6) a lack of government funding for sociological research in this area, (7) an anticipated lack of interest on the part of other sociologists and/or limited opportunities for publishing in this area,[16] (8) a lack of conceptual tradition in this subject matter,[17] and (9) a definition of some sociologists as "their mission being that of critics of capitalist society."[18]

There is a sociological literature pertinent to business, but much of this material has remained subterranean relative to the discipline, and very little integrative work (or even cross-referencing) exists. As a result, this literature is very uneven in character and emphasis. Other than the present project, there has been little attempt on the part of sociologists to approach systematically the larger field of marketing and sales.

For those wishing to familiarize themselves with the range of this literature, the following listing is provided:

In brief reviews of the literature, Lazarsfeld (1959) and Foxall (1974) lament the neglect of business and consumer behavior by sociologists; while Tucker (1964) posits that there is a "social base to economic behavior."

Among the inquiries into the retail sector, some consideration has been given to department and other store settings (MacLean, 1899; Donovan, 1929; Lombard, 1955; French, 1958, 1960; Sofer, 1965; Caplovitz, 1973; Greenberg, 1980), mall life (Jacobs, 1984), automobile sales (Miller, 1964; Browne, 1973; Valdez, 1984), real estate operations (Angrist, 1955, 1984; House, 1977), and time-sharing programs involving vacation accommodations (Katovich and Diamond, 1986).

Other retail endeavors sampled by sociologists include antiques (Maisel, 1966), flea markets (Maisel, 1974), street markets (Pinch and Clark, 1986), auctions (Clark and Halford, 1978); Olmstead, 1986); Smith, 1986), home party plans (Peven, 1968; Prus and Frisby, 1989), door to door sales (Bogdan, 1972; Stets-Kealey, 1984); hippie enterprises (Cavan, 1972), art markets (Levine, 1972; McCall, 1977; Becker, 1982), and "race horse sales" (Lilly and Ball, 1979).

As well, attention has been directed toward a variety of service-related exchanges such as those involving junk dealers (Ralph, 1950), watch repairers (Strodtbeck and Sussman, 1956), cab drivers (Davis, 1959; Henslin, 1968), milkmen (Bigus, 1972), contractors (Glaser, 1972), doctors (Hayes-Bautista, 1976; Kasteller et al., 1976), insurance adjustors (Ross, 1970), and lawyers (Darden et al., 1981).

Also noteworthy in the retail setting are materials focusing on consumer behavior (Stone, 1954; Caplovitz, 1963, 1974, 1979; Glock and Nicosa, 1964; Nicosa and Mayer, 1976; Wallendorf, 1978; Wiseman, 1979), fashions (Kaiser, 1985; Sanders, 1985, 1988; Solomon, 1985), "troublesome customers" (Roth, 1965; Siporin, 1967; Eaton, 1980; Karikas and Rosenwassen, 1980), and debt collection practices (Rock, 1973; Bass, 1983). Additionally, some attention has been directed toward market research (Jacobs, 1979) and advertising (Schudson, 1984).

At another level, sociologists have also tapped into buyer-supplier relations (Kriesberg, 1956; Macaulay, 1963), purchasing departments (Strauss, 1962, 1964), and franchisee-franchisor relations (Sklar, 1973,

1977). While much neglected, Simmel (1900, 1978) provides a most valuable statement on the "philosophy of money" and the relative relationships of price, value, and supply and demand. Nevertheless, some of these themes have been explored in studies of financial markets (Glick, 1957; Adler, 1981; Smith, 1981; Adler and Adler, 1984) and the setting of rental fees (Gilderbloom, 1985). Some consideration has also been given to the "selling of communities" to corporate investors (Prus and Fleras, 1987). Others have studied self-images and status problems of salespeople (Howton and Rosenberg, 1965; Ditz, 1967), elements affecting success (French, 1960), vendor-seller traits (Evans, 1963), and the professionalization of real estate (Hughes, 1979) and insurance (Bain, 1959) sales-related groups.

Finally, albeit involving "disrespectability," some valuable insights into the practice of business may be gleaned from the deviance literature. Relevant in this respect are studies of black market operations (Clinard, 1969), fencing (Klockars, 1975; Walsh, 1977), fiddling and pilferage (Ditton, 1977; Henry, 1978), bookmaking (Hindelang, 1971; Lesieur, 1977; and Prus and Sharper, 1977), drug dealing (Carey, 1968; Adler and Adler, 1983; Fields, 1984; and Adler, 1985), and the sales of sexual and related entertainment commodities (Cressey, 1932; Velarde, 1973; Hong et al., 1975; Rasmussen and Kuhn, 1976; Prus and Irini, 1988; and Luckenbill, 1984). Additionally, one finds some consideration of trust violations within legitimate businesses (Sutherland, 1949; Cressey, 1953; Quinney, 1963; Leonard and Weber, 1970; Farberman, 1975; and Clinard and Yeager, 1980).

Despite the seemingly impressive array of sources just cited,[19] and the value of each item included in the preceding listing, it is important to recognize the limited forays of sociologists into the interaction dynamics characterizing the marketplace. The marketplace may be seen to epitomize human interchange, but we have learned little of the social dynamics of exchange from this setting. Insofar as any theme may be seen to dominate the literature, it reflects the desirability of studying the marketplace in ethnographic (observations, participation, interviews) terms. Even here, however, one finds relatively little attempt to locate these studies within the broader dimensions of the marketplace. Accordingly, by focusing on activities generic to a wide range of products and marketing formats, it is hoped that the present undertaking will also serve as an integrative frame for subsequent inquiry.

Basic Premises

Within the social sciences, one finds two basic approaches to the study of human behavior. The more prevalent or mainstream perspective is that of (quantitative) *positivism*, which assumes that people can and should be studied in much the same ways that one might study other physical entities. The emphasis in this approach is on causation (what makes people do this or that) and is accompanied by a search for "factors" thought to determine people's behavior. While some researchers envision their tasks as contributing to the accumulation of knowledge, a prominent objective is that of predicting human behavior with an eye to controlling or redirecting human behavior.

Although characterized by significant conceptual (causal foci) variations, positivism in the social sciences is very much rooted in the works of the French sociologist Auguste Comte (1830-1842), and the British psychologist John Stuart Mill (1843). Defining reality as rather synonymous with quantitative data (especially survey and experimental data),[20] positivism operates with a mechanistic (robotoid) view of human behavior. People are seen to react to (presumed) objective conditions because of internal (psychological) or external (sociological) forces or factors acting upon them.

Positivists vary considerably in the attributions they make to the people they are purporting to study, but the dominant image that emerges is that people operate in a singular, objective reality, engage in little or no consequential reflective activity, operate largely autonomously (disaffiliated manners) both in the short run and the long term, and produce behavioral outcomes by virtue of various factors acting upon or through them (i.e., the term *billiard ball determinism*).[21]

In contrast, those assuming an interpretive approach to the study of human behavior contend that we need to study human behavior as it is experienced by those whose lives we are purporting to understand. This approach is grounded in the everyday experiences of people and focuses on the ways in which they work out (construct) their associations with others. It is not proposed that we be "unscientific" in the process. However, if we are to study human behavior, then we have an obligation to recognize that people are different from other objects in some very basic respects, and to incorporate explicitly these features into our theoretical and methodological approaches to the social sciences.

Building on "symbolic interactionism" (Mead, 1934; Blumer, 1969) and "reality construction theory" (Berger and Luckmann, 1966),[22] one may delineate five premises central to understanding how people work out their interests and activities with one another on a day-to-day basis.

These premises or baseline assumptions are: (1) the world can have multiple meanings to people (people act toward objects in terms of the meanings they have for them); (2) people have capacities for taking themselves (and others) into account when developing lines of action toward objects (including self and others); (3) meanings are shaped by people's interaction with others, (4) people develop particular bonds with others, and (5) human life has an emergent nature. In short, human behavior is seen as perspectival, reflective, negotiable, relational and processual. This approach is concerned with studying and analyzing human behavior, mindful of the perspectives of the people involved, the ways in which these people interpret situations, the ways in which they influence one another's actions, the particular interconnections people establish with others, and the ways in which the participants actively (in process) construct their activities. Given their centrality for the approach undertaken in this volume, each of these points will be examined in greater detail.

INTERACTION AS PERSPECTIVAL

> Sales is much like performing. I've worked on stage. . . . There's a lot of similarity between stand-up comedy and pleasing the client, bring a smile to their face and making a sale on a one-to-one basis [mixed sales].

As the preceding extract suggests, whether people make sales or are successful as entertainers depends on their abilities to relate to their audiences; and audiences may have quite different notions of desirable goods and enjoyable entertainment. Rather than presuming an objective or stimulus reality that all persons experience similarly, it is more accurate to envision multiple (and symbolic) realities. Objects do not have inherent meanings for humans. Humans attribute meanings to objects, and these meanings reflect the perspectives (frames of reference, worldviews) to which those people have been exposed and presently operate. One can find all sorts of variations in meanings attributed to objects (e.g., sex, religion, and policies) in our own society,[23] and one has only to watch the socialization of the young to realize that meanings (and valuings) of objects are learned. Objects become meaningful when located within a group's symbolic system. Thus parents may buy children toys that they (the parents) find attractive only to find the children more interested in the packaging than the toy. To play appropriately, children have to acquire perspectives on how to play with toys; that a toy gun is not a hammer, or that a doll is not a projectile, for instance. Likewise, a wooden chair may be seen as something to be sat upon, but this phenomenon can also be used as a weapon (in barroom brawls for example), a means of defense (from a lion), a stand for giving speeches or for a flower pot, a door jamb, kindling for a fire, an eyesore, an antique, and so on.

Consistent with this discussion of the chair, we can intend or presume objects to have specific meanings, but we are always dependent on the interpretations of others for the confirmation of our reality. Clearly, the same objects can have different meanings to different audiences at the same time. They can also have different meanings to the same audiences at different times, and even to the same audience at the same time. Orrin Klapp's (1962, 1964, 1971) analysis of "heroes," "villains," and "fools" is illustrative here. From Klapp's discussion of the processes by which people become known as "social types," it becomes readily apparent that one audience's villain may be another audience's hero, and yet be considered a fool by a third audience. In the sales setting, this suggests that each customer may view the same product differently, and that products thought to be attractive or good buys by a vendor may be perceived in similar or different ways from one customer to the next.

It is also evident that the same audience can attribute quite different meanings to the same object over time. A person earlier defined as a hero (as a result of a particular activity) may later be redefined as a fool or a villain by the same audience when it is reconsidering the very same event. Formerly stylish clothes (once much desired) may be given away to obtain closet space when newer styles are popular. Similarly, customers happy with purchases at one time may, upon further reflection, decide to return the goods. These goods need not have changed in any way for these people to now define them as inappropriate, too costly, and such.

People may also attribute different meanings to the same object at the same time. For instance, one may define another as a villain, but simultaneously admire his resourcefulness, defiance, courage, and so on. An attractive item may also be defined as costly, fragile, dangerous, and the like. These multiple and potentially shifting definitions have important implications for understanding the valuing of goods by prospects and their willingness to enter transactions with particular vendors. They are critical for vendors as they endeavor to assess prospects, do presentations, attempt to compete sales, and build a repeat clientele. From the vendor's perspective, it means coming to terms with multiple and shifting sets of meanings that prospects (and existing customers) attribute to and/or associate with themselves, the items under consideration, and the vendors involved.

While the meanings of objects are audience-specific and reflect the perspectives of those audiences, one also encounters a sense of objectivity in reference to object definitions. Thus, although I may never have met the reader, I presume that the reader will have somewhat shared interpretations of the symbols (letters and words) printed on this page. A sense of objectivity seems evident. It should be noted, however, that our sense of objectivity in this instance (and in all others) rests on the presumption of shared perspectives (those with which others would agree). People unfamiliar with the English language may be able to make little (if any) sense out of this material. People unfamiliar with books may view this phenomenon in untold ways, possibly using it as a window prop, a projectile, an object on which to stand, material for starting a fire, and so forth, ad infinitum. What is considered objective seems better recognized as reflecting "intersubjective consensus" (Schutz, 1971); an affirmation of shared perspectives and definitions on the part of communicating parties.

This sense of objectivity, however, is promoted from first contact with a group. Thus, for instance, newborns enter a social world, but one that has no immediate meaning for them. As they acquire rudiments of the symbolic realities of others, and begin to internalize the perspectives to which they are exposed, we may speak of them becoming "minded beings." They will be taught to identify and label objects in manners approximating those with whom they have contact. They will be taught value systems and shown techniques for doing things. They will be given perspectives for interpretation and communication. And, unless this knowledge about the world is challenged, it is apt to be considered natural and objective, denoting paramount reality.

INTERACTION AS REFLECTIVE

As perspectives are internalized, they represent "frames of reference" (Shibutani, 1961) for the actor's behavior. The world becomes known through (and acted toward in terms of) these perspectives. It is in this respect that we may speak of people as having minds or as engaging in minded activity. Mind develops through interaction with others, as persons acquire perspectives for interpreting and conceptualizing the world they encounter. Although minded activity takes place within the brain, the two are not synonymous. The brain is the physiological locus of mental activity, but the mind denotes the ongoing process of acquiring perspectives, interpreting, and conceptualizing the phenomena one encounters.

Especially significant in the acquisition of perspectives is the *definition of oneself as an object* in a world of other objects. The capacity of humans to be *self-reflective,* to be objects unto themselves, to have a self-identity is one of the most crucial elements in the understanding of human behavior. It means that humans can communicate or converse with themselves, about themselves. People thus not only interpret all phenomena from certain perspectives, but they can fit themselves into their interpretations and their anticipated lines of action. They are recipients of action, but they are also planners and doers. As entities capable of making self-indications and fitting themselves into anticipated lines of action, humans not only live on the past but also invoke images of the future ("What if . . . ?") as they work their way through the present. People interpret (define, assess) their situations on an ongoing basis, and they can act back on (plan, maneuver, accept, resist) those acting toward them as their encounters take place.

Another aspect of minded behavior is the recognition that others also operate from particular perspectives and have the capacity for self-reflective behavior. These realizations seem to occur on a variety of levels, but (regardless of levels) have important implications for one's interpretations (and behaviors). One may take others into account in both specific and general ways. The term *role taking* is used by the interactionists (Mead, 1934) to refer to situations in which people try to define the perspectives from which another (specific) person is operating (i.e., achieve some understanding of the other's concerns, interests, values, meanings). Denoting role taking on a more extensive basis, the "generalized other" (Mead, 1934) signifies a sensitivity to the perspectives of people more generally (i.e., What would they think?).

The value of these concepts (mind, self-reflectivity, and role taking) for understanding marketing and sales activity seems indisputable. Both vendors and buyers have perspectives on the marketplace and both may take themselves and others (generally or specifically) into account interpreting the activities of others and developing strategies of their own. Both may also attempt to manage the impressions they give off to each other. As objects unto themselves, people not only interpret the activities of others, they can intentionally construct their own activities in an attempt to promote selective interpretations of the part of others. While they need not be accurate in their predictions of others' definitions of them, actors can endeavor to "present themselves" (Goffman, 1959) in ways they feel would most facilitate their interests (i.e., exercise control over how they present themselves to others); and may assess one another in terms of strategy and sincerity.

INTERACTION AS NEGOTIABLE

Notions of persuasion and resistance are also central to an analysis of human behavior. While people may define objects in an infinite number of ways, and can engage in conversation with the self, these capacities are predicated on persons actively participating in a world of other people. Through those with whom they associate, people not only develop their preliminary symbolic systems (language) and their senses of self (as symbolic essences), but it is with other people that they work out their lived experiences on an ongoing (day-to-day, moment-to-moment) basis. Thus we attend to the manners in which these minded, reflective beings shape their realities in conjunction with others.

By depicting objects (regardless of whether they are, so called, tangibles or intangibles) in certain ways, people may be able to alter the meanings others hold for those items. Similarly, by providing alternative perspectives, actors may dramatically affect the ways in which others interpret the same situations. In all cases, however, the success of attempted redefinitions of symbolic significances is dependent on acknowledgment by the other party or parties. Negotiations may be largely promoted by one party, but both parties to an exchange may attempt to redefine the significance of any exchange. And both parties may be somewhat successful in doing so, all the while realizing that they may both be doing this. The participants to an exchange may also find their objectives (relative to one another) shifting considerably as the interaction sequence unfolds. Likewise, actors may intensify or reduce the significance of their interests (those of self and/or others) as they interact.

People may invoke a wide variety of strategies (sequentially or simultaneously) as they attempt to work out their interests (preexisting and emerging) in an interactive context. Beyond ongoing interpretations, comparisons, and evaluations, people may (for instance) reveal, conceal, stall, hedge, joke, and bluff. Likewise, they may exhibit enthusiasm, surprise, skepticism, condemnation, become intimate or distant. They can seek support from others as well as make compromises to others. In the process of interacting with one another, people may move far and in unexpected directions from their earlier anticipations. This means, for example, that an agreement on the purchase of a particular item is much more a conclusion of an exchange than the embodiment of the exchange. Similarly, settlements or agreements to exchange specific items need not signify the end of exchanges in which buyers and sellers are involved. Were one to focus only on the actual changing hands of goods, one would miss the large substance of doing business.

INTERACTION AS RELATIONAL

Insofar as people tend to develop particularistic bonds or affiliations with others and take these relationships into account in developing their activities, these interconnections represent additional elements to which we would want to attend in developing a more complete awareness of human behavior.

In discussing relationships, we would not only want to recognize the capabilities of people to become involved in multiple (and possibly conflicting) relationships on an overlapping basis, but also the unfolding or processual nature of these relationships, the abilities of people to redefine the viability of these relationships over time, and the precarious nature of people's relationships with others. These associations may vary greatly along several dimensions (e.g., fleeting versus enduring, limited versus unlimited choices, specific versus multicontext). But insofar as people take these associations into account in formulating and implementing their lines of action, these relationships emerge as exceedingly central to an understanding of human behavior.

Given both the immediate impact of sales relationships on buyers' purchasing commitments and the significance of repeat patronage to the success (or demise) of most businesses, a consideration of relationships is most consequential to a fuller appreciation of buyer-seller exchanges. This seems especially important in view of the alternatives buyers have in "free choice" markets. Thus, for instance, while buyers seem most amenable to vendor influence (negotiation) when they experience higher levels of ambiguity and urgency, vendors who are accorded higher levels of trust seem especially effective in this regard. Not only do the suggestions of vendors with whom buyers have established trust relationships seem more likely to be accepted, but these vendors are also more likely to be sought out when these buyers feel more uncertain of their options. Representing a collage of competitors and an ever-shifting assortment of customers, combined with vendor concerns for both immediate purchases and long-term buyer loyalty, the marketplace is a most exciting arena in which to consider the dilemmas and processes that relationship work entails.

INTERACTION AS PROCESSUAL

The preceding concepts of perspectives, interpretations, negotiations, and relationships are best understood in the dynamic context of interaction. Focusing on the processes by which interaction emerges, one finds that exchanges are built up over time, with participants more or less continually interpreting other people, themselves, and other objects in the ongoing situations in which they find themselves. By viewing interaction as a dynamic quality, one becomes aware of the ongoing definitions, decisions, and selected lines of actions leading to (or away from) exchanges. While more aspects of new situations remain to be interpreted and considered in developing one's line of action, all situations are problematic in their outcomes. Each and every situation needs to be interpreted anew (if only as a confirmation of earlier expectations). This is not to suggest that situations may not become considered routine and predictable by the participants; but that all routines presume consistent (and cooperative) behavior on the part of all participants.

As outcomes are predicted on the basis of past experiences, frequently encountered situations (or types thereof) tend to be defined as more routine. Over time, people tend to develop somewhat standardized ways of assembling these encounters. In this sense, recurrent situations tend to acquire a normative quality. Others develop ideas of our interactional styles and we do the same with them, all parties anticipating activities accordingly. As patterns or routines become more firmly established among the interactants, we may speak of a "taken-for-granted" reality (Schutz, 1971), in which participants assume that others will maintain existing arrangements and understandings. Thus, for instance, one may find that store hours in an area are 9:00 a.m. to 9:00 p.m., Monday through Saturday. There is nothing intrinsically objective about these hours. They can, however, define shopping times and will take on an objective appearance (so long as all abide by these hours). However, as Schutz (1971), Berger and Luckmann (1966), and Garfinkel (1967) note, reality is quite precarious. Our notions of reality are dependent on ongoing acceptance by others for their continued validation. Generally speaking, the more widespread a practice becomes, and the longer it persists, the less vulnerable it is to successful challenge. And, in the interim, all practices in line with the prevailing style serve to affirm its reality (appearances thereof). However, each time that situation is encountered, the possibility of alternative forms of exchange exists. And, as any alternative becomes more widespread, it threatens the earlier practice. It challenges the integrity or objectivity of the earlier routine.

Whenever two or more people come together, they do not know how their encounters will end. Each may have certain objectives and may plan for certain conclusions. However, as minded beings, continually assessing incoming information relative to self and other, participants may find that their eventual outcomes take them some distance from their original anticipated outcomes. While one person may anticipate another (with considerable accuracy in some cases), each action of the other remains to be interpreted (and potentially negotiated) within an emergent context.

METHODOLOGICAL IMPLICATIONS

The methodological implications for those accepting these premises are as follows. First, researchers should at the outset and throughout the entire research and analysis stages of the study exhibit a fundamental concern with uncovering, elaborating upon, and conveying the meanings (of objects) of those they are purporting to study. The emphasis is on providing an account of the world of the participants as defined by those participants in as careful, thorough, and representative a manner as possible.

Second, researchers should be profoundly sensitive to people's capacity for reflectivity. If researchers can think, experience dilemmas, develop strategies, selectively present themselves to others, and make ongoing adjustments through internal conversations, would it not also make sense to see if other people could do likewise? Thus we would

ask questions around issues such as the following. How do the participants make sense of their worlds? How do they envision their situations,
their activities, their relations with others? This means not only recognizing people's main viewpoint(s), but centrally attending to the interpretations that people make as they do their activities. These interpretations are individualized and personalized, but they should not be
dismissed as subjective, peripheral, or epiphenomenal. Since people
know the world only as they experience it, these meanings are as
objective, central, and basic as any other piece of information we may
possess about the world. The meanings that people attach to things may
vary greatly in longevity and the extent to which they are shared by
others at this or that point in time. But this does not make these
meanings any less consequential for understanding the production of
human behavior.

Third, recognizing that people's behaviors cannot be reduced to their
individual properties, researchers would want to examine the ways in
which people interact with others. As reflective entities (objects unto
themselves), people can take themselves into account not only in developing their own lines of action, they can also endeavor to shape the
ways in which others define, experience, and act toward the world. As
well, they may attempt to resist the possible influences of others. Here
we would want to ask about any preparations people make in anticipation of encounters with others, their styles of approaching others, the
ways in which they attempt to understand (i.e., take the role of) others,
the practices they employ to shape meanings (and interests) on the part
of others, and the ways in which they deal with resistances and pursue
commitments from others. Viewed thusly, we ask about influence as
practical, ongoing accomplishment on the part of people interacting
with one another.

Fourth, researchers in this tradition would not only acknowledge
people's tendencies to form particularistic bonds with others, but would
also ask about the short-term and long-term implications of these
relationships for people's activities more generally. It is not simply a
matter of asking who interacts with whom, but rather attending to the
developmental aspects (i.e., initial involvements, continuities, disinvolvements, and reinvolvements) of people's relationships with others,
as well as acknowledging the ways in which people take these particular
others into account in formulating their own lines of action.

Fifth is the focus on process. While the concept of process implies an ongoing, emergent, or unfolding dimension to human behavior, its relevance is much greater for students of human behavior. Not only does process cut across notions of perspectives, reflectivity, negotiation, and relationships insofar as all of these elements assume a temporal quality (however short-lived or fleeting some instances may be), but process also offers us a comparative, transsituational feature on which to build as we work toward a theory of human behavior. The methodological implication is that researchers would want to attend to the sequencing or natural history of each episode that they encounter, seeing how people formulate their activities in process. And, indeed, this is central. For it is only by examining the ways in which particular instances of human behavior take their shape that we can more fully appreciate the significance of people's perspectives, reflectivity, negotiations, and relationships. Then, by focusing on parallel occurrences across situations, we may begin to arrive at a fuller appreciation of the more basic processes of which each case is but an instance.[24]

As may be quickly surmised, survey (standardized questionnaires, administered by interviewers or oneself) and experimental research do not generate very much depth along these lines. These modes of research may be useful in other respects, but they are too presumptive, decontextualized, and cursory to shed much light on the lived experiences (and emergent practices) of human beings. We need a methodology that will provide us with greater levels of intimate familiarity with the life worlds and activities of those we are purporting to study.

No technique will give us a perfect representation of the data one would wish (mindful of these premises), but participant observation (researcher as participant) and open-ended interview formats seem especially valuable in this respect.[25] These materials may be supplemented by a variety of other procedures, such as direct observation, audio-visual recordings, and the use of diaries and other documents. In each case, however, the task remains that of obtaining a full account of the situation examined, being especially mindful of the perspectives, reflections, negotiations, relations, and processes experienced by the people we are purporting to study.

Buyer Behavior

In discussing interaction as socially constructed activity, we have been considering the formulation of what Blumer (1969) terms "joint activity." Examining interaction as perspectival, reflective, processual, negotiable and relational, it becomes apparent that the behavior of individuals cannot be adequately understood without reference to the social settings in which people find themselves and the ongoing adjustments that minded, reflective beings make in the process of interacting with others. If sales are viewed as two-way exchanges, then every model of marketing activity implicitly assumes a model of buyer behavior and vice versa. Thus, while necessarily brief, it seems instructive to provide a statement on buying activity. Given the relative emphasis of the present project on vendor activities, this statement on buyer behavior should be regarded as more tentative. It relies on a model derived from research on people's involvements in a wide variety of other settings. These include studies of union organizers (Karsh et al., 1953), check forgers (Lemert, 1972), delinquency (Matza, 1964), religious recruitment (Lofland and Stark, 1965; Prus, 1976), collective behavior (Klapp, 1969); and hustlers, thieves, hookers, entertainers, violence, drinking, and a bar life (Prus and Sharper, 1977; Prus, 1978; Prus and Irini, 1988).

One might ask what relevance these studies have for buying behavior. My answer is this. Unless we require a separate theory for buyer behavior versus other involvements, we should be able to learn about buying behavior by examining the participation of people in other settings and the relationships these people develop therein. Indeed, if one looks past the content to the processes of interaction, extensive similarities emerge. For instance, whether one focuses on the activities of clergymen, hookers, or businesspeople, one typically finds that all are concerned about building up clienteles; location is important to their overall success; all not only find themselves in competitive contexts, but are also highly dependent on the cooperation of others; all have their better customers and their troublesome characters; all engage in public relations work; all develop reputations within their communities relative to the notions of morality prevailing within these settings; and all are subject to the problems of sustaining enthusiasm. This is not to suggest that these people share the same belief systems, only to draw attention to the fundamentally social nature of people's involvements.

Thus, while the contexts of people's involvements may vary greatly, the studies on which this model is based are exceedingly relevant to buyer behavior. They focus on the processes by which people become initially involved in situations; they continue (and intensify) other involvements; they become disengaged from these involvements; and they become reinvolved in earlier situations. The buyer analogues are first-time purchases, customer loyalty, dropping products (brands, suppliers), and revitalizing patronage.

The model outlined appreciates the perspectival, reflective, processual, negotiable, and relational nature of group life. Judging from its applicability across other settings, it should have considerable generalizability to the marketplace.[26] Consistent with earlier work (Prus and Sharper, 1977; Prus and Irini, 1988), the term *career contingency model* (or *involvement theory*) is used to refer to the general model introduced here.[27]

CAREER CONTINGENCIES (INVOLVEMENT THEORY)

Denoting a history of people's involvements in particular settings, we may envision persons as having "careers" in each of the situations in which they participate. Thus, one might have a "career" as a drunk, a thief, a parent, a purchaser of clothing or a buyer of Brand X office supplies, for instance. It should however be noted, in reference to the aforementioned processes (initial involvements, continuities, disinvolvements, and reinvolvements), that not everyone will experience each of these processes for each possible involvement. For instance, many will not become involved initially in particular situations; while others, once involved, may never become disinvolved from particular situations. Likewise, some will leave particular involvements never to become reinvolved in these situations again.

We should also recognize that each involvement is likely to be only one of several that people experience at any given time. Thus the existence of multiple involvements should be noted, for it is within the context of one's other involvements that each single involvement is located. Multiple involvements are not only commonplace and inevitable, but each involvement may interfere with a person's other involvements. Thus disinvolvement from *B* may be significantly related to an earlier involvement in *A*, a later involvement in *C*, or even a chance to become involved in *D*. With this notion of multiple involvements in mind, we may consider the career contingency model in reference to purchasing situations.

Initial Involvements (First-Time Purchases)

Reflecting people's participation in a wide variety of contexts, the literature suggests three basic routings by which involvements may occur: seekership, recruitment, and closure.[28] When people pursue situations they define as attractive, interesting, enjoyable and the like, the concept of seekership is applicable. When their involvements are promoted by others who solicit their participation in situations, that constitutes recruitment. Closure comes into play when people engage in activities as a means of realizing pressing obligations. While one of these routings may clearly dominate in any given case, many involvements reflect combinations of these. Thus, for example, a young man may want to own a car (seekership), find his employer requires him to have access to ready transportation (closure), and be approached by a friend now in the car business (recruitment).[29] It is most important to view involvements as perspectival, reflective, processual, and negotiable.

Involvements presume some contact of the person with others involved in the situation, but involvements are also affected by the perspectives (viewpoints, frames of reference, ideologies) from which persons interpret their situations. In addition to the other ways (seekership, recruitment, closure) in which people define situations, perspectives are also important with respect to any reservations persons may have in reference to particular involvements; the restraints (moral, financial, physical safety) persons experience at particular times.[30] To follow the car example further; while the young man may buy a car from his friend, he may also buy elsewhere. For example, although he may consider the price of his friend's line reasonable, he may define the safety features of his friend's cars to be inadequate (for him, a noteworthy reservation). His friend may or may not be successful in moving him past these concerns by stressing the images associated with style and performance.

An issue of considerable significance to those involved in marketing, is the question of how people initially make product purchases. The following four points are central to this process.

Seekership. Prospective buyers (purchasing agents, dealers, consumers, and so on) may pursue particular products/brands on their own.

Products do not have inherent meanings, but are defined within the prospects' frames of reference. These assessments of desirability may occur prior to, or after contact with particular products (or their representatives).

Recruitment. As part of their promotional effort, vendors may attempt to define products as more favorable to their prospects by relating products to these people's situations. Indicating how their products would help prospects realize their interests, solve their problems, and the like, vendors may generate relevance, establish worth, and justify purchases of their products. Should the prospects not be initially inclined to view products favorably, vendors may also attempt to shape the ways in which prospects envision products by suggesting alternative viewpoints and interpretations. Other modes of recruitment reflect the initiative of third parties, such as friends, relatives, and other associates.

Closure. Albeit reluctantly, people may also consider involvements that they would not have chosen when they envision these as meeting their obligations. Thus, for instance, vendors may carry lines that they personally despise in attempts to generate profits. Or many people may buy sump pumps to maintain dry basements rather than because of any particular interest in their inner workings or exterior appearances. Likewise, many products are purchased at Christmas because someone needed "something" to meet their familial obligations. Recognizing these sorts of obligations, vendors may attempt to promote purchases more generally and immediately by creating closure. To the extent that vendors can intensify existing (product-linked) obligations, indicate urgency, and provide more exclusive routings to solve pressing problems, they increase the likelihood of obtaining target investments.

Reduced reservations (drift). Even when prospects are inclined to make purchases, they may still consider the implications of particular purchases for other aspects of their situations. Recognizing that prospects have other commitments (obligations), vendors may be concerned that these other commitments not interfere with the present transactions. To the extent that vendors can eliminate or minimize the significance of other obligations, they increase the likelihood of obtaining investments in the products being promoted. Should prospective buyers be skeptical of vendors (products, warrantees, and so on; thereby reflecting concerns about losing money, making unwise commitments, and such), then notions of trust become more central to the purchasing decision. Recognizing concerns of this nature, vendors may attempt to promote definitions of themselves (and products) as sincere, knowledgeable, reliable, and such; thereby potentially reducing people's reservations concerning particular purchasing commitments.

Continuity (Buyer Loyalty)

Once people have become involved in situations, the question of when and how they are likely to continue (and intensify) their involvements becomes prominent. Continuity may reflect earlier routings of involvement, but persons may continue to participate in situations on bases other than that related to their initial involvements. Since repeat customers represent the basis of most successful businesses, it is essential to ask how this repeat patronage comes about.

Assuming that repeat purchases represent feasible options, we can ask about the elements affecting continuity of the buyer-seller relationship. The earlier cited literature suggests that customer loyalty would depend on the extensiveness of the patron's involvements in the use of the vendor's product. In this regard, customer loyalty seems largely contingent on: developing more comprehensive perspectives (justifications) for continued use and patronage of particular products; achieving more extensive and exclusive identification as buyers of particular products; making larger, irretrievable investments in particular products or getting involved in more comprehensive product programs; incorporating particular products more fully into their routines (activities); and becoming more fully involved in ongoing relationships with product-supportive others (vendors and/or loyal patrons). To the extent that vendors recognize these bases of continuity, they may endeavor to generate loyalty by providing justifications, fostering identification, obtaining commitments, facilitating patterns of use, and promoting supportive associations. Finally, although buyers in pluralist societies typically have a number of product and vendor options from which to choose, it should be noted that there may be cases in which people may continue making particular purchases when they fail to perceive a lack of feasible alternatives (i.e., continuity by default).

Disinvolvement (Dropping Products/Brands/Suppliers)

As with initial involvement and continuity, it is important to envision disinvolvement in process terms. While any reassessment of one's current situation may generate definitions conducive to disengagement, the multiple involvements (and other options) in which people find

themselves are especially consequential for disinvolvement from particular situations. Given the existence of competition and the shifting
situations in which buyers find themselves, it is important to ask when
buyers are likely to switch products (brands, suppliers). While some
terminations of purchasing involvements reflect the lack of applications, other instances denote opportunities for purchases elsewhere.
However, these alternative involvements are most likely when combined with: shifts in perspectives, changes in identities, reassessments
of existing commitments, reevaluations of product-related activities,
and redefinitions of product-related associations. Although disenchantment may arise on any of these bases, it should be noted that its
significance may be offset by positive definitions of involvements in
other respects. And, insofar as disenchantment need not result in disinvolvement, in itself, the timing and nature of buyer contacts with
vendors representing alternatives can be critical for determining subsequent involvements.

Reinvolvement (Revitalizing Patronage)

Should disinvolvement (and any alternatives) be defined as unsatis-
factory, reinvolvement becomes a viable option. As former customers
are familiar with the routines and styles of vendors with whom they
have dealt in the past, reinvolvement in these earlier relationships
becomes more likely when current situations are deemed inadequate.
Reinvolvement presupposes (re)acceptance of buyers by the vendors to
whom they return. And, as with initial involvements, reinvolvements
may be sought out by buyers (seekership), be promoted by vendors
(recruitment), or reflect buyers' assessments that these involvements
are the best or only ways to meet pressing obligations (closure).

Reinvolvement seems most likely when former relations were dis-
solved on a more congenial level, patrons experience some disenchantment with their new products, and some changes have taken place on
the part of either the buyers or vendors considered that could be used
to justify renewed contact.

Some attention will be given to this model in the chapters following.
However, the material is focused primarily on the recruiting activity
(preparations, presentations, strategies, dilemmas, and so on) of vendors rather than on the involvements of buyers.

The Data Base

The salesman, he is the person in the center of it all. If he doesn't sell it, the orders don't come in. If the orders don't come in, the machines don't move, and the people don't get employed, and on and on and on [wholesale— giftware].

This project began as an examination of retailer activity. As the study developed, however, it became evident that in order to better understand this realm of activity, it was necessary to learn more about the retailers' suppliers and their relationships with the retailers. Subsequent visits to trade shows and ongoing interviews with suppliers and buyers confirmed the value of this strategy. As a result of attending these trade shows, and talking with the people involved, the base of the project was expanded considerably. The retail element remained central to the project, but it was now located within the more general realm of sales activity. Thus, in addition to retail sales, the participants include those involved in wholesale, manufacture, and promotional (advertising agencies and mediums; premiums and incentives programs) trade.

While questions may be raised about including both a wide range of products and multiple levels of enterprise in the analysis, these strategies have considerable merit. Once one moves past the mystique surrounding particular products and levels of merchandising, the parallels are striking. For example, vendors can sell candy in a wide variety of ways, but others can also sell clothing, appliances, and automobiles in similar ways (and vice versa). Likewise, manufacturers, wholesalers, retailers, and those involved in promotional trade all deal with suppliers, face pricing decisions, rely heavily on repeat trade, face troublesome customers, and so forth. Qualifications will be made as these seem appropriate (e.g., regarding organizational complexity), but once one looks past the "content" to the "forms" of association (Simmel, 1950), it becomes evident that one does not need a separate theory for each product, industry, or level of sales. The advantage of this wider scope is considerable. It provides invaluable comparisons and contrasts across a wide range of products and styles of marketing. The result is a much more balanced statement, and one that sheds considerable light on marketing and sales activity in a variety of settings.

COLLECTING DATA

Three modes of data collection were used in this study: interviews with businesspeople, observations of trade shows, and participant observation in a craft enterprise.

Interviews

The (118) interviews were obtained largely on an individual basis and reflect a variety of contacts with vendors. These ranged from a few preexisting personal contacts with vendors to a majority of people encountered as relative strangers at their places of business, at trade shows, and in other settings. Despite adages such as "Time is money," the businesspeople encountered were generally quite receptive to the study. While some were "too busy" to be bothered with the research (no particular pattern emerged herein), most of the vendors encountered were willing to assist me with the project. As a result, I was able to locate many more willing participants than I was able to interview (geographical accessibility, mutual schedules).

As is the case with all interview research, some participants were more helpful than others. Some were willing to explain situations more fully and candidly than others, some were more informed about more areas of activity than others, and some had broader bases of experience upon which to draw. Overall, more attention was given to the retail market than to other categories of sales, but the emphasis was on marketing as a process rather than on any given product or realm of sales. Thus, while most of the participants worked primarily in retail sales (n = 71), others pursued trade in wholesale (n = 12), manufacture (n = 21, and promotional (n = 14) sectors at the time of interviews. Given the multifaceted nature of salespeople's careers, however, these numbers considerably underrepresent the effective base of the study. These multiple involvements consequently afforded a much greater base of comparison and information than the numbers of interviews indicate. Most people had worked for more than one company by the time they were interviewed, and of these, a large proportion had worked for companies selling different products. Salespeople often remain within the same realm of sales (e.g., retail versus manufacture), but it is not uncommon to encounter people who have worked at several realms of trade (e.g., retail, wholesale, and manufacture) on a simultaneous and/or concurrent basis. To this end, statements from the participants have been coded in accordance with the categories of sales that participants referenced at particular points in the interview. Although vendors' activities are not so sharply defined, participants were placed in the following categories as a result of their primary activities in order to provide readers with a sense of the sample:

Retail: those who sell directly to the public. While primarily retailers, some of these vendors also have significant wholesale ventures in their enterprises.

Wholesale: those who sell (pre)manufactured goods to other vendors.

Manufacture: those who construct, process, make, or assemble products to sell to others. It should be noted that many manufacturers also serve as distributors (e.g., wholesalers, retailers) for products manufactured by others.

Promotions: those involved in the sales of advertising and other promotional materials (e.g., media, packaging, incentives, premiums).

These categories are further qualified in the extracts (quotations/observations) in reference to the products (e.g., shoes, real estate) involved. While references will be made within the text relative to both company size and participant position within organizations, neither the size of organization nor the positions of the participants are indicated in the extracts.[31] Table 1.1 shows how the sample distributed itself, relative to the position and category of sales the participants found themselves in at the time of their interviews.

Trade Shows

In addition to providing further insight into buyer-supplier relations, the trade shows (32 attended) were especially valuable in providing firsthand material on large scale and international levels of trade. Featuring items such as giftware, clothing, luggage, hardware, computers, office supplies, and a wide range of industrial supplies, these exhibitions were extremely important for generating sources of interviews; making observations of multiple levels and areas of trade; providing opportunities to make related inquiries of vendors, albeit generally on a more fleeting basis; suggesting new realms of inquiry; providing opportunities to observe ongoing buyer-supplier exchanges; and assessing the validity of materials that emerged in other contexts. Thus, in

TABLE 1.1

Participants' Positions at Time of Interview

Category	Manager (owner)	Salesperson	Total
Retail	41 (12)	30	71
Wholesale	6 (3)	6	12
Manufacture	10 (4)	11	21
Promotions	5 (2)	9	14
Total	62 (21)	56	118

NOTE: Since the owners interviewed were also managers, it was decided to include these in the general category of managers (the numbers of owner-managers are indicated in brackets).

addition to providing innumerable specifics, the trade shows have been invaluable for developing a more complete understanding of the marketplace.

Craft Enterprise

The interviews and trade show materials were supplemented by three years' involvement in a craft enterprise. This business microcosm not only generated insider contact with a number of craft show vendors, and provided opportunities to experience most aspects of marketing (from product design, purchasing, and manufacture to completed sales, repeat patronage, and doing exhibits), but it also provided practitioner access to a number of suppliers in several different product lines and facilitated access and acceptance at trade shows. Like other small businesses, craft enterprises provide limited insight into the internal organizational exchanges characterizing larger businesses. However, since small operations involve the same basic marketing activities as larger companies, and those participating in small businesses are more likely to experience all these elements themselves, the craft enterprise generated a more holistic sense of marketing than that commonly achieved by individual functionaries in larger operations. Nevertheless, it was most valuable as an analytical device when my experiences therein were assessed relative to the experiences of the vendors encountered in other contexts.

An Overview

Selling is selling. If you are good, you can sell anything. It's how you approach the people, how you present yourself to them. If you do that well, you should be able to sell anything [women's clothing]!

Focusing most directly on the presentation of products to prospects, Chapter 2 attends to vendor concerns with impression management, customers approaches and qualification, and tactics for developing interest. Although these features of interaction may be more apt to be taken for granted by prospective buyers than are vendor attempts to close sales, these preliminary persuasion processes can be vital in building a base from which to pursue customer commitments in both short-term (i.e., immediate purchases) and long-run (i.e., repeat patronage) respects.

Building on notions developed in Chapter 2, Chapter 3 considers the ways in which vendors attempt to generate a greater sense of trust on the part of prospective buyers. Attention is given here to portrayals of vendor integrity, product quality, and the minimization of prospect obligations (and risks). As well, since it entails presumptions of trust, this chapter also attends to "suggestive selling" (vendor attempts to promote purchases of higher-priced lines and/or multiple items).

Chapter 4 focuses on the sorts of resistances salespeople encounter and the ways in which they attempt to overcome these obstacles. Of particular significance here are notions of price resistance, skepticism, and indecision, existing loyalties, and comparison shopping. It is in Chapter 4 (and in Chapter 5) that we find vendors most cognizant of buyer abilities (as elusive targets and tacticians) to withhold cooperation or otherwise attempt to shape the direction of the encounters they have with vendors.

The pursuit of prospect commitment is explored even more explicitly in Chapter 5. In addition to considering vendor perspectives on, and tactics of, completing (closing) sales, we become increasingly aware of the dilemmas vendors face in their attempts to secure sales in single as well as multiple buyer situations.

Chapter 6 sheds further light on the discordant aspects of saleswork, by focusing on troublesome customers. The uncertainties and disruptions these people's shopping styles represent makes salespeople's activities and plans a little more precarious. Attention is given to annoying shopping styles and the problems associated with returns, complaints, shoplifting, and financial difficulties. Ironically, not only are troublesome customers typically bad for business in themselves, but vendors may find themselves devoting proportionately so much time and energy to resolving these disruptions that they may neglect more valued aspects of their enterprises. This is an area much neglected by marketing experts, but one that deserves genuine attention as this realm of customer activity is responsible not only for many of the "abrasive policies" stores implement, but for negative vendor dispositions more generally. This material also depicts the dilemmas the vendors encounter, as they attempt to achieve a diplomatic balance between keeping order and keeping customers.

Concentrating on what is often described as "the backbone of most successful businesses," Chapter 7 is devoted to the forms, processes, and problematics of customer loyalty as seen from vendors' viewpoints. This chapter reflects earlier discussions of presentations, trust, commitments, and trouble, but it more specifically examines the ways in which vendors actively foster long-term relationships with their customers. In addition to dealing with the variations repeat customers assume, we consider vendor attempts to develop customer perspectives, identities, activities, investments and relationships conducive to continuity.

"Holding 'Sales'" (Chapter 8) serves to illustrate and summarize a number of themes earlier developed. Consideration is given to the vendors' use of price reductions as a marketing tool, and to the contingencies affecting decisions to engage in price-cutting promotions. While "sales" customers are seen to epitomize troublesome shoppers, "sales" bring most of the earlier discussed marketing activities into sharp focus. "Sales" are designed to create action, but they also generate a number of noteworthy dilemmas for vendors becoming involved in these marketing formats. Especially noteworthy in this regard are the problems associated with "sales" shoppers, the unpredictability of "sales," and vendor concerns with loyalty, images, and being competitive. The excitement and frustration of both buying and selling become intensified during "sales," and the strategies and dilemmas of the involved parties become more evident.

Chapter 9 ("Maintaining Enthusiasm") explicitly attends to vendors' assessments of their own situations. Thus consideration is directed to elements serving to diminish as well as enhance salespeople's careers and successes on both a short-term and long-run basis. Particularly significant in these respects are elements such as the pressures and unpredictability of sales on the one hand, and the support afforded by families, companies, and co-workers on the other. Attention is also given to the affiliational networks that develop in sales settings. Beyond their implications for friendship and recreation more generally, these networks also affect sales, careers, and identities within the business community.

Addressing themes developed in the preceding chapters, Chapter 10 ("In Perspective") is first used as an opportunity to reflect on the ethnographic experience this project entailed. It is hoped that this discussion will better help readers to contextualize the project from which this statement was derived as well as to develop a fuller, more general appreciation of the ethnographic research process. This is followed by a consideration of buyer behavior as situated activity (and the implications of target capacities for reflective enterprise for our understanding of the roles of tacticians). Then, using the insights gained from the present study, 10 processes central to our understanding of influence as interpersonal accomplishment are delineated. In developing this material, we derive a conceptualization of influence (and human behavior), which is not only interactive in its essence but is also fundamentally rooted in reflectivity.

Notes

1. For a fuller appreciation of the extent to which vendors (themselves) are buyers and the targets of other sales endeavors, see *Pursuing Customers* (Prus, 1989, especially Chapters 4, 6, and 9).

2. A companion volume to the present text, *Pursuing Customers* (Prus, 1989), focuses on the ways in which vendors set up businesses, do management, purchase products for resale or manufacture, price goods, and promote products through the media, field sales campaigns, and showrooms and trade shows. Taking us behind the scenes in a highly detailed and intimate portrayal of vendor activities, this volume provides invaluable material depicting vendor preparations for customer encounters.

3. This position is developed in more detail in the literature section of this chapter.

4. Although vendors sometimes work with scripts (also spiels, patters, canned presentations) more closely approximating those of the theatre (i.e., extensive, explicit, tightly focused), we should recognize that prospective buyers are much less ready to assume roles as supporting casts than are their counterparts on stage. More accurate, in a great many cases, would be the realization that people's scripts as both buyers and sellers are apt to be ambiguous, open-ended, often mixed (sometimes ridden with conflicting images and dilemmas) in content for each participant, and reactive (rather than preplanned) in their implementation.

5. Focusing on the preparations vendors make in anticipation and pursuit of customer encounters, the companion volume, *Pursuing Customers*, also addresses yet other basic features of everyday life. Included here are discussions of the processes by which people become involved in situations; gamble, and attempt to reduce ambiguity and risk-taking; define the parameters for exchange vis-à-vis requesting and acknowledging commitments

from others; and endeavor to access mass or unfamiliar audiences via the media, direct (agent) canvassing activities, and the use of exhibits.

6. The emphasis on activities contrasts significantly with Borden's (1964) conceptualization of "market mix." Thus, while material central to Borden's "4 P's" (product, price, promotion, and place-distribution) will be given much attention; of primary importance are the ways in which people work out marketing activities with others (ergo, the "P's" of people and process).

7. This is consistent with Merton's (1957) broader notion of system interdependence, but practicing functionalists generally do not consider the ways in which people actually work out their activities with one another. As a result of these interdependencies, certain ways of doing particular marketing activities may be facilitated (or inconvenienced) relative to other ways of doing the same activities. This sense of interrelatedness is also expressed by Bordon (1964) who contends that each aspect of one's market mix affects the other aspects of one's marketing program.

8. Insofar as the boundaries of the disciplines within the social sciences are relatively arbitrary, I would argue that the more consequential demarcation is between those who assume an interpretive approach to the study of human behavior and those who do not. This statement clearly assumes an interpretive frame and builds on the lived experiences of the participants (vendors in this case) as the primary data or reality for the study of human behavior. Although they did not anticipate what was later to be called naturalistic inquiry (Chicago-style interactionism), much of the conceptual ground work for this interpretive approach may be traced back to the works of Wilhelm Dilthey (1833-1911; see Ermarth, 1978) and Georg Simmel (1858-1918; see Simmel, 1900, 1978, 1950; Levine, 1971; Frisby, 1984).

9. It is ironic that while most social psychologists in both sociology and psychology ardently reject the concept of *needs* as developed by Maslow (1954) and others of that genre, this scheme has become central to many discussions of marketing motivation.

10. The interactive aspects of sales have not been entirely neglected among those in marketing. Thus, although not as fully developed as is the present project, the works of Bonoma and Zaltman (1978), Levy (1978), and the Reingen and Woodside (1981) collection of articles directly address this topic, as does Swan (1986).

11. One could level similar charges at most social scientists. One may ask to what extent their lived experiences in human groups are accurately reflected in their (largely quantified) academic depictions of human behavior. Academics in marketing as well as those in the social sciences more generally have heavily imported conceptual frames and methodological practices from the physical and natural sciences. They have done this without much regard for the centrality of human experiences (ongoing interpretations and interaction) for their alleged subject matter (the study of human behavior). The issue raised here is not a new one, and can be traced back to Dilthey (Ermarth, 1978) and Mead (1934). It is most cogently addressed in Blumer (1969). Working from a philosophy of science (interpretive) perspective, Anderson (1983, 1986) provides an astute in-house critique of the positivist orientation academics have taken toward marketing and consumer behavior.

12. Those interested in cross-cultural material on marketing are referred to economic anthropology. While minimally concerned with the actual processes by which exchanges occur (compared to the functions of exchanges for life within the groups studied), readers may find the collections of Bohannan and Dalton (1962), Brookfield (1969), and Smith (1978) valuable.

13. This is even more ironic in that one may argue that the marketplace is the base of urban society!

14. This point is addressed somewhat by Zakuta (1970).

15. This may have been encouraged by the exchange theorists (e.g., Homans, 1958; Blau, 1964) who in attempting to apply an economic model to social exchanges (relationships), provide very simplistic and misleading images of economic exchanges! The components of exchange need to be explained as social phenomena. There are fundamental elements of (social) exchange that exchange theory neglects. Particularly significant are the perspectival, emergent, and negotiable nature of meanings; reflective planning, variable strategies, impression management (Goffman, 1959), and possible deception; the uncertainties of characterizing the future (e.g., an evershifting marketplace); and desires on the part of participants to maintain working relationships (on any number of bases).

16. Although the marketplace is an area of considerable significance for sociology, most of the publishers with whom I discussed this project have indicated that they did not perceive a market for this subject matter (citing the absence of sociology courses in the area) and did not want to become trail blazers.

17. Of the early theorists, it is Georg Simmel (1900, 1978) who most incisively addresses matters of the marketplace. Unfortunately, The Philosophy of Money was not published in English until 1978. Weber (1947) also considers matters pertaining to the marketplace, but at a much more general level. Ralph Turner (personal communication) expressed this position most clearly, saying that the neglect of business by sociologists might be expected since no one had yet laid out a theoretical scheme to show us how we might go about studying the marketplace.

18. Perhaps it is worth noting that these critics (Marxists, especially) evidence little familiarity with marketplace exchanges in any society.

19. In addition to my own efforts, this review reflects the contributions of a great many scholars who have discussed the project with me.

20. Durkheim's (1897) rate-data study of suicide was to play a major role in plotting a methodological course that (positivistically oriented) sociologists have followed, while the laboratory Wilhelm Wundt established in 1879 provided an experimental model that (positivistically oriented) psychologists have followed.

21. Some might argue that this portrayal of positivism is obsolete, or at least not accurate for many of today's social scientists. I would agree that this statement is very cryptic and approximates something on an "ideal type" in Weber's (1947) terms. And I would acknowledge that the theoretical underpinnings of logical positivism, vis-à-vis the social sciences, were largely destroyed on philosophy grounds in the 1950s. I would also note that many contemporary quantitative social scientists endeavor to distance themselves from positivism in one or other ways when discussions of interpretive paradigms surface. They sometimes contend that aspects of interpretation are assumed, implied, or incorporated into their conceptualizations, measurements, and analysis. In other cases, they appear willing to concede the viability of interpretation if challenged, but posit that interpretation is not relevant for the question at hand. Nevertheless, quantitative social scientists have given only minimal attention to the ways in which human behavior is accomplished by the people they are purporting to study, they have almost entirely neglected the interpretive aspects of human experience (and behavior), and their methodology (while more sophisticated in some respects) remains essentially unchanged vis-à-vis positivist assumptions. The emphasis on rate data (factors-outcomes) remains

preeminent. Matters pertaining to human agency are generally relegated to the residual, inconsequential, subjective, social psychological, or speculative in their overall projects. That social scientists would persist in this direction is even more amazing in that those in the physical sciences have not only begun explicitly to incorporate an interpretive paradigm into their knowledge of the world, but have begun to question the assumptions of the positivist model vis-à-vis the substance(s) with which they work. For other discussions of these and related issues, readers are referred to Winch (1958), Kuhn (1962), Blumer (1969), Harré and Secord (1972), Bloor (1976, 1983), Giddens (1976), Barnes (1977, 1982), Gergen (1982, 1985), and Roth (1987).

22. As the material develops, readers will also recognize my indebtedness to Goffman (1959; 1963); Garfinkel (1967), Schutz (1971). Those familiar with the works of Harré and Secord (1972), Giddens (1976), and Gergen (1982, 1985) will note strong conceptual affinities with these materials as well.

23. As we take much of our own reality for granted (Schutz, 1971), the most compelling evidence for multiple realities and its relevance for people's activity may come from cross-cultural research. Weston LaBarre (1947) aptly illustrates that the meanings of gestures and emotions are *not* universal, while others, such as Malinowski (1987), Mead (1950), and MacAndrew and Edgerton (1969) provide powerful evidence suggesting that all our behaviors are culturally situated.

24. For a more comprehensive statement on generic social processes and their implications for theory and research, see Prus (1987).

25. Those working in this (ethnographic/interpretive) tradition would argue that methods books are a poor substitute for methods in practice (i.e., one is much better advised to read ethnographic research reports). However, readers may find the following discussions helpful relative to fieldwork techniques: Glaser and Strauss (1967), Bogdan and Taylor (1975), Johnson (1975), Sanders (1976), Shaffir et al. (1980), Emerson et al. (1983), Hammersley and Atkinson (1983), and Lofland and Lofland (1984).

26. As some might realize, this statement denotes the base of a study on buyer behavior in its early stages at the time of writing.

27. The term *involvement theory* was casually coined by my colleague Frank Fasick, but seems entirely appropriate.

28. As noted in earlier studies (Prus and Sharper, 1977; Prus, 1978; Prus and Irini, 1988), the career contingency model builds on Becker's (1963) work generally. The concepts of *seekership, recruitment,* and *closure* indicate our indebtedness to Klapp (1969), Lofland and Stark (1965), and Lemert (1972), respectively.

29. Two other modes of involvement might also be noted. In some cases people find involvements imposed on them, as when an engineer specifies the supplier and the product a purchasing agent is to buy. Inadvertent involvements denote unwitting or unintended events, as when a shopper mistakenly grabs a new or less preferred brand of canned goods in a rush to the checkout counter.

30. Matza (1964) uses the term *drift* to refer to situations in which persons experience decreased levels of responsibilities from their usual obligations.

31. The matter of people's positions in particular organizations is considerably complicated, not only as a result of the different positions people have held in one organization over time, but also as a consequence of occupying different positions in different organizations over time, and the relative lack of (internal) comparability noted in positions such as managers, assistant managers, representatives, and clerks, for instance. A concerted effort was made to contact managers (and owners), but it should not be assumed

that information from those higher up in the organization is necessarily more valid, more thorough, or more insightful than that of other staff people, simply because they hold a higher position in the organization. Those in higher positions can indeed provide valuable and unique information, but people's experiences with, and observations of, the front lines are no less valuable in arriving at a more complete understanding of the marketing and sales process. Likewise, it should not be assumed that those operating as salespeople have little insight into other aspects of marketing (e.g., ordering, pricing, managing). Many have worked in a plurality of companies and have held positions entailing more responsibility than the title of *salesperson* suggests.

Chapter 2
PRESENTING PRODUCTS

> You have to have a liking and an understanding of people because, first and
> foremost, it's a people business! . . . If you can handle people, you can sell
> them anything. If you are an affable person, if you can talk to people, relate
> to kings or peasants, whether it's an upper-class person who wants to buy a
> top line or someone who is wanting to buy our least expensive model, that's
> a big part of your success [auto].

How do vendors present products to prospects? What concerns do they
have? What preparations do they make? How do they approach prospective customers? How do they arouse interest in their products?

In contrast to those involved in media sales, vendors operating in the
field, in showrooms, and at trade shows, find themselves in direct
interaction with prospects. Those selling through the media may attempt to qualify their audiences, and may make subsequent adjustments
to their messages after assessing the effects of the preceding one-way
communications. But salespeople in these other settings find themselves in more dynamic two-way exchanges. These encounters need not
last long, nor need they result in purchasing commitments on the part
of their prospects. However, to the extent that vendors are concerned
with selling to all (eligible) buyers, the relationships they develop with
prospective buyers assume considerable importance.

Some purchases would likely occur regardless of prospects' assessments of particular sales encounters, but since sales depend on buyer
cooperation, presentations are best seen in the context of the ongoing
interaction vendors have with their prospects. Salespeople may attempt
to determine the directions of these encounters, but so may their prospects; and vendors are always dependent on their prospects' willingness to cooperate with them.[1]

The sales relationship clearly transcends the material discussed in this chapter, but of immediate concern are vendor (1) preparations, (2) styles of approaching customers, (3) attempts to qualify prospects, and (4) means of generating interest. These elements will be discussed in a particular order, but it should be appreciated that these are very much interrelated. Not only can these processes occur more or less concurrently, but also in sequences at variance with the ordering presented herein. Thus, for instance, vendors may qualify prospects before, during, and after the approach; or promote interest before qualifying or approaching prospects. Before considering these processes, however, it is valuable to consider the sales encounter more fully as this pertains to joint activity, including exchanges of symbols and impression management. This will allow us to appreciate more adequately the social nature of presentations.

Selling as Joint Activity

Blumer (1969) uses the term *joint activity* to refer to the processes by which people work out lines of action with respect to one another. Joint activity acknowledges people's abilities to take both their own interests and those of others into account as they interpret situations and make ongoing adjustments to those with whom they associate. It entails a reflective linking of the activities of two or more interactants. This concept is most relevant to the sales setting as buyers and sellers take one another (and themselves) into account and proceed jointly to construct their encounters.

The notion of joint activity does not presume that the parties involved take equal initiative or that they have equal impact on the emerging interaction. However, it does alert us to the cooperative and processual nature of interaction. It means that no matter how convincing vendors may seem to be, sales encounters are subject to definition and negotiation (including termination) on the part of the prospects involved. Vendors' successes (making the sale) are contingent on their prospects' willingness to make the appropriate commitments. Even though vendors may plan and attempt to move the interaction in specific directions, the ensuing interaction may assume directions (and outcomes) quite at variance from those attempted by either the vendors or the prospects.

Vendors may sell products, but they are selling products to people. In contrast to those who work with aluminum or plastics, for example (in which quality control can be rather sharply defined), salespeople face the task of working with "entities" that are variable, complex, and unstable.[2] However, prospective customers can also assess the vendors' procedures as these pertain to their own situations,[3] and act back on vendors via concealment, deception, and other strategies of influence and resistance. Thus it is one thing to know one's products and be able to present them in a general sense, but it is another thing to obtain purchasing commitments regarding those items from others. In this respect, it is essential that vendor-buyer relationships be considered with regards to symbolic activity and impression management. These are elements that are not only inseparable from the buyer-vendor relationship, but are relevant to it at all points in the encounter.

SELLING AS SYMBOLIC ACTIVITY

You sell the "sizzle," not the steak. That's the key. [wholesale—giftware].

Stripped of their contexts and applications, objects have no inherent value (qualities, properties, worth). The meanings attributed to objects reflect prospects' perspectives, ongoing exchanges with vendors, and anticipated lines of action. The desirability of the products (images) vendors are attempting to sell is contingent on their prospects' interpretations of those objects.

You'll get something in, the hottest thing around. Seems like you can't order enough. Then all of a sudden, the sales slow down. Pretty soon, no one wants it any more. The product hasn't changed. It's the way people look at it [jewelry].

It changes also in the life cycle of the products. A product goes through an introduction, a growth, a maturity, a decline, usually. Now as the product gets older, there's less knowledge needed of the product. So how you're selling an item can change that way, too. As more people own the products, see more about them, they learn more about the product, so you do less explanation as time goes along. Now the only thing that upsets the life cycle, the explanations too, is the innovations. Then it goes off on another level. So one of the things you do in marketing is ask, "Where is my product on the product life cycle?" If you're at the maturity stage, what you need is product differentiation, new innovations, new ideas, new changes, so you try to come up with changes that spark your product, revitalize it for the consumer. . . . You see the same thing with soaps as with television and cars. . . .

You can also have a brand life cycle. And you're always faced with the problem, "What do you do when it's in a decline stage?" Do you ride it out? Reinvest in it? Drop it for a new brand name? The same thing with beer, wines. You want to know how well your image is doing. What you really sell is the image. The product is basically the same [manufacture—appliances].

In contrast to the tendency to view exchanges in reference to "objects for cold, hard cash" or "supply and demand," it seems more accurate to define exchanges in *symbolic* terms.[4] At issue is not the mere exchange of two objects, but the exchange of two objects whose meanings (symbolic significances) inhere in the assessments of those objects by those contemplating exchanges.

Perhaps the daily newspaper will serve as an example. Most people do not purchase today's newspaper to obtain a few ounces of paper and ink. Nor are many people interested in buying yesterday's paper today, even though it might have been larger than today's (a better buy, more paper and ink; possibly a lower price, too). It is not the ink and the paper people are buying, although people may have become habituated to this medium. It is what the newspaper symbolizes to them—entertainment, weather, stockmarket reports, job opportunities, and the like. The same holds true for clothing, food, automobiles, computers, buildings, and so on. Their value lies not in their physical structures, but in what they symbolize to prospective buyers. Any number of other items may serve the same function, indicating that physical qualities (e.g., weight, constitution, texture, form, and the like) are relevant only in reference to what they symbolize to prospective buyers.

The vendors, on the other hand, do not accept people's money (paper, metal, shells, and so on) because they like paper, metal, shells, and so on, but because of what this medium symbolizes to them. And the worth of this medium (e.g., dollar bill) is defined not by what it is, but by what it symbolizes to others with whom the vendors may wish to make exchanges. In this vein, one finds governments using currency to facilitate trade, and they may attempt to define its worth (by basic units, e.g., dollars). However, like other objects, the worth of money (units) is reflected in what people (regionally, nationally, and internationally) will offer in exchange for it. Exchanges frequently involve physical objects, but it is most fundamentally symbols that are exchanged.[5]

Insofar as people are exchanging symbols, and can influence one another's symbolic realities, it becomes exceedingly important to examine the ways in which vendors present products to prospects and attempt to come to terms with the symbolic significances prospective customers associate with objects. While some of the symbolic significances of items may be well established by prospects before they make contact with vendors (e.g., through associates, advertising, self-reflection), salespeople can significantly alter these definitions. Prospects sometimes are highly resistant to any definitions suggested by salespeople, but vendor behaviors represent elements of some consequence to all prospects.[6]

SELLING AS IMPRESSION MANAGEMENT

When you're selling, it's like you're putting on a show for the customer. . . . Sometimes I stutter, I get excited, but we've memorized our presentation, all our lines. And it is like being an actor, but you get tested more. And you have to give your version, but you have to watch it. It has to come out more naturally. Not like Shiela. She didn't last because of it [cosmetics].

Since purchases reflect the images that prospects associate with purchasing situations, it is to the vendors' advantage to present themselves (and products) in ways that prospects will find appealing. Nowhere is the practice of impression management more fully explicated than in the works of Erving Goffman. In his classic, *The Presentation of Self in Everyday Life,* Goffman (1959) outlines the significance of impression management for ongoing interaction. Like the interactionists more generally (e.g., Mead, 1934; Blumer, 1969), Goffman's position reflects four basic assumptions: objects (including people) are defined and named; meanings are attached to objects through group interaction; people act toward objects in terms of the meanings they have for them; and as self-reflective beings, humans can take themselves and others into account in developing lines of action. Recognizing that actors are self-reflective beings able to take themselves and others into account, Goffman shows how people may selectively present themselves to others to promote particular definitions (of self) by others. In this way, persons may attempt to influence how others act toward them, thereby attempting to shape the nature of their relationships with these others.

In examining impression management, Goffman is not concerned with people's "true selves," [7] but with their "projected selves;" the images that people present to others. Appreciating that people may find it advantageous to be seen in certain ways and may attempt to influence the ways in which others define them, Goffman shows how people may promote (give off) particular images of themselves to others.[8] Thus, for instance, people may prefer to appear bright, nice, and honest, rather than slow, rude, and dishonest. Regardless of how they may wish to be seen, however, people are dependent upon the interpretations of their presentations by others. People are ultimately reliant on others for affirmations of projected images and identities. These (ongoing) presentations and interpretations, Goffman posits, are central to the emergence and maintenance of social order. While any presentation may entail some insincerity, Goffman views impression management as an inevitable aspect of group life. It represents people's attempts to deal with others in ways they most prefer.

Using a *dramaturgical* (theatrical) model, Goffman (like Shakespeare) contends that "All the world is a stage . . ." As actors in the drama of everyday life, people have "back regions" in which to prepare themselves and "front regions" in which to give performances to others. And, while people may attempt to exercise control over their personal appearances and manners, like actors on stage, so may they also use settings, props, and supporting casts to make their presentations more convincing.[9] Although everyday scripts are generally much less well defined than those of actors on stage, people may develop rather elaborate scripts (as indicated by some sales presentations) on the stage of everyday life. Similarly, people can develop styles of presentation and they can rehearse more complicated and/or important communications. But, unlike their stage counterparts who assume cooperative others, cooperation in everyday encounters is much more precarious.

Everyday audiences (viewing the world as a stage) are all those who witness people's activities. Like audiences in the theatrical setting, these everyday audiences may judge people from afar. In contrast to theatrical settings, however, these audiences may also get on stage. In the process, all involved can be seen to develop jointly (negotiate) the scenarios they experience. Each participant may have certain objectives in mind, but so may the others. And, although some participants may assume the role of supporting casts, others may be much less cooperative. Hence, a central task of everyday actors is to make ongoing adjustments to others, to fit their lines of action into the emergent (and negotiable) encounters in which they find themselves. In everyday life, people find themselves in much more dynamic (although not necessarily more dramatic) contexts than do their counterparts on stage. Their obstacles are greater, but their resources, subsequent lines of action and outcomes are much less clearly defined. Seen in this manner, people are not just actors, they are *interactors* whose life chances are dependent on how their performances are received by others.[10]

Reflecting a mixture of viewpoints, unfolding exchanges, uncertain outcomes, and opportunities for input from all parties, sales-related encounters can be considered in dramaturgical terms. As with actors in a play, salespeople can be seen as on stage as they enter the prospect's presence. But, unlike those witnessing plays, the vendors' audiences play direct, interactive roles. As in all everyday encounters, salespeople are dependent on the cooperation of those with whom they interact. Vendors may have scripts from which to work, but they will also find themselves negotiating encounters with prospects and making ongoing adjustments as these encounters take place. Impression management, thus, is best seen in processual terms as buyers and sellers make ongoing adjustments to one another. Each party may have his or her own anticipations and experiences to draw upon, but the encounter is to be worked out with much less certainty as to outcome.

To say that sales encounters are jointly constructed by the participants adds a vital element to the dramaturgical model. It does not, however, indicate what role vendors may play in the process; nor does it reflect the difficulties vendors may have in attempting to construct their versions of the emergent scenarios. From the vendor's perspective, a more complete unfolding of the sales drama would include (1) getting prepared for customer encounters; (2) approaching customers; (3) qualifying customers; (4) arousing interest; (5) establishing trust; and (6) closing the sale (and overcoming any resistance). Since these processes may occur concurrently and/or intermittently, they do not follow a necessary sequence. Further, these elements are not equally important across situations. While one or more of these dimensions may be inconsequential in specific encounters (a sale is still made), each may represent a major impediment in any given encounter. Recognizing variable vendor-buyer concerns and inputs, each of these elements will be discussed in an attempt to indicate what each entails, when and how each may be problematic, and the ways in which vendors endeavor to come to terms with these contingencies.

Getting Prepared

Beyond all of the activities that "set the stage" (e.g., setting up, purchasing products, pricing, promotions, display work, and the like),[11] one may ask how vendors become immediately prepared for their forthcoming contacts with prospects. Vendors vary greatly in the amount of preparation they do, but two concerns many salespeople share with their stage counterparts reflect scripts and stage fright. Scripts may be extensively prepared in advance or emerge more casually over time, while stage fright denotes concerns pertaining to receptivity from others, self-confidence, and acceptability of the products they sell.

GETTING SCRIPTED

When readers think of salespeople using scripts, they are apt to envision the sort of standardized presentations they might encounter from door-to-door insurance, encyclopedia, or vacuum salespeople, or telephone solicitors.[12] The scripts used by many of these companies are extensive, and salespeople are expected to learn these in the same ways that one might prepare for a play on stage. Not all scripts are as explicitly formulated as these, but most salespeople use scripts of some sort as they approach and present products to prospects. Further, scripts need not be deliberately contrived. Many are, but vendors can easily and unwittingly routinize styles of presentation. And while there may be a tendency to view more extensive presentations as artificial, our primary concern is with their deployment as interactional tools.

Prepared Presentations

The standardized presentation (also "track," spiel," "canned talk") represents a way of organizing any and all of the following tasks: approaching prospects, qualifying prospects, arousing prospect interest, developing trust on the part of prospects, facilitating purchases, closing sales, and working out financial arrangements. Incorporating as many of the sales features as desired, a standardized presentation can be a very efficient method of organizing sales activity. It not only enables script writers to build on the past experiences of salespeople in the field, but allows them to integrate images of product, user, company, and so on, in a more complete, precise, and systematic manner. The sales track can not only expedite the entire transaction, but, as Bogdan

(1972) notes, may also provide a quick training routine (product knowledge, style, confidence builder) in itself.

Standardized presentations are often criticized for being too inflexible and limiting target participation. More importantly, however, set presentations may require certain amounts of time to develop in their entirety, be more vulnerable to interruption, become redundant when dealing with repeat customers, and be more cumbersome when wider ranges or changing sets of products are being sold.[13]

The following quotes outline some fairly extensive scripts along with some of the variations vendors find themselves making. It is worth noting that agents involved in the more extensive presentations are usually provided with some props (e.g., folders, presentation kits, audio-visual equipment). These help direct the presentation and facilitate agent recall. In addition, these props may represent mediums of interest, as well as suggesting that the agent is a member of a larger team capable of some planning.

> Our agents use standardized presentations and flip charts, as well as audio-visual equipment that we can set up in the person's home. This way, they can do a better presentation than they could do on their own. . . . These sorts of materials, the audio-visuals, selling tracks are also used by other large companies, like _____ and _____ . We have audio-visual presentation materials that we use in dealing with the vendors (home owners), a format that we use, a planned presentation on why you should list with us, why you should get us to sell your home for you. There are other areas of planned presentation, such as qualifying buyers. You can save a lot of time and effort by getting their requirements early on. We use audio-visual because of the greater attention it commands. We also have other material we can leave with the people. We try to get the person involved in the material both visually and mentally [real estate].

> We have sales tracks that we memorize. We practice these in the office, raising objections and trying to deal with these. Then when you're feeling more comfortable with them, or the supervisor figures you're ready, you go and try these on actual prospects. . . . I think that as far as approaching the individual at first, most of the salespeople will use a standardized sales track, to get the ball rolling. But once you get started, you may, as you're interviewing the person, drift away from the sales track. You still like to follow the basic outline of the presentation, you concentrate on the basics, but you have to adjust to the people, their questions, and such. It also varies with the policy. Some policies have built-in presentations in folders, charts, and such. They make it very easy for you to go through the presentation. Then if there's a question along the way, you can deal with it and then get back to where you left off, or you may tell them that they will be explained in

the next section. But there will be other situations where you may be more flexible, where you empathize more with the client, maybe stressing things that are not built into the presentation, or maybe explaining things to them in ways they might better understand [insurance].

While companies using scripts tend to be especially concerned that newcomers learn these verbatim, one finds a general tendency among salespeople to improvise within the general guidelines of the script.

You use songs that are played on the instruments more specifically, and you have a variety of tunes, a whole repertoire in your presentation, a variety of tempos, beats. It's all part of the canned presentation. You can vary the tunes a little, something that's more contemporary, something you feel more comfortable with. But the basic presentation's pretty well set. . . . We also shop the competitors, see how they're doing their presentations. And it's so pat, you sort of smile. Sort of, "Where have I heard this before?" Most work from the same sort of presentations, and it's so pat, and, of course, the problem is to appear natural. . . . But you have to vary the presentation with the people you're dealing with, as they're talking about this and that. So sometimes, you'll go through your routine pretty well the way it is laid out, but at other times, you will try to emphasize these features as you are talking with them, because they want to talk more. They interrupt with questions, make comments, things like that, more. But after a while you realize that the questions are much the same, and the lines you're showing them, they're much the same, just different features you're trying to emphasize in each case [music].

Despite their apparent advantages, not all vendors like preset presentations. Thus, while some may feel phoney or unduly challenged in memorizing scripts, others (usually salespeople with some prior experiences) may view them with some disdain.

Presentation kits, demonstrators, video machines, slides, all these things are window dressing. The prime thing is the salesman. . . . The props help, but it's the person that does it, and most really good salespeople shy away from the gimmickry [manufacture—industrial].

Emergent Scripts

A major advantage of a script is that it makes it easier for salespeople to deal with prospects. Thus, even in situations in which no particular scripts were used originally, many vendors find themselves developing scripts as they go about selling their products. These tend to evolve as salespeople begin emphasizing certain features of the products being sold and/or find that certain gestures and/or expressions seem better received than others. Although these vendors need not define their habits in reference to scripts, spiels, or presentations, many come to realize that it is profitable to present themselves and their products in certain ways, and those explicitly thinking in script terms seem advantaged.

> I don't have a standardized track, but what happens is that as you make more and more calls, you do get a more standardized presentation. It becomes more standardized. With the graphic material I was selling before, it was more standardized than with the appliances now. But you do develop styles of presenting the product to the people. Maybe you don't use the exact same style, but there is a certain routine that you've found maybe works best for you, and so you follow that along as you are making your presentation. But we don't actually have a format we instruct our people to use in making their sales [manufacture—appliances].

> I really hate canned presentations, but what happened was that I eventually developed one, but one that I felt comfortable with. I want to sell quality items, and I believe that I can help them through the promotional materials. But if I am to help them best, I will need as much information as I can get about their business and their clientele, things like that. You have to know how much they want to spend, how many items they want, something to start with at least. There are 10,000 items, more, so I need to have some idea of what they are wanting to accomplish with the specialty items, what their budget is like. Things like that. . . . Are you trying to dig up new clients? Are you trying to say "Thank you!" to those you already have? Trying to increase worker morale? And it needn't be expensive to work, to get people thinking about your company, help them remember you [promotions—agency].

MANAGING STAGE FRIGHT

Scripts provide guidelines for interaction, but another aspect of preparation involves the management of "stage fright" (Lyman and Scott, 1970). Like actors on stage, vendors anticipating encounters with their audiences do not know how they will fare. Denoting concerns with customer receptivity, stage fright tends to be especially common among novices, but it is by no means so limited.

> You have some people who are nervous when they start out, and then some of them end up doing a very good job selling suits, for instance. But you also get a lot of the ones that think they can do it, and then, when it comes right down to it, they get nervous because there is a strange person standing there and they have to go

over and ask them. You'll also get the ones that you pretty well have to push out there, "Why don't we just let them look around." And you have to, "Go on. Get your ass over there! Go and ask them if you can help!" They might do well when they got there, but you would have to get them out there [men's clothing].

I've been in sales for five years now, so it shouldn't bother me, but it does. I still haven't really gotten used to the idea that I'm in sales. It's been my livelihood for five years, and I still get nervous when I approach new accounts for the first time [manufacture—industrial].

Feeling Comfortable

Some people reported little initial reluctance to approach people in sales contexts, but for many others, stage fright is best overcome with coaching and/or experience.

I didn't think I could sell. I thought I wasn't aggressive enough, but it's amazing how it makes you that way, more aggressive, more outgoing. I found it was a tremendous change. The first time you walk up to someone, "May I be of some assistance?" You're so afraid they'll say yes. And yet you're afraid they'll say no. . . . But now, there's no hesitation. I just walk up to someone, start chatting, pass the time of day. If they don't want me to help them, fine. If they do, well I know how to do that well. I know my products, and I'm confident. But initially, you have all these fears, reservations. . . . It took me about a year to get to where I felt really comfortable approaching people like that [jewelry].

Now it's so easy for me to approach customers. It feels so natural now. And there, the owner had been really helpful. He would sit us down at meetings and discuss how we're selling with people, how we're approaching people and all. And it made a world of difference to us, it really helped. You learn some things on your own, too, but it's good to have someone to point these things out to you [women's clothing].

Even those who have overcome their reservations on a general level indicate that their sense of confidence is somewhat situated, reflecting those with whom they are dealing.

Strangers are a threat. If you don't know them, they're a threat. . . . When I first started into sales, I was always reluctant to knock on that door. I was fearful because you don't know what is going to happen every time you walk in a room. Now, I really don't have that reluctance. . . . Sometimes it creeps up on you, like the first call of the week is the roughest one. You've sat back over the weekend, and now you've got to get back into it. . . . Or if you know you've got a hassle, you hate to confront it, but you've got to. If you go in and try to do what you can for them, they may be mad when they call you, but if you can go in and show them that you do have their interests at heart, they'll buy from you again. They've thought that you've sold them a bill of goods, which all salesmen are noted for, but if you can put those fears aside, you can deal with them [manufacture—industrial].

Although open insults are generally infrequent, it is the salespeople's awareness of the potential negativity the next encounter may bring, together with general anticipations of customer distrust and distancing, that promotes timidity. Prior sales tend to nullify these hesitations, but upon experiencing negative and/or unproductive encounters, salespeople tend to feel less prepared to approach subsequent prospects.

The customers are getting pretty wary of salespeople. "Just browsing." "Just browsing." That's what they say as soon as you approach them. Say anything to them and it's, "just browsing." Usually, I give them a few minutes to look around, and then if I see them looking at something or waiting for you to come over, then I'll go over and ask them how they're doing today. Something like that, "May I help you?" "Can I give you a hand with something." But usually, it's "I'm just browsing." "Fine, take your time, look around." [men's clothing]

Some of the customers don't want to talk to you. They want to try things on, but they want to be left alone. That's kind of hard to deal with when they ignore you when you go up to them [department store].

Common Reservations

Like actors feeling uncomfortable with "the character" into which they've been cast, salespeople may find that certain aspects of particular sales situations make successful performances more awkward. Thus vendors may find themselves reluctant to sell items that they consider costly, unpopular, or inferior in quality.

Price concerns. Although customers would seem most concerned about prices, vendors who feel that items are overpriced, priced above most incomes, or priced at levels apt to arouse buyer resistance, tend to have difficulties promoting those goods.

You have to get comfortable with your prices, like $40 for a [skin] cream. You have to get comfortable and not feel guilty. That's really important! Like myself, and the other staff, we would never spend the kind of money we are trying to get our customers to spend on cosmetics. . . . "And this is $40, but well worth it in terms of what it can do for you." . . . You try to show them that if they spend more, they'll look better for it. They're buying an appearance. Essentially, you are appealing to their vanity. And then they think that if they pay more, it will do more. And that is true to some extent. And it helps if you have more confidence in your products [cosmetics].

In general, price reservations tend to be short-lived. Some employees may be dismissed (or quit) because they were unable to deal with this concern, but most of those remaining eventually define appropriate prices relative to the competition and/or justify them in other ways.

One of the things I had to get used to when I first started was the prices. I'd think, "Oh my gosh! Do people really pay this much for this jacket?" But I've noticed in the past couple of years that the prices of some items have doubled or even tripled in some cases, and it doesn't really bother me any more. You say say, "Well, the blue jackets are in," and you just go and sell them. Every now and then you realize that an item is more expensive than you thought it would be, but then you realize that manufacturers have costs and that other kinds of things do go up, and you just don't think about it the same way. . . . It's good looks and service that we provide, and the price is something you don't worry about. You sell the appearance, the image that you're creating. Also quality is important, so you emphasize that, quality, and durability, how these items will hold up better than some that may cost you less. "Cheap," that's a word you try not to use. Some things are less expensive or inexpensive [women's clothing].

Initially, before you know the industry, you might think that the machines are really costly, but when you see the competition, and when you realize how much the [purchasing] company will save, compared to what it would cost them if they had to do the job manually, then you realize that it's a small price. It really is [manufacture—office equipment]!

Unpopular merchandise. As with merchandise thought to be too costly, vendors may have difficulty selling goods they consider personally and/or generally disliked.

It's hard to sell something that you don't like. Even when someone comes in and says, "Oh, that's really neat." [You think] "You like that? Okay, fine, we'll ring it up for you." But it's not like something that you really like, that you think really looks good on the person. Those things are a pleasure to sell!. . . . So some things, the things you thought looked nice, you would suggest these more. Also, the way you arranged things in the store. If you thought that something looked nice, it would get a better spot in the store. Something you didn't like, it would get buried somewhere in the store. If you didn't like the cut of a pant, it ended up in the store room, things like that [mixed clothing].

In every shipment, you'll get some "dogs." That's what we call them, items that just don't move. . . . We have our buyers, and they order the merchandise and set the prices. They send them to us, and our job is to get rid of them. . . . If they're not selling here, in this area, then we can move them to another area. They may do better there [shoes].

Quality concerns. Vendors are also more reluctant to promote merchandise (and/or service) that they consider to be of poorer quality.

We have some watches that I don't like selling. We've had a lot of problems with one of our lines, and I don't like to sell a watch that someone has to bring back in three weeks. So even though we're running a "sale" on them now, I will try to get them to move up to a better line. If they want to take their chances with that watch, they can. But even then, when they come back, they're upset with you, "You sold me this watch!" So I'd rather not sell that watch [department store].

We deal with a lot of suppliers, and for sure there's a difference in quality, although it's not always related to price. . . . So there are some lines I push over others. You know they will hold up better. If somebody really wants the other, okay. But after you see that they don't hold up as well, and I'll often tell the person that, it's harder to push them [men's clothing].

Approaching Customers: Initiating Action

Customers will sometimes initiate encounters with salespeople, but on a great many occasions vendors assume the responsibility of approaching prospects. The approach marks a mutually evident beginning of the encounter, but its significance may be much greater than this. Thus, while sales encounters are fragile, subject to skepticism, and ultimately dependent on buyer cooperation, approaches may be used to qualify customers, generate interest, and promote trust. Since they tend to shape first impressions, approaches can have considerable effect on the prospects' assessments of all that follows.[14]

As the following materials indicate, vendors may adopt a variety of fairly standardized approaches. These include the "nonapproaches" characterizing self-serve stores, general offers of assistance, conversational approaches, delayed approaches, and approaches involving those recognized as repeat customers.

Serve Yourself

Denoting a nonapproach format, self-serve stores tend to minimize vendor-customer contact. It is in these settings that buyers have to assume the greatest initiative for purchases.

> We've living proof that customers can serve themselves. For the most part, at least. We operate self-serve, but so does [deep discount store] and even [department store], basically. But display is more important, your signs and all, because that has to do the talking for you. Packaging too is very important. Is it attractive? Does it tell a customer enough information? Because that'll make a difference in how much we sell. And name brands do better than the lesser known brands. But we have a pretty good return policy, so we generally do pretty well with our [store] brand too [discount department store].

Offering Assistance

When vendor initiated contact is made, this most often involves vague inquiries regarding potential aid. This tends to be especially true of those working in self-serve stores, but emerges as common practice in a great many other settings.

> Usually, it's "May I help you?" "Can I be of some help?" Some such thing. And usually the reply is "No, I'm just browsing." "Just looking, thanks." And that's the problem, because it typically stops there. Or sometimes the clerk will say, which is better than nothing, "Well, if you need any help, I'll be over there." But that's not selling [department store]!

Making Conversation

Although they seem relatively ineffective in promoting alternatives to general offers of assistance, most training programs (and marketing manuals) discourage this tactic. The major alternative they propose is that of developing conversations with prospects. This strategy may reflect any of the following concerns: it is more difficult for prospects to decline interest in casual conversation, prospects may dislike or become weary of "May/Can I help you?" approaches, conversation is a less obtrusive means of showing products and generating interest; and conversation allows vendors to develop more fully relationships with their prospects.

Although salespeople may feel very comfortable about making conversation, this alternative is generally more demanding than general offers of assistance. It entails a comment (e.g., compliment or question) seemingly appropriate to the situation. Commonly, salespeople using conversational approaches draw attention to the prospect, the prospect's experiences (including the weather), the products featured, or even themselves (or the company they represent).

You approach the person. You try to approach everybody. That's our policy. You never say, "Can I help you?" or "May I help you?" It's too easy for the person to say "No" or brush you off. You try to get into a little bit of conversation with them. Try to get them involved talking with you. . . . Like with luggage, if they're looking at a piece of luggage, I'd say, "Would you like to see the inside?" and start to open up the case for them, explaining some of the features to them. Or I might think, "Are there particular features they're looking for?" So I might ask them if they had a particular color in mind or size. I try to find out what the person's needs or wants are [department store].

This strategy seems most effective when the vendors' comments appear nonthreatening and suggest more extensive interest in prospects.[15] Viewed in this way, the conversational approach is not only a means of initiating an encounter, it is also a technique for promoting relaxation, developing relationships, and generating interest in the company's goods.

When someone walks into your store, you have to assume that they are coming in to buy something, so you want to say hello to them, give them a greeting, be friendly, let them know that you're a friendly store and that you're aware that they're there. You don't want to ignore them because people don't want to be ignored. You don't want to hover. I don't like to have someone all over me when I go into a store. I want to be free to look. You have to find a perfect balance between letting a customer know that you know they're there and you're friendly and you're ready to help them if they wish it, but you're going to let them alone and let them look. . . . There are certain approaches, some approaches that you use that demand a negative answer and you don't want that, so it's a difficult situation to know exactly what to say, to be friendly but not to be pushy. . . . You just have to learn what's comfortable for you. If it's comfortable for you to just walk up and say, "Hi, how are you today? Isn't it a beautiful day?" Or "That's a lovely dress you're wearing!" Or "Did you just get your hair done?" It's more comfortable for some people to go along with that than it is for other people, and some salespeople, when they start, it's

"Can I help you?" If the customer says no, they have nowhere to go from there, but to slink off [jewelry].

If you want to sell more, first, you have to be willing to approach all the people who come into the store. And you do not approach them, with "Can I help you?" That's the worst way of approaching people. The best thing is to try to build up a conversation with the people. . . . Now everyone will get in a routine, where they get slack, especially after a slow period, but if you can make conversation, maybe comment on something they're wearing, or that some color would look lovely on them. That's the ice breaker, and from there you can move into your sales very easily. . . . Sometimes, if they're looking at a dress, say, you might ask them if they would like to try it on. Or you might assure them that it is a good price. You might say something about the fabric, that there's cotton in it and it breathes and all, and how it cleans. And it is difficult, because you don't know just what they're looking for, but it gives them a chance to tell you, "Well, I'm not too concerned about this or that. Basically, what I had in mind was . . ." Then you can help them a little more, go into other things, but you really can't do that until you can get them to open up to you. And that's not always easy to do, because they think that you're just there to make a sale, that that's all you do! . . . With your name brands, you've got another in, "Are you familiar with _____'s line?" And even if they're not, they get to be more aware of this line, and start to think more in these terms. But a lot of people love to talk and they do like help, so if you're nice to them, it's so easy to make a sale [women's clothing].

Not all salespeople are attuned to conversational modes of approach or are sufficiently interested in pursuing these when they are aware of their advantages. However, even those aware of, and interested in pursuing, conversational modes of approach tend to find that this is a difficult posture to maintain on a consistent basis. Apart from very limited patterns (e.g., "Hello. How are you today? Nice day, today."), conversational approaches involving strangers (minimal background information) entail creativity in the face of uncertain receptivity. While these elements cut across vendor-buyer encounters, they help account for the tendency of salespeople to revert to general offers of assistance, even when they personally oppose this style of approach.

Delayed Approaches

Regardless of whether salespeople offer general assistance or attempt conversation, another way they may vary their approach is to allow customers some time with which to become acquainted with the setting before being approached.[16]

> When people come in, we let them have a minute to browse. Then we approach them carefully, slowly, very low key. They're frightened to death of these high-pressure salesmen [appliances].

> We like to let them browse. When they come in, we don't attack them. Not even "Can I help you?" or anything, right off, because some people are just scared. They just want to take their time and look around, and if someone is on their back all the time, they'll just leave again. We let them walk around for a while and then we approach them, ask them if we can help them with something. It makes them feel more comfortable that way, and some people come in quite regularly and browse. . . . We just let them browse, because if you don't do that, you might make one mad out of a hundred, but if you attack everyone, you might scare away twenty [furniture].

However effective the delayed approach may be, it also creates dilemmas for vendors. Vendors may wish to give prospects time to acclimatize themselves to the setting, but in doing so, they risk departures prior to contact (and, it is usually easier to approach prospects before they give indications of leaving).

> If a customer came in, we would give them half a minute, tops, and then we were supposed to approach them, "Good afternoon. How are you today?" . . . "Is there something in particular that you were looking for?" that kind of thing. Try to coax them into something [department store].

> We usually give them a few minutes to browse, before we approach them. I like to do it the same way, when I'm shopping. I like to have a few minutes to look around. So I'll greet them, and if they want to ask any questions right away, they will. Otherwise, they can browse for a few minutes. . . . We all have our different styles of approaching people. But I think you also read the signs too, so that if someone looks like he's in a hurry to get something and get on his way, you can often tell that, so you try to help him right away. We're out there, so if someone needs our help right away, we help them, but we let them browse around most of the time before we go up to them [jewelry].

Approaching Repeat Customers

One of the most important elements affecting salespeople's approaches is the recognition that someone is a regular customer. Although some repeat customers may be disliked, most are seen to represent more receptive and predictable prospects. Further, insofar as relationships have already been established with these persons, vendors have other bases on which to initiate subsequent encounters and promote sales more generally.

New customers are my more difficult sales because you don't know what they're looking for or how much they can buy. And you can't judge by how they look when they come into the store. Usually, people who are dressed better will spend more, but it's just not that simple. So those sorts of things, plus they don't know who you are, if they can trust you, things like that, make first customers more difficult [women's clothing].

Everybody's different, but you know the regulars in a different way. You get to know more about them. Their likes and dislikes, habits, something about their families, the things they do. So it's a different situation. And usually you're much more comfortable with them. And they're more trusting. There's more joking, more of a conversation. It's more of a friendship thing, which is nice [department store].

The regulars are generally more predictable,[17] but each exchange remains to be worked out anew. Salespeople may make more assumptions about regular customers, but the following discussions of qualification and interest are relevant to this subset of prospects as well.

Qualifying Customers

Vendors' attempts to qualify customers provide living instances of what Mead (1934) terms "role taking." Role taking or contemplating the perspectives of the other is another commonplace activity that appears in a more crystalline form in the marketplace. Here as well, it rests on the premise that by knowing the other better, one can more readily construct lines of action that the other will find acceptable.

Qualification appears minimal in some sales settings,[18] but it is apparent that vendors may begin to qualify prospects as soon as prospects enter their awareness (even before making an approach). Thus surface information (e.g., appearances, companions, occasions) may affect the ways in which vendors approach prospects and their willingness to consider further the prospects' situations. And any information obtained at any point in the encounter may be used better to define prospect perspectives and interests. In these respects, qualification may be seen as an activity occurring throughout the encounter.

If you can get a better line on your decision maker, find out more about the person, what they like, dislike, you can work more effectively on that person. You know how to appeal to the person [appliances].

What I try to do with each of my accounts is sit down with the people and get some ideas of their sales totals for the year before and such, and also where they are wanting to go with their sales, and sit down and plan an advertising budget with them. You also want to take into account what it is they want to achieve in terms of products they're putting out. . . . When you are selling advertising to these accounts, you become like an extension of that company. You become, in a sense, their promotions officer. I'm an extension of their business [promotions—newspaper].

By qualifying customers more fully, salespeople may be better able to match prospects' interests (existing and/or to be developed) with their own line of products. Additionally, by suggesting elements to be both incorporated and avoided as their encounters unfold, qualification enhances vendors' abilities to establish working relationships with these people. Vendors are not always accurate in their assessments, nor do they make effective adjustments even when they intend to do so, but qualification represents an attempt to define better those with whom vendors interact (and must satisfy to make sales). The job of qualifying prospects may become very intensive when large orders are at stake, and the term *qualification* is more likely to be used explicitly in reference to higher-priced items, but qualification is by no means so limited.

You pick up all the information you could from the person coming in the store. And then you try to relate to them, on general terms, in a way they would feel comfortable, so you'd react a little differently to someone who's maybe more professional looking than say some 18-year-old. You try to relate to the person as you perceive them to be [shoes].

When a customer comes in, we have a brief consultation with her, inquiring into her life-style, her activities, her color preferences, and all. From that we make a judgment on what they want. Do they want a natural look? Do they want a _____ look? Do they want an evening look? . . . You try to find out a lot about the people, as much as you can, although some people are very closed. . . . It's good too, in relating to people, having something to talk with them about, along with your presentation [cosmetics].

Vendors are very uneven in their qualification efforts, but frequent areas of inquiry pertain to prospects' seriousness; background situations; potential product applications; and personal preferences. These areas of information often overlap, so an inquiry into one realm often produces information on other areas as well.

ASSESSING SERIOUSNESS

One of the dimensions on which customers (new prospects especially) are most often assessed is in reference to their seriousness (perceived willingness and/or abilities to make purchases). Vendors vary greatly in their definitions of particular people as serious, but this definition can have strategic implications for the ensuing encounters. Some vendors try to approach everyone as if they were serious, but those defined as less serious tend to receive less attention.

> One of the things I do to tell if someone is serious is to ask them when they might be interested in making a purchase. Like if he says not until next spring, and he says that he's happy with the present car and that his wife is shopping next door, where he is just filling in time, I'll hand him my card and tell him to feel free to look around and, if he has any questions, to feel free to ask. . . . You've got to qualify the customer. I've seen a salesman spend an hour and a half with someone just browsing while his wife is grocery shopping. That's a waste of time. His time should be more productive [auto].

This appears to hold true even when deliberate efforts are made to the contrary.[19]

> If people seem to be looking at something more carefully, more intensely, you assume that they're serious. But if someone is looking at a wide range of things, sort of flitting around, you will probably approach them, but you expect that they're not all that serious, that they're just browsing, perhaps killing some time while they're waiting for a friend, husband, or whatever. . . . But that's the one thing about sales, everybody is different. You can't really treat everyone the same way! And that's part of your job, to move someone from a browser to a buyer. That can be done many ways. Like you may see someone with a pendant on, "I see you have a very nice opal there, may I clean it for you?" Or "By the way, I have a pair of earrings that would match that beautifully." But that's hard to do, to remember to do that every time, especially when you're busy. . . . You have to be very alert, and very outgoing all the time, and it's also a very strong, selling type of thing. It's difficult to do [jewelry].

It's difficult to act towards everyone [at craft shows] as if they were good
prospects. I've been trying to do that consistently, but after a number of futile
attempts you find yourself being more selective. At the same time, however,
I've also found that people who seem too poor, or young, etc. to buy your
goods often have the money required. It's their money, and they have the same
rights to buy things as anyone else [notes].

The preceding instances reflect the retail walk-in trade, but similar
concerns are evident at trade shows and in field sales where the vendor
seeks out prospective customers. As with salespeople in busier stores,
vendors in these other settings who have other prospects are generally
less attentive to those thought less serious.

You can often spot the serious ones, but some of them will let you go through
the whole spiel, and then they tell you that they've got one in the back room
that they're still planning to set up when they get around to it. But usually, if
someone asks more questions, they're more serious. . . . If I can see that
there's no damn way I can sell to the person, I'm gone like a flash. You thank
them and out you go [promotions—signs].

You try to concentrate on those people who seem more interested in your product.
There are a lot of prospects out there, so you spend your time and try to make
your money on the people who seem the most interested [promotions—magazine].

Although lessened effort seems likely when prospects are thought to
be less serious, it should be noted that salespeople may assess seriousness on quite different bases. Thus interest may be inferred on the basis
of appearance, presumed item appropriateness, or even mere presence
in the setting.

Some salespeople claim more ability for detecting serious from
nonserious shoppers, but most view this as problematic even though the
person's presence may suggest some degree of interest.

You really can't tell if they're lookers or buyers. Sometimes we'll ask one
another that, when a customer comes in the store. You'll sometimes joke that
way, before you approach them. And you guess, but then, there are times when
you think you've got it sold, for sure, and they'll say, "Well, we'll think about
it," and other times, they're buying [luggage].

Given this uncertainty and the negotiable nature of sales encounters,[20] the tactic some vendors define as safest is to assume that all
prospects are serious until proven otherwise."[21] While not uniform in

their orientations, salespeople operating from this perspective also seem more likely than others to envision their task as one of developing interest on the part of all prospects.

You really can't tell whether someone is serious or not, but that's something I really don't worry about. Some people say that they're "just browsing," or "just looking," but I figure that everyone is looking and that everyone is a customer. If they didn't think there would be something that they might like to see and possibly buy, they wouldn't be going through this store. I just assume that everyone is a prospect, a customer. Also you get some people who are afraid to say that they want something, because they might be worried about getting pushed into something. So people saying that they're "just browsing" isn't something that's important to me in doing sales work. I assume that everyone is there to buy. . . . It's the same thing with the way they're dressed. You might get some that look like they couldn't afford our clothes, but you never know. Someone can look down on a particular day and yet have a fair bit of money to spend in your shop [women's clothing].

Beyond assessments of prospect interests in the items at hand, other realms of qualification pertain to prospect backgrounds, product applications, and personal preferences.

OBTAINING BACKGROUND INFORMATION

Insofar as purchasing activity reflects the more general contexts in which prospects find themselves, it is generally advantageous for vendors to learn more about their prospects' situations.

You try to qualify the customer in terms of what his needs are. Like if it's a man with four children, you forget about the smaller car, you would talk in terms of station wagons, a full-size car, whatever. If it's a young couple, and they show an interest in a sports car, you might steer them to what you have there. Now if it's an older couple who like the comfort, you try to sell them a larger car, and you ask them if they have friends their own age. Then you would try to suggest a four-door, because it's a little easier for passengers to get in and out of. So qualification, figuring out what would be most appropriate for them, that would be one of your first concerns. . . . The basic steps are meeting and greeting, qualification, presentation, demonstration, and then the close. That is how all sales should work. Those are basic, the fundamentals. Now, you can embellish each one, but there are a lot of salespeople who talk themselves into a deal, through the deal, and right out of the deal. You have to be a good listener. . . . If a person is a referral, you've won part of the battle. If you've been recommended, then you know you've crossed the bridge, because you can build on that, how you've given this other person a good

deal, good service, and such, and would like to do the same for them. . . . I try
to find out why they came to our showroom. Whether it was because of an ad in
the paper, whether it was because of a referral or what. That's part of the qualifier,
you try to get a little background information on them. That's so important! . . .
You have to deal with people and so you have to get to know more about them
to see how they might be fitted up with your products. . . . You sell three things,
and in this order: yourself, the product, and lastly the price. That's so important!
If you can sell yourself first, you gain some yardage [auto].

UNCOVERING PRODUCT APPLICATIONS

Although knowledge pertaining to applications often overlaps with
background information or other aspects of qualification, vendors may
endeavor to define more precisely the "tasks" expected of products in
order more effectively to relate products to prospects. Salespeople
attempting to determine applications may not only find themselves
trying to define the locus of applications, but also ascertaining prospect
familiarity with the products considered.

The first thing you have to do is to find out what the customer is after. You have
to find out what price range, what they need the shoe for, and you have to do
this without the customer really realizing that you're trying to find that out. . . .
Also, if they use words, like a "casual shoe" or "dress shoe," you have to be
careful, because their ideas of casual or dress shoes may be different from what
the other people mean, or the way you think of them in the store. You want to
find out what they're thinking. And with some, it can be either. . . . Also, you
want to know how often they're going to wear the shoes, where they're going to
be wearing them. Sometimes people will come in with a piece of material and
say, "I need a pair of shoes to go with this," and that's all they will tell you to
start with. So you have to ask them. If they say, "It's for a suit," you have a
little better idea there, but then, depending on if it's a younger person, say,
they might want a more casual dress shoe than someone else [department store].

In selling luggage, you want to find out what kind of traveling they're doing. And
then with the people, like a little old lady, she'll want a light bag, something easier
for her to handle. You have to feel your customer out, see what they might have
in mind, and what they might like, how much they're traveling and all. And
people will ask us how much luggage they need, and that's a very hard question
to answer, because we really have no idea of where they're going, how long
they are wanting to stay, and what they're doing. . . . But most of our luggage
can be bought separately, so basically, what we do is to show them the different
lines and show them the features, the prices, and all, and let them choose [luggage].

DETECTING PERSONAL PREFERENCES

Since applications are often colored by tastes, vendors more able to define personal preferences pertaining to color, style, and the like, may be able to facilitate purchasing decisions. As well, they reduce the risk of losing more impatient prospects. When vendors are able to offer a wider range of choices, they may use these options as a means of providing service. In settings in which desired options are not available, preferences may represent obstacles to be avoided or negotiated should these appear unavoidable.

How you approach the people, depends on the person. Like some are very serious. They don't want you joking and laughing. They want the thing to be presented with no nonsense, and that's it. And you try to figure out who's price-conscious of quality, name brands, and so forth. And then there's people that come in that you can joke around with, so it all varies. . . . The things you stress will vary. An older man's more apt to want comfort. A younger man wants to look dressy, wants something to make him look smashing, something very stylish. And you'll get the people who look at prices, so you direct them to certain items that are a better deal. Some people don't care about the price, they just want something really good, or maybe a certain brand name. . . . If it's someone that you've dealt with before, you might know what other things you've sold them. You have a better idea of what's in their wardrobe. You don't have to ask them so much about that. You know more what they need, where the gaps are in their wardrobe. You know more about how they feel about prices, quality, etc., etc. And if they're a real good customer, you may know that you can show them three or four things and that they are not going to get intimidated. You know that they buy a lot of things when they buy. With a new person, they might get very offended if you're suggesting accessories or a second suit, thinking that you're trying to push them, but if you know the person, then that might be just what they expect you to do, to provide a more total service like that [men's clothing].

QUALIFICATION IS COOPERATIVE ACTIVITY!

Since it requires ongoing enterprise on the part of the salespeople involved, it should not be surprising to find that salespeople do not qualify prospects as fully as might seem ideal. Indeed, as with role taking more generally, salespeople not only tend to assume that others will share their own viewpoints, but may also find that their attempts to gain greater insight into the perspectives of others may be ineffectual. While there is no assurance that salespeople will be accurate in their "readings" of their customers, they are fundamentally dependent on the

willingness of these others to disclose accurately and fully their situations to them. Despite major advantages of qualifying prospects, role
taking entails cooperative behavior on the part of targets. It is one thing
for vendors to attempt to qualify prospects. However, should vendors
lack opportunities in which to do this, or should prospects be reluctant
to "open up," these efforts can be readily frustrated.

As their counselor, you try to get them to give you more information about
their situation. And that's the hard part. They may not trust you enough to
give you all the information you really need to do a top rate job for them. If
you just get a little information, you go away, work up some ideas, and then
when you come back, it's "Well that's not quite what we wanted." And in
graphic designs, if you go back and it's not something that they wanted,
you've wasted hours and hours of time. And in copy, every time you make a
change, it costs money. So you want to be very careful in trying to determine
what they want [promotions—agency].

It's not so much that they don't want to explain their situations, but until
you've instilled that confidence in you as a person, they don't want to open
up all that's good and bad about their business. . . . Once you get to know that
businessman and show him that you're up front with him, then he'll let you
know, "I'm having trouble in this area." They don't want you to go to another
businessman and tell him, "Joe Blow down the street is really having troubles
selling so and so's." Once you've established confidence with him, then he's
not afraid to let you know what his problem is. And then you can really attack
that problem. You can push, you can come up with creative ads. Something
that is going to work for him. Sometimes it can take a couple of years before
that happens. . . . With repeat people, the more you work with them, the more
you realize what it is that they really want to push. You begin to understand
more about their businesses. . . . When is the best time to push them? Should
you be going for it? . . . You sit down and talk to a client. You have to listen.
That's number one! The clients really do want to let you know about their
businesses, because otherwise you can't help them. And I think that a lot of
salesmen find that one of their biggest downfalls, they talk too much. And if
you're talking, you're not listening. What you have to do is listen [promo-
tions—radio].

Under these circumstances, vendors may work their way through
encounters by relying on general product appeals, descriptions, and the
like, making specific assumptions about the buyers and the possible
applications of their products to the buyers' situations; or asking if they
can be of assistance.

Generating Interest

As suggested by the preceding discussions of approaches and qual-ification, prospect interest may be affected by everything prospects associate with the products, vendors, and their own situations. Prior to discussing the ways in which salespeople promote interest, however, it is valuable to consider the interests with which prospects enter purchas-ing situations. Salespeople may be highly instrumental in prompting certain purchases, but in other instances purchasing decisions may be made without (or in spite of) their efforts.

PREEXISTING INTERESTS

Insofar as prospects may develop interests in purchasing particular products on their own, this capacity should be acknowledged relative to the vendors' pursuits. Of particular relevance here are prospects' self-defined attractions and obligations.

Seeking Products (Attractions)

As self-reflective entities, people may define certain situations (and products) as "desirable for persons like themselves." These definitions may reflect earlier experienced advertising campaigns and input from friends and other associates, as well as more privately attributed self-interests. Regardless of origins, however, these self-attributed interests suggest lines of action persons may independently pursue. Self-serve stores have long acknowledged the abilities of people to seek out objects, but people seeking out products represent some of the easiest sales all vendors experience.

> People that come up to the cash register with something in their hand, that's the easiest sale. . . . Or if someone is there, with two things in their hand, and they're going, "I don't know which one I like better." I will go, "I like this one better." And they usually go, "Yeah, I'll take this one." Those are the easy ones. I will make the decisions for them, and tell them what I like about the one I've chosen [department store].

> Fashion conscious people are the easiest people to sell because they're buying for fashion and fashion is changing constantly. So they're the easiest people to sell to. . . . As long as you've got what they want to buy. You've got to have it! If you don't have it, then it can be pretty rough [shoes].

CLOSURE (MEETING OBLIGATIONS)

Another source of preexisting interests involve people who feel obliged to make certain purchases. Perceiving particular purchases to represent solutions to pressing problems (i.e., necessary), prospects may "close" themselves into sales.

> You get a lot who come only when they need something. They're very specific, "I need a hammer, some glue, this size screws." We probably get more of that than some other places, but I've also gone into clothing stores, say, when I needed a shirt for some formal outing. Not really caring too much about this or that, so long as it's a shirt that fits, looks not too bad [hardware].

> Easy sales are like husbands at Christmas time who come in the last day and who could really care less what they're going to buy. They will pretty well go along with any suggestions you make. Like a guy might be willing to spend a thousand dollars, but he doesn't really know what, so you make a few suggestions, "That's fine, that's fine." [jewelry]

These self-defined interests (i.e., attractions or obligations) on the part of buyers may facilitate sales work overall, but as implied by the earlier discussion of qualification, it may be difficult for vendors to discern the direction and intensity of any interests the buyers may consider relevant to the case at hand.

Recognizing that vendors may attempt to promote interest from their first contacts with prospects, attention is now given to the ways in which salespeople attempt to cultivate interest in their products.

SHAPING INTERESTS

Vendors may attempt to intensify interest on the part of prospects who already have existing interests in their products (via seekership, closure),[22] but they may also attempt to develop interest in products where little or no interest previously existed. It is in reference to these situations that vendors envision themselves most as "selling" and in which we most clearly see interest as negotiable. Nevertheless, as in sales encounters more generally, the *promotion of interest* is best seen within the context of the entire interaction sequence. Thus, from first contacts to later points at which prospects make irrevocable purchasing commitments, interest remains a problematic and negotiable feature of sales encounters.

You try to get people to buy things, but to make it seem like it was their own idea. You tell them what it does for them, how it makes them look better, get them to want to get the item for themselves. Nobody wants to be shoved into these things [mixed sales].

You have to lead people sometimes. Like this one man, I [female] made a couple of good sales on him the other night. We got around to a suit and I looked along the rack and I looked at him, and I said, "This is the suit for you," and I picked it off the rack. He said, "I don't like it! Not at all." I asked him, "What don't you like about it?" "I don't like the colors, the stripes. No, I don't like it at all." "Well it's going to fit you better than anything else on the rack." "I always have a hard time getting things to fit." I said, "Put the jacket on." "Gee, the jacket does fit nice." "Put the pants on, put the whole thing together. See how it looks as a set." So he went into the fitting room and came out, looked at himself in the mirror, says, "Looks really good, doesn't it?" And yet, five minutes before, he didn't like anything about the suit. But, once he got it on, and saw it would fit him. . . . This is where knowing your products is such a big asset. He started liking it on him, and he bought the suit, a [top line] suit. So sometimes you can lead them, even when people are exactly sure what they do like, so sometimes it's just getting used to the item on yourself. You might just say, "Wow, that looks really macho!" Or "That looks sexy! It brings out the blue in your eyes." But you don't do that with an old man. There, "It looks nice. The color looks good on you." You tone it down. But with a young guy, kind of a swinger, you play up to that. You kind of judge them and try to put the kind of thing on them that they might go for [men's clothing].

Vendors in any situation may use the media and/or displays and demonstrations to promote generalized interest in their product, but they may also do so on more immediate interpersonal levels. Three major ways of generating interest are considered here: focusing participation, defining significance, and arousing discontent.

Focusing Participation

One way of generating interest is to encourage prospects to attend to particular products with the vendor. "Focusing" may be incorporated into one's approach or qualification procedures, but it may be prompted at other points in the encounter as well.

When combined with an introductory line, this strategy is easily invoked and can provide the basis for further dialogue.

When people are looking at flatware or at dishes, you don't just stand there and hold up the dishes and say, "Oh yes, they're pretty, aren't they?" You get out a placemat and say, "What is your decor at home? What colors will fit in?" You get a placemat in that color. . . . You put the plate and a cup and saucer on it and you maybe get some flatware to add to it, so that they can see that apart from all the sea of dishes. They can see that set apart, so that they can appreciate the beauty of it, if you make it look attractive [jewelry].

If somebody's been looking at something, I'll often go, "Nice, isn't it?" Just to make that initial contact. Then you go on to tell them something about the fabric, the tailoring, the style, who makes it. . . . That way, you have more of a conversation with them, give them more information [mixed clothing].

In another variant of focusing, prospects are encouraged to test or sample the products featured.

The suppliers will sometimes do that. Have someone giving out samples. It gets attention, and it does work. Sales on those products usually go up [grocery].

One of the things about trade shows is that they can actually see the equipment in operation. Everything is set up, "Here, you push these buttons." That's very impressive, compared to what you can show them in their office, when you're working out of your car [manufacture—industrial].

Should prospects not be receptive to immediate product involvements, vendors may attempt to establish a secondary focus en route to a primary objective.

If you have a person who's being reserved with you in his office, then you haven't done an adequate job of presenting the product. You want the person sitting up, paying attention. . . . If you've done a good job, and the person still isn't paying any interest in what it is you're selling, it may be any of a number of things. It may be the Monday morning blues, Friday afternoon golfing. It may be that he's thinking about the new secretary, a new account, anything, but it's not because your product won't fit or that he couldn't use it. He may already have previous commitments he's not telling you about. He may be already signed up with somebody and he might just be listening to see what's going on. You've got to get to that person, and say, "Look, what do you think of the product? Do you like it? Is there anything that you would like to know about it that I haven't told you about? And what you're doing is getting that person from whatever in the hell it is that he's thinking about and you're getting him involved. If you can get interaction between you and that person, and here, I don't care if it's hostile interaction, if you can get interaction between you and that other person, you've got a better chance of selling him. He may hate the color of the machine you're selling or something, but they may not tell you that. There are people who will sit and let you talk, and then when you're finished, they say, "Thank you very much. Bye." And the reason is that you haven't got interaction going with that person, and without that, it's hard to sell. You've got to get him thinking about your product, relating to it. . . . So even if it's a negative response, at least you've got something to work with. But the stirring up is a unique thing. You've got to get them going, get some enthusiasm. Maybe you can't get it going with your product, so maybe you've got to talk to him about golf clubs, or boating, or girls. You've got to get something going in that person. If you've gone into his world and you haven't aroused any excitement within him, you've wasted your time. You've got to stir something within that person [manufacture—industrial].

Defining Product Significance

Vendors frequently attempt to generate relevance for their products by highlighting particular features and functions of the item in question. Here, salespeople portray definitions of products as fitting the tasks at hand (i.e., being reliable, durable, exciting, "hot," and the like). Thus even those who have extensively qualified their prospects may still describe products more fully in attempts to enhance their desirability (see Angrist, 1984: 141).

The more you can tell people about your products, the better. Tell them what it's made of, what it can do, that a lot of people really like it, very popular, that it's easy to use. Anything you can tell them, actually, that makes something more interesting and more worthwhile. Give them more reasons to buy something [department store].

I like the promotional side of it, walking in and giving presentations. I go in and tell jokes, try to get the audience to respond, I like doing that. Normally it's a slide presentation, and slides are nice because you can adjust the slides to get more of the kind of shows that would appeal to the particular group you're dealing with at the time. More on golfing, sporting facilities for some; for others, more on meeting rooms, things like that. With slides you can move the material around a lot more. . . . You should adjust to the time of the day you're meeting with them. At the end of the day, you might start with the more entertaining parts of the presentation, "Hey, look at this one in the bathing suit!" Work on their interests that way. . . . If you go in the morning, they want to get down to the facts, so there, start with the facts and work your way up to the other. When I go in to see these people, I try to put myself in the other person's position, and what are they wanting right now? What will appeal to them right now [promotions—travel]?

Should vendors anticipate that prospects would compare their products with others, they may also outline the relative advantages of their products over others.

You don't want them to comparison shop, at least not any more than you can help. So you stress the features of your systems. Tell how these compare with the competitors. And there, you point out their shortcomings. Show them how it's going to save more money, time, less maintenance. You sell them on the benefits of yours: "It's got all the bells and whistles you'd ever want." [manufacture—computer]

The key to selling is FAB, F-A-B. You want to show the features of your products, the advantages they have over the competition, and the benefits to the prospective buyer. That's what you have to do [wholesale—giftware].

It is in the comparisons intended to invoke discontent, however, that attempts to define product significance assume their sharpest forms.

Arousing Discontent

If they're unhappy with their present product, you've got something to work on. You can go in and maybe get them to change because of that. But if they are happy with their machines and equipment, then probably you are going to lose them, because if they want a new model they will probably get the same kind next time [manufacture—appliances].

Recognizing that people content with their present situations are generally poor candidates for new product purchases, some vendors (as part of their presentations) question the validity of their prospects' assessments. As self-reflective entities, people may "sell themselves on products," but salespeople may also generate reappraisals of prospect definitions by providing alternative points of reference. By indicating discrepancies between present situations and more desirable states prospects could experience, vendors may be able to create dissonance, provide rationale for change, and suggest means of reconciling the dilemmas they've helped define.

The concept of *cognitive dissonance* was introduced by Leon Festinger (1957) to refer to the discomfiture persons experience on recognizing seeming contradictions. Festinger contends that people find inconsistencies troublesome and try to resolve these discrepancies (i.e., change their present situations). The marketing implication is that upon encountering prospects too content with their present circumstances to consider change, vendors would only need to invoke discontent to make these prospects more receptive to their products. However, we should note some limitations to this notion. First, all discrepancies are subject to definition and interpretation. This means that even when these are clearly recognized by the prospects, the significance of any inconsistencies are problematic. Salespeople may attempt to dramatize the dissonance prospects experience, but the impact of any (recognized) inconsistency varies relative to the context in which that discrepancy is interpreted. Prospects may recognize inconsistencies on their own or with assistance from others, but they also tend to assess the significance of particular discrepancies and the integrities of those introducing these dilemmas. Vendors may attempt to define dilemmas as more intense and immediate, thereby defining "problems" where none were previously considered, but dissonance arousal seems most effective when some disenchantment preceded their efforts.[23]

Dissonance can be defined in either negative or positive terms. And, while either mode of arousing discontent may be used in any instance, they may also be combined for stronger contrasts between present undesirable situations and more desirable alternatives.

Problems defined in negative terms are designed to accentuate existing undesirable situations (inconsistencies are often presumed to be recognized by prospects).

"Is your car unsafe?" (Safety is important!)

"Trouble getting the dirt out?" (Cleanliness is desirable!)

"That's an inefficient way of doing _____." (Don't waste energy, time!)

"Is your furniture showing its age?" (Don't be ashamed; newer is better!)

"You're not going anywhere for holidays this year?" (Be somebody!)

"Feeling like a loser?" (Be somebody!)

"Are you wasting your hard earned money?" (Don't waste money!)

Dissonance defined in positive terms generally emphasizes desirable future states, but presumes more interpretive work on the part of prospective buyers.

"These improvements make this model much safer!" (Your old model isn't that safe. And, safety is important!)

"_____ will get your clothes whiter and brighter."

"With _____ , it's no fuss, no bother, and it's fast! That way, you'll have time for more important things."

"This is very popular, very contemporary!"

"Wouldn't you like to spend two weeks in exciting, romantic _____ — ?"

"Like to be more successful?"

"You can save money with . . . !"

Clearly, dissonance may be directed at any concerns prospects presently have or could be expected to entertain (e.g., physical safety, financial well-being, entertainment, and so on). And, to the extent vendors are successful in defining problems for prospects (indicating significance and urgency) and presenting more exclusive means of resolving these dilemmas, they will have promoted closure on the part of their targets.

Both positive and negative modes can generate and focus problems and interests, but they need not be equally effective in given instances. By defining problems in more direct, negative (painful) terms, vendors may more abruptly arouse dissonance. However, this may also promote greater hostility and/or distancing when interpreted as an insulting (or embarrassing) imputation. This effect seems less evident in mass media advertising (e.g., television) where the "targets" are more diffuse, and prospects may assume that statements were directed at others more than themselves or feel less embarrassed as a consequence of the more autonomous conditions in which these messages were received. In personal encounters by contrast, negatives are assumed to be more directly aimed at prospects ("Because you have bad breath . . ."). It is for these reasons that some vendors have opted for positively oriented dissonance messages in media and (especially) personal communications. In either case, the effect of vendor input in defining relevance remains.

If someone knows exactly what they want, that can be some of your easiest sales. They are, however, some of the sales that you'll make the least money on, because if someone doesn't know what they want, you can usually lead them int buying something more expensive or spending a larger amount. If someone knows what they want when they come in, you just get it for them and total it up, but if someone comes in and they're not sure, there you will usually work on the highest priced items, and it's easier to get them to buy them. . . . You might get them to go for the fancier packaging, how it looks nicer as a gift. . . . If they seem concerned about price, I'll tell them which is the best value for their dollar. But if they don't, I'll push them towards the better lines, the richer, more expensive lines. There, you'll stress the quality, tell how it's imported, things like that. We'll tell them that _____ is our most popular mint, and they are, that they are the richest, that they have the most flavor, that they have less sugar, more cream, fewer preservatives, additives. You can also stress the wrapping. And, if it's imported, that's something else that seems to impress people, "Oh, imported!" And you can usually tame down a customer over the price, by telling them that it's imported and all. . . . I think some of the things that we carry are pricey, for what you get, but they sell. . . . You have to feel the customers out along the way. Some of the customers you know, so you know what they like, what's been successful before [candy].

You're saving them time and money. That's what you're selling. So you show them how much more efficient your processing equipment is, "Look at the wonderful things it can do for your profit margin. Look at what you can accomplish with the same man-hours!" [manufacture—industrial].

Should vendors find positive contrasts ineffective and/or want more immediate action, they may emphasize negative possibilities.

I'll tell them, "I don't know if good looks are important to you, but when I'm buying a suit, I don't want it getting all wrinkled up and having to worry about it holding its shape every time I go out. This [brand] suit costs more, but you'll never have to worry about being embarrassed." Something like that [men's clothing].

Sometimes it's not good to have them too much at ease, because if you're talking about some problem, you want them a little concerned about it, you want them to take it seriously. . . . If you've gone over the whole thing, and they're in a situation where they don't have money to invest, they should feel uncomfortable about it, like, "Are you happy with that?" Now, I wouldn't say this to everyone, but there are some people who have a very lackadaisical attitude, sort of, "I don't care." Whether they really feel that way or not. You have to give them a little jolt by saying, "If continue this way, do you see what's going to happen to you? Do you understand the consequence if you continue to borrow, and your debts get bigger and bigger, and there'll be a time when you cannot meet those obligations?" So you don't always want them to feel completely comfortable. . . . If they don't see themselves as having any problems, how can you solve them? And that's basically what I'm doing [investments].

ONGOING ASSESSMENTS

While vendors may encourage prospects to view products in favorable terms, their efforts (as well as earlier prospect definitions of products) are subject to ongoing assessments. Thus the impact of sales technique and earlier prospect product orientations may be nullified as prospects consider products in other ways (e.g., utility in various settings, costs, prestige) over time.[24] Thus as prospects acquire more information or consider existing knowledge in other contexts or from other viewpoints, products may seem more or less desirable, more or less essential to realize their interests or obligations.

> You can move people around to your way of thinking, but you can lose them too. They may come in wanting to buy, full of enthusiasm, and then something bothers them, and they talk themselves out of it. Sometimes, it's some feature of the product they weren't aware of, but they've changed their mind, and there's nothing you can really do about it [department store].

> You can talk yourself into an order and talk yourself right out of it again. I've done that and I've seen others do that. . . . Or they want to think about it. And there, I always try to be as friendly and helpful as I can, even when it seems that they're just wasting your time. Because some of them do turn around. Somebody can be very difficult, very skeptical, sometimes downright insulting, and turn out to be a good customer [manufacture—computers].

In Perspective

This chapter began with a discussion of selling as symbolic activity. Exchanges commonly involve physical items, but exchanges are fundamentally contingent on the symbolic significances that people attach to the objects being exchanged. And vendors can greatly influence their customers' willingness to entertain particular purchases by the ways in which they present these objects to these people. Building on Blumer's (1969) notion of "joint activity" and the dramaturgical metaphor Goffman (1959) developed, consideration was given to the ways in which vendors present products to prospects.

In this regard, we first find vendors getting scripted and experiencing stage fright in anticipation of encounters with their audiences. Once contact is made, the focus is on vendor-prospect encounters as experienced by the salespeople. Here one finds vendors approaching customers, qualifying them, and attempting to generate interest. Although each encounter is apt to differ from the next, we see the value of attending to the social construction of sales encounters. It is "strategy in process," with background preparations and concerns subjugated to the "nowness" of the encounter, and the necessity of fitting one's line of action into those of others.

Not all salespeople will be attuned to the impact of various modes of approach, the value of qualification, or the significance of developing interest on the part of prospective customers. Further, some will not be interested in doing "relationship" work even when they are aware of their implications for sales. However, should salespeople be both aware of these tactics and interested in pursuing them, it becomes evident that seldom are they able to do as much relationship work as they might desire. Ultimately, this reflects salespeople's dependencies on the willingness of their customers to cooperate with them in reference to mutual time frames, attentiveness, openness, and the like. But it also is indicative of the ongoing reflectivity these interactional tactics entail and the uncertainty each encounter represents.

Having considered vendor preparation, approaches, qualification, and concerns with prospect interest, attention now shifts to the problematics of establishing trust. Although often taken for granted by both buyers and sellers, trust can also greatly affect immediate purchasing decisions as well as long-term buyer-seller relationships.

Notes

1. Cooperation, in fact, is mutual. In some cases, vendors may have more veto power than do prospective buyers, but for most goods in pluralistic society, it is the prospective buyers who can be more selective in choosing those with whom they deal.

2. The term *unstable* denotes the abilities of people to change their viewpoints, emphases, and strategies in very short periods of time. Thus, in contrast to properties attributed to inanimate objects, those attributed to persons are highly vulnerable to error.

3. As Mead (1934) indicates, this capacity for "self-reflectivity" (to be an object unto oneself) fundamentally distinguishes humans from other objects. As "objects unto themselves," humans may not only take themselves into account in planning lines of action, but also recognize the abilities of others to do so as well.

4. If one accepts the premise that "objects do not have inherent meanings," then exchanges can only be defined in symbolic terms.

5. Should people agree on the value of an object relative to some other object(s), then as a "standard" these first objects may be thought to have an "objective" worth. In actuality, however, the worth of any standard (e.g., gold) requires continual confirmation on the part of those involved in its definition.

6. For example, even those "self-sufficient" shoppers who try to avoid staff exchanges in selecting merchandise may become indignant, pleased, or (remain) indifferent each time they deal with a clerk. Likewise, people making vending machine purchases still arrive at assessments of the service they receive (witness battered machines) or be critical of the goods available. Thus even people engaged in "highly impersonal" shopping are apt to be sensitive to staff exchanges (including those as indirect as the operators of vending machines).

7. Goffman avoids the very thorny and elusive phenomenon of the "true self" by concentrating on the selection, presentation, and interpretation of people's "social selves."

8. It needn't be assumed that people are always concerned with "giving off" and/or "reading" impressions. The participants can vary greatly in the degree of concern they experience in either "portraying" or "monitoring" impressions.

9. In a much neglected account of the saleslady, it is Donovan (1929: 188) who first explicitly defines the marketplace in theatrical terms. The applicability of Goffman's (1959) "dramaturgical model" to the sales setting is also illustrated in works by Miller (1964) and Stets-Kealey (1984). For extended depictions of impression management in other contexts, see Goffman (1963), Edgerton (967), Haas and Shaffir (1977), and Prus and Sharper (1977).

10. It should be appreciated that stage performances (and performers) vary in degrees of sensitivity to their audiences.

11. See *Pursuing Sales* (Prus, 1989) for a detailed presentation of vendor preparations in anticipation of customer contact.

12. Telephone encounters are generally less demanding performances in the sense that those selling over the phone may rely heavily on written scripts.

13. The first two criticisms seem to reflect definitions of particular spiels and are more valid for some tracks and/or styles of delivery than others. Long, elaborate presentations can be personalized and allow for audience participation (albeit in more defined manners). As with players acting on stage, the script need not be improvised to appear natural or be impressive.

14. Although denoting a first interpersonal impression, it is more accurate to envision approaches within the context of any images (of the vendor) prospects may develop through the media, location, display, from associates, and so on. It is within these contexts that prospects define encounters.

15. It should be noted that any personal contact may be seen as threatening or distracting by prospects.

16. Shopping autonomy is a dominant element in self-serve stores and likely accounts for much of their popularity since prospects may study goods at their leisure.

17. The forms of repeat patronage and vendor attempts to cultivate customer loyalty are discussed more fully in a later chapter.

18. In self-serve stores, buyers are presumed to "qualify themselves" up to the point of ascertaining sufficient monies to pay for the goods.

19. The immediate concern with seriousness pertains most directly to qualification (and approach), but prospect interest is apt to be a matter of concern throughout the encounter.

20. It should be noted that prospects may intentionally indicate disinterest as a means of maintaining control in personal encounters with vendors.

We wanted to look at some cars on the lot, and when the salesman came along we said we were just browsing. He said, "Okay folks, look around all you like," and left. We were sort of taken aback by that, because we actually wanted to be shown some cars, but hadn't wanted to make it too obvious [male].

21. Although this strategy seems beneficial regarding success, it should also be noted that it is not an easy stance to maintain, especially after a number of unsuccessful endeavors.

22. Not only may vendors not be aware of the base or extent of prospect interest, but even when a strong interest seems apparent, they may not know if this base of interest is sufficient in itself to promote purchasing commitment.

23. Although they do not use the term *cognitive dissonance,* Karsh et al. (1953) provide a most insightful statement on the creation and use of dissonance by union organizers (who promote disenchantment and subsequently sell employees on membership). While focused on religious recruitment, Prus (1976) provides an explicitly sociological statement on cognitive dissonance. Particular attention is given to the roles others may play in promoting as well as diminishing the dissonance people experience.

24. This may be one of the reasons fast-talking salespeople are subject to higher levels of skepticism. They may be seen to interfere with people's abilities to assess situations as fully as they would like.

Chapter 3
GENERATING TRUST

A premium salesperson is someone who's sold the person so that they're happy about the sale long after you've gone. You've delved into his mind sufficiently, that you've linked it up with what he really wants. The item has been incorporated into his mind. So when you come back next, he's still thinking that way. Your product may not be the best product for him or the best one on the market, but you make it fit in for him. Now there, when you return, you may have to reinforce that image for him. Time and duration will thin out the effect of what you've been saying, so then it gets down to how well you got along. And if you were able to relate to that person better, then it's more likely that he'll do business with you over someone else who hasn't developed that with him [manufacture—industrial].

What role does trust play in the sales process? How do salespeople attempt to convince prospective customers that they have their best interests in mind? How do salespeople convey integrity and product quality? How do they offset the obligations purchases imply on the part of prospective customers? What are the practical limitations of vendor attempts to invoke trust? Building on materials developed in Chapter 2, these questions suggest the central thrusts of this chapter. Insofar as it operates on presumptions of trust, this chapter also represents a viable setting in which to locate a discussion of "suggestive selling" (attempts on the part of vendors to sell more costly lines and/or multiple items). This latter material provides a stronger appreciation of trust and the relationship work that salespeople do more generally.

The Social Construction of Trust

Trust does not guarantee sales, but its presence (or absence) can greatly affect prospects' willingness to make the commitments necessary for sales to be completed. Further, while this discussion considers trust with regards to immediate purchasing decisions, it is important to recognize the significance of trust for long-term buyer loyalty. Once established, trust not only seems more likely to be taken for granted in subsequent purchasing contexts involving the same set of traders, but may also be very instrumental in shaping buyer preferences for particular vendors.[1]

Concerns with (and assessments of) trust vary greatly from one prospect to the next, as well as across the particular products people are considering and their experiences therein. People may define purchases by the items of which they assume possession, but the meaning of these items are not mere functions of these items' physical properties. Prospects are purchasing all that they associate with the products they are considering. Thus, in addition to anticipations of product performances, for instance, purchases may also reflect the images buyers develop of vendors as well as buyer concerns with their future financial solvency. As long as prospects take these sorts of elements for granted in reference to exchanges, trust (or lack of) is relatively nonproblematic. Purchases are contingent on finding vendors to complete transactions. However, should any element be subject to uncertainty or doubt at any point in the encounter, sales may be lost.

To minimize the significance of any doubts, vendors may do both *preventative* and *remedial* work. While remedial strategies are designed to deal with concerns seemingly disrupting sales, preventative strategies are intended to reduce the prominence of these (or other) concerns before they become disruptive to sales encounters. Vendors using the media to establish credibility for their businesses may be seen as engaging in preventative strategies. So would those who do more preparation for prospect encounters, qualify prospects more fully, and present products more completely to prospects. Vendors attempting to develop trust earlier and more extensively throughout the encounter would seem less likely to require remedial strategies. They may still need to invoke remedial strategies to make sales, but their "repair work" should be less extensive and less consequential for their sales overall. Although the division is not so simplistic, the present statement emphasizes preventative work, while the chapter following (focusing on resistance) depicts repair strategies.

For our purposes, *trust* is a quality attributed to persons (groups, vendors, suppliers) by others; it denotes an anticipation that these persons will act in manners consistent with one's interests. Viewing trust thusly, we would not only expect variations in the extent to which people trust one another in a general sense, but also anticipate that people would more readily trust the same people in some areas of pursuit than others. From discussions with vendors, three dimensions emerge as central to the social production of trust. These reflect the extent to which vendors are seen to (1) portray vendor integrity, (2) indicate higher levels of product quality (performance), and (3) minimize buyer obligations. It is not suggested that any or all of these elements of trust are necessary to all sales, but they appear relevant to a great many purchasing situations.

Prospects tend to use the term trust (or some presumed synonym such as integrity or confidence) rather vaguely. They may impute trust (or distrust) to vendors on one or more of the preceding dimensions, and there is no assurance that the same people will make the same inferences or assumptions regarding trust from one encounter (or even from one part of one encounter) to the next. People seem unlikely to consider all these dimensions in all cases, and the relevance of any dimension can vary greatly from one instance to the next. As a result, vendors cannot know in advance if their approaches will be effective as actual encounters take place.

Although vendors are unevenly concerned with (or attuned to) developing trust, the following elements indicate the basic range of trust-inducing practices vendors employ.

Portraying vendor integrity
  Finding effective product applications
  Expressing sincerity
  Personalizing encounters
Evidencing product quality
  Demonstrating products
  Providing abstract evidence
  Indicating external consensus
  Displaying vendor accountability

Minimizing buyer obligations
Conserving prospect resources
Making it easy
Providing greater purchasing autonomy

Each of these points will be examined in the discussions following.

PORTRAYING VENDOR INTEGRITY

The portrayal of images of integrity refers to vendor attempts to achieve definitions of personal acceptability from the buyers they face. At an interpersonal level, vendors may try to convey integrity at many points in their encounters with prospects, including their initial approaches, quests for background information, and modes of answering questions. Integrity work reflects three major, but frequently interrelated forms. These are finding effective applications (i.e., that products would serve the tasks prospects have in mind); expressing sincerity (honest, truthfulness); and personalizing encounters. Prospects need not be equally concerned about these matters, nor need they agree on definitions of effective applications, sincerity, or genuine friendliness. However, they commonly appear to assess their situations relative to these concerns. Although prospective buyers generally realize that their assessments of vendors represent limited indications of product performance, prospects may nevertheless envision these assessments as providing them with some protection against their other purchasing inclinations (e.g., "media hype," surface quality).

Finding Effective Applications

While it is not uncommon to encounter some buyers more knowledgeable than some vendors in almost all areas of sales, people more uncertain of their purchases are apt to be more dependent on salespeople to define effective applications. Thus vendors may endeavor to foster trust by presenting their products in ways thought to be more consistent with prospects interests.

> If you're selling diamonds and watches, you have to know a little more about the product. It's something like selling a horse or a car. The people want to have some confidence that you know something about what you're selling them. . . . A younger couple, when they come in, it doesn't really matter, but a lot of other people, if they're buying a certain size, a larger diamond, they would like to speak to someone who knows diamonds. If it's for an invest-

ment, what size, what quality would they like? They would like to speak to someone who knows more about diamonds. I have people that I've sold diamonds to, that have brought in their friends for me to sell them diamonds. . . . So when we hire someone we'll usually start them off on something more straightforward, like chains, smaller items. The idea is that they graduate from selling chains and charms to pearls and colored stones, gems, and then if they're doing well there, you might graduate them to diamonds [jewelry].

You might know one specific more than the doctor does, and you've got to try to convince him that you've got something worthwhile, back it up somehow. Because otherwise, he sees himself as much more knowledgeable than you and he won't like someone telling him how to practice medicine. You can do it, but you have to be a little diplomatic. . . . But it's the same in any sales. The people, the engineers, whatever, you have to watch that they don't get the impression that you think you're superior to them, in their trade. You might know more about one product or a few things, but you have to watch how you present it to them [manufacture—pharmaceuticals]

As Gross (1959: 93) suggests, product knowledge variously may reflect awareness of distinctive product characteristics (within and across product lines), uses and applications, manufacturing processes and situations, and marketing information (sales, policies, and service). Clearly, all of this information is not available to all salespeople, even were they willing and able to retain all this knowledge. Vendors dealing with more limited lines (e.g., specialty shops/departments) seem generally more knowledgeable about their products, but as with other aspects of the sales encounter, the *adequacy of the vendor's knowledge* reflects the interests (and perspectives) of the buyers.

Expressing Sincerity

In this context, the emphasis is on honesty as *conveyed* rather than complete and open revelations of information as known to the vendors involved. This is not to imply that the two are necessarily incompatible or that vendors inevitably deceive prospects; only that buyer trust may be shaped by the ways in which sincerity is projected. Prospects appear unevenly concerned with vendor sincerity, but when surface impressions of products seem incomplete or otherwise disquieting, more attention tends to be directed towards the vendors involved.

Recognizing that people considered to be more honest are more apt to have their claims acknowledged, some vendors indicate specific efforts to be honest.

Something I try to get across to the staff is that in making a sale, you're giving the customer the best advice you can. That's how you're closing the sale, by fitting up the product that's best suited for them in terms of their circumstances [appliances].

Don't bullshit for a sale. Never! Back off. You'll never get back in that door, and that one guy will bad mouth you to other people too. If you bullshit, sell the guy the wrong thing, you'll screw your reputation. . . . Know your product fairly well, if you're going into sales. Learn what you can about the competition as well and your own product [manufacture—industrial].

Although many vendors believe that higher levels of openness will result in greater trust on the part of prospective buyers, it is generally recognized that complete candor may disrupt sales.[3] Honesty (and it's interpretations thereof) creates particular dilemmas for vendors wishing to make immediate sales and also develop a repeat clientele.

If they ask for my opinion, and I don't think it suits them, unless I figure that she's going to buy that shoe regardless of what I say, I'll try to be honest with them. I figure that way, they're more likely to come back. . . . I've had that experience myself, where I've gone into stores and whatever you try on, "Oh, doesn't it look lovely!" and you would know it wasn't true. And I never went back to those places. So I sort of learned from that that honesty pays off. So as much as I like to make sales, I try to be honest as well [shoes].

We're in a pretty competitive market, and every system, I don't care whose it is, has certain strengths and weaknesses. So when someone says, "Well, what about _____ or _____? I hear they have a pretty good system," that gets a little sticky. "Well, yes they do, but here's where ours is better." And you play up your strengths, and downplay your shortcomings. . . . Now if it is going to be a really bad fit for them, then there is no point. But if we can do as well as anybody else on the overall, well, we might as well get the business if we can [manufacture—computers].

Somewhat related to attributions of sincerity are perceptions of fairness, denoting the vendor's perceived willingness to play by the rules.[4] As with other aspects of trust, definitions of vendor fairness are not only subject to (mis)interpretation, but also reflect vendors' attempts to promote perceptions of fairness.

Our prices are a little higher than some other places, but we stand behind our products as much as anyone. That's something we try to communicate to our customers, the service we provide and the way we back our products. Some people don't seem to appreciate that, at least not until they try taking something back to some of the other places, like _____ or _____, but we've built up quite a clientele on that basis. It's not just money in the till. It's treating people fairly all the way along [department store].

Personalizing Encounters

While all interpersonal encounters denote personal relationships of sorts, vendors may also promote definitions of integrity by more explicitly *personalizing* relationships with their prospects.[5] Of particular relevance are attempts on the part of vendors to *fit in* with their prospects; and signify that their prospects are worthy of consideration (i.e., a "somebody").

Fitting in. This refers to the process by which persons acknowledge (or assume) the perspectives of others and take these perspectives into account in pursuing lines of action that these others would find compatible.[6] From the vendors' viewpoint, fitting in is contingent on sharing general understandings with their prospects, but it is also facilitated by attempts to gain more complete appreciations of prospect viewpoints as sales encounters take place and subjugate their behaviors to images with which their prospects feel comfortable. Prospects may also attempt to comprehend vendor perspectives and adjust to these positions. However, fitting in (and the development of more personalized relationships) is an undertaking more likely explicitly to be assumed by vendors.

You have to get the customer to trust you, like you, trust your judgment. I have to establish the needs in the customer, let them know what their needs are. Then, once you've established the need, the interest, then it's a matter of showing them the features of the items you think are best suited for that person, what each appliance in a line can or cannot do for them [appliances].

In selling, you've got to build that bond between that other person and yourself. You've got to get on their wavelength. You want to be able to communicate with them, where they're concentrating on what you're telling them. Get eye contact. You don't want their thoughts wandering all around, looking over here and there [manufacture—industrial].

Although salespeople are concerned about presenting products, those who indicate greater awareness of prospects' perspectives (and situations) seem more effective in generating both interest and trust. Vendors can create atmospheres prospects find more relaxing through decor, lighting, climate control, and the like, but on an interpersonal level vendors may also begin fitting in with prospects when they first make contact. *Conversational* and *delayed* approaches seem particularly effective therein.

In approaching people, you don't want to say, "May I, or Can I, help you?" It's better to start a conversation, and maybe pick up on something that they're wearing, or something on the news, or some item in the store. Not where you're trying to sell it, but just breaking the ice, getting them started in a conversation that's not really related to selling them something. Now some people, they may not warm up to you. Then you try to be very nonchalant in making the sales, but you go on talking to the person, showing them the item, where the actual sale is not the most important thing. . . . With me, if someone says that they're not interested, I look at that as a challenge, so I'll try to show them things, arouse their interest. If I can do that, and sell them the accessories, that to me is the challenge. That's sales work! . . . If there's time, you talk more. If it's busy, you can't do that so much, but if you don't talk to the person, you really can't develop them as a customer. . . . The experienced salespeople in this business, that's what they do. They do talk to the person. Then you figure that you've got a chance, because if you get talking with them, you can then show them things easier. And they're more relaxed, so the chances of the sale are greater then [women's clothing].

We approach the people first. Not "May I help you?" but you try to make some casual conversation with the people, or if they have children, you might start talking with the children. Basically, in starting you talk about other things, and then you lead into the sales. You let them warm up to you, get used to you in this time [stationery].

In addition to preexisting understandings of a general cultural nature, vendors may also attempt to arrive at a greater awareness of their prospects' perspectives by qualifying these prospects more extensively. Beyond initial projections aimed at promoting a sense of shared understanding ("We speak your language."), vendors may attempt to develop this aspect of trust further as the encounter unfolds. Salespeople who listen more carefully, ask more questions, and acknowledge patron viewpoints more fully seem more effective in not only finding out more about their prospects, but also arousing product interest, and establishing higher levels of trust. Some talk will likely center around

the items being promoted, but the extra time spent in the setting may
afford prospects greater opportunities to become familiar with both the
vendors and their products, as well as to consider a wider range of
applications.

If you can talk to the customer easier, that should help in sales. And it's surprising sometimes, just the different things you might get into talking about
when you're showing an item to the customer. You don't neglect other people,
but with the customer, you try to get them to feel relaxed. . . . If they're not
familiar with some of your lines, you might try to start with the better known
lines. You can start showing their features, and as you're doing that, you can
compare them with the lines that they're not so familiar with. Then they can
make their own decisions [department store].

When a good salesman gets a hold of him, he spends time with them, and time
is an important element. If you spend time with somebody, show them the car,
demonstrate the car with them, listen to them, there's an obligation there. Because all the dealers sell for pretty close to the same amount as the others, so
more [important] than the money is the time you're spending with the customer,
the camaraderie, the trust you establish with the people, the confidence you
establish [auto].

Beyond attempts to understand better the viewpoints of their prospects, salespeople may also influence the amount of trust prospects
associate with them by the ways in which they "custom(er)ize" their
roles. In this sense, by making adjustments to accommodate prospects'
concerns as encounters develop, vendors see themselves as "being on"
or being more chameleonlike.

When you're selling, you're always on! You have to watch yourself, and you
have to watch the customer, be aware of their moods. You have to adjust yourself
to them. You have to judge them, see how receptive they are to different styles.
Like some people I hardly talk to, and others you can joke around with, and
some you'll have to explain things to carefully. This is something you try to do,
to adjust yourself to your customers [women's clothing].

It was a question of being able to identify the customer. And you sell better if
you have a technique, although for each person, the technique could be different. You have to relate to the customers, you have to match up with the
clientele. And there, if the staff could relate better to the type of customer coming
in the store, those people would sell better. . . . You have to take on the image
that they want you to be, and that will differ from one customer to the next [shoes].

Thus no less important on many occasions than one's level of product knowledge in establishing customer confidence is one's ability to explain features in terms with which the prospect feels comfortable.

Usually, I just explain policies in laymen's terms. You tell them, "Basically, this is what it says." But you do get some people who love the terminology and you can usually tell that, by the words they use in asking you questions. But my whole speech pattern will change, depending on who I'm with, adjusting to the people, the sorts of things they seem to expect [insurance].

I try to chat with them. I try to make them feel at ease and I try to give them that confidence. I don't bullshit them and baffle them with all kinds of theories and weird terms and so on just to prove that I know what I'm talking about. I try to talk to them on a level that I think that they are going to get to trust me and know me and understand me and not pressure them [jewelry].

As with other aspects of the sales encounter, fitting in represents both a means of success and a dilemma to be resolved.

In meeting people I basically try to be myself. I think you have to be somewhat chameleonlike to fit in, but at the same time you also feel more comfortable being like yourself and you are also concerned about the professionalism that you project in selling products [promotions—magazine].

I find it very hard to disguise my feelings, to be something other than I am when I'm selling. . . . But you do have to isolate yourself from maybe how you're feeling about home, things like that, and in some ways that can be good, because it gives you a chance to get away from that, at least temporarily. But you do have to concentrate on what you're doing, you can't let something else get you down [music].

Signifying prospect importance. Also subsumed by the notion of personalizing relationships is trust reflecting indications (and assessments) of prospect importance. *Signification* may assume many forms, ranging from service, attention, a willingness to listen, and attempts to promote creature comforts, to overt expressions of importance. All efforts are subject to customer interpretation. Nevertheless, vendors may endeavor to promote a greater sense of trust by being more attentive, more considerate, more willing to make concessions, and providing more explicit indications of appreciation (e.g., "This [item]. . . . is for you." "You're important to us!"). While indications of appreciation and/or interest in the prospect are sometimes interpreted as appeals to vanity, they often represent viable means of generating trust. Even spending more time with prospects may be seen as acknowledging their importance. Thus all activities directed towards particular prospects (e.g., approach, qualification, presentation) may foster signification.

> You try to show that you're interested in them. So when they come in, after their tour and introduction to all the benefits, I would take some time and try to find out more about them, to get to know them and what they wanted to do. Try to get them to feel more relaxed before going into the costs and all [fitness center].

> The kids are great. Sometimes you won't even bother with the parents, you just dote on the kids. The parents figure that if you like their kids, you must be okay. It puts them in a more receptive mood. You're not jumping on them. You're letting them feel more relaxed, creating a nicer atmosphere. You're being really friendly, but not to the point where you're saying, "I want your money." But if you really show an interest in people, like whether it's with their children, their vacation, or how they are, then they are more likely to like you, to buy from you [shoes].

As the preceding discussions of vendor integrity indicate, people may try to portray confidence in themselves by indicating how their products would coincide with the applications the prospect has in mind, that they are sincere in the information they provide, and that the buyer is someone worthy of their attention and consideration. In all instances, however, these efforts are contingent on ongoing buyer interpretations and may be contraposed, relative to other concerns (especially matters of product quality and buyer obligations), that buyers may have.

EVIDENCING PRODUCT QUALITY

The second major element affecting trust is the quality prospects associate with the products (goods, services) being considered. Notions of quality encompass attributions of competence (task applications) and reliability (consistency). Vendors sometimes specifically emphasize one or both of these dimensions in their presentations, but they are often blurred together in communications with prospects.

Vendors attempting to promote higher levels of confidence in products commonly demonstrate products, provide abstract evidence of product viability, portray external consensus regarding products, and indicate higher levels of vendor accountability. Insofar as quality ultimately can only be known after products' actual uses, each of these endeavors may be seen as attempts to "objectify" (Schutz, 1971) quality in advance of buyer commitments.

Demonstrating Products

> Your demonstration is a way of overcoming skepticism. If you can get past their doubts, and a demonstration usually does that, they're going to buy. If you can demonstrate, eight out of ten times they will be buying. So a big thing is getting to that point. Getting good leads, and finding the right guy in that company, getting to him, that's central [manufacture—industrial].

Demonstrations are sometimes used to spark interest, but they can also be very effective ways of generating trust. Some demonstrations may be dramatic and complicated, but any "witnessing," "handling," or "sampling" activity on the part of prospects is likely to foster buyer familiarity with both the products featured and the vendors involved.[7]

> You want to get them to try the item on, to see it on themselves. Then, if they like how it looks, then nine times out of ten, they'll buy it. . . . That's a big part of it, to get them to put it on, "Why don't you see how it looks on you? Come on try it on." And you take it off the hanger, head toward the fitting room. And most people will follow you along. Sometimes you might feel a little silly, where you've left them standing there, but most will go along with you. . . . Once they've tried it on, you assume the sale. If it fits them and looks good, how could they not want it? And you're there, "Looks, great! Good set! And we can do this and this to it. Here, let me pin the bottoms, and you can wear this shirt with it. Here's a nice belt." And it's theirs! All of a sudden, it's theirs [men's clothing]!

> [With incentive travel programs] they're investing a quarter of a million dollars sometimes, and they don't see exactly what it is that they're getting, so we will offer to take the reps from the companies down [to the vacation spot], show them the setting, a couple day package for them. . . . That's something we'll build into the costs, because very few companies will spend that much money without wanting to see what the place actually has to offer for themselves [promotions—travel].

Providing Abstract Evidence

In addition to, or in lieu of, demonstrations, vendors may provide additional product descriptions as a means of establishing buyer confidence. Especially effective are references to testing, quality control, and conditions of use. These other materials may also be used to verify vendor claims.

There are customers who are totally skeptical, not just of you, but of all salespeople, because it starts right from the beginning. . . . I give them information, the factual information that backs up what I say, so they're not just trusting me, but also so that they're trusting a brochure I can show them from the manufacturer, a written guarantee from the company, as well as telling them the store policy on returns, things like that. That helps build up trust. That way, they just don't have to rely on your word for something. . . . Like even where you can point to a label and say, "That's washable. You don't have to get it dry cleaned." Or if they don't believe a glove you are showing them is actually leather, you can tell them to smell it, or show them that the manufacturer has put a tag on the inside saying "genuine leather." . . . If it can appeal to their own senses, holding something, feeling it, touching it, that's good too. But you can't always do that with some products [department store].

If you are going to approach someone analytical, then it is imperative that you have a lot of charts, graphs, information, so they can relate to that. Get them to feel comfortable with what you've got to offer [investments].

Indicating External Consensus

Vendors may also attempt to define quality by indicating consensus concerning the viability of the items featured. In these instances, trust is based on the anticipation that "others would concur" in the wisdom of making particular purchases and/or dealing with particular vendors.[8] One way vendors indicate consensus is through reference to name brands. Insofar as these labels signify purchases widely accepted by others, vendors featuring name brands invoke higher levels of credibility.

You'll get a boot or a shoe that's a hot item, where you'll get a lot of people coming in and asking specifically for it. And that can be a problem, if you don't have it. You might have an item that's better, but because the people, the teenagers especially, saw this or that, and they want that name brand, you can't do anything with it. With the younger people especially, you would just be wasting your time to try to show them something else along a similar line, even if it were better, less money, etc., etc. [shoes]

Your name brands will move better. People trust them. They have come to associate a certain level of quality with them. . . . We had a man in from [supplier] the other day, with a new line of televisions. A brand I haven't heard much about. I had to tell him no. They're selling on price and a few dealers have started carrying them, but they'll be harder to sell because they don't have the name, the track record the others have. You want your space for brands that are going to move better [appliances].

Recognizing that prospects may be unable to unwilling to define products as "good choices" on their own, vendors may provide prospects with other indications of more general approval. Thus, references may be made to the popularity of items ("Look at how many we've sold!"), the prominence of the vendor ("We're the biggest!"), and the viability of the choice ("Examine these testimonials!"), as defined by others.

If you sell for a big name company, and you say, "I'm so-and-so from _____." that'll help you get their attention. Or if you have a good reputation among people they know, that'll help too [mixed sales].

We've been around for a long time, placed a lot of units. It's that track record we build on. It gives you a lot of credibility [manufacture—computers].

Heightened credibility represents a reason that recommendations from friends (and others) tend to be effective.

The recommendations are easier sales. It's like you've got a friend waiting for you [appliances]

The referrals are easier. Oh yes, very much so. Somebody's been talking to his friend with this other company or somebody else he feels he can trust and now he's contacting you. It's good. He's interested enough to find out about you and then there's the added trust or assurance that he got from a satisfied customer. A satisfied customer can be your best salesman [manufacture—industrial]!

Exhibiting Vendor Accountability

Another means of generating confidence in product performance is to provide insurance against product failures. Vendors may do this on both informal and more formal levels. One way vendors claim accountability is to indicate their dependency on the buyer's continued good will.[9] Vendors may also propose contracts to formalize conditions of accountability. Although most customers seem to recognize that the contracts implied by guarantees, warranties, and the like have an uneven quality to them (e.g., from company to company), these are seen as elements inducing trust. Similarly, vendors offering more liberal return or refund policies (e.g., "satisfaction guaranteed") indicate other forms of vendor obligations that salespeople may use to promote sales.

Some of the sales are pretty easy because you just tell them, "If you change your mind, or you're not happy with the merchandise, just bring it back and we'll give you a replacement or a refund, whatever you want." That's our policy and it makes selling so much easier than at _____ where I worked before. . . . I know that people abuse the policy, but it breeds confidence. It does a lot for the company, because people develop confidence [department store].

I started to try to create credibility by putting down as much as possible in writing for the customer, and tack that on the customer's sales form. And say, "Here it is, in writing. The only thing that can go wrong is that the store can go broke." . . . And it did. But you can't control everything [stereo].

As with their attempts to find effective applications, salespeople's attempts to convey images of quality are rather uneven. In the main, however, they employ the practices of demonstrating products, making abstract claims for products, referencing external sources, and indicating their own responsibility for buyer satisfaction. Still remaining is the matter of the obligations that purchases entail from the buyer's end of the agreement, along with the tactics vendors use in their efforts to minimize the threats these commitments represent to prospective buyers.

MINIMIZING BUYER OBLIGATIONS

Somewhat related to indications of vendor accountability are attempts to generate trust by defining initial prospect commitments (and risks) in less consequential terms. Vendors choosing this strategy commonly promote trust by conserving prospect resources, making purchasing seem easier, and providing greater purchasing autonomy.

Conserving Prospect Resources

Insofar as monies expended in one exchange may interfere with people's abilities to obtain other desirables, saving money becomes a consideration in many transactions. However, it is very important to appreciate that the price tag associated with a particular item (e.g. $100 for a certain pair of shoes) does not have the same meaning for all customers (or even for the same customer from one time to the next). Likewise, vendors note that the relationship between people having particular sums of money and their willingness to part with some or all of this money for a given item is an erratic relationship at best. Not only may prospects assume a variety of orientations toward spending in particular situations, but their assessments of product worth and the significance of the financial sacrifices involved can also change during the encounter. Nevertheless, vendors showing concern about conserving prospect resources seem likely to fare better generally.

You're selling a savings of time, of money, and that has to be proved to the prospect. You try to draw upon labor studies and draw upon the savings of the machines over manual systems. Then you show how that will account for buying the machines. You always try to apply it to what they have in the office, you adjust to it, but you try to show how they can save money by having your machine [manufacture—office equipment].

You don't like to sign them up for one year. You try to sign them up for two years, five, a lifetime, whatever you can do. . . . You'll also sign people up in groups, give them package deals, if that's what it takes. . . . When you're selling long term, you point out the advantages, how they're going to save money in the long run, and how they don't have to worry about any price increases. The facilities may expand, and the new memberships will have that figured in, but the existing members, they're already covered, protected from that [fitness center].

In a more direct, obvious sense, vendors may put items on "sale" in an attempt to show that they are mindful of buyers' interests in minimizing expenditures. Nevertheless, as noted in Chapter 8 ("Holding 'Sales'"), price reductions can create a variety of tactical and practical dilemmas for vendors. "Sales" can foster trust on the part of some buyers, but these events may also generate vendor skepticism and product disdain, as well as notions of irrelevancy and hostility. Although not necessarily saving buyers money, vendors may generate an appearance of savings or minimized expenditures by introducing extended payments, calculating costs over periods of usage, or providing additional "throw ins".[10]

Something like a fridge and stove can run a fair bit of money. So there you emphasize how long it is going to last, and how in the long run we will value the larger size or these additional features. . . . Our prices are pretty competitive, but we also offer a pretty good credit plan. Some people have the money right then and there, but we offer everyone at no additional charge a three-month payment plan, which basically makes it easier on everyone's budget [appliances].

We usually do our presentations in terms of the monthly costs, say over a 12- or 24-month period. It seems a lot less that way, a lot less money to have to invest right away. So there, you work towards a monthly payment that they feel comfortable with [manufacture—computers].

Making It Easy

Since some reservations about products may reflect the complexities of change, salespeople may attempt to provide assurances of minimal disruption. Vendors using this strategy typically stress the functional convenience of the product and/or its applications.

So there's two parts to the program, one the destination. The other is the way to get there. And that's our advantage, we're not just selling the destination, which is what most of the competitors are doing. So I can walk in and say, "You don't have to do anything. We have computers that'll take care of the mailing and all. You don't have to do anything. We'll take it off your desk." All you'll get is someone coming in, "Hey Harry, what a neat beach towel! This is terrific! Thanks a lot!" If you can walk into the vice-president, and say, "I'm going to make you look like a star, and you don't have to do a thing," then they just love it. Usually, travel is an extra on their desk, and when you add an incentive program, they ask themselves if they have time for it. And so the biggest thing you can do is show them that they don't have to do any worrying or any work to have it work for them. Stress that, and they're more likely to listen. Because everybody goes, "I don't need any more work. You say it's going to create more profit, but if it's going to cost me 30 hours of time, I'm not so interested." [promotions—travel]

Noteworthy too, are vendors' willingness to allow some more tentative testing of products on the part of prospects before requesting more sweeping commitments. While this tactic may cost prospects more in the long-run (i.e., at variance from conserving prospects resources in this respect), these options provide another avenue for ascertaining quality prior to making more extensive commitments.

These trial-size packages have worked fairly well for us. You don't get as good a deal quantitywise, and in part because the smaller packages cost pretty well as much as the larger ones. But it means that people can try something out before making a bigger investment in a product they're not familiar with. . . . We'll sometimes put coupons in these packages, but they go towards their next purchases, the larger sizes. Not everybody who's interested will buy the testers. Some would rather get the larger size right off, but some are a little more conservative that way [manufacture—food products].

If you're a brand new customer and you're with us for the first time, I don't want to suddenly have you locked into a whole year when you may not be paying your bills. Maybe you'll run into some sort of trouble. And you probably wouldn't feel comfortable signing a year's contract. So let's go with a shorter campaign, and if it works, we'll go for another one. And if it continues to work, then you look at an annual campaign and the saving that you will get. But for the extra dollars that you're not going to make [as a rep] because you didn't go with an annual campaign, you're probably ahead not to tie them into a long campaign for the first couple of campaigns. I just think that if I was a businessman and someone wanted me to sign a year's contract on a media that I'm not familiar with and have no loyalties, and have never tested, I would want to test this product before I commit myself to 12 months of it. And I would want more than one test. I would want to try it two or three times before I would consider going for a year [promotions—radio].

Providing Greater Purchasing Autonomy

Signifying a greater sense of freedom, purchasing autonomy takes two major forms: shopping autonomy, and greater selectivity.

A higher level of shopping autonomy is a clear and major advantage of self-serve operations. However, similar tendencies can be noted in other settings when prospects see vendors occupied with others. This also suggests higher levels of purchasing autonomy.

If one shopper comes into your department, it'll draw others. People are afraid to go in and be the only person in the department. They think they are going to be attacked by the salespeople [department store].

A lot of customers like to be able to look around without someone hovering over them, "This is nice! This is really great! This is new." . . . That's one reason it's good to have more customers than salesmen on the floor. You can be attentive and yet people feel they have a chance to sort things out on their own [furniture].

Salespeople sometimes provide prospects with more shopping autonomy by stepping back from encounters with prospects.

I'm not a high-pressure salesperson anyway, and I've told people that are looking at something, a high-price item, and they're maybe very close to buying it but I can sense that they just have that little bit of apprehension and they're not sure. I will say to them, "Go home and sleep on it. Think about it. Like this is a big decision that you're making, and I would rather that you go home tonight and think about it and come back in the morning and say, 'Yes, I've slept on it. I want it,' than to buy it right now when you're not absolutely sure, and then have a sleepless night and come in tomorrow all sheepishly, 'I want to bring this back because I shouldn't have bought it.' " With big things like [more costly] paintings and things, I will say, "Take it home, put it on the wall, look at it. If you like it, great, then we'll write up the bill. If you don't, bring it back." I'm not a high-pressure salesperson. There are a lot of high-pressure people who will, just to get it sold and get the money in the cash register. They don't care if the person likes it or is going to sleep that night or not. I can't deal that way. My store would probably take in more dollars and yet I don't believe that, because I think in the long run I have built up a clientele of people who believe in me and trust me. I think, in the long run, that's a much, much better way to go. . . . Or "Why don't you go have a hamburger and talk about it and come back. Here's my card. I'll hold it for you because I want you to be absolutely sure." If they are trying to decide whether they trust you or not, that's going to get them to trust you because they're going to say "This person isn't pushing me. They're willing to tell me go, and I'll hold this for you." That instills confidence in you, that you're not pushing them and you want them to buy your product but you're not grabbing on their ankle and pulling them [jewelry].

The worst thing in the world, when a man walks in the door to sell something, is when the potential buyer knows that before you leave you're going to ask him to make a decision. Now, if that's the case, all defensives are up. He doesn't even hear half of what you're saying. He's thinking about his defenses. He's protecting his bank balance. He's not convinced he wants to be involved, therefore, the message is not coming through. . . . If you become more of a friend than an antagonist out to catch his dollars, then the man is going to relax with you and you're going to be able to make your point. He knows you're not going to ask him to quickly make a decision. You may not ask him to make a decision at all. Indeed, I'll go further and say that after a period of time you aren't asking him, he's asking you. So it's this method that I encourage. All the people that work with me don't use that method. They have their own style [promotions—television].

A greater sense of choice represents another form of purchasing autonomy. People may find it confusing to choose from multiple options, but the availability of two or more options provides prospects with a greater sense of control over their own destiny. When only one product is available, prospects seem more apt to anticipate pressure from vendors to purchase that product.

You really notice it when your stock is getting low. It gets harder to sell a car even when it's almost exactly what somebody wants. They like to have other things to compare it with. The same options, but another model, or the same model with a few different options, a different color, so they can pick the one they want. That way they don't feel that they were pushed into buying the one you wanted to sell them [auto].

If you get down to one style and color, it can be really tough trying to sell it. You're much better off to have more colors or more styles, more selection in the same thing. People like to compare it to something else [women's clothing].

Although vendors seem less attuned to the practices entailed in minimizing buyer obligations than in invoking images of vendor integrity or product quality, their efforts (conserving prospect resources, making purchases easier, and providing autonomy) are extremely valuable in sensitizing us to this more general aspect of relationship work. The neutralization of people's obligations seems a fundamental element fostering participation in situations.[11] Still, as with others who would involve us in their pursuits, vendor practices in this area are also subject to ongoing buyer interpretations and adjustments.

SOME PRACTICAL LIMITATIONS OF TRUST

Taken together, the preceding elements suggest that trust reflects assumptions and assessments on the part of persons that they will be able to maintain control of their fate through others. That is, people seem to trust others to the extent they assume (or anticipate) that others will act in ways consistent with their interests. However, there are some practical limitations to this notion of trust.

In some cases, people may not wish to be bothered assessing trust in reference to purchases they consider more inconsequential. In other instances, they may lack either the luxury of time in which to consider trust as fully as they might like or viable alternatives from which to choose. In these latter instances, people may find themselves trusting in others (or suspending distrust) as a matter of urgency or limited choice.[12] Under these conditions, vendors' relationship work may be greatly nullified, at least in terms of immediate purchases.

From the vendor's viewpoint, trust is even more elusive. Since trust is a quality attributed to vendors by their prospects, vendors inevitably live with uncertainty. Vendors seem able to invoke higher levels of trust by embarking on certain lines of action on an overall basis, but each encounter is much less certain. In each instance, they are dependent upon their prospects' interpretations and ongoing assessments of these efforts.

Suggestive Selling

When you go to write up the bill, you pick up the jar of polish that matches, and say, "We recommend that you use this on your shoes." You don't say, "Buy it!" but you sort of put it with the shoes. . . . With the shoes, and purses, when you're showing them the shoes, you hand them the handbag that matches, and you say something like, "Doesn't this look nice with these shoes! We happen to have this one that matches." . . . We use the term *suggestive selling* mainly [shoes].

Should prospects seem willing to purchase particular products, vendors may attempt to increase the dollar value of their customers' total purchase by having customers purchase more costly items and/or additional items at the time of purchase. Regardless of whether vendors are *selling up* (promoting more costly products) or are engaged in *second selling* (promoting multiple purchases), *suggestive selling* is a powerful marketing tool and one worthy of attention.

The existence of trust is largely taken for granted in the following consideration of suggestive selling. It is quite apparent, however, that varying levels of buyer trust can greatly affect vendors' abilities to accomplish these objectives.

Suggestive selling may seem most familiar in retail settings, but it is by no means so limited. Any vendor (e.g., manufacture/wholesale) may elect to use this option by presuming a sale at one level and then proceeding to "suggest" further and/or more costly purchases than those the customer had intended. Although this is the intent of those who use explicitly suggestive selling as a technique, other vendors may accomplish the same ends in their attempts to be helpful or provide better service.

There are three major dangers associated with the practice of suggestive selling. Customers may not make initial purchases even though these seemed forthcoming, may return most or all of the goods purchased, and may avoid buying from those vendors in the future.

We don't push the add-on sales all that much, but in showing them the item, we do try to indicate how this or that item would be handy for them. Say suggesting a carry-on bag if they're considering a basic suitcase, telling them how this smaller bag would be useful if they're traveling in the plane, things like that. Or we'll maybe suggest that they might like another bag, one more than they had in mind, because if they're taking along shoes and sweaters, they may need more room than they had realized. So we'll mention things. . . .

But you have to watch it too, because if you're too pushy you'll get more returns, where people get home and think of things, and then they'll bring it back, so there you want to get that happy medium [luggage].

As the following material indicates, however, these risks can be minimized, depending on the ways in which suggestive selling is done, and ongoing vendor sensitivities to customer situations. While promoting greater buyer expenditures, suggestive selling can even consolidate buyer-seller relations!

SELLING UP

Insofar as higher-priced items generally carry the same ratio of margins, it is usually to the vendor's advantage to sell the more costly items.[13] At the same time, however, vendors may believe that higher-priced items are of better quality and well worth the price differences. Thus attempts to sell up (step up) may be to the advantage or disadvantage of the buyer.

As the following strategies of (a) defining quality and (b) "assuming the best" indicate, selling up operates on the more general notion of selling the customer on the symbolic significance of the items promoted.

Providing Definitions of Quality

One way of selling up involves vendors disparaging their lower lines, once prospects seem interested in purchasing these less costly items.[14] Vendors depicting less costly lines as inferior may generate some skepticism about their products more generally, but this strategy appears to work in many cases. Some attempts have been made to discourage vendors legally from bait and switch practices in reference to advertised "sales," but it is virtually impossible to prevent the practice of vendors denigrating less costly lines in routine selling situations (and, the vendors may be completely sincere in pointing out shortcomings).

We [staff] don't like the [watches] line, and you hate to sell these products to anyone, but if you don't have them, you're going to lose sales. They want to see the cheaper items, and this way, they can at least see the differences, whereas if you didn't have them, they would be less likely to buy anything from you. So we don't push this line. Not at all. And you actually try to persuade people not to buy them, telling them that they just won't hold up very well [jewelry].

We were encouraged to sell the better items, but I think that in most cases people do that automatically anyways. Like with myself, I don't like cheap quality things. The cheaper things won't look as good, they won't hold up as well, and I'll point that out to the customers [department store].

Vendors may also promote purchases of more costly items by attaching comparison points (e.g., "Good," "Better," "Best") to their merchandise either in personal communications or through the media (including displays).

We do that in our catalogues. You want to show differences in quality, especially since they can't really see for themselves. So you get these things, "Economy," "Heavy Duty," "Super Value," "Best Buy," and what not [hardware].

If the differences are not so apparent, we'll sometimes use signs to tell them which is better. . . . Your better lines usually cost more. It's not just that it costs them more, but we will usually spend more to get a line we think is better . . . or a line [name brand] that people think is better, and that price gets passed on to the customer [department store].

In contrast to those denigrating lower-priced products, vendors providing indications of greater product worth may avoid some of the distrust that may arise when lower lines are slighted. Thus some vendors stress the value of the higher-priced versions relative to images, convenience, and such.

If you can move them to a higher-priced line, you're bringing in more capital. It's good for the company, the store, and it's easy to do. . . . You might start out with a guy looking at one of your "sale" priced suits. So he comes in and, "Not a bad price!" So he looks them over. Nothing he really likes, "Oh well, I wasn't really looking for a suit anyways." "But I've got a nice one back here, a good color for the fall, and it's only $____ . I'll just show it to you. It doesn't hurt to show it to you while you're taking that one off." So he tries it on. "Well, that's not too bad, better quality." "No? . . . I've got a better one." . . . And it starts out the guy wasn't really interested in a suit, and you end up selling him a good quality suit. He just happened to like the price of the first ones, and he walks out of here, happier than a pig in shit! And he's bought this suit that cost three times what the first one did, and he only came in because he saw the "sales" sign. That happens a lot of times. . . . At first, it scares the hell out of you when you do it, you think, "Oh, this guy is going to get hot at me if I show him this. I wonder if I should do this?" That's how you see it, when you're first learning. . . . The customer seems really appreciative too, "Gee, thanks, I'll be sure and ask for you whenever I come back." And you sort of wonder, "What happened?" [men's clothing]

In selling cosmetics, you're selling beauty. You're fulfilling people's hopes and dreams. You don't grab them and say, "You've got to buy this!" It's more suggestive selling, "This would look pretty with what you just bought." Or "Oh, this shade would look lovely with this." . . . You try to sell them the higher-priced lines. It's not that there's anything wrong with the lower-priced cosmetics [department store].

Assuming the Best

Unless prospects indicate preferences for particular price levels, vendors may promote higher-priced lines by presuming that prospects want (or are willing to purchase) "top line" merchandise.

If someone came in and asked for a kettle, and didn't give you a price, you would bring out one of your best, the nicest. Then if they said that they were looking for something for less, you could direct them to something for less. And there, with your better ones, you use the old line, "We've had very few come back." Or "I rarely see any come back. They're really a good make!" [discount catalogue house].

Quite often when people come in, it's with the approach, "I don't want to spend a lot of money." "That's fine. Let me show you what we have." And I always start at the top of the line. They can see the most beautiful, the most deluxe. They can see all the features. Then we work down, right through the line to the bottom. And then I'll say to them, "Is there one there that looks as though it has all the features that you would be interested in?" And usually, they'll go back towards the middle and will look at the features, and then I'll go to the next one up and, "This one has this and that. Would that be important to you?" . . . And nine times out of ten they'll pay the extra. But you have to be able to show them just what the worth is, and they have to decide in their mind that those features are worth that to them. . . . Now sometimes we feel that we neglect our second line. It's good quality and all, but it's just not as attractive, doesn't have the same features as the first line. But you just can't do it both ways. . . . We've tried selling the lower ends through newspaper ads and all, but we just can't seem to move them the same way. We seem to be able to sell the high ends and our customers are happy, no complaints. In fact, they'll come back and tell us that even though they didn't expect to put out that much money for appliances, that they're glad they bought the one with the extra features. But we have had the other, where people have bought the more stripped-down version and later came back a couple of weeks later, saying that they made a mistake, that they should have bought the one with the extras. So now, when they come in, I stress these features. You know how people may feel a bit short when they've got to make a purchase, and a couple of months later, find that they should have spent the little extra for what they want [appliances].

Vendors inclined to engage in selling up also face the possibility of losing customers who may be unwilling and/or unable to purchase the higher-priced units, but who now have begun to question the value of purchasing the lower-priced items. To avoid this situation, salespeople often find themselves trying to assess the prospects' abilities (or willingness) to be moved up to "better lines."[15]

You want to sell your higher-priced items, but you have to be a little careful. . . . You can sell somebody on a better line, but he may not have the money for it. Only now, the lower line is not good enough for him anymore, so he wants to put off buying for now, which isn't good [jewelry].

SECOND SELLING

The other thing we do is to try to make add-on sales, where you sell them one item and then try to get them to buy some related product. That can add a lot on to your sales totals, "Would you like a whatever it is to go with it?" [department store]

Just as vendors promoting better lines tend to bring more money into the business, so does the practice of *second selling* (also: multiple, tie-in, add-on, tack-on, associated, combination, and cluster selling; accessorizing). Second selling may involve multiple purchases of the same items and/or different items. Customers will sometimes spontaneously select (convenience, preference) several items, but their purchases may also reflect vendor attempts to promote multiple purchases.

Second selling may be combined with attempts at selling up. Both forms of suggestive selling are greatly facilitated, however, when prospects have made initial purchasing decisions.[16]

Suggestion selling is the key to the whole business. And you can sell one item to five people or you can sell five items to one person. And if you can sell the five to the one, then probably you've gained a friend in the process. . . . What I've found is that it's the first item that's really the hardest. Once you've sold the first item, you've made an opening. You can add the others on rather quickly. It's easier, and you can keep going, except that the total price may prevent them from going higher. But it is easier, because the first one, that's the one that really breaks the ice for you. . . . What I'll do, say if a person wants to try on an item, like a blouse or skirt, I'll bring something to complement it, suggesting that they might like to wear this while they're trying the other one, to get a more accurate impression of the article they're wanting to consider. Then later, you just tell them that it looks really good together, or they'll see that the outfit matches up nicely. And they'll say, "Well, I've got blouses at home," whatever. And you let them try it on and, "Just a minute, I've got something else you might like to try on, you might like to pick up later on. We've got two of these in stock in your size, and if you decide later to add it to your wardrobe, just give me a call. If we have it in stock, we'll be glad to hold it for you." You're always building up a set for them, so it just keeps going! It's not just a pair of slacks or a skirt, but it's a whole set of items. And as I say, you usually have gained a friend in the process. . . . Or you might ask her if she would like to try this other item on to go with it, telling her that it's intended as a set, but that we haven't seen it as a set on anyone. You ask her if she would model it for us. So you might get her to put on the skirt, the blouse, and the vest. That way she'll get the effect of the total look [women's clothing].

If someone is buying a stapler, you ask them if they would like staples. Or if they're buying a filing cabinet, you ask them if they would like file folders, file separators, and such. The same thing with a desk, you try to suggest all the accessories. Add-on sales can really make a difference to your sales totals. You want your people to do that! It brings more sales into the shop [stationery].

Despite the overall advantages of selling higher-priced lines and/or multiple items, these practices are by no means uniform. Hence, even when explicitly encouraged, considerable discretion may be exercised by the salespeople involved.

We're encouraged to sell second items, especially around the popular seasons. Say, for example, you learn that they're getting some nuts for a party, you might ask them if they would like some after dinner mints to go as well. Or if they're getting ice cream, you might ask them if they would like a cake to go along with that. . . . They encourage us to do that, but most of us, actually, very seldom will do that. It's too much like high pressure. Because to me, I know how I feel when I go shopping, and if I have someone ramming something down my throat, "Buy! Buy!" I'm more than likely not to go back to that store again, or if I see that clerk, to avoid that person. I don't like high-pressure sales. So usually, once they've made their choices, I'll say, "Is there anything else?" and that's about it. Not "Would you like this or that to go along with it?" . . . If we have a "sale," we might remind them of that, "By the way, we have this type of candy on "sale," right now. Would you like to pick some up?" I'll tell them things like that, but otherwise, just ask if there's anything else [candy].

> When I sell a pair of shoes, I'll ask them if they would like to get anything else before I ring up the total, but I really don't try for the second pair of shoes like some people do, or like they say you're supposed to do. But it's the same with myself. If I go into a store, I wouldn't want people pushing a lot of things on me, and that's how I operate. I go by what I like to have done to me [shoes].

The emphasis so far has been on second selling at an interpersonal level. It should be noted that vendors may also promote multiple selling through display, packaging, and pricing styles. Thus, for instance, by putting items in sets, or larger size containers, vendors may offer convenience or (small typically) savings to those making larger purchases. In these ways, vendors may promote multiple sales beyond that which might be generated by the interpersonal efforts of the staff.

> We do a lot of things that way, especially during "sales." "2/79¢," "3/$1.00." That way, people buy more than they would otherwise. They may not be back so soon for those same items, but they bought a larger amount from you. So it's good that way [groceries].

> We want to get as many combinations as we can, so we do that a fair bit, "Two for so much," "three for whatever." You knock off a little, but you make up for it in the volume [discount department store]

In Perspective

Like the preceding chapter, ("Presenting Products"), Chapter 3 provides us with much valuable insight into the ways in which vendors strive actively to shape encounters with their customers (and the relationships these encounters signify). Defining trust as an assumption or assessment that others would act in accord with one's interests, this chapter outlined three major dimensions along which vendors attempted to invoke trust. Thus attention was given to the portrayal of vendor integrity, product quality, and the minimization of buyer obligations.

Despite the value of trust as a preventative tactic, we find that salespeople are very uneven in implementing trust-inducing practices. First, as with other aspects of relationship work, the development of trust entails ongoing reflective activity. Second, the promotion of trust should also be contextualized relative to other kinds of information salespeople may wish to convey or manage to obtain from their customers. Third, even when they make deliberate attempts to invoke trust, salespeople must contend with diverse customer concerns and shifting interpretations. Not only are salespeople likely to find considerable variations in the ways in which particular trust-invoking tactics are acknowledged from one customer to the next, they are also apt to find that the same customers are unevenly receptive to particular tactics from one encounter to the next or even throughout the course of a particular encounter.

Attributions of trust appear to foster purchasing decisions in a great many settings, but also noteworthy are situations in which buyers find themselves either forgoing or suspending considerations of trust (e.g., minor purchases, time pressures, limited choices). These elements tend to negate the impact of relationship work on the part of the salespeople involved. Even here, however, the significance of trust for sales should not be discounted. We have been discussing trust in more fleeting or situated contexts, but it can have very consequential long-term effects as well (see Chapter 7 on buyer loyalty).

Including both the practices of selling up and second selling, the phenomenon of suggestive selling casts further light on the significance and fragility of trust. While these practices can dramatically increase the cash flows vendors achieve, they presume levels of trust that customers may be unwilling to attribute to vendors both in immediate encounters and over the long run (repeat patronage). To the extent that buyers interpret these practices as consistent with their interests, trust may be sustained and even further consolidated by suggestive selling. Otherwise, the same efforts may be construed as evidence of pressure and may result in immediate distancing from and subsequent avoidance of particular vendors.

Depicting the ways in which vendors attempt to deal with customer resistance, the next chapter further examines the negotiable aspects of sales encounters and the relationships they denote. It more fully expands on the challenges and dilemmas salespeople face in their dealings with others. It illustrates the ways in which salespeople try to manage the more unpredictable features of impending sales encounters.

Notes

1. For other process-oriented statements on trust, see Garfinkel's (1963) ethnomethodological depiction of "rule violations," Henslin's (1968) interactionist statement on trust and the cab driver, Bigus' (1972) portrayal of the milkman and his customers, and

Browne's (1973) material on trust and the used car salesman. Luhmann (1980) and Barber (1983) provide functionalist interpretations of trust.

2. The reference here is to those holding synonymous interests for the same target. This contrasts with those holding parallel, but competing interests (i.e., both parties want to win); intersecting, possibly competitive interests (people interacting, but with different ends in mind); and nonrelevant interests (no interests of consequence regarding one another's activities). Since in trusting, one is "betting on the future," all assessments of trust are based on assumptions or anticipation.

3. This point is also made by Angrist (1984: 141-142). For a more general statement on "designating discretion" (the when and how of truth telling), see Prus (1982).

4. Although Garfinkel (1963) defines a perceived willingness on the part of others to play by the rules as fundamental to trust, this seems only one element that may be taken into account by people trusting others. And, buyers may specifically request that vendors (trusted otherwise) give them special concessions (ergo creating some more particularistic understandings; i.e., redefining the rules).

5. Angrist (1984: 141) also addresses this theme.

6. Fitting in clearly involves what Mead (1934) terms "role taking" (taking the other's point of view into account), but it also involves an attempt to develop relationships with others that these others would find acceptable.

7. "You try it" demonstrations also tend to promote a sense of obligation on the part of the participants. Having embarked on particular lines of action, people may experience some loss of integrity when later forgoing these options.

8. Insofar as our notions of reality reflect perceptions that "others would agree" (Schutz, 1971), objectivity is no more than the intersubjective consensus we perceive ourselves to share with others.

9. Normally, this would seem to work best when buyers envision themselves as having subsequent occasions to do business with these same vendors as opposed to one-time only purchases.

10. Price resistances will be considered more fully in the following chapter.

11. See Matza (1964) and Prus and Irini (1988) for depictions of the significance of "drift" for people's participation in deviance.

12. Lemert (1953) uses the term *closure* to refer to situations in which people experiencing pressing obligations act in terms of short-run options.

13. Even if the margin is greater for a lower-priced item, the overall outcome of selling a more costly item may be a better return in dollars (e.g., buy for $1, sell for $3 versus buy for $5, sell for $10). Vendors on commission may benefit more directly from suggestive selling than their noncommission counterparts, but higher sales totals generate job security for all.

14. See Caplovitz (1963) for a depiction of this strategy in "selling to the poor."

15. Similar dilemmas are noted by French (1958: 40-41).

16. Not unlike the bar staff (Prus and Irini, 1988; Prus, 1983b), who rely on tips for a significant proportion of their income, salespeople on commission are especially likely to see the value of suggestive selling.

Chapter 4
NEUTRALIZING RESISTANCE

They'll [merchants] give you lines like "Business is tough," "Inventory is high, I have year-end coming up," "No, I have a big order, two big orders placed at the gift shows; I can't have any more," "My girl doesn't like it," which is a bad one. . . . You think, "Your girl doesn't like it? Who runs your business you or your girl?" . . . "I just don't like your packaging, but I do like what is inside it." You have to break that down! These are some of the pitfalls you have to deal with. These are some of the things you have to break down. They use every excuse in the book [wholesale—giftware].

What sorts of resistances do salespeople encounter in pursuing prospect commitments? What strategies do they employ in overcoming people's doubts and reservations? What makes it difficult for salespeople to be successful in these endeavors? As these questions suggest, Chapter 4 is a natural extension of the relationship work implied in vendor approaches, qualification, attempts to generate interest, and the development of trust. It builds directly on themes developed in the preceding chapters and forms a particularly vital bridge to Chapter 5 on obtaining commitments.

The material in this chapter assumes more of a "remedial quality" in the pursuit of cooperation, but it is best located in the more general realm of *relationship work*.[1] Individual salespeople are unevenly attentive to both the impact of relationship work on immediate purchasing commitments and the effects of relationship work on future transactions, but the management of resistance represents a valuable dimension for a fuller understanding of buyer-seller encounters. Vendors may want to consolidate sales and work diligently to that end, but they are ultimately dependent on prospect cooperation. Reflecting the perspectives and interests of the participants, sales are subject to ongoing negotiations.[2]

The following discussion first gives attention to buyers as "elusive targets," indicating the uneven, unpredictable, and often nonexplicit nature of prospect resistance. The focus then shifts to the ways in which vendors deal with resistances pertaining more specifically to skepticism, price concerns, existing loyalties, and comparison shopping. This is followed by a summary statement on the general strategies vendors use in dealing with resistance.

Elusive Targets

As a consequence of vendor dependency on buyers, any resistance can represent a major impediment to a sale. And while some reservations may be most evident toward the end of encounters, any buyer concern may become extremely consequential at any point in the encounter. This means that any time vendors deal with prospect reservations, they may be seen as moving sales toward completion. In some cases, vendors encounter no resistance when they attempt to complete sales. The prospects may be willing to make purchases, but have not assumed the initiative necessary to complete these transactions. In other instances, completed sales may be only one reservation away, or many.

Although we will be discussing sales encounters in general terms, each sales encounter is somewhat unique. Vendors may encounter a fairly consistent set of prospect styles and reservations, but they never know just what resistance(s) they may get next, at what point in the encounter resistances will emerge, the ways in which reservations will be expressed (or concealed), and the number of resistances they may encounter in specific episodes. These uncertainties introduce elements of challenge and frustration. They also tend to frustrate "quick-fixes" or "magic formula" approaches to saleswork.

Noteworthy in this respect are buyers' capacities for self-reflectivity (Mead, 1934; Blumer, 1969) and "resourcefulness." Both imply unevenness and unpredictability within sales encounters. In discussing reflectivity, we might first address the variable levels of attention with which buyers attend to particular reservations. Some reservations may remain at the forefront of prospects' consciousness throughout sales encounters (and may very well nullify the intended effectiveness of vendor presentations). Other concerns are more fleeting and may be readily forgotten as prospects consider other aspects of their purchases. These elements make sales activities particularly problematic. Not only may salespeople be unaware of concerns of significance to the prospect, but even when specific concerns are evident, salespeople may have considerable difficulty in accurately determining how significant any concern is, how long any concern will persist within the encounter, and whether, once a particular concern seems resolved, it will become a problem at a later point in the encounter. Salespeople may pride themselves on their abilities to understand the perspectives of the other (what Mead, 1934, terms "role taking"), but the matter is further complicated in that prospects may be reluctant to reveal their actual concerns for a variety of reasons (e.g., embarrassment, distrust, bargaining leverage) and may intentionally mislead vendors. This means that not only may buyers' expressed reservations be misleading, but vendors may also have to contend with reservations not indicated to them by their prospects.

> You'll get all these comments, "This is too big," "This is too small," "I don't like this finish," and on and on. You don't know if someone is trying to get out of buying something or what, or if there is something that they've really been looking for. . . . Some of them, to get away from you, they will ask you about something that they know you don't have on your table [crafts].

> Often they don't tell you what's bothering them. Often they just say, "Well, I'll have to think about it." They don't really say whether it's the price, the color, whatever [department store].

While resourcefulness is contingent upon people's capacities for self-reflectivity, it also denotes the "stock of knowledge" (Schutz, 1971) people acquire through their own direct experiences and those shared with them by others. Recognizing that buying decisions can easily become complicated, prospective buyers may use certain strategies to avoid making commitments. To this end, prospects may "reserve overt indications of relevance" until they've had opportunities to learn prices and assess purchasing situations; distance themselves from vendors, lest these vendors establish higher levels of relevance and immediacy than that desired; provide indications of nonserious shopping to avert sales presentations or generate greater shopping autonomy; engage in comparison shopping to obtain a better sense of product knowledge and prices; stall for time (e.g., "I want to look around a little more," "I want to think about it," "Do you have a card?"); and use companions (family, friends, and other "experts") to offset vendor influences. Thus, while salespeople may misrepresent their situations, there is no assurance that buyers will be truthful. Vendors may have experience as salespeople, but prospects also acquire experience as shoppers. Further, knowing their situations more completely than the vendors do, prospects are advantaged in contextualizing both products and expenditures.

Beyond sorting out their own roles (concerns with immediate success, integrity, stage fright, customer loyalty, and so on), vendors are faced with the task of achieving the cooperation of people who may experience uncertainty, not only in reference to the products under immediate consideration, but also in reference to other aspects of their situations (e.g., financial concerns, major objectives, accountability to others) as well.

Major Obstacles Encountered

Four major realms of purchasing resistance that vendors commonly encounter in pursuing sales are (1) skepticism, (2) price concerns, (3) existing loyalties, and (4) comparison shopping. While vendors may face any number of objections in any given encounter, each of these forms of resistance will be examined, indicating some of the ways in which vendors endeavor to deal with these. Vendors may have difficulty determining the existence (and direction) of particular resistances, but their adjustments to buyers will depend on how they interpret these resistances (e.g., an instance of product quality versus price resistance) as well as upon the "practical limitations" (e.g., awareness of tactics, time constraints, prospect styles and interests) of the situations that they experience.

SKEPTICISM

Even vendors who do extensive trust-promoting activity often cite skepticism as a major obstacle in making sales. A closer examination of this obstacle reveals that this reservation may have several bases. It is by no means limited to qualities directly attributable to the product.

Thus, in addition to product skepticism, one may also encounter doubts regarding vendors and prospective owners.

Product Skepticism

A great many reservations that people have regarding products reflect the images of quality (performance/reliability) that they desire in products. Hence, vendors able to demonstrate or guarantee products to the satisfaction of the prospects are advantaged.

If they're not sure about a product, they'll ask you more about how they will hold up, but usually, that's not until they're more serious about the product. There, its nice with some of our lines because we have more confidence in the manufacturer, that they will stand behind their products. You can tell the customer with more assurance that the item will hold up better. And that is good in terms of sales too [men's clothing].

The most common question of that type is "How do I know it's working? "How do I know it is going to work?" And that's one of the most frustrating questions I get. And I get that all the time. . . . And I can't say, "This is a tape recorder. I'll turn it on and you're going to hear it. See how it works." I haven't got something concrete. . . . I can't just produce it for them. All you can do is take the radio audience ratings, and they do break it down into your age groups and malefemale. . . . We can take that information and we know who we reach. And to be realistic, it's not going to be accurate. . . . All you can do, really, is explain to them that this is the type of people you are reaching, and perhaps they can talk to other people who are advertising on the station. Listen to the station. Hear the sound. Hear who advertises. And phone them up, if they're not competitors, and ask them, "Is it working for you?" If it wasn't working, they wouldn't be on the air. And you find that the people who are on the air consistently, the reason they're on the air consistently is that it is working for them. And they just keep on going and going and going. If it wasn't working, why would a businessman invest $20,000, $30,000, $40,000 in a medium and just throw that money out the window? It doesn't make sense! So all they can do is do what he did. It's like going into a job you're not too sure of, plunge in with both feet. Do it right, and wait for the results. And hopefully, those results will be good. I have confidence that they will be. That's all you can do, but you don't know until you try [promotions radio].

In other instances, vendors may attempt to redefine the prospects' expectations.

The guy that comes to buy a used car, you've got to get it through his head that he's buying a used car, not a new one. Most used car buyers, they'll go home and say, "I've just bought a new car!" He hasn't bought a new car, he's bought a used one. So you've got to get that into his head because otherwise they'll pick your cars to bits, that scratch, that mark, "Can you have that fixed for me?" You got to get to him, "Look, you're buying a used car." And they'll start dickering over mileage, "There's too much mileage on it." And you have to tell them, "You're not buying a car for what it's done, you're buying a car for what's left. If you want one with no mileage, have you thought of a new one?". . . . We can't do it anymore, but in the old days, it was "Well, how many miles do you want on it?" [auto].

You'll have people and they don't have the money, but they want top quality. There, you try to explain the situation to them. They can't be as fussy. Nobody makes them for that, with all the features they want. You try to get them to compromise, because if they can't lower their standards, you can't make a sale [men's clothing].

Since buyers tend to associate quality with price, products priced less than expected may also generate some skepticism.

If the price is reasonable, you'll often get people who want to know "What's the catch?" So there, you tell them that you're dealing in volume, that a lot of the activities are group events, so you don't need as many instructors, that the programs have been streamlined so that we don't have to spend much time in the office. "So we can spend more time on the floor, having fun with you." . . . But, you see, a lot don't follow through actively in the program. It's the same in everything, there's a lot of joiners, but not all that many follow through. So you overbook. The traffic is moving all the time, through the sauna, the exercise rooms, and all, but if everyone came all the time, we'd be in trouble. So you oversell, on the assumption that they're not all going to come all that often and that a lot are going to drop out. . . . And after that person pays their membership fee, you're not really making anything on them, so that's why you get into these other services, give them something else to get, shirts, bags, beauty services, things like that. Get in these other things to get their money [fitness center].

The objections you get varies with your products. If you have a low-priced line, people want to know "What's wrong with it?" If you get a higher-priced line, they want to know "Why is it so much?" So you're defending your products in both cases, trying to show that the cheaper things are still good quality. We've actually had to raise some prices because of that [men's clothing].

When prospects have had negative experiences with identical or similar products in the past, vendors are especially apt to encounter distrust. Although prospects may endeavor to avoid situations of this nature, vendors encountering those who have been "stung" may face additional skepticism.

You'll have people who've had bad experiences with other magazines that've folded. There, they might have signed a contract for so many ads, paid in advance to get a discount, and then found that the company with the magazine went broke. . . . Those are tough! You might have to take some heat over that, but if you are patient with them, take your time, you might be able to overcome that. Explain things more fully, go short term with them. And make sure, if you get their business, that everything goes right, and keep in touch with them, because they're more distrusting [promotions—magazine].

Someone's said to them, "Well, I wouldn't deal with _____ because I lost money with them." . . . Sometimes you can overcome that. Sometimes, you can't. It depends on the relationship and how credible the other person was, etc. . . . I've done business lots of times with people who've said, "I don't know if I want to do business with your company because my father invested with you [company] 20 years ago and he didn't like the guy he was dealing with." So there, you try to relate to situations where they can see that it can make a big difference who you're dealing with in any situation [investments].

Vendor Skepticism

Skepticism is not limited to products. Some skepticism may also be directed toward the company and/or the particular salesperson (honesty, competency, and the like) involved. Given the relative anonymity of many sales encounters, vendors may find that their own credibility represents an impediment to sales.

We get a lot of people who come in and say that they buy from us because they know they can depend on the quality, that they know that they're getting good stuff, something like that. But we do have people who don't trust you when you weigh up candy, "Are you taking into account the weight of the box?" . . . Nothing all that serious, but they want to be sure that they're getting what they're paying for [candy].

They're never sure who is telling them the truth. It's sad to say, but there's an awful lot of misinformation that gets fed to them, stats that get bent, as you and I well know. It's the old story that figures don't lie. So they're afraid and, you know, there's very little area for them to go and get that unbiased

opinion. . . . Television is a very big part of most people's lives and yet,
because it is so intangible, the biggest problem we have is the skepticism that
I'm [advertiser] going to invest a lot of money and lose it. So the big thing is
that here is this mystery. They don't know how to measure it. . . . They're a
little distrustful of media people because everybody's number one. They can
show on some short of a chart or graph that, indeed, they're number one. This
the client doesn't understand. He doesn't understand why everybody's number one. How come there's not somebody number two. You can have four
radio stations and each one of them are number one. Well any damn fool
knows that that isn't true, but it may be true if you start to jack around and
find some spot at 2 o'clock in the morning where you dominate the audience.
The fact that there's only 350 people there doesn't become a part of the
discussion. So they're distrustful. Here's this person coming along and they
are very skeptical. . . . The same faces coming in the door all the time (i.e.,
repeat calls). If they're performing as they should, and indeed they do, then
there is a trust that builds up, and that's one way of bringing them in
[promotions—television].

Skepticism Regarding Prospective Owners

Prospects may have confidence in both products and vendors, but be
uncertain whether the impending owners (themselves or others) would
have sufficient skills, opportunities, or desires to use products in question (thus justifying expenditures). One important dimension of owner
skepticism emerges with respect to people's self-concepts and the
images that they associate with owners of particular products.

It's interesting to watch people trying on cowboy hats. They wonder [some-
times openly] how they look in them, how they will look to others, and where
they might be able to wear a hat like that [notes].

You might think it looks good on them, but they have to think that, too. [mixed
clothing].

Similar concerns are noted relative to owner abilities to perform the
tasks that purchases imply.

If they [merchants] tell you that sales are slow [too slow to order], you might
say something like, "Maybe you have the wrong products. Maybe you need
to change your products. Try something new. Try something different." And
I think there's benefit to that [wholesale—giftware].

A musical background is of some help because, that way, you can pick up on some of the things a little faster, but the main thing is being able to sell because you don't want to show them what you can do. You want to be able to show them what the organ can do. So in some cases, people who are very good at playing the organ can find that it works against themselves. People who have never played before will say, "Oh, I could never do that!", especially adults who want to learn for the first time. And a lot of people buying these organs are people who don't want to devote ten years of their lives to learning how to play the organ. . . . It's set up so that any child can do it, but you have to watch it if the parents come with a child. Because in a situation like that, in a strange setting and all, they [children] may not be able to sit down and do it, and the parents may think, "Aw, forget it." So you don't really want to have people just sit down and try it, because they may be discouraged off the bat. Some salesmen will get the people sitting down right at the start, so there it would depend on the system that you've developed. With the new salespeople they try to discourage it though [music].

Here vendors have the options of trying to locate products more suited to the buyer's definition of the user or redefine the interests of the user.

You get, "Well, it's nice, but I don't know if it's really for me." They think it's a little too flashy or colorful, something like that. So you might have to go to work on them a little more, "Look Harry, this is where the fashion is going. It takes a little while to get used to these new things. But, hey, if you don't jazz up your wardrobe a little here and there, you're going to feel left out along the way. Makes it a little harder to fit in. What do you say you try it on and see how it looks. I think you may be surprised!" [mixed clothing].

Regardless of the basis of buyers' skepticism [product, vendor, owner], vendors encountering skepticism also face the decision of whether to try to allay the doubts of particular prospects or to pursue seemingly more promising buyers.

Each call is costing you money and taking your time. So there comes a point where you figure you're better off to try approaching someone new and forgetting about this other guy. Even if you're on salary, it's still going to show up on your sales volume, which might determine whether you get a raise or promotion. So you have to stop. Usually, I cut them off at three calls. If they seem sincere to me, I'll let them have a few fouls, but usually it's three strikes and they're out. But you have to read people along the way. You can't use that as a strict rule, and sometimes you're more abrupt. And some people are too skeptical, so there you might just say, "Here's my card. You know where to reach us. If we can help, give us a call." [manufacture—industrial].

If other prospects are readily accessible, salespeople will often define a lack of expressed interest as the basis for disinvolvement. However, it is also recognized that this "lack of interest" may be insincere (i.e., an evasion tactic) and/or reflect other concerns (e.g., preoccupations, skepticism, indecision). Assuming these latter sorts of interpretations, vendors may attempt to probe for (and resolve) any underlying reservations and/or promote their products more intensively in an attempt to move past these concerns.

> If someone tells you that they don't need a policy, it's up to you to create a need. "No hurry?" Well, there you might give them a story, a "for instance." "No time to sit down and talk right now?" There, I ask them if they don't think that their financial future is important. "Oh yeah!" "Well, let's sit down and talk about it." . . . If it's a lack of confidence, I just have to try to show them that I'm honest. You try to give them more information [insurance].

> "No time," that is another common one that you get. There, you might tell them that if they don't have time to prepare an ad, then we can do that for them [that would cost them extra]. . . . If they say that it's not convenient for them, that's what they mean when they say they "don't have time," then what we will do is try to find another time that is more convenient to talk with them about it [promotions—magazine].

PRICE OBJECTIONS

Since the monies offered in exchange may be used for other purchases, one of the most common purchasing reservations salespeople encounter pertains to price (i.e., the commitments purchases entail). Since price resistances may reflect many concerns other than the immediate objects being exchanged, vendors attempting to deal with price objections may touch upon any and all elements of financial concern to prospects. Although not always successful, the major ways in which vendors attempt to handle price objections are locating limits, providing price comparisons, stressing worth, minimizing sacrifices, explaining prices, and making concessions. These tactics are generally not mutually exclusive, and, as with other strategies, vendors may use these in combinations or in some sequence.

Locating Limits

One means of dealing with price objections is by locating the prospect's price limits. Should vendors encounter prospects expecting to pay less than that which vendors consider acceptable, vendors face the task of redefining "good prices." Some salespeople endeavor to uncover buyer limits in anticipation of price resistance [through qualification], while others may attempt to determine this once the prospects have indicated price reservations.

I ask them, "How much are you prepared to spend?" If it's a small company, there's no point showing them this $100,000 system. You see if they can go $20,000, $10,000, then maybe tack on a few things, but get an idea of their upper limits, what to show them. Get them on the right track sooner [manufacture—computers].

One of the things you have to realize as a salesperson is that some people want good quality, but some don't care. They just want the cheapest instrument that they can get and still have one. So your main thing is to sell someone what they're after. So you try and determine, in talking with them, what it is that they want. So if they're more concerned with quality, you would try to emphasize the value of the better instrument. Show them how this instrument costs more than the other, but how it's so much better. . . . With someone else, you might not show them the more expensive item, you don't want to confuse them. They just want something to play around with, and you can scare them off if you get too expensive, too complicated. They'll just get confused! . . . Also if they don't have the money for the better organ, and then they go to the less expensive model, it's not going to sound as good, and they're going to be disappointed. You may lose them. So you try to ascertain what they want and what they can spend and work towards that. . . . So you try to determine what price range they have in mind, and what use they will be putting the instrument to. Generally, people will not tell you as much as they might be willing to spend, because they hope that they won't have to spend quite that much, but you start in that range. And what it's for? Is it for lessons? Is it for home entertainment? You try to find out if they've got any experience in music or if they are just starting out from scratch. Whether they want a basic instrument or they want the automatic features. . . . Some have no idea of what they may want to buy or spend, but most have looked around before they come to buy, so they generally have something in mind. . . . Now if you find basically what they want and they don't seem to want to buy, you have to try to find out what's stopping them from buying. So you ask, "Other than price, are there any problems involved?" You try to get around it, make it seem like it's in the context of friendship. You have all the sales pitches, try to get them to make their decisions right now, but a lot of them sounded phoney to me, and pushy, something that I couldn't do all that much. . . . If money's a problem, we'd arrange for a bank loan on the instrument, stretch the bank loan out, "only so much per week." But it might be for a lot of weeks [music]!

Providing Price Comparisons

In their attempts to deal with price objections, vendors may also provide comparisons designed to generate favorable definitions of product worth. Two common modes of comparison are providing a range of prices and making general comparisons.[3]

Vendors using the first strategy may opt for a number of differentially priced lines and/or carry a basic line with a variety of options. The advantages of these price ranges are to offer goods within more budgets, to enable vendors to define quality against standards owned by the same vendor, and to reduce comparison shopping. This does not eliminate the problem of uncovering the buyer's spending limits, but allows some selection for those more concerned with price.

We'll get people who'll come in here and they don't realize that we carry the more expensive lines, and they get flabbergasted at the prices. And it's kind of hard, because you know that you've not made the sale, where you might have sold them another shoe if you had a more economical line. And even we carry a few urethanes to make our products more competitive. Like this one, a leather lined urethane. . . . But you pay for what you get. If you're not hard on your shoes, you might find that it's quite serviceable, but overall, it's not as good. We put it with our leather lines, and if people don't ask, we don't tell them that it's a plastic upper they're getting. If they seem to be willing to buy a better line, we'll point that out, but if they're looking for a bargain shoe, that's the one we have for them [shoes].

The second means by which vendors deal with price objections is by making comparisons in the abstract, indicating what similar products could cost elsewhere.

In jewelry and clothing, say, the mark-up is usually double, or more. . . . But most people don't realize what the mark-up is, especially if they're not in sales. If someone says something about an item being high priced, I'll say, "Well, everything seems high priced these days. . . . Or if it's a good quality item, I'll point that out, showing them how they will get better wear, etc., for the extra money [department store].

Stressing Product Worth

Regardless of whether vendors have only one line or whether buyers are making decisions on particular lines, another way salespeople handle price objections is to indicate that the product's value is greater than it might first seem. While vendors may try to define product worth through their presentations, they may also find themselves doing remedial work in this very same area. Building on the prestige of ownership, quality, and long term benefits (e.g., savings, convenience, performance), vendors using this strategy try to define the object being considered as worthy of greater sacrifice than the buyer had intended.

> The important thing is what it will do for you. If it's worth it to you that way. "And here's what this will do for you." You try to show them how the product is worthwhile getting. . . .
> Sometimes you'll get, "I don't have the money. I can't afford it now. I'll be back." Sometimes, it's the truth. Sometimes it's an excuse. We'll suggest putting it on their charge cards. . . . Or something that I'll use is "Well, I know it's a lot of money, but it is an investment in your complexion, and after all, you only have one face for life. It's not like a dress that you pay $100 for and it goes out of fashion in a year. Taking care of your complexion is like brushing your teeth, and when it comes down to it, who wouldn't spend the money to take care of their teeth." Something like that. . . . Another common one is that their husband wouldn't let them. He wouldn't let them spend that much money on cosmetics, or that they wouldn't spend that much on cosmetics. Not that they don't spend money, just not that much on cosmetics. I try to sympathize with them, win their approval, that way, so then it's "Yes, but if you get this, your complexion will be . . ." You're sympathetic, but then in turn you turn it around. . . . Also, I feel that a woman, especially if she's in business, to be successful, you really can't ignore your femininity. No man wants to deal with a butch! The beautiful people, they're more influential all over, so if the woman looks better, she'll probably do better [cosmetics].

When vendors are dealing in comparatively costly lines, they are especially apt to be concerned that they be able to establish the worth of their products (preventative strategies) prior to discussing prices.

> When people ask you, first thing, "What's it going to cost?", it can bother you. Especially at first, because we were told not to discuss prices until you're well into your presentation, maybe even a demo if you can swing that first. But I find that if I'm up front with them if they ask, and then you kind of move past that, "Where else are you going to get a product like this?" Or then go

on to tell them, "Over a five year period, it's going to save this much money."
So you can work around it that way [manufacture—industrial].

They always want to know what the rates are. That's the bottom line with most
people when you call on them, "How much is it?" . . . And the problem with
that is that until you explain the merits of something, any cost is going to be
too much. If somebody isn't convinced that they're going to benefit from
something, they're not going to spend the money on it. . . . So they want to
see the rate card. Our rate card is also very confusing, because we work on
an inventory system. If a lot of the minutes of the day are still for sale, the
rates are low. Around Christmas time, or in the fall, we sell an awful lot of air
time. And we can't add pages like a newspaper does, so we bump our price
up. So in December, for instance, you will pay more for the same commercial
than you would in February. So that's confusing too, and it's all on the rate
card, so when you look at it the first thing somebody says is "I don't
understand this. Take it away." So I try not to say to somebody, "Here's the
rate card. If you want some prices, here's what it's going to cost you." It's not
fair to them and I haven't done my product a service either. If anything, it'll
probably hurt it. Because they'll look at it and say, "Holy smoke! X amount
of money for a commercial! You must be kidding!" "Yeah, if you're only
buying one commercial, it wouldn't be worth it." And this is where you have
to have a chance to explain the whole thing to them [promotions—radio].

Minimizing Sacrifices

When prices seem prohibitive, vendors may contextualize prices
within greater time frames than that presently envisioned by their
prospects. Thus, in addition to defining costs relative to smaller units
(e.g., cost per day, per potential application, and so on), vendors may
also suggest series of (smaller) time payments, offer low base prices
with the intention of selling accessories later, minimize initial investments by incorporating product costs into subsequent billings, and use
less costly purchases as a means of later converting prospects to more
costly versions.

If I get price objections, I'll usually make reference to the fact that everything
is going up. But I won't go in and, "Here's this sign, it's so much." You try
to get around to the price later, and then, "For pennies a day . . ." You take it
inch by inch. If you tell them that it is only going to cost them pennies per
day, and it will result in a traffic flow that will yield thousands of dollars in
business, it sounds much more attractive [promotions—industrial].

In selling these systems, I'll be talking in terms of their long-term benefits, and it is kind of interesting to see the different companies that you deal with. . . . Often, you have to let the company absorb the cost over the long run. So there, you might hold down their initial billing but increase their billings for their service following with that. It seems to bother many companies less that way, to charge less initially and then to charge them larger service costs. So if that's what it takes to make the sale, you go through that route (manufacture—industrial].

Explaining Prices

Though a less compelling means of establishing worth, another technique vendors sometimes use in dealing with price objections is to account for the cost of the item in question. Vendors using this strategy may sympathize with the buyer in reference to costs, but need not do so.

If they're telling you it costs too much, you try to switch them to a lower line. If they want higher quality, you switch to a higher-priced line. Or if they don't seem to realize that the cost of leather has jumped 20% since they've been out looking, you try to point out things like that to them. Or you might examine the features of the higher-priced item and try to explain why it's worth getting the more expensive item [department store].

You'll have someone who hasn't bought a car in 10 years. He probably expects to pay more, but he doesn't really want to. "Boy, are these ever expensive! Wow!" So you might try to explain how, with inflation over the past number of years, everything has gone up all along the line, including his salary. And maybe talk to him about the extras he's getting and the costs of technology [auto].

Making Concessions

Should vendors be unable to implement the preceding strategies, they may consider price concessions. While vendors may lower the price for entire lines (either on a regular basis or as a "sale"), they may also dicker on the price (and/or include other extras) on a more individualized basis.

In general, larger businesses are more resistant to individualized price negotiations. Although some department managers in larger operations will bargain with prospects, "firm asking prices" not only tend to be a matter of policy, they are also supported by the problems individualized deals create for bureaucracies. Even in these settings, however, managers may find some offers difficult to refuse. Thus prospects attempts to bargain are apt to be more successful in reference to larger orders, damaged goods, and slower moving stock.

We're flexible, where if they're getting a larger order and they suggest it, we'll give a little. But it's the manageress, like me, who approves it. So there, you can give a little, and you pretty well have to take it as it comes. Some customers feel that they have to have a discount to buy it [luggage].

You can dicker in furniture, appliances, carpeting, something like that, here. But not on the smaller things like clothing, giftware, shoes [department store].

Price negotiations can also create other problems for vendors thusly involved. As a result, the reluctance of vendors to dicker on prices is by no means limited to larger businesses.

Normally I try not to dicker. I am quite firm on the prices. I've found that dickering can be rather awkward. It is awkward for the merchant and the customer. And it is especially awkward if other people are around. If you can stay away from dickering, you can also avoid an image as someone who will go down. I have been known to dicker, but it is something I try to avoid [women's clothing].

You get some people who never seem satisfied with what you're doing for them. If you give them a better price, they'll take it and want more. Sometimes, it'll come to the point where you just say, "That's it! That's all I can do for you. If that's not good enough for you, perhaps you should go elsewhere." They want to keep getting more and more and more [appliances].

Despite its drawbacks, dickering can be an important means of consolidating sales. Thus, if vendors want more action for their stores (or themselves), they are more likely to make price concessions.

There's dickering in our store. Definitely! Sometimes I wish there wasn't, but people have a tendency to think that the mark-up in jewelry is so fantastic that the jeweler can come down in price. And, admittedly, the mark-up is better than in most retail places, but we have other costs that some other places don't. You can dicker and you do, but still you don't like to, because you're losing some of your profits that way [jewelry].

EXISTING LOYALTIES

A third major set of obstacles that salespeople encounter pertains to people's current patterns of product purchases. These loyalties have three major roots: brand mystique, satisfaction with existing products (suppliers), and inconveniences of change.

BRAND NAME MYSTIQUE

One of the most specific forms of loyalty pertains to name brand purchases. While vendors carrying requested brands may find these relatively easy sales, merchants not carrying those brands are disadvantaged. Many vendors simply tell prospects that they do not carry specific brands (possibly indicating who does), but some will attempt to switch prospects onto the lines they carry.

> Some people come in asking for particular brands. You can get some of them to switch. The others have got their minds set on a particular brand or model and there's really nothing you can do with them [mixed clothing].

> We went through one Christmas season without a [A] watch and that was devastating because [A] had done a fantastic job of advertising. Everybody wanted to own a [A] watch. Every second person that came in the store to buy a Christmas gift wanted a [A] watch. And when you say, "Sorry, but we don't have any [A]'s, but let me show you our line of [B]. Let me show you our line of [C] . . . ," and out they go. They wanted a [A] watch, so we [managers] all screamed and yelled and hollered so much that [head office] says, "Okay, bring them back in." . . . It's the name and that's what they want [jewelry].

Satisfaction with Existing Products

Should vendors encounter prospects content with existing products, they have the options of disengaging themselves from further association with those prospects, arousing discontent with existing products, or maintaining contact with those parties.

When purchases represent one-time and/or long-term involvements, vendors tend quickly to disregard parties already involved with their competitors.

> If you learn that they've just bought a car, you drop it there. No point going on. Find a better prospect. . . . You might ask them what kind they have, but that's about it, and that would just be small talk anyways [auto].

Say they've just bought a new system, you just move on to someone else. They're still mesmerized with that. . . . Maybe a couple years down the line, if they're having problems or making changes, it might be good for you to get in there. But not now [manufacture—computers].

However, vendors may still try to generate interest in their products by "planting the seeds of discontent." Thus, by arousing doubts about existing suppliers or their products [e.g., efficiency, image, convenience, service], salespeople may promote reevaluations of those suppliers.

We have an exceptionally good warranty on these units. Much better than most of our competitors. So that's one thing we'll use if they say, "Oh, we've always bought _____ before, or _____ ." "Well, do they back up their products that well? Do you know what repairs cost these days?" . . . You may be able to turn the corner with them that way [appliances].

If they say they already have a supplier, you might say, "Well, I'm sure that they do give you very good service, but you might find that it's worthwhile to have another source in the event that for some reason or another they have a backup, discontinuations," or just to keep them on their toes a little. . . . Give them a justification for dealing with you. Now you might say, "We do have a minimum order, but it's not very large, so it shouldn't create a problem for you. But at the same time what you'll be doing is establishing an account with us. And as we pick up new lines, things that you might like better, you may find that it helps get you better and faster service." [wholesale—giftware].

In other cases, vendors may maintain contact (albeit generally lighter) in the hopes of an eventual product application and/or in attempts to provide a new basis by which the competing products may be defined. This option is more apt to be pursued when the prospects are more limited in number and/or represent more significant sales.

If they already have a program and they're happy with it, what I'll do is call them every now and then, send them material on new programs we have in the offing. Just keep plugging away. Now we might not see any returns on that for a year or two, but it may turn around for you [promotions—travel].

Inconvenience of Change

When product purchases entail changes in other aspects of prospect routines, these may represent significant obstacles facing vendors. Thus, in addition to promoting products, the salespeople involved may also have to justify any disruptions the prospects anticipate.

> People hate change, any change. Anything new or different, and I think that's at all levels. That's something you run up against, right off the bat [manufacture—industrial].

> You'll get some who say, "Well, I really don't want to open another account, I've got enough suppliers already," something like that. That's hard. That's been one of the things I don't really have a good reply for. And I know that that's how I was when I was buying. And yet, I know that I would buy on a new account if I thought I was getting a bargain. So that's probably what I should be pushing now, that it's a really good deal, worth the extra effort [wholesale—giftware].

COMPARISON SHOPPING

Whereas existing loyalties reflect buyers' preestablished preferences, comparison shopping represents an active effort on the part of buyers to assess the relative value of the products (and vendors) they are considering, prior to making purchasing commitments. Denoting a range of external options (i.e., third party reference points), comparison shopping significantly redefines the buyer-seller relationship. Comparison shopping frequently reflects more than price, but since price represents a readily standardized measure, it tends to assume considerable importance.

> Most of my customers are from around this area. You get the odd one coming from a distance, often because they think they are going to get a better deal here. A false economy, because they'll spend a lot on gas, looking around for a deal, and, in terms of service, they're better off dealing with the place they've purchased the car from. If the service is bad, they can always go to the salesman. And if he values his customers, he can back them up [auto].

> Most people will do comparison shopping. They'll go to the neighboring cities if they think they can get a better deal. . . . If it's just a few dollars less, it's not worth it to them. They won't get any service, and they'll have to pay for the delivery. They would have to get it for considerably less. Otherwise, it's just not worth it. If they get it home and it has a little scratch on it and

they call someone out there, they're not going to come out and take care of it. Where here, we'll go out and take care of it [furniture].

As a result of their research, comparison shoppers are apt to learn more about the market situation than other shoppers. Thus they are likely to be more aware of prices, quality feature differences, selection, and other readily standardized elements, such as warranties and return policies. At the same time, however, they appear more indecisive, more skeptical, and less loyal than other customers. Further, to the extent the items they are comparing are made by different companies, involve different features, come with different "protection plans," and so on, comparison shoppers also seem likely to experience more dissonance (and the resulting frustrations) in reference to their purchases. As the material in this section suggests, merchants do not like dealing with comparison shoppers, experience increased levels of urgency to close sales when dealing with comparison shoppers, and prefer to encounter people who are determined to shop around at later stages of their buying expeditions.

They can comparison shop at a couple of the department stores, and then hit the other men's shops on the strip here, but when some have done a bit of that, say they get to the end of the mall, they will just compromise. They've got to leave or they're just getting tired, "Let's take this. I'm not walking all the way back there to get that." They get tired of walking around on hard floors all the time. And if it's crowded, people just say, "Let's get this. It's too busy down there . . ." So if you're the fourth store they've hit, you might get a break on that. Although you'll also get the ones that come in in the morning, and you'll see them still going at four in the afternoon [men's clothing].

"Be backs," that's the man who says, "I'll be back." You can pretty well forget about them! If they come back, fine, but usually they don't. . . . Mostly the people are unsure, just plain unsure. Some of them shop, shop, shop, and the further they go, the more confused they get. Now, if you get someone who comes in and tells you that they're totally confused and that the appliances are all starting to look alike to them, you're in a pretty good position to sell them something. . . . But if they come to you and, "Well, this is just the first place I've looked," you can pretty well forget it. If you do your job well, you might be able to sell them, but they're often bent on shopping around [appliances].

People who intend to shop further before making their purchases create special dilemmas for vendors. A preliminary concern is that of uncovering the bases of the reservations (e.g., prices, brand names, specific features, warranties, and so on) implied by prospect desires for further comparisons. Vendors may reduce comparison shopping somewhat by offering a wider range of prices and products. But even here, prospects may want to gauge the overall competitiveness of those lines.

You show them what you have at the price they want to pay, and then you show them the leather shoes, your less expensive ones that have the features they want. Now if they're concerned about the price, they'll often say that they want to look around, but then they'll realize just how expensive shoes are, and they'll usually come back, because we do have the better prices in the area [department store].

With all the clothing stores in the area, people want to shop around more, compare prices. We carry quite a wide range of prices. We're a little slower in our styles though, and if someone is really particular about new styles, they may decide to buy elsewhere [department store].

As a means of circumventing price comparisons, salespeople sometimes emphasize features such as quality, uniqueness, prestige, and service.

If you get someone who says they can get a lipstick or whatever for less someplace else, you try to emphasize quality. If that doesn't work, it's "Sorry, I can't help you. Thanks for dropping by." . . . But we have different lines too, different prices for different levels. There, you try to bump people up to a higher level. But something else you'll do sometimes is to show people the most expensive line first and then show them a less expensive line. It's an alternative, "And it's almost as good." Then a lot of times, the second price seems like a relief to them, "I'll take that." . . . But you try to sell your better lines. You bring in more money that way, more for you in commission [cosmetics].

They may be able to get a similar item more cheaply at some other places, like _____'s, right around the corner. We stress our three-month warranty on our products, that if they should have any problems with the products, they can return them to us. Whereas with the high-volume dealers, where things are cheaper, they're not as reliable in making replacements and adjustments [stationery].

When the items being compared are identical, vendors unable to compete on other grounds may be willing to "match prices." As with dickering, matching is a matter of store policy, but the two are not uniformly in evidence. Some vendors, unwilling to dicker, will match prices (i.e., "will not be undersold"), while others, more disposed to dickering, will match prices only if the price to be met is within an acceptable range. Those unwilling to be undersold tend to reason that the practice of matching prices is a means of maintaining customer loyalty.[4]

You'll get an idea of prices from the customers, they'll often comment on prices, how they compare with other stores in the area, because they've been comparison shopping. . . . If it's a matter that someone else has a watch on "sale," and it's so much off, I'll usually match that if the customer asks, and I know that that's probably what they're selling it for. But you don't get that all that much [jewelry].

There's no dickering here, but if we find out that someone else had the same thing on "sale," we'd be able to match the price. You want them to shop here [department store].

General Strategies for Neutralizing Buyer Reservations

Having examined the ways in which vendors deal with resistance associated with skepticism, price concerns, existing loyalties, and comparison shopping, it is valuable to consider strategies that vendors may invoke on a more general basis. These tactics may be used at any point in the encounter at which vendors experience reservations, and, theoretically, would apply to any realm of resistance.[5] Although they may overlap somewhat in actual deployment by salespeople, three major sets of options are in evidence: (1) affirming product desirability, (2) more explicitly engaging in role-taking activity, and (3) making concessions.

AFFIRMING PRODUCT DESIRABILITY

The affirmation of product desirability emerges as the dominant overall tactic by which vendors attempt to manage resistance. It encompasses a wide range of activities intended to define (or reestablish) products as possessing the qualities prospective buyers want or require. Included in this category are challenges of unwanted definitions, qualified acknowledgments of customer claims, attempts to generate favorable comparisons, explanations of limitations, attempts to overlook objections that cast doubt on the products being featured, and efforts to refocus prospect directions.

Challenging Unwanted Definitions

Vendors using this tactic question prospects' assessments of products (or applications). Thus, in response to objections, such as, "It's too expensive, poor quality, wrong color, etc." salespeople may challenge the claim, possibly elaborating on this contradiction.

> You try to be diplomatic with people, but sometimes they're just so wrong about something that you have to correct them. Or sometimes you just lose patience with them, "No, that's not true." And you go on to correct them. Sometimes they get offended, but there are times when you have to set the record straight [men's clothing].

Another variation of the challenge involves using the prospect's objections as the basis for promoting products. Thus prospects indicating that they don't have the time, the money, the applications, and so on may be challenged on that very basis ("That's exactly why you need . . ."). Perceiving these objections to reflect interests of significance to their prospects, vendors may be able to redefine their products in ways that illustrate particular advantages to their prospects.

> You have people, "Oh, I'm too busy to get into that." And there, you can either accept that or you can say something like, "Well, Mr. Jones, that's exactly why we might be able to help you. Our system is designed for greater operating efficiency." That way, you and your staff will have more time for other things that need to be done [manufacture—office equipment].

In contrast to some other situations in which people may challenge one another, salespeople are dependent on maintaining the good will of their prospects. Hence, they tend to be concerned about challenging prospect definitions in nonoffensive manners and providing supporting information. This often leads to qualified acknowledgments.

Making Qualified Acknowledgments

Vendors using this strategy typically project some validity to prospects' claims while attempting to redefine product significances for their prospects ("Yes, but . . ."). Indicating that their prospects' objections are reasonable, this strategy is generally less offensive than more direct challenges. Vendors using this strategy acquiesce somewhat, but still emphasize the overall wisdom of the purchase.

> Depending on the buyer, I'll sometimes say, "Well, yes, it is a lot of money, but . . .", and then go on to talk about the benefits [manufacture—industrial].

> It they're [merchants] saying it's too expensive, I sort of, "Well, I realize that it's expensive." I usually try to agree with them. And then I'll say, "But there's crazy people like me, who if they really like something, they'll buy it!" And that's really how I am. No matter what the price is, if I like an item, I'll usually buy it. And there are people that way, where price is no object. Unless things are really tough for them [wholesale—giftware].

Generating Favorable Comparisons

Recognizing that customers are often in the position of choosing between suppliers, salespeople commonly find themselves attempting to establish the relative virtues of their products over those of their competitors. Regardless of who (buyer or seller) makes the comparison explicit, salespeople may invoke any reference point that seems relevant at that particular time (e.g., product construction, service, price).

> Given the choice that people have, your job is to show them that you've got the best deal for them right here. You try to justify them buying from you. Most are serious about eventually buying, but they want to know that they're getting a good deal. That's why it's good to take your time with the presentation. You show them all the features and tell them how this is going to do this and that for them. That's where your product knowledge comes in. . . . They watch TV and read the papers, especially when they're thinking about buying something like a fridge or a video recorder, say. So whatever they're comparing it to, my job is to show them that this is the best [appliances].

Explaining Limitations

Although it assumes more of a defensive posture than some of other tactics, vendors sometimes find it different to counter customers' claims. Under these conditions, they sometimes resort to a "true confessions" stance. Salespeople adopting this approach may vary greatly in the depth or extensiveness of the accounts they provide, as well as in the sincerity, but the implication is that by providing prospects with more background information, vendors may develop customers who are more favorably able to contextualize the shortcomings that they presently associate with the exchange at hand.

Sometimes, all you can do is to try to explain things to them, "Well, you're right, it would be nice to have a bigger selection, but we only have a certain budget to work with, so we try to order the lines that we think will be most popular. Would you like to take another look at what we do have, maybe we can find something that might be pretty close to what you had in mind." [mixed clothing].

Overlooking Objections

Another means by which salespeople endeavor to neutralize customer concerns assumes a more elusive posture. While sometimes genuinely insensitive to concerns that prospects express, vendors may also attempt to ignore objections. The hope is that prospects will either forget these issues or consider them less consequential as the encounter unfolds. Insofar as they find themselves unable to ignore completely their prospects' expressed objections, salespeople using this strategy frequently acknowledge these concerns in passing, often with an implied promise to consider them more fully later in the encounter.

If you can't deal with the objection effectively, I think you're better to go past it, and maybe they will forget about it. A lot of times the objections aren't that important overall. It's just something they thought about, so you just go past it and end up making the sale [mixed clothing].

I do that a little, but mostly I've learned that from Paul. He often does that. . . . Somebody doesn't like the color, Paul says, "Uh huh, hmmm . . . What do you think of the interior? Would you say you've got pretty good room? Why don't you get in and see how it feels?" He does that a lot. Certain things you can't change. You've only got so many cars on the lot, so you try to sell what you've got. And it seems to work. They sort of forget about this and that [auto].

Refocusing Prospect Directions

Not unlike clergymen who sometimes generate relevancy by giving prospective followers a clearer sense of purpose (Prus, 1976), vendors may also try to enhance buyer receptivity to their products by recasting their buyers' frames of reference.

If someone's less certain, you may have to lead them. They simply may not have thought out what they need. So there, you take more initiative. You know what things people generally look for, and then if they have children or don't drive or whatever, you tell them why this or that house is the one for them, "Of course, you'll want to be nearer to a school, or a bus route." Or "This is a nice quiet neighborhood. That's something you'll really appreciate about living here!" You can lead them that way too [real estate].

Direction is also sometimes provided as vendors seek acknowledgments from their prospects on route to a sale. The objective here is to establish shared understandings about the nature of the exchange. Allowing prospects to participate more fully in the transaction and feel more comfortable about the terms of sale, these agreements tend to facilitate commitments.

As part of our presentation, we try to get people to accept parts of the plan as we go along, "And this is important to you, isn't it?" You know, money, security, the future. . . . Essentially, you try and lead them along with all these agreements. Then it's harder for them to refuse. You've closed them along the way [insurance].

You try to get them to make commitments to your product as you go along. You try to get them to say, "Yes, that is important to me." "Yes, I like the things you can do with this." That sort of thing. Not saying that they're going to buy, but getting them to agree that your product is what they want or need. That way, you sell them on the product as you go along. And if they're hesitant later, you've got that to work on [manufacture—computers].

ROLE-TAKING TACTICS

Attempts to gain a fuller sense of prospect perspectives and product applications may be used in conjunction with other tactics, but insofar as vendors assuming other tactics need not engage in extensive role taking (Mead, 1934), these more explicit pursuits deserve independent attention. Thus consideration is given to vendor attempts to be attentive, probe for more information on prospect situations, and define better the limits under which buyers may be operating.

Being Attentive

Since prospects' definitions of sales situations (e.g., interest, trust) are uneven and may change extensively over the course of the encounter, vendors may be concerned about their abilities to relate effectively to their prospects. It is in this vein that salespeople are often encouraged to watch for "closing signs" (when to try to complete the sale). They may be instructed to be attentive to the prospect's body posturing, eye movements, eye pupil dilations, and the like, as signs of "when to ask for the order." However, the major value of these observations seems to be that of alerting vendors to the importance of relating more intently with their prospects.

> I look at it this way. You're only going to have a few seconds, maybe a few minutes to relate to this person. So I'm watching them, trying to see what I can say, show them what they understand, what they like. . . . You try to establish a relationship with them in that time, however long they give you. It has to happen there! So even if they're [just] looking at something, I'm thinking, "What can I do to make it happen?" [men's clothing].

> When you're dealing with a customer, that becomes the most important thing to you. You have to concentrate on them, and how they're seeing things. See if you can get a fix on what's concerning them. Try to take care of that. Get one step closer to the sale [manufacture—industrial].

Inquiring into Expressed Concerns

On encountering objections, vendors may also ask about the origins and substance of these resistances (e.g., "Can you tell me more about that?" "Why do you say that?"). While this (qualification) strategy often elicits background information, it may be used in conjunction with other purposes as well. In addition to inquiries intended to help vendors better sell to or service these prospects by learning more about buyer concerns or situations, questions may be used to relieve pressure from vendors by asking prospects to explain their situations more fully, and intimidate customers (especially when vendors ask "Why?"). Any inquiry may have all of these effects to some extent, depending on how it is interpreted by the buyers. However, vendors asking about the basis of objections in lower-keyed or less direct manners not only seem less likely to be defined as "pressuring" prospects, but also are apt to obtain more information on buyer circumstances.

> You have to watch you don't answer their objections too quickly. You have to have more of a conversation with them, "Well, have you thought of the fact that . . . ?" Another thing you might do is to sort of ignore their objection, sort of "Mmm." You pause, and then go on to something else. Sometimes they're commenting more than objecting, so that will work out sometimes. Or if it's something you can't deal with, you might say something like "Hmm, that's a good point. We'll have to get back to that later." . . . If I've gone over the whole thing and I ask them what they think, and they're, "Well, I don't know." Then I will usually back up a few steps. And I'll say, "We've established such and such and such. Now is there anything in here that is not perfectly clear.

Something that you don't like about it? Because if there is, let me know. I
want to make sure that you really understand it." That sometimes helps.
Sometimes, the person is just a blah person, "Yeah, I guess it's okay." Then
you just proceed as if they want it. That's their way of reacting. But usually,
their hesitation is because of some objection and you want them to get it out
so that you can try to work with it, get them feeling more comfortable about
the product [insurance].

Something I'll do if they're objecting to the price or something, I'll ask them
to explain that. "You say it's too costly, too big, whatever, for your purposes.
Can you explain that?" . . . If I can find out more about them, maybe I can
deal with that. Arrange longer payments, find him a smaller model, or maybe
you'll see that there is no application for you there [manufacture—industrial].

Locating Limits

Regardless of whether or not buyers express particular concerns,
salespeople may also attempt to define the constraints under which
buyers may be operating. Some of the clearest instances of limits reflect
buyer price concerns, but vendors may also endeavor to define the outer
tolerances people have for other aspects of products, such as that
pertaining to quality, size, or style of the products under consideration.

You're not just selling prices, although sometimes you will get stopped there.
It's the whole package. How much scope do they have regarding budgets, quality? The actual size of your products compared to the space requirements they
have? Would we have to retool? It may not be feasible. [manufacture—industrial].

More extensive role-taking activity may reduce buyer reservations
by encouraging trust on the part of these targets. As well, buyers
will sometimes resolve their own dilemmas in the process of articu-
lating their concerns to salespeople. However, once this additional
information is obtained, salespeople typically attempt to deal with
buyers' remaining reservations by (re)affirming product desirability in
the manners outlined earlier or by making concessions along the lines
following.

Making Concessions

Representing compromises of sorts, concessions denote concerns
with expediency (quick fixes) as well as "last resorts" for dealing with
matters vendors have been unable to resolve in other ways. Compromise
solutions may be initiated by either buyers or vendors. Sometimes these

involve specific terms (e.g., "If you do this, I will . . ."), but on other occasions the parties may use (looser) proposals as a means of either maintaining the other person's interest ("What would it take to make a deal with you?"), or locating the limits under which the other party is operating ("What is your bare bones price on this?").

Compromises in the sales setting may involve direct price cuts, but other concessions may pertain to matters of quantity, quality, service, warranties, or "throw in" goods, for instance. Insofar as each compromise breaks with existing or anticipated vendor practices, it introduces more uncertainty. In each instance, questions may surface regarding the nature and extensiveness of concessions to be made, along with their anticipated implications for profit margins, repeat patronage, and other buyers. As well, salespeople may experience dilemmas regarding the styles and intensity with which these deals ought to be pursued. And, while vendors may wonder about the viability of immediate transactions, they may also find themselves reflecting upon the existing premises under which they are operating more generally (e.g., are their prices too high, is their service adequate, will these sorts of concessions become more routine in their businesses?).

> The problem is how much can you give and still maintain the integrity of your business? Say someone comes and gives me a big order. Well, if he asks for a little something off or some throw-in, I'll be happy to go along with that. In fact, I'll try to do a little extra for him, just to let him know that I really do appreciate his business. But some people, they want to work you for every nickel. And the more you give, the more they want. Those are the killers! They are the ones who will give you problems again and again and again, until you draw the line. And then they might get upset with you, but otherwise they start taking too much out of your hide. And often, they're more vocal, so it's bad all around [appliances].

> We have discounts based on volume and we can do a few extras, say on service, delivery, that sort of thing. But you do have to keep your head up on these things. If you make a deal with this one and this other one finds out, well you pretty well have to do it for him too. Or if you send out another salesman [to the same buyer], he'll run into this: "George always did this for us." "Well, we can't do that." And then they're unhappy with him and we may lose orders over that. But that's the sort of thing you run into with these deals [manufacture—industrial].

As noted earlier, many businesses (especially those involving larger bureaucracies) try to avoid individualized concessions and the disruptions these represent. Like vendors who feel particular deals are too

costly to pursue, they are prepared to "let customers walk" rather than
jeopardize their images or organizational routines. Albeit by default in
most instances, disengagement emerges as a fourth option vendors may
implement in dealing with customers that they have been unable to
accommodate in other respects.

In Perspective

Examining the ways in which vendors deal with buyer reservations,
this chapter provides much insight into the problematic and negotiable
nature of human interaction. Salespeople are unlikely to be aware of all
prospect reservations, but even when particular reservations surface,
salespeople do not know how long these concerns will last, how consequential they are for the sales at hand, or how successful they will be
in dealing with these obstacles.

To appreciate vendor situations better, consideration was first directed toward the major substantive objections encountered. Here,
vendor strategies for dealing with resistance pertaining to skepticism,
existing loyalties, price reservations, and comparison shopping were
examined, indicating the more common variations thereof.

Working with the tactics vendors invoke in dealing with these substantively situated buyer resistances, three sets of general strategies
vendors use in uncovering and managing prospect resistance were
delineated along with the subprocesses of persuasion they assume. Thus
we find salespeople affirming product desirability, more extensively
engaging in role taking, and making concessions. Affirmation strategies include the following: challenging unwanted definitions, making qualified acknowledgments, generating favorable comparisons, explaining limitations, overlooking objections, and refocusing prospect
directions. While the success of any tactic (or any combination of
tactics) is problematic in any given instance, these affirmations emerge
as central in tacticians' attempts to neutralize target reservations. Thus
salespeople using more intensive role taking often revert to these
affirmation practices, as may those proposing various concessions to
their targets. The practice of affirming product desirability generally
serves to maintain the viability of vendors' existing marketing programs, as does more extensive role-taking activity. However, the introduction of concessions creates tactical dilemmas of both short-term and

long-run natures. A great many concessions emerge as quick fixes as salespeople attempt to offset other problems. But, in addition to the immediate dilemmas each concession creates ("How much can I afford to give up?"), concessions may introduce some unintended long-term consequences. As these practices become more commonplace in any marketing context, they effectively redefine vendors' overall marketing programs.

In concluding this discussion of the neutralization of buyer resistance, it seems fitting to consider the dynamic features of the marketplace as this pertains to ongoing vendor adjustments, ongoing buyer experiences, and the interrelatedness of the various components of vendors' marketing programs.

First, in addition to being prepared for encounters more generally (e.g., displays, presentations), salespeople may also prepare for objections. Insofar as vendors are apt to encounter many somewhat similar reservations on the part of their prospects over time, they may endeavor to work out more effective ways of dealing with them. Thus, beyond adding new lines (thereby circumventing some concerns), vendors (individually or in groups) may develop strategies for recasting particular objections in more favorable terms.

> When you get the same objection a number of times it sort of bothers you, so what I try to do is work out some kind of response to it. If you can do it, then you have the advantage. . . . But in the meantime, it bothers you. It costs you a sale or a number of sales, and you can lose more because of it. So you try to get past it, and you want it to sound natural, reasonable. And you don't want to argue about it, so it has to be smooth too [mixed clothing].

> If someone's had problems with a sale, we'll often talk about it. You see how other people might have handled it. The other people may have had similar experiences. Maybe someone's found a way of dealing with that situation. . . . That way, you might be more able to deal with that one again [real estate].

Second, it seems appropriate to reemphasize the practical limitations of tactics designed to overcome customer reservations. Vendors are ultimately dependent upon the cooperation of their prospects. As reflective entities, customers are able to make adjustments to vendor strategies as well as learn from their earlier experiences. Buyers may also learn from experiences relayed to them by other people. Hence, despite the seeming sophistication of some of these modes of dealing with prospects' reservations, we find that prospects also become quite adept at shaping the outcomes that sales transactions ultimately assume. In conjunction with this, vendors also face shifting prospect distractions (including time and resource limitations), personal fatigue, and the problematics and dilemmas of selecting and implementing lines of action within unfolding (and ambiguous) contexts. Consequently, even when salespeople are well versed in the sorts of remedial strategies considered in this chapter, they are apt to find that the unpredictable, emergent, and reflective nature of group life makes it difficult for them to be as effective in implementing these tactics as they might like.

In a broader sense, we are also reminded of the interrelatedness of all of the features of vendors' programs. For instance, the sorts of resistances vendors more commonly encounter, as well as the resources that they have for dealing with the resistances they face, are related to the lines they carry, the prices they request for their products, the manners in which they promote these products, and the styles in which they present these items to their prospects. Although perhaps not so evident in this chapter, it is equally noteworthy that the resistances that vendors encounter also affect other aspects of their marketing programs. Thus, however bothersome this feedback may be for immediate sales, it may profoundly shape vendors' subsequent dealings with suppliers, as well as their pricing practices, media promotions, and presentational styles.

Notes

1. For other indications of remedial interchange or repair work in everyday interaction, see Goffman (1967: 5-112; 1971: 5-112). Both Goffman's work and the immediate analysis address the cooperative nature of group life. However, Goffman's material is more oriented toward "face-saving" or "image-salvaging" activity. The repair work discussed herein has a more explicit "recruitment" or promotional cast. Concerns with personal images are subjugated to the task of obtaining commitments from prospects.

2. Anselm Strauss (1978) provides an overview of the sociological literature on negotiations. Also relevant is Glaser and Strauss's (1964) depiction of "awareness contexts."

3. The discussion of comparison shopping (also in this chapter) further addresses comparison concerns and tactics.

4. Fortunately, from a bureaucratic point of view, buyers use this option far less than possible.

5. See Hewitt and Stokes (1975) and Prus (1975b) for other statements on how people resist unwanted imputations.

Chapter 5
OBTAINING COMMITMENTS

There are a lot of houses out there, they get confused. They get confused on what they really want. They don't know really what they want, and some want to know every house in the marketplace before they make a decision. And maybe there's one other house they've not seen, and they have to go see that one, just to assure themselves that they made the right decision. Or maybe another house might come up next week, so they vacillate. . . . And I guess that most people don't like to make a decision. It's easier not to make decisions, especially when you're making a large investment [real estate].

If sales are to be completed or "closed," the parties involved must agree that a "bargain has been struck."[1] While customers sometimes take initiative in completing sales transactions (e.g., "I'll take this"), commitments are not always so readily assumed by prospective buyers. How do vendors handle those other more ambiguous situations? What sorts of strategies do they invoke? How do they develop these lines of action? And, what makes it difficult for them to close or complete sales as often as they might like or consider feasible?

Reflecting questions of the sort just indicated, this chapter has two major objectives. First, attention is focused on the consolidation of sales. Consideration here is given to the perspectives, tactics, and dilemmas vendors experience in their attempts explicitly to obtain buyer commitments. The second part of the chapter deals with vendor attempts to pursue commitments in group (multiple buyer) purchasing contexts. As will become evident as this latter dimension is developed, the pursuit of buyer commitments becomes even more precarious when salespeople encounter buyers making decisions in preestablished groups.

Closing Sales

Regardless of what has transpired previously, vendors not receiving explicit purchasing commitments from prospects (at times they consider appropriate) may attempt to close sales.[2] It matters not whether vendors attempt to obtain purchasing commitments during or following a presentation or before or after dealing with buyer objections; a central task is to obtain the commitments necessary to complete the transaction. It also means that everything salespeople have done to establish favorable product definitions (and alleviate reservations) may be instrumental to obtaining commitments. Some vendors will have done more extensive qualification work, given elaborate presentations, and dealt with more reservations before attempting to consolidate sales, while others may be seen to have sought out purchasing decisions very early in their encounters with prospects. Likewise, salespeople differ in the extent to which they are explicitly aware of closing as an element of selling, concerned about completing sales and attentive to the prospects with whom they are interacting.

Salespeople may learn closing techniques from managers and co-workers, how-to-do-it books and/or courses, or they may develop these through client interaction and self-reflection. Vendors are not equally aware of, or concerned with, closing techniques and their applications. But since closing techniques tend to facilitate sales and expedite encounters with prospects, one finds few contact situations in which they are not used (if only naively).

Seven general strategies dominate the sales setting. On a solitary basis, salespeople may attempt to close by inquiry, assumption, justification, indicating limitations, indicating openness, and default. In some cases salespeople may be able to involve co-workers (i.e., definitional support, "turn overs") in attempts to obtain commitments. It should be emphasized that these strategies are not mutually exclusive. Thus one may find salespeople using multiple strategies concurrently and/or in some sequence as prospects evade earlier attempts to "be closed."

CLOSING BY INQUIRY

Should prospects not overtly indicate a willingness to purchase goods, vendors may "ask for the sale." In a very straightforward version of inquiry, salespeople may ask if prospects are ready to buy

(e.g., "All set?" "Will that be it?"). In other settings, inquiries may
be more abrupt or presumptive (e.g., "Do you want this or not?" "Why
don't you buy it now?" "Would you like A or B?"). Should resistance
be encountered, vendors may then attempt to inquire into its basis
and then deal with these objections, following this with further attempts
to close.

> You come to a point where you know you've done everything that you can do and
> then you say, "Now how would you like to pay for this item?" And they say, "Oh,
> I'm not ready to buy," or whatever. If they are going to buy at that point, they get
> out their money. So closing a sale is the most important thing that there is. You
> can't always close every sale. . . . "How would you like to pay for this?" or "Can
> I wrap it up for you?" or "Do you want me to deliver it?" Just little things like that
> to let them know that you've done everything you're going to do and now's the
> time. If you want this, take it [jewelry].

> The best close for me is to find out if the guy is satisfied. . . . If I ask, "If you're
> satisfied, can I take your order now?" and if he says, "Well, I don't know," then
> you know you haven't got it, and then you can start going back over it again
> [manufacture—industrial].

In an another variation of closing by inquiry, salespeople attempt to
consolidate purchases on an ongoing basis. Thus, although they needn't
ask for a sale until later, they may endeavor to build commitments
through ongoing inquiry.

> Closing is essential, because in 90% of the cases, if I don't ask for the business
> right then, they would just say, "Well, this is all very nice. I'll think about it." I'd
> probably do the same. . . . But when I say I ask, I may not always ask, because I
> close right from the very beginning. Right from when I enter their home or when
> they're here in my office. And in going through the presentation, I'll say, "Do
> you see yourself as having these goals?" "Does this seem like a reasonable
> approach?" These are all little closes, because you're getting them to say yes, yes,
> yes, and they're making commitments. So we're closing all the way along, on
> everything. We talk about their goals. "If I could show you a way in which you can
> save, would you be interested?" And they're going to say "Yes." How can they say
> no? So they're making these little commitments to themselves and to you all the
> way along. . . . Now the final close is dependent upon all those little closes, so I
> don't always come right out and ask. Because of the way we've done it, I will
> assume that because they've agreed with everything I've said so far that we're
> going to do business. So I'll say, "All I need now is a check and a social insurance
> number." And they may or may not say, "Just a minute," or they may say, "Fine."

And I'll say, "I'll need your signature right here." Actually, I'm telling them that we're doing business. . . . It depends. If you're dealing with someone who is very reticent, I wouldn't work that way. I'd say, "Well, we've agreed all the way along. I suggest that we start tonight." And he may or may not say "Yes." Or he may not say "Yes" right off. He may say, "I'd like to think about it." And I might say something like "That sounds reasonable, I like to think things over myself, but what do you find that concerns you about this?" or "Is there something that concerns you?" Now if there is no real objection, then I might do something like this. I'll say, "When you buy things, like a car or television set, there are three decisions you make. One, can I afford it? Now we've already established that you can afford this program. Second, do you like it? Thirdly, do you need it? And if there's yes to all those things, what did you do? You bought it." And I get them to participate in that, and then I ask them, "Do you like the kind of program we've been discussing?" And you've ascertained that they do like it, because you've been asking them that all along. "Yes, I like it." "Does it fit your needs?" Yes, it does, because we went over all that before. And then you go back and say, "Well, why don't we start it tonight?" You'll still get some who want to think about it. So fine, "How about if we get together tomorrow night or two nights away, and then we're going to do business, if you're happy with the program." You don't try to harass them, but you want to make a decision [investments].

Vendors closing by inquiry may also allow prospects to participate in defining the terms of sale. To this end, salespeople may suggest or acknowledge concessions in the form of extra merchandise, delivery, price, and the like, in attempts to strike agreements. These compromises may be used to "sweeten the pot" (create more pressure to buy) when prospects express other concerns as well.

If you can't close, you can't sell! It's the hardest part of selling. You can give them a really strong presentation, and they'll say thank you, and out they go. And you know you've lost them. They've learned a lot about appliances, but you've missed the sale! . . . "Is this the unit that you like? Great, I'll get the invoices on it." "Does this one have all the features you want? If I give you a meat rack that you need, will you take this one?" "If I call head office and I can get a better price on this unit, will you take it?" . . . Everyone wants a bargain, so if I can establish in my close that I'm giving the customer a bargain, whether it's [extra] merchandise, a discount whatever, it's a super close [appliances].

We'll have throw-ins, little extras, like so many seats free with so many being purchased. That varies with the time of the year, so when you're busier, you'll give away almost nothing, but when it's slower for you, you might try to make the package more attractive to get the business at that time if you can. . . . But every time you give away something, you're giving away revenue, because you still have to pay for that space on the plane or the hotel room [promotions—travel].

CLOSING BY ASSUMPTION

When closing by assumption, salespeople act "as if the bargain has already been struck." By taking the sale for granted, they define only one line of action (purchasing) as appropriate for the prospect. While some attempts to close by inquiry seem quite presumptive, vendors assuming sales may seem even bolder.[3] In some instances, salespeople may begin totaling bills or wrapping merchandise in the absence of explicit approval from their prospects. In other variants, vendors may "assure prospects that they have made the right choices," before the prospects have given these indications.

Closing is the most important part. Your approach is important, the way you sell is important, the way you get the confidence of the buyer is important, but the closing is the most important because you can have them smiling and all, trying everything on, but if you can't close properly, they can say, no, and you can lose the whole sale. . . . Or, if you even hesitate on your closing, you could lose the whole sale. They think that you're unsure of something. So they'll say, "Well, I better check around." If they're getting some hesitation (from you), they're thinking, "Maybe the suit looks wrong on me. Maybe it doesn't fit quite right." You go, "There's no reason why you shouldn't be wearing that suit tomorrow. I'll have that taken care of, for you, right away." If you're more ambiguous, you may lose it, right there [men's clothing].

If they're wavering, I'll say, "This is the better one of the two. We've had really good results with it. . . . That'll be $15.95 plus tax." And you just do it. Usually, it works out well, but sometimes you have to backtrack a little, "Oh, I'm sorry. I thought you had decided." [giftware].

CLOSING BY JUSTIFICATION

Although rationale for purchasing may be given at any point in the encounter, the justifications offered at closing time are generally characterized by a "greater sense of urgency." More fundamentally, however, they endeavor to build on the buyer's sense of responsibility or obligations. These messages (e.g., "You owe it to yourself/your loved ones. . . .") may reflect concerns expressed earlier, or ones freshly introduced, but the task at this point is to dramatize the relative short-

comings prospects will experience by not taking immediate action
(purchasing this product). And while many justifications may be directed at the prospect (obligations to oneself), other messages may
stress the responsibility the prospect has for the well-being of others
(e.g., family, company).[4]

We place a lot of emphasis on the closing of sales, "If you had a machine that
produced money, you would insure it wouldn't you?" "Oh yes, of course." "Well,
as far as your family is concerned, you are such a machine." And you might just
leave it there. Let him tell you what his objection is. You've put the ball in his
court. . . . You might also build situations that they can empathize with, perhaps
you've had a friend or whatever, "Suppose that . . .", and you can use that to
promote the decision. You try to make it relevant. You've got to do it! You've got
to be a little blunt sometimes. . . . Sometimes you get people who don't want to
talk about life insurance because they don't want to think about dying and such.
There, what you do is stress the savings part of the program. How, if they build up
their policy, they can build up a nice little nest egg for retirement. Or this you may
have to stress more with people who aren't married, who don't have the responsibility to others [insurance].

If they say that they couldn't afford it, I tell them what a good bargain it is and that
most of the other shops, especially the smaller shops, will be more expensive, "So
if you really like it, get it. Treat yourself!" I often add that, and the ladies go, "Yes,
I think I will treat myself." They end up buying it. . . . But I've done the same kind
of thing when I was waitressing. If someone was debating about having a dessert,
or a drink, where they're debating between a gin and tonic and one of our more
exotic drinks, "Hey, you only live once. Have an exotic drink! For medicinal
purposes." [laughs] And that works a lot of the time [department store].

CLOSING BY INDICATING LIMITATIONS

Vendors sometimes promote closure by indicating that the product is
offered for a limited time only, in limited supply (and/or in great
demand), or subject to future price increases. Suggesting a last chance
to obtain a desirable item or an opportunity to save money, this strategy
may redefine the significance of other reservations.

Some people are not sure what they want. They want to look around more. Others
are just browsing. Sometimes it's not exactly what they want. . . . Some of them
are students, so there, "I'll bring my mother back on Friday." . . . Sometimes I'll
ask them if they would like me to hold them [shoes] for them for a while, and if
they say, "No, uh, don't bother," you realize that they're not coming back. If they

liked it, were quite interested, they would like you to hold it for a while. And many times, they will come back. . . . Sometimes I'll tell them, and I usually only do this if I only have one or two, I'll say, "If you're really considering this shoe, don't leave it. I only have one pair, whatever, in your size." And a lot of people think that that's just a pushy way to get you to buy. And it's not. And I've had other people tell me that they really appreciate that, because they realize that you have only got so much stock, and that you might not be getting any more like that in for the rest of the summer or season. Some people, though, do feel it's high pressure, so there I have to feel out the person, the customer, before you tell them that, because some people can get quite annoyed. And it's something that you can't tell for sure. . . . They think you've got back-up ordered. That's it! The company doesn't want to overbuy, and the factories are into the next season. And they're saying, "Well, can't you order it from the factory?" "No, that shoe company only makes what they get orders for, and right now, they're into manufacture for the fall." There's no way you can get more, but people think you can [shoes].

If they were being indecisive, you would say, "Well, it's the last one." And usually, everyone bought, because they had no way of seeing that there was more unless there was one in the show case. But then it would be sticky if the next person behind them wanted the same item. But then you would go, "I don't think there is any left, but I'll double check, just to make sure." So you would go back, and in a few minutes, come out with it, "You were sure lucky on that one. Someone stuck it in the wrong place, and I just happened to notice the box." [discount catalogue house]

CLOSING BY INDICATING OPENNESS

In contrast to the preceding strategy, which relies on a projected limitation of options, vendors may also attempt to close sales by indicating that prospects have greater ranges of options than immediate purchases would seem to indicate. Contextualized in this manner, purchasing commitments may not only appear less binding, but may also signify options which redefine the "product" (more versatile) being purchased.

Our policy is "satisfaction guaranteed or money refunded," which is also a good selling feature. "If you change your mind later, you can always bring it back." People will buy more because of that. Say they're getting something for children, but they're not sure it will fit, they can still get it. And if it fits, we've made a sale. If not, they can bring it back [discount department store].

If someone is more tentative, I'll go into more detail about our trade-in program. The idea is that they can start with a less costly unit. If they find that satisfies their demands, fine. If not, we can put that purchase price towards one of the bigger units. We install the system for them and then give them maybe a month to get a sense of their applications and then decide at that point. . . . It's the demonstrator concept, basically, which is something else we can do too. We can bring in a demonstrator unit, with no purchase necessary. It's a little riskier for us, but we'll bring a unit in and let them try that out for a couple of weeks. The idea is that they're going to get excited about the system and see how indispensable that unit is [manufacture—computers].

CLOSING BY DEFAULT

Should salespeople be unable to close sales, they may attempt to place the onus for doing so on the prospect. Although this is a strategy much relied upon in self-serve stores, it may also be used in other settings.

If you just can't seem to help someone, you might just have to say, "Excuse me, I don't think I can help you any more right now. Maybe you would just like to look around yourself and if you see something you like, let me know." Sometimes, people like a little time to themselves, or they just don't know how to get out of the situation [department store].

I've found that with some people, if you leave it with them with a chance to think about it, you'll get a sale the next time, whereas if you pushed, you might lose out. But maybe I'm losing out by not pushing more at the time. You just don't know [wholesale—giftware].

CLOSING WITH ASSISTANCE (T.O.S)

Lest they "walk" (lose) prospects, vendors who encounter difficulty satisfying particular prospects may "turn over" (T.O.) these cases to their co-workers.[5]

If one of us is having problems with a customer, where she can't seem to satisfy the customer, can't find something to sell her, she may come over to a rack where you are, and while pretending to look through the items on the rack for the customer, tell you what sort of problems she's having. It's good to get another person's opinion like that, because sometimes you'll get caught up in the sale, where you lose track of other things, where another salesperson might be able to suggest something or say something to the customer to make them feel more at ease, "Say, Deb, have you tried this one on her? I think she would really look fantastic in it!" . . . Sometimes, if you have a few people free at that time, you might joke about it with the customer as you're trying to find her something, "Where else would you get three people waiting on you?" But you do learn from the other people and you can switch off customers sometimes, where the person didn't take to your style or someone else's on staff, where your style wasn't quite right for the customer and someone might be able to handle them better [women's clothing].

T.O.s, turnovers, you'd do that especially on slower times when things weren't moving as fast. Then you could do a T.O., do a job on the person. There's really an art to doing a T.O. because you've got to redirect the person that's there to buy something. It's a "no-no" to "walk somebody" without trying to turn them over to somebody. And it doesn't have to be the manager, just so long as you let someone else take a shot at the customer, because a second viewpoint, anything, something, might just do it. T.O.s can be a big thing! . . . There's two ways to do it. One is the person who's trying to make the sale can just grab somebody, "Oh, this gentleman buys all the women's shoes for our store, maybe he can help you." Like it doesn't matter who the hell it is, could be a part-time staff. Or if it's a man you were dealing with, it's someone who buys all the men's shoes for the store. That way they feel like they're getting a little more expertise. But you can do that a lot of ways, introduce the manager as someone who might be able to help, things like that. . . . The other way, I will sometimes step into a sale, make a comment so that I can introduce myself, if they [staff] seem to be having trouble handling the sale. . . . You can tell most of the time whether or not the person is going to be able to wrap it up or not. It really helps your prestige with the staff too, if you can step in and make a sale when they're having a lot of trouble with it. Boy, I'll tell you, you're right up there! . . . You don't want to do it too often, and a lot of times, you don't have time. A lot of times you get walk-outs because you're too busy yourself. But you really don't like to see walk-outs [shoes]!

Not all turnovers involve new customers, but the objectives remain the same.

Some of the people are tough to deal with. They're usually people that you can't hit it off with. Like this one girl [buyer], when she comes down to our shop, I let Harry deal with her. Some of the people you can get along with. Some, there just is that friction between you, so there you switch them off with someone else they feel more comfortable with too [manufacture—clothing].

Encountering Shoppers in Groups

So far, attention has been largely directed toward two-person encounters. As Simmel (1950: 135-169) so aptly notes, however, the presence of third parties leads to much more varied and unpredictable patterns of interaction. The turnovers just discussed provide an indication of how sales encounters may be affected by the addition of a second salesperson. The emphasis now shifts to the ways in which third parties, presumably in alliance with the buyer, may influence buyer-seller encounters, and vendors' attempts to deal with these third-party influences.

While not a form of resistance per se, some of the more challenging sales encounters that vendors experience involve people making purchasing decisions in group contexts. The effects of groups on sales are far from uniform, and groups may facilitate as well as disrupt sales for the vendor. However, an examination of group shopping is important for a more complete understanding of sales encounters and the obstacles vendors experience therein.

Group shopping may result in multiple purchases for vendors, but encounters with groups are even more unpredictable than those involving solitary prospects, and the vendor's influence with reference to any prospect within a group is contingent upon the cooperation of the other persons in that group. Group shoppers may approach (or be approached by) vendors under a number of different conditions.[6] Thus group buying (shopping) may reflect elements such as convenience, entertainment, shyness, confidence in others' opinions, or anticipations of better volume prices, and financial interdependency. Once groups are encountered, however, salespeople may find themselves caught in a set of perplexing relationships. In addition to the difficulties involved in sorting out the preexisting relationships of the groups encountered, vendors face more frequent and more varied obstacles as they strive for prospect commitments.

HEIGHTENED VULNERABILITY

Vendors often describe group situations in either/or terms, with the prospect's companions either promoting or nullifying sales. Insofar as all sales have an either/or quality, this depiction is somewhat misleading. Nevertheless, the presence of third parties can significantly complicate purchasing situations.

In a group, you've got to sell that many more people, and all at once. Sometimes it can work more positively, because say the manager might think, "Aw, to heck with it." But you've got the foreman there, and he sees something there he wants, so he might push for you, maybe win the case for you. . . . The negative would be where say the manager's sold, but the two foremen are not. The foremen may want something that's just not available, impossible to purchase. There, you might just try to convince them that there is just nothing out there that can do all these things they want, and what you've got will do the job better than anything else they can get anywhere. And sometimes the manager will make the decision over them. It can be a good thing, or it can be a real drawback [manufacture—industrial]!

Sometimes they can be very frustrating because one will really like something and they'll be ready to buy it and the other one will say, "Oh, but what about the one you saw over at so and so." And you could just plow them, you know. You wish that that person had come in alone. Sometimes it's fun. Sometimes the other person will say, "Oh, it looks gorgeous on you. Buy it!" Maybe if they had come in by themselves they wouldn't buy it. So it works both ways. The other person can deter them or the other person can give them that extra little push that they need. A wife will want something and a husband will say, "Sure, buy it," or a husband will say, "You don't need another ring," and away they go. So group shopping can be fun, it can be exciting, it can be yuck. So, you get them both. You get them all. . . . Every situation is different and you don't know what it's going to bring. In some groups, you can kind of have a fun thing and you involve everybody in it and you create a fun atmosphere and then they're all going to be happy and they're going to buy it. They're all going to talk this person into buying it along with your help. So you have to figure out each group, what they came in for and why they're there and whether you can work a sale or whether you can't [jewelry].

In addition to facing possible rejection by the third parties, vendors in group settings also find themselves less able to define specific targets to whom to direct their attention. Thus groups create definitional dilemmas as salespeople endeavor to determine who or how many people might be making purchase(s), those for whom purchases may be intended, and significant points of influence within the group. The matter is further complicated in that the members of the shopping group may be uncertain about these points as well.

When you've got two or more shoppers it's a problem sometimes because you don't know whether one is buying or if both are buying or if they might be buying for themselves or for someone else. So what I try to do there is let them talk to themselves a little bit and try to pick it up on who it might be for, or if it's a gift. . . . Sometimes you come right out and ask them if they are thinking of it for themselves or as a gift [department store].

Further, it may be more difficult to access or assemble the relevant decision makers in larger settings.

I would rather sell to one. It's easier to convince one person than two or three. . . . And the accounts where you've got to deal with two or three people, it takes so long. They've got to communicate between each other, and it's just harder for them to make up their minds [wholesale—giftware].

What happens is that you'll make a contact with one person, so you'll make arrangements to sit down and talk about it. If the first person likes it, then you'll probably have to go and give one or two more presentations to the other people in the company. . . . The company is putting out a very large amount of money for fifty or a hundred or more people to travel, so normally I will only deal with vice-presidents, presidents, national marketing managers, and people on that level. So if your initial contact was with a salesperson, that might be the only actual contact you have with them in putting the package together for the company. . . .

If you are going to make a presentation to a group, you try to get straight before hand, how the person is going to introduce you or what they are going to do or say during the presentation. . . . If your contact likes the idea, that person might be really helpful, tipping you off on the people, what their reservations, fears are. Sometimes people have these little fears, concerns. . . . You also have to be prepared, because they will tell you that they will present the program or part of it and then sort of fade away on you when it's actually time to get into the presentation. So you have to watch it. It's one thing for them to say they will do it and another thing to actually do it. . . .

It's frustrating when you're dealing with one person who's told you that he makes all the decisions. So you've gone through the whole thing with this person but, sure enough, he'll have this board of directors meeting or something and he'll take it in and say that he's got this great idea and they'll turn it down flat! That's happened a few times, and it's really annoying because you're not dealing with the people who are making the decisions. And they won't let you into see the people who would be making the decisions, like the president or the marketing manager. "No, you can't see the top guy." And the top people, they've allocated this job to this guy, but the problem is that when they're making the presentation, it's not the same way as you would do it. Either he leaves out half the stuff or he's not hitting the right points or whatever. And you just don't know. You've got no control over it. That's the worst part. You've done your job and you feel that you've got a good program for them, but you can't get to the right people. And that's disappointing because you've spent a lot of hours on it and it looks like the company is very happy with it and they are going to go. Then all of a sudden, you get a phone call out of the blue and they decided not to go [promotions—travel].

GROUPS AS HELPFUL

In some situations, vendors very clearly define third parties as having been instrumental in facilitating sales. The value of groups in these settings reflects a greater number of prospects, favorable third-party definitions, image concerns, and the practice of gifting within groups.

You will get cases where the friend comes in and does the job of selling the item to the other person for you, where they might have been a little reluctant otherwise. But you don't know what to expect. It's more difficult that way [luggage].

You can play on that, but you don't actually have to say anything. They have this other person here, so often they're more concerned about feeling cheap or getting better quality than if they were on their own. . . . I've noticed that with myself too, and my wife. She'll buy things when she's out with her sister or her friends that she wouldn't buy alone. . . . You have an image to keep up. That's why a lot of people like to shop alone. It's hard to be as frugal or picky or whatever when you have these other people watching over you [mixed clothing].

They might have bought the same thing if the kid wasn't there, but the child being there is a reminder even when they're not asking for something. . . . And they will ask, and it's not that they get everything, but the parents will sometimes soften up. Grandparents are maybe even better that way. So there's another sale for you. . . . You wouldn't want to rely on those sales, but they help pay the bills [giftware].

GROUPS AS THREATENING

However helpful salespeople may find some group shopping situations, those in which salespeople anticipate and/or encounter resistance from persons other than the immediate prospect can be highly disquieting.[7] While group situations tend to be more challenging overall, salespeople tend to define group encounters as particularly disconcerting when the troublesome third party is seen as vocal, unknowledgeable, or as someone with whom the buyer is not financially interdependent.

The husband and the wives are one of the worst. The husband will come in and he'll often like the first thing you put on him. So then he might try six suits on, but she finds something wrong with every one, "We should look elsewhere, Henry!" It can just drive you to drink! Really, it can. . . . You have days where it seems like those people wait in line to come in, and each guy brings his wife. And there are many, many times we come to the back and, "Why do they bring their wives along?" . . . Or you'll have the guy in a suit, a shirt, a tie, and he's all set to buy, and she comes walking up, maybe she's been looking around elsewhere in the mall. She'll walk in and, "Where did you get that from? You look the pits! Who picked that out for you? Who works here? Who's the manager?" You're coping with something you have no control over. The only thing you can do is say, "Lady, pick out a suit and put it on him. If you like it, fine." You can only do so much. It's especially a problem if it's one of my salesgirls selling. And they put together an outfit for him, really nice. Makes him look great! Then you can almost sense the jealousy there. They don't like anything she picks out for them. She's picking out great outfits, bang, bang, bang. She's got the guy dressed great. The wife is there, "Nothing in here!" dragging the guy out by the ear, "We're never going in there again! The girl doesn't know what she's doing. She shouldn't be selling suits!" Meanwhile, all the abuse you're getting, six o'clock comes, you're ready to let off some steam. Especially if you know what you're doing, and you know that the suit fits great on the person, and she's saying, "It doesn't fit!" [men's clothing]

The ones that really get me are the loud obnoxious, know-it-all friends. They know it all, and they're rude, "That's too much!" "Looks like junk to me!" "You don't want that, do you!" They didn't really give you or the other person a chance [mixed clothing].

DEALING WITH GROUPS

While vendors may use many of the same strategies in dealing with groups that they would in meeting individual resistances, some strategies unique to groups were also noted. These include vendor attempts to solicit favorable definitions from others in the group, pitch to persons seen as more influential to purchasing decisions, seek agreements among group members, blend into the group, discredit disruptors, and create two-person encounters. While interrelated, and often used in some combination, each represents distinct lines of emphasis.

Soliciting Favorable Definitions

A very common tactic salespeople use in group settings is that of attempting to elicit positive assessments of the products featured from within the group.

Sometimes you'll wish they left their friends at home. And you have to watch, especially with younger women, their friends, because sometimes their friends could be jealous. So you can have an outfit that really looks phenomenal on one girl, but the other doesn't have the same kind of money or the same build or looks, and she'll be down on it. . . . Sometimes you'll get women who, before they buy something, will ask you to hold an item until they can bring a friend to get another opinion. . . . Sometimes it'll work the other way around, where a friend will say it looks gorgeous on her when it looks really bad on her, when it's just not right for her and you feel bad then because that purchase is not good advertising for the store. . . . Sometimes you'll get situations where you show the item to the one person and you end up selling to both of them, a double sale. . . . I usually try to draw the other person into the sales, trying to get their opinions to work for you. . . . But one-on-one is much easier, but if it gets busier, that can be a problem because you're getting spread around too thin to be able to give anyone good service. But I sometimes fix that by having the customers sell to one another, where they don't realize it, but they're giving opinions on how they like this and that item that the other women are trying on. And of course, the outfits all look pretty good, so that can help you out sometimes. . . . Like if someone is trying on an outfit and it looks pretty good, you can say, "Gee, I think that outfit looks really good on you! What do you think, Lotta?" or "Wouldn't you agree, Grace?" And if somebody who doesn't know you at all says that she thinks it looks good on you, then you're more likely to go along with it. A completely unbiased opinion [women's clothing]!

Sometimes it's nice to have two people come in together because the one might help sell the product to the other. But it can work for or against you. I prefer to have it one to one. If you have two, though, you can sometimes double the sale, maybe more if they both get excited about it. . . . With two people, you're not sure who you're selling to. If it's a man and a woman, I try to please her first and then use him to get an opinion, "She does look good, doesn't she?" [cosmetics]

Pitching to the Influentials

Salespeople adopting this strategy attempt to define the persons in the group most central to purchasing decisions, and concentrate their efforts accordingly. Assuming uneven intergroup influences, those using this tactic are less concerned with those paying for purchases than with those they envision as shaping purchasing decisions.

You get a feeling, ultimately, never mind who's got the money, who's going to make the decision. There's one person that's always stronger and they're a spokesperson, so you know that's the mouthy person. They're the one that everyone else is going to look to. You know that they're the boss. Whether they've got the money in their pocket or not, they're the boss. So you talk to them. Maybe you don't look at them and talk to them, but you say things that you think they want to hear because you know, ultimately, they're in charge [jewelry].

Group sales are different. There, you try to work on two or three key people. So in a group of ten, there will be two or three that are going to be critical in making the decision. The other seven will go along. Out of the ten you are probably going to get a few objections, but they may be minimal in effect. You may get a real nasty son of a bitch in there as well. The ideal way would be to bring them along at the same pace. That's the nice way. You introduce yourself, the product, and get the interaction between all of them. If not, you try to get it out of them, get them involved in the presentation. Now there are cases where you can't get those other seven going. If you can't get them all going, you try to look for the leaders, find out who has the authority. Who says, "Go ahead!" Who signs the checks? Then pour a lot of juice on them, but still try for the others. Never let the others feel that they've been left out because then they're going to be a pain in the ass! They're going to drag their feet, they're going to feel rejected, and they're going to reject you. . . . The decision makers are going to be the people who go over the literature more carefully usually. Try to get to know the people with the titles, they're usually the signers. So you try to sort the group out that way [manufacture—industrial].

Pursuing Group Consensus

Should customers be seen as financially interdependent or readily accountable to one another, vendors may be particularly concerned about achieving acceptance of the product by all parties involved. Salespeople may attempt to reconcile group member viewpoints in all group settings. Mediation becomes especially important under these conditions.

> Given our range of prices, you could overcome most price objections, so our most difficult sale would be something like where a father and daughter come in, and the daughter wants this very expensive brand of jeans. The father is perfectly willing to spend an average amount, and all the jeans look the same to him. That's the most difficult, something like that [mixed clothing].

> In selling home items, selling to two people is not so different than selling to one. In many cases, one will be the leader, primarily the wife, who will then do most of the selling to the husband. So in those cases, you will sell to the wife and give moderate attention to the husband. If it's something like a swimming pool, you'll probably sell more to the husband than you would with indoor furnishing, for example. . . . But you have to sort of generate an excitement, an enjoyment to encompass the customer. If you can radiate a confidence, an understanding, a belief in yourself in what you're selling, in what you're doing, without being antagonistic to people, that'll help. . . . And always include them, get them communicating back and forth with you. Keep a solid strong point and get them involved in it. Make them feel part of it so that they believe that they know everything there is to know about the product and what they're buying. They not only want to have a product, but they want that product to fulfill their wants, and if you can fulfill their wants, they'll buy your product [home improvements].

Given the generally acknowledged interdependency of spouses, the need for approval can also represent a significant "dodge" one party may employ in the absence of the spouse. Regardless of its sincerity, it becomes a noteworthy group-based obstacle to the vendor.

If they say they've got to talk it over with their husband, that pretty well does it. You realize that they don't want to risk him not liking the expenditure, and some of the things are a bit of money. There's not much you can do there [women's clothing].

The biggest excuse, then, is "Well, I've got to talk it over with my wife." The husband on his own has always got the excuse of talking it over with his wife. So "Talk it over with her." "She's at work." "Take it there," or "Here's the phone, call her." And most customers will follow you at that point. "Here's the phone." Force them to do it. Don't give them an opportunity to say no [auto].

Blending In

Beyond the preceding tactics, salespeople sometimes deal with groups by becoming "friends" or "insiders." Their success in assuming this role is clearly contingent on being accepted by members of the group, but the trust this acceptance implies can be very instrumental in fostering sales.

Sometimes, with a group, you can get right in there. You can't do it with everyone, but with some you can. . . . If you can joke around with them, or maybe they just treat you more friendly, like at the start. If you can build good rapport with them, that'll help in a lot of cases [department store].

Everybody's different, but if you can become, well, almost an instantaneous friend to one or more people in the group, that can be a real advantage. . . . You might pick up on a hobby or where they worked before or something they're wearing. But you've changed the relationship to where it's not strictly a financial one. It's more personal now, more relaxed. You can be more open about your products and they're still going to give you a shot [manufacture—industrial].

Discrediting Disrupters

Just as vendors may sometimes challenge prospects' definitions of situations, so may they also contest definitions promoted by third parties. In both instances, one notes vendor concerns regarding the impact of their challenges for subsequent purchases.

I don't like doing that, but sometimes you find yourself in that situation. The friend has made a comment about your products and it's chancy to contradict him or her, but if you don't, you've probably lost it anyways. . . . You might offend both people because they're friends, family, but you don't want those doubts there either. You try to be diplomatic, but if it's a strong statement that's really difficult to do [men's clothing].

It depends on who it is. If it's a mother saying, "You wouldn't like that," to her child, you can't say much. But if it's two friends shopping together, you might confront the friends, "Why do you say that? That's one of our best selling shoes!" You hate to do that, but if it's all you can do I'll do that, if I think there's a chance of getting the sale from the other one [shoes].

CREATING TWO-PERSON ENCOUNTERS

In partial response to the risk they run in trying to discredit disruptive third parties, some salespeople have developed tactics designed to distract or otherwise isolate third parties from the central transaction.

It's harder to manage a group than a single customer by yourself. So if Jane is dealing with a couple of women and I'm not occupied, I may step in an start up a conversation with her [customer's] friend. It lets Jane concentrate on the first one without the distractions. And I have a chance to keep the other one occupied, so she's not getting as bored or critical, and I may be able to get her to try something on herself while she's waiting. Maybe ring up a sale on her too, which is nice! So that's something else you can do in that situation. We'll do things like that [women's clothing].

That's where it's nice to have a couple of people in the booth. You might let one person do the demonstration and then, as they're asking questions, you might start to deal with them more individually. They might have different questions, or maybe this one hits it off better with this other salesman. So there, you can begin showing them different features or applications that the other one wasn't interested in. Or you might just shoot the shit with the one while the other one is getting all the technical information [manufacture—computers].

In Perspective

When I first started, I didn't realize that there would be as much customer resistance as there is. You have to lead people to what they want. They know what they want, but you have to give them that little extra push to make them get it. You have to help them make a decision, which I didn't realize. I hadn't anticipated that amount of resistance in decision making. I figured that if people wanted something, and they had the money for it, they just went and got it [hobby].

Regardless of whether or not vendors deal with all their prospects' reservations, a critical aspect of sales work is that of closing or completing sales. Salespeople do not always assume initiative in consolidating sales. However, when they do pursue buyer commitments, they commonly attempt to confirm purchases by inquiring about buyers' willingness to make purchases, assuming agreements, providing justifications for purchasing decisions, indicating pressing limitations, noting commitment options, and closing by "default." Likewise, the practice of seeking assistance in closing sales (T.O.s) appears typical of the more common strategy of letting others deal with people when one's efforts at persuading these others have failed.

These practices seem similar to those employed by others who wish to attain commitments from people in other contexts (for instance, see Karsh et al., 1953; Prus, 1976; Prus and Sharper, 1977; Prus and Irini, 1988). Closes may be more explicit in sales settings (in which people are asked to put their money down), but the pursuit of cooperation (and commitment) is very much an element of everyday life. Consider the following in a dating or friendship context: "Like to go out?" (inquiry); "Why not?" (inquiry); "I already bought the tickets!" (assumption); "You'll have a really good time! You deserve a break" (justifications); "We may not get this opportunity again." (limitations); "If you don't like it, we can leave early" (openness); "O.K., I'll leave it up to you" (default); "Mary, would you tell Cindy how much fun it will be. She seems reluctant to go. Talk her into it" (turn over). And people may be asked to make even more extensive commitments in other settings (e.g., consider religious or political conversion, marriage).

When discussing the closing of sales, we should also be attentive to the dilemmas salespeople experience regarding the selection and implementation of particular tactics, the intensity with which they pursue these, the points at which they invoke these strategies, and when they back off from particular tactics or prospects. Similarly, while faced with the task of making sales in an immediate sense, vendors may be concerned about the significance of their present pursuits for subsequent encounters with these same prospects (i.e., trust, repeat patronage).

Relevant, as well, as the uneven relationships between overall efforts, specific tactics, and eventual purchasing decisions. Reflected here is some sense of buyers' willingness to be closed as opposed to feeling as if they had been "bamboozled by some slick, fast-talking salesman." In

this same vein, we may expect that some customers may resist immediate purchases (possibly as a result of image concerns) even when they
have accepted the feasibility of making particular purchases. Later,
these prospects may even seek out those very products, so that the
salespeople who next encounter them may find that they are very easily
closed.

The examination of the role of third parties in group purchasing
contexts adds further insight into the commitment pursuit process.
While vendors may benefit from group shopping (e.g., assistance from
the third party, multiple sales), these encounters are much more unpredictable than those involving solitary prospects. Thus, although vendors
find themselves both helped and hindered by third parties, they recognize their susceptibility to third party definitions. To this end, they
commonly solicit third party definitions in an effort to buttress their
positions, direct their communications toward those they define as more
influential, and assume mediator roles as they strive for consensus
among members of the groups they encounter. As well, they sometimes
attempt to neutralize group effects by gaining personalized acceptance
in the group, discrediting those they see as disrupting impending sales,
and breaking the group into (more manageable) buyer-seller dyads. In
all cases, however, salespeople remain vulnerable to inputs, interactions, and the preexisting as well as anticipated relationships that
members of the shopping group have relative to one another.

Notes

1. For other sociological depictions of attempts to close sales, see Donovan (1929: 46-59), French (1958), Miller (1964), and Stets-Kealey (1989).

2. Closing is a featured topic in most sales texts. Gross's (1959) statement was found particularly valuable.

3. Some closing by assumption reflects naïveté rather than technique, as when vendors innocently presume a sale and act accordingly.

4. Although friends and family seem more apt to make explicit use of this tactic (e.g., "How can you let me down at a time like this?"), vendors will occasionally stress obligations buyers should feel toward them (vendors). For example, "We've been good to you in the past. You owe us one."

5. For other discussions of turn overs, see French (1958: 36, 43-44; 1960: 128-134). Goffman (1959: 178-180), and Caplovitz (1963: 17-18).

6. One of the most successful instances of marketing pitched at shoppers in groups involves "party plans" (or "home parties"). For two sociological statements on this phenomenon, see Peven (1968) and Prus and Frisby (1989).

7. As Donovan (1929: 53-54) indicates, this denotes another common vendor experience.

Chapter 6
ENCOUNTERING
TROUBLESOME CUSTOMERS

You can't please everyone. There are a lot of customers who want the impossible. They don't look at what they're buying, they're careless with what they buy, and then they expect the store to keep them happy. And some of them are very adamant when they come back and find that there is no refund. And some of them, they try all the scare tactics, threats possible. Or they won't keep their sales receipts, and they have a responsibility too. . . . In that sense, we find that our best customers are often salespeople because they realize the problems involved in retail work. They know that you're trying to make money for the store and they realize that they, as consumers, have to take some responsibility for what they're getting [music].

What sorts of shopping practices do vendors find annoying? What strategies do vendors use to deal with these situations? What dilemmas do these efforts at control pose for vendors? What are the implications of these episodes for vendor enthusiasm? What about repeat patronage?

Defining Trouble

Some difficulties pertaining to saleswork have been discussed in earlier chapters. Thus, for instance, attention has been given to a number of resistances including price objections, skepticism, indecisiveness, existing loyalties to competitors, comparison shoppers, and group shoppers. But as a consequence of their effects on salespeople's dispositions and effectiveness, troublesome encounters deserve more attention.[1]

In addition to other aspects of marketing for which they may be responsible, salespeople are also expected to "keep order" within the boundaries of their businesses.[2] While vendors will call the police in some cases, most disruptions are handled informally. And perceiving themselves to be dependent on the good will of their customers in reference to both short-run and long-term purchases, vendors are more constrained in how they handle trouble than would the same people in other settings. Sales work thus becomes an exercise in self-constraint and composure, deference (acknowledging the other as someone worthy of consideration) and demeanor (styles of expressing oneself to others).[3] The amount and variety of "troublesome customers" encountered will vary somewhat with vendor products, promotional styles, policies, and volume of customers, as well as salespeople's personal tolerances. But all businesses seem certain to have some troublesome customers.[4]

If *trouble* (or deviance) is defined as any human activity considered offensive, disturbing, or threatening to some audience,[5] one finds two basic themes around which vendors define troublesome customers. These definitions reflect concerns with implementing all aspects of marketing (e.g., making sales, keeping the merchandise and store safe and presentable, providing service, collecting fees, and promoting repeat patronage), and maintaining personal notions of integrity and fair play. These shape perspectives from which shopper activities are defined as troublesome. As Emerson et al. (1983) note, trouble represents an important feature of the workplace. Not only may trouble result in much internal discussion (and dissension), it may also generate new operating policies.

Given the greater volume of shoppers involved, vendors in retail settings are very likely to encounter not only more troublesome customers but also a greater variety. Still, those dealing with "trade" more exclusively will find many parallels (also see Chapter 4 in *Pursuing Customers*). In addition to (1) annoying shopping styles, other commonly defined troublesome behavior includes (2) returns, (3) complaints, (4) theft, and (5) financial difficulties.

Annoying Shopping Styles

An examination of annoying shopping styles reveals a number of practices that vendors frequently find disconcerting. Of particular relevance here are careless shoppers, time consumers, impatient shoppers, and those with "difficult dispositions."

CARELESS SHOPPERS

One group of annoying customers are those thought insufficiently careful in how they act toward the merchandise and/or the displays in which these items are located. While notions of "messy" shoppers reflect vendors' desires for neat displays, customer insensitivities to attractive displays represents one of the most commonly mentioned forms of troublesome shopping styles. Carelessness may result in some destruction of products, but merchandise need not be damaged to result in losses for the vendors. Some shoppers may find disheveled displays too unattractive to examine further, and to the extent that staff time is diverted by rearranging displays, other shoppers may feel sufficiently neglected to leave without making purchases.

Not all careless behavior is witnessed in time for vendors to take action, but even when they directly witness these occurrences, vendors are generally reluctant to chastise the "culprits," lest they offend prospective customers. However, since carelessness may result in more work, damaged goods and displays, and lost sales, vendors experience frustration in their attempts to be tolerant.

> I can't believe how sloppy people are! How they take things off the rack and put them back. And they'll just pull the pants out of the stacks and here a pair and there a pair, "No, I can't find anything." And they'll walk away, and you just want to bang them against the wall and beat their brains out. And you'll have people say, "You've got nothing to do all day. You can fix that." [men's clothing]

Stores frequented by parents with disruptive children create control dilemmas for the staff. While concerned about maintaining order within the store, salespeople are reluctant to impose controls on the children lest they offend their parents.

> I love children! We like to sort of play with them when they come in the store, but it's the kind that they let run loose in the store that gets to me. . . . You worry about

them knocking things over or breaking the glass, things like that. And you get worked up about that. You don't know what to do. Sometimes you try and distract them. You can't expect them to be perfect, but you do get some brats in sometimes, pulling on the clothes and all. You'll get some little terrors! And if you're on the phone or something, then it's really awkward. Sometimes you'll have to chase them down yourself [women's clothing].

TIME CONSUMERS

Salespeople often appreciate the opportunity to chat with customers during slow times. Especially at busier times, however, vendors are apt to find indecisive shoppers or those requiring more assistance very frustrating. Those on commission are more likely to be bothered by time consumers, but all salespeople may be concerned that other sales not be lost as a consequence of these slower shoppers.

You'll get people who can't make up their minds. And it will be a small item, and some of them will take so long to make up their minds. You'll spend 20 minutes showing them this item, and then she still can't make up her mind. That's a difficult thing to handle, the indecisiveness of some people [jewelry].

IMPATIENT CUSTOMERS

In contrast to the time consumers, impatient customers generally want immediate and efficient attention. Ideally, vendors would like to serve time-consuming and impatient customers in isolation from other customers, for both can interfere with the salesperson's ability to serve other customers. However, impatient customers put additional pressure on vendors, for impending sales may be lost if these people are not given prompt attention.

Impatient customers, they bother me. If you're busy and having problems looking after a number of customers in a very short time, you try to acknowledge them, you indicate to them that you have seen them, that you'll try to get to them as soon as you can. Then they're usually more at ease, but that doesn't always work with some people. They get huffy and walk out [stationery].

Not all impatient people are bona fide customers, but their interruptions can be just as devastating.

If there's any distraction, it's enough for them to get away.... Some might not buy anyway, but some I'm sure you lose, maybe 50%. They'll say something like "I'll be back later." Or someone interrupting your conversation with customers to ask you the price. That's another thing I find annoying. Any of these things, they can lose you a sale [crafts].

Likewise, it should not be assumed that impatient shoppers are efficient customers themselves.

Impatient people are usually the worst, and they're usually the people who want to pay by the slowest means. They're really impatient to get to the register, but when they get there, instead of paying cash, where you could just whiz them through, they take out a charge card or a check. In a line-up, they're hemming and hawing because someone else is writing a check, but when they get there, they do the same thing [discount department store].

DIFFICULT DISPOSITIONS

Customers perceived as unfriendly, pompous, in bad moods, discontented, or rude represent another group of troublesome shoppers. And even when they accept the challenge of "talking prospects into sales," vendor satisfaction is apt to be diminished.

Some people are very unfriendly. Like you'll approach them with a smile, a friendly hello, and some of them are very, very nasty. For no reason. And that's hard to take. Mind you, I wouldn't say that that's a larger percentage, but you do get a few.... Eventually, you just realize that there are people like that, and just take it as it comes, try not to let it get to you [music].

Rudeness

Whether behavior is interpreted as indicative of difficult dispositions or rudeness is a matter of vendor perspectives. But behavior defined as rudeness tends to be taken more personally, as a challenge to salespeople's integrity. One form of action often taken as an indication of rudeness is a failure to respond to the vendor's introductory comments. Likewise, a perception that shoppers consider themselves superior to the salespeople is also taken to reflect rudeness. In both respects, it is worth noting the relative vulnerability of salespeople, for any exchanges that become bitter may end in lost sales and/or create additional problems for salespeople should customers (justified or otherwise) complain to their supervisors.

You just give them a couple minutes in the store, and then go over with a smile, "Hello, how are you doing today? . . . Something special you're interested in? . . . Looking for something for a special occasion?" And most times, you get "I'm just looking." "Just browsing." You get that all day. You hear that in your nightmares! You can see them coming. And then you get the ignorant ones who say nothing. They say nothing. You walk up to them, "Hi, how are you doing? Are you interested in the suits?" Nothing! That's it, that's my level. I'm not going to push, I'll just say, "That's it!" to myself, and I'll walk away. And I'll tell the rest of the staff "He didn't say a word." And everyone knows: "That's it. If they want help, they've got to come to us, call us over." Because that's really rude! . . . I've seen some of our staff really get mad about that. I've had some that will just come storming back. And what can you really ask them to do? Go back and be nice? She's tried that already. You can try to be congenial, friendly, and it's just like there's a wall, and they're not even listening. It's rude, but you get that a lot, and if that happens two or three times in a day, you're burning! You're ready to kill the next one who does something really stupid or rude. That's horrible [men's clothing]!

Rudeness appears especially debilitating when it is unexpected and/ or occurs in group settings. Thus, for instance, while vendors realize that not everyone will like their products or consider their prices to be reasonable, open criticism is seldom welcome. These criticisms differ from objections in that people making these statements are typically not interested in making purchases.

One of the things I find frustrating is with people who find your goods too expensive. If they just look, and you can see where they're maybe a bit surprised. Sometimes they expect handcrafts to be priced like the things in your discount stores imported from Korea or someplace. Well, that's not too bad. But where it really gets me is where they have to tell you that's it's too expensive or they get a little rude about it, especially if other people are around and had been making motions as if they were intending to buy something. Now often, the other people will make some little comment to you, like this grumbler has been unreal, and often they will still make a purchase, but this other one has made the whole thing a little more tarnished, not as pleasant. And you don't know just how much their stupidity has cost you, all in all [crafts].

Dealing with Returns

Signaling "failed sales," customers making returns are approached with some trepidation by most vendors. Some offer generous return policies, guaranteeing satisfaction or money refunded, but returns may represent lost sales, result in displeased customers, signify losses through damaged goods, and cause some inconvenience. With these concerns in mind, the three R's of returns (repairs, replacements, and refunds) are considered. Vendor return policies are influenced somewhat by those of their competitors. However, one finds considerable variance in policy not only in reference to particular products across stores but also in reference to the range of products individual stores feature.

REPAIRS

When returns reflect problems with the merchandise, repair is a common first line of action, especially when more costly items are involved.

They don't get their money back. We will fix the car, get it in satisfactory condition, but we will not give them their money back. It's a machine that's been used, been driven, licensed in their name, and the car depreciates the minute it moves off the lot. I would be losing a lot of money that way [auto].

REPLACEMENTS

Should repairs be not feasible or inconvenient or irrelevant, a direct exchange or credit generally represents the next preferred alternative.

If something goes wrong with something you bought here, we'll fix or replace it. We try getting it fixed first, and if we can't do that, we'll replace it. . . . You try to avoid giving a direct refund because that way you lose the whole sale, and in this business you're out to make a dollar and you just don't want to give refunds [women's clothing].

REFUNDS

A lot of refunds can kill the day. You could be having a great day, then if you get a few refunds in a row, it can really put you down. I have had days that have been a minus situation, where I didn't end up with enough money in the till to make the float. . . . They do happen, but fortunately not too often [shoes].

Vendors provide customers with refunds for two reasons. First and foremost, it is intended to promote customer confidence and long-term loyalty. Second, some vendors realize that it increases the likelihood of other sales at the time of returns. While any store may vary in its practices from case to case, it seems valuable to distinguish "easy refunds," "negotiated refunds," and "no refunds" arrangements.

Easy Refunds

In the retail sector, "hassle free" refunds tend to be most characteristic of larger chain stores, especially department stores. But because of their problem-solving potential, easy refunds are by no means limited to large department stores.

> It's just much easier to give them a refund, if that's what they want. Often you've got other people around and you don't want to create a scene, but the other part of it is that you don't want to get into an argument and all that goes along with it. When you're selling, you have to be in good spirits and it's disappointing when you lose out on a sale through a refund, but it's not as upsetting as an argument [giftware].

However, even when companies guarantee "satisfaction or money refunded," the sales staff may not be as tolerant as head office intended.[6] Depicting some other ways in which consumers may attempt to take advantage of vendors through returns, the following extracts also indicate the personalization of "generous returns" by salespeople.

> Our store is too generous with their return policies. Someone might use a mascara or lipstick once, sometimes halfway through, and decide that they didn't like it and come back for a refund. There's nothing wrong with it. You can't return it to the manufacturer, and yet you can't sell it because it's obviously been used. Things like that really get to me! We're too easy with people that way [department store].

> One of the things I didn't like about the department store was that if the customers didn't like something or something was wrong with it, they could bring it back. No problem! You always were to be cheerful. The customer is always right! . . . That bothered me a lot because you're there working and doing your best, and here comes the customer and takes advantage of the store. Of you too, because you and the other people who work there, you have to work harder to make up for the loss that that person caused the store by their stupidity, their carelessness in the way they treated the item [department store].

Negotiated Refunds

Should vendors wish to maintain greater control over returns, they may request further evidence of purchase and/or more intact packaging.

Consistent with Karikas and Rosenwasser (1980), it may be noted that customers who appear more sincere generally fare better in situations in which vendors have more discretion in accepting returns.

> You have to watch the returns, especially with the more common lines. If they don't have the receipt or if you don't remember the customer and they're bringing in some item that they could have purchased at any number of stores, you get more wary. Our policy is to require the receipt, but we will make refunds if it's our own line or if we remember the customer, something like that [luggage].

Refusing Refunds

Vendors seem most concerned about avoiding refunds when large-ticket items are involved and/or returned items cannot be resold as new. Some vendors have consistent no-refund policies, while others vary policies by products and problems.

> With the diamond rings, I suggest that they consider putting the diamond in another setting. That's the first thing. If that doesn't work, if they're too distraught about it, then I guess the only other suggestion is to suggest that they sell it. . . . There's no reason for us to buy a diamond back at the cost of a new diamond to us. We have to spend additional time on it and there's got to be some money there, so they wouldn't get the cost of the materials back, so I try to stay clear of that. I will appraise it for them so they can try to sell it themselves in the newspaper, things like that. But to buy it back is something we do not like to do. . . . With gifts, they can exchange it for whatever they like. You sometimes get people who want their money back. But the way I look at it is that if someone has bought something, you have to take some responsibility for it. They shouldn't expect to spend your time and all and then turn around and get a refund on the item. They get this idea from the policies of the large department stores, and it's not good really, at least for an operation like this [jewelry].

Optimizing Returns

Although returns are often viewed with some trepidation on the part of vendors, it is worth noting that returns may also be used as occasions to sell customers higher lines and/or additional items.

> I would rather have them make the return than sit at home and grumble to all their friends about how they got ripped off by us. I'm not sure that my staff sees it that way, but if they [customers] come in, you at least have a chance to work things out with them and maybe keep them as a customer too. It's a chance to do some P.R. work, and maybe make another sale in the process [women's clothing].

Nobody really likes to get returns, but it depends on how you handle it too. If you can take the situation more in stride, you can make it work to your advantage. Now if the person comes in yelling and screaming, it's going to be more difficult, but even there you might be able to turn it around. . . . You try to get a handle on the problem and see what you can do for the person. Sometimes they just haven't used the product the right way or didn't realize it had some feature, so no real problem there. But even if there is a problem, if you relate to them you can often find something else that will do the job for them. You might be able to sell them some attachment or a better model, get it resolved that way. The idea, though, is to keep them happy, and then you might do a little second selling, find something else they might be able to use. Even one more try, "Is there anything else we might be able to help you with today, Mrs. Whatever?" . . . But that is a more difficult situation, and they will take you by surprise, so you're just not as effective as you should be [department store].

Handling Complaints

Some complaints involve returns, but others may reflect any aspect of marketing, including such things as the selection of goods, pricing, sales techniques, service, and advertising. If complaints reflect general concerns, they (along with other customer suggestions) may be valuable in enabling vendors to improve aspects of their business. In most cases, however, complaints are seen as unpleasant nuisances with which to be dealt, albeit with the recognition that styles of dealing with complaints can affect business.[7]

As with effective "confidence men" (Goffman, 1952; Prus and Sharper, 1977), vendors often find it very worthwhile to spend some time with concerned customers.

A lot of your complaints have to do with the charges on their bills. Occasionally you get complaints about the salespeople. Or if we refused to authorize an account sale for some reason, the customer might get upset about that. You try to be patient with them, because how you treat them can affect whether they do business with you in the future [department store].

Like policemen in the field (Black and Reiss, 1970) whose judgments of validity reflect the demeanor of both the complainants and the targets involved, managers' assessments of complaints also seem affected by definitions of both the buyers and salespeople involved. Where customers are known, past encounters with the same people may serve as a basis for assessing subsequent complaints.[8]

> You sort of judge the validity of the complaint by the way the customer acts towards you or the [store] manager. Like if you get someone who's threatening the manager next, the complaint is usually not taken too seriously, just a bad apple in the bunch [discount department store].

> It depends on who it comes from, and with the regulars you get to know them, so that with some of them they are of no use to you at all. You listen to them and agree with them and just let it go at that, because they're basic complainers [hardware].

PERSONALIZING TREATMENT

While denoting general practices, the preceding material on returns and complaints may be further qualified by the customers involved. Important in this regard are preferred customers, regular returners, and persistent complainers.

Preferred Customers

Some people may be given better treatment as a result of family and friendship ties, but regular customers (and particularly larger buyers) typically tend to be given more considerate attention.[9]

> Fortunately or not, some people are better customers and you have to treat them better. It's not fair, but it is in a way too. You don't want to risk losing them, because they do so much for you. So unless it's a real big problem for us, we'll absorb it. But overall, they more than make up for it. They pay the bills [women's clothing].

> We try to treat people much the same, although if they're better customers, you're going to go out of your way to make sure they're happy with you. You have to! There are many other stores around, and if you want to keep getting their business, you've got to show that you're interested in solving their problems. They expect it [giftware].

Regular Returners

Among those making returns, vendors may encounter "regular returners." Some stores attempt to keep track of returns by having customers fill out return slips, but those in the "front lines" are most apt to recognize frequent returners.

We've got a few people who are always returning things, and when they come back, they'll often get something else, but you know that they'll be back a few days later to return what they got this last time. Finally, you have to cut them right off. You do get people like that [jewelry].

Persistent Complainers

Returns can be "dramatic encounters" (Klapp, 1964), with the participants variously playing the roles of heroes, villains, victims, and fools. It is apparent, however, that vendors are generally more concerned about "scenes" than are shoppers.

It's the people who want to make a scene, rant and rave on your floor, they want to be as obnoxious as possible, and they try to turn off the other customers because they know that you hate that. That's your biggest problem [shoes].

Recognizing their dependency on community goodwill, vendors view persistent complainers as definite liabilities. Shoppers sometimes attempt to intimidate salespeople by threatening to report them to superiors, to report businesses to community agencies, and otherwise "blacken their reputations." In each case, salespeople have to make decisions as to whether to give in or resist shopper demands. Thus, although they may lose time, energy, and respect in the process, persistent complainers generally tend to benefit in returns over their more complacent counterparts. It might also be noted that concessions needn't reflect judgments of correctness as much as evaluations of costs vendors incur as a result of customer persistence.[10]

On a "sales" item, they can't get their money back. On a "sales" item, we'll give them an exchange or a credit, and we tell them that. The item is on "sale," because you wanted to clear it out, and they're sort of penalizing you by bringing it back. And they will scream and holler and fight with you. And this person will rant and rave at you, and there may be other customers watching too. And there, you have to decide whether to give in or stand your ground. They can storm out and never come back. If you're trying to build your clientele, whether or not you want that kind of customer is up to you. . . . If it's a steady customer who's been in before and you know that they're just a little upset today, you might be wise to do it for them, maintain them as a customer. But some of them, they really make a fuss about it [men's clothing].

COMPLAINTS AGENCIES

Many communities have agencies to whom dissatisfied customers may make claims against particular businesses.[11] The following material from one such agency provides further insight into customers' complaints. Like most complaints agencies, the one assisting us with this project is supported by local businesses (and local offices of larger businesses).

> Being a member of _____ gives credibility to the business. It instills confidence in the consumer because he or she feels that dealing with someone who's a member, that they have to live up to our standards and have to be approved by our board of directors. And if he or she has a problem, then certainly that business will cooperate in helping to get it solved with the agency. . . . There's actually been very few businesses that have had to be turned down for membership. One of the criteria is that they look after their consumer complaints, that they cooperate with us. We don't get into the financial end of the credit reporting. It's strictly a reputation-reporting business, so we go by what is on our files. If we feel that something is not proper in their advertising, we'll bring it to their attention and let them try to correct it, that sort of thing. . . . Our only source of funding is from the membership fees. . . . The membership fees are based on the number of employees the companies have. . . . The more revenue I bring in [by getting more members] the more services I can offer [complaints agency].

When complaints are received, the standard procedure goes like this:

> If it's a complaint, we first want it in writing, and we send a copy of that complaint to the company involved and ask them to respond to it, to get their side of the story. And that's how we start mediation. And we mark our files accordingly. If the business cooperated with the consumer, we mark that. If the complaint wasn't valid in our opinion, we make note of that for our files. If the business doesn't answer us, we mark it as uncooperative. Then when the next consumer calls in to inquire about that company, we give our the information that we have on the business from what's in our files. . . . When they phone in a complaint, we always ask them if they have gone back to the business to discuss the matter with them. A lot of times they'll say yes, and we'll find out the owner hasn't heard about it. And a lot of it is the business's fault too, because they'll talk to the service manager, say, and they'll be frustrated with him, and they won't let the person speak to the owner. And so who's telling you the truth? Often I think, somewhere down the middle is the truth, and then you hear both sides of the story. It's very, very difficult, and you're having to take people at face value. You just sort of develop an intuitive nature after a while, but it is difficult, it really is, trying to mediate a complaint. You can hear both sides of the story, but then if you start making some recom-

mendations and both of them won't budge, you're just sort of stuck in the middle and all you can do is just throw up your arms and say, "Look, I just can't help you. Obviously someone is going to have to make a decision if you want to pursue the matter from here." . . . This is where the arbitration comes in, which is a much better way to go rather than one forcing the other into the court, with the expense, the time off work, the nastiness that can be involved. . . . But some people are vindictive. They figure they'll get the other person better if they take them to court, and they just don't want any part of the informal hearings to try to get something solved. They figure that they're right and they're going to get the other person, come hell or high water! And that's fine too, if that's what they want to do. There's really nothing we can do about that. They certainly have been offered the alternative [complaints agency].

There is also the perception at the agency that persistent complainants get better treatment, regardless of the validity of these claims.

If a consumer is complaining more, the business will often do something just to get the person off their back. . . . There are a lot of consumer complaints that are not really valid, and they fail to realize that when they make a purchase they've entered into a legal contract with the vendor. But when you get the sort of return policies that the big retail giants have, the consumer is so spoiled that they now feel that it is their right and it's not the courtesy of the store. And we tell people that when they purchase something they have to find out the policy of the store regarding those sorts of things. . . . The consumers think that the business can afford it, the business can afford to write it off. And businesses are trying to make ends meet too, and they can't afford to write things off. And people abuse the privileges of the large organizations with refunds and exchanges, and they don't realize that they are paying for it in the end. These big companies have to make money too. So they just jack up the prices next year to make ends meet. But you can't tell some people that. And there's always that hope that they'll get something for nothing. But the truth of it is that there just aren't freebees in this world. You get exactly what you pay for, and a lot of people get into trouble because of that and they'll go with a cheaper item or someone whose workmanship is not up to par at a lower price, people not looking after their problems the way they could. . . . But it's funny. They get themselves into these jams, and then they want you to get them out of them: "You better do something about that guy. He rooked me!" But a lot of times it's because they didn't do their homework first that they got into that trouble [complaints agency].

As might be imagined, these agencies also represent levers that dissatisfied consumers may attempt to use in dealing with vendors.

We'll get people threatening to go to us if they're unhappy with the business. . . . And when they do that, some of our members will tell them that they would prefer that they did that, that they are members of the organization, that they support it, and that we may be able to help in this case. And that's what we're here for, to help iron out these differences, possibly help the business keep a customer [complaints agency].

Generally speaking, mail-order services, auto repairs, and home repairs tend to dominate the agency's complaint files.[12] As the following extract suggests, however, many complaints tend to have seasonal qualities.

In the fall and the winter you get insulation complaints more. In the summer you get more about the siding, the roofing, waterproofing, house repair industries. . . . Then some other things won't be a problem until the spring of the next year. Some things take more time to surface, and sometimes you'll get people calling, afraid that their year's guarantee is just about up. Waterproofing is another thing. Often you won't hear about it until there's been a terrible rainstorm, and if there hasn't been that type of weather, it won't show up. And all of a sudden, you'll have people after a bad storm with a lot of water in their basement, yelling blue murder! . . . It can really be difficult sometimes, to sort out where the blame should be, especially if the business has subcontracted part of the job out to someone else [complaints agency].

Consistent with the experiences of those in other businesses, people working with agencies of this sort find that managers have greater definitional power than staff when dealing with complainers.

It's unfortunate, but it does happen. Sometimes if a person is talking to the manager, they'll be more cooperative than if they think they're just talking to staff. It's a bit ridiculous because sometimes the staff can handle it more competently than I can because they're more familiar with the situation. . . . Or someone will phone and want to speak to the manager and the girls will put the call through to here, and I'll end up going to the girls to find out what they want to know anyways. . . . But people are funny. They often think that the person at the top knows all, that you've got all this information at the top of your fingertips, and it just isn't the case [complaints agency].

Files are generally kept on businesses rather than on complainants. Even here, however, "regulars" tend to emerge.

We don't keep a file on the complainers, because the complaint is filed by the business involved, but you do get to know after a while the chronic complainers who complain about everything they can think of. And after a while, you more or less just try to calm them down, but you can often tell that it's not a legitimate complaint. . . . Certain segments of the population are more likely to complain. . . . [Robert Prus: I imagine that university people are among your more frequent sources of complainants. I don't know.] . . . What is there to say? I didn't want to be heard on tape. I was almost going to, and then I thought, "No, I'm not going to say that." But that is very true! They're the number one! They're the most difficult to reason with. I swear that they have absolutely no business sense! Their academic minds do not see beyond. And they're the tops [complaints agency]!

Finally, even these agencies receive complaints about their operations.

A lot of people complain about us, that we're useless, that we really didn't do what they hoped we would. We didn't solve their problems, we didn't protect them when they inquired. It's because they don't know what we are. They don't realize that because we give them a report, it's not a guarantee of satisfaction. It's not a recommendation or an endorsement. It's factual information, and beyond that they're on their own. . . . We offer to try to solve disputes, if we can. But we can't take a gun to the guy. . . . They have the alternative of taking it to small claims court or getting legal help. We're only here to help. We can't guarantee anything [complaints agency].

Shoplifting

Shoplifting represents another form of trouble vendors encounter. Those selling smaller items in high traffic and "rougher" areas are apt to be victimized more often than other vendors. But regardless of incidence, it is difficult to assess accurately losses due to shoplifting. Some "inventory shrinkage" may be attributed to shoplifters, but other losses may reflect short shipments, damaged goods, nonsalvageable returns, price markdowns, and employee theft.[13]

I don't know what our losses are, or how much is due to theft. A lot of times you really don't know where the merchandise has gone. You can't keep track of everything, and then you're not the only one ringing up your sales, so you can't keep track of things all that closely [children's clothing].

I was talking with the manager about that [theft] the other day, and he was saying that he figured that we were losing more from theft by the staff than by the customers. And when I think about it, I have to agree. And you can do a lot of markdowns of "damaged goods" [for employees to purchase at discounts], things like that [discount department store].

Despite its uncertain nature, businesses may compute losses due to theft (and other unexplained shortages) into their budgets (and markups).

We budget for a 7% loss in dollar value. It varies by store, but overall, you are going to lose about that amount, and there is nothing you can do. If you add more staff or a better security system, it'll probably cost you more than what you're losing in theft [mixed clothing].

Since much shoplifting goes undetected, empty hangers and packages, open shelf spaces and such are often taken as theft. Some vendors report frequent encounters with thieves. Others report few actual first-hand encounters with shoplifters. Additionally, while the thieves are apt to be upset at discovery, salespeople may also become somewhat distraught over these incidents.

It is embarrassing to catch someone stealing because you don't really know what to do in that situation. It happens, and yet it is something you don't really expect. Like this one time I caught this girl stealing a necklace. She was only about 16 and I felt sorry for her; I ended up letting her go, but I suppose I should have called security. But she seemed very upset and embarrassed and it is just a difficult situation to deal with [jewelry].

It still shocks me to see someone stealing, like I just wonder how they get the nerve to do it. ... They'll take everything, big things and little things. Often you'll notice that they've taken the item out of the package, and then it gets more difficult to prove that the item is really from the store. Like you'll come across these empty packages [department store].

Even when security people are employed, the apprehension of persons suspected of theft by salespeople remains problematic.

Sometimes you'll see people holding something and then a couple of minutes later you'll see it's not in their hands and it's not back on the shelf, so you know it has disappeared. ... In those situations, we just call security and tell them who it is that you're suspicious of, or saw them do something, and they'll follow the person, check them out a little. ... But it's frustrating, because you have to call the central office and they relay your message to security and by the time they arrive the person is often gone. ... Also, a lot of times I didn't actually witness a theft, I just noticed that the merchandise disappeared, so I can just tell security that I suspect that person and security can follow that person to make sure that they don't take anything else [department store].

In a department store, it's more of a problem with people walking around with merchandise, saying they'll pay for it later in another department. You lose track of who has what. If they seem suspicious to you, you can call security, but you can't do that every time someone walks away with an item into another department [department store].

Some stores (including some with very liberal return policies) have strict policies of prosecution, but others prosecute inconsistently. Many seem more concerned about reclaiming their goods than prosecuting offenders.[14]

Tagswitching

Although a generally less risky form of deception, "tag switching" (the practice of moving tags from lower-priced items to the more costly items people plan to purchase) denotes another form of trouble vendors encounter.

We do get some tag switching, and some of it gets by. If you come across an item that has the wrong ticket on it, you would suspect that something has been switched. . . . But there are so many different prices, and things are always coming in and going up, to where it's hard to keep full track of your prices. You know the prices on most things, but it can get by you and the staff, even more with them, because they're less familiar with the prices. . . . Sometimes if someone brings something back without the bill, we may not know what the price on the item was if we don't have anymore in stock at the time. Like we'll have baby dresses from 9.99 to 34.99 and you know where the different lines are, more or less, but for sure you don't know. And then as things come in, they're usually a little more than what they were last time [children's clothing].

Given these practices, vendors may take a variety of precautions such as using "fail safe" stickers and tickets and/or providing employees with incentives to minimize tag switching.

We try to use tickets that are designed to stop switching. They will tear off [in small pieces] before they can be transferred [discount department store].

In working cash, you have to watch for switched tickets. And that can get embarrassing too. . . . But then they have a whole reward system for that and at the end of the month they have a little gift certificate for the winner of the switched-ticket award [discount department store].

Financing Problems

Some other trouble has its roots in the financial arrangements the traders make. While vendors may experience occasional counterfeiting, a great many problems emerge as a result of accepting "negotiables" other than cash. However beneficial these "trust arrangements" are for business, they also introduce other risks for the vendors involved. Thus, in addition to attempts to assess people's purchasing power, attention is given to concerns with checks, credit cards, charge accounts, collection agencies, and consumers in heavy debt.

ASSESSING PURCHASING POTENTIAL

One way in which vendors may attempt to reduce the risks is by qualifying prospects prior to approving purchases.

> With financing, you want to know if they have any outstanding debts, especially against the car they're trading in on the new one. . . . You do have to watch it because some people are so far into debt that you can't sell them the car. You would have to go out and repossess it, first thing. . . . I've had some who were so far in debt that I've simply told them that I couldn't sell them anything, let alone this [top line] they're wanting. But you know that somewhere along the line, they'll find someone who wants to make a sale and doesn't want to check up on them or doesn't do a very good job of it. . . . Most people finance their cars. Most don't have the money to buy the car outright [auto].

Prepurchase qualification can reduce risks, but vendor desires for sales may generate a willingness to involve poorer risks.[15]

CHECKS

Most of the bad checks that vendors report involve "naive" as opposed to "professional" bad check writers.[16] Typically, vendors accepting checks require multiple pieces of identification. However, the ways in which "NSF" (nonsufficient funds) checks are handled varies considerably with the operating policies of the stores involved. Some vendors will immediately inform the police of the potential fraud, but

many commonly attempt to contact the purchasers themselves to arrange for repayment. Collection may be less assured when informal
routes are pursued, but these approaches are less likely to distance
customers from the businesses involved.

> We get many NSF checks. We get a lot! Out store is very lenient. Usually we'll
> call them through security. Let them know that we've had this check that's bounced
> and ask them to come down and take care of it. Try to work out a time that is good
> for them. Usually they come in then, but you do get some that still don't make it
> in. And with them, we usually give them a second chance before we turn it over to
> our company's credit bureau. . . . We also have a policy about not refunding money
> for goods paid by check for 14 days. You'd think that that would be enough, but
> we've had refunds like that where the check didn't clear in that time, so we've
> gotten stuck that way a few times [discount department store].

Merchants may attempt to reduce NSFs by maintaining "bad risk"
lists, using centralized credit files, sharing information regarding bad
risks with other vendors, and policies such as accepting checks only
from people registered with the business.

> You can call _____ . It's computerized. They can check their files to see if
> anyone matching the driver's license or the other ID you're using has been a credit
> problem. That helps to cut down on NSFs [shoes].

CREDIT CARDS

In discussing credit cards, it is important to distinguish vendor credit
cards from those of credit card companies. Vendor credit cards are
accepted by particular businesses only (and possibly affiliates), but
those promoted by credit card companies may be honored by any
merchant establishing an account with that credit card company. In
these latter cases, the vendor agrees to pay a percentage (e.g., 2-5% of
card sales, decreasing with volume) for the privilege of accepting cards
from that company.

Generally speaking, vendors accepting credit cards gain relative to
those who do not do so.[17] Not only are they more likely to make sales
when prospects have insufficient cash on hand, but purchases on credit
are often more extensive. In both respects, the percentage paid to the
credit card company is offset by the increase in sales. A further advantage in accepting cards from credit card companies is that of reducing
the risks (and inconvenience) normally associated with checks. So long

as vendors abide by the rules of the card company, they will receive payment for the purchases.

> We find that most of the people pay cash, but at most shows you will have a few who want to pay by card. In some cases, it's because they are short on cash and it's a sale you probably would have lost otherwise. . . . We also prefer cards over checks, it's a lot more convenient, and we've been stung on a few checks. We've found the cards very worthwhile to have, certainly worth the percentages you pay in sales [crafts].

> With our checks, we get the ID and all, but it's not an easy thing in a lot of the cases to chase everyone down. It gets quite costly. And if you have to get a collection agency to chase them down, there goes any profit you might have made on the merchandise. . . . So the charge cards are much better that way too, but even there you have to watch that the card isn't one on your list as having been terminated, stolen. You also want to check the expiry date, make sure that it's still valid, check the signature [luggage].

When vendors use their own credit cards, it represents an attempt to minimize the overhead associated with credit card companies. However, companies large enough to generate their own credit cards would likely get very favorable rates from the credit card companies (e.g., 2%). These vendors also assume the risks of collecting for credit card charges. When vendors use their own cards, the system becomes basically that of a direct credit account, the cards adding convenience and prestige to previous charge accounts.

CHARGE ACCOUNTS

In efforts to variously promote immediate sales, foster long-term purchasing relations, and/or earn interest on delayed payments,[18] vendors may allow buyers to make purchases on credit.[19] With vendor originated charge accounts, relationships become somewhat more complex as vendors simultaneously attempt to collect debts from patrons and promote future purchases from these very same people. Ideally, as Tyson (1966) suggests, company collectors would pursue three objectives: creating goodwill, generating subsequent business, and collecting payments due. Viewed in this manner, collection may become an integral component of one's marketing program. Operating with these concerns in mind, collectors commonly stress the value of good credit standings and attempt to sell debtors on the virtues of marketplace integrity. Collectors may threaten and intimidate as last resorts, but appeals to fair play, integrity,

and loyalty are more apt to promote continuity of the buyer-seller relationship than those threatening repossession, garnishment of wages, and
the like.

COLLECTION AGENCIES

When other means have failed, vendors wishing to pursue debtors
may contact collection agencies. These agencies either buy out contracts from vendors or charge fees on accounts collected.

> You don't want to go to a collection agency if you can possibly avoid it. The markup
> on appliances is such that you would lose money on the deal, never mind your
> profit. It's really a last-ditch thing for us [appliances].

> The collection agencies charge 50%, but that's still better than nothing. Now
> sometimes you find that the same person has done this a fair bit, and you may have
> to stand in line to collect on his outstanding expenses. . . . Also, you would like to
> put the skids on the person too. But by the time it is all settled, if you include my
> time and all as well, we will get very, very little from it [jewelry].

As Tyson (1966) and Rock (1973) note, collection agencies initially
attempt to pursue debts in a firm but generally polite manner. Should
payments not be forthcoming, they are apt to pursue accounts more
aggressively than would vendors (creditors) attempting to maintain
customer loyalty. With difficult debtors, collection may assume a "cat
and mouse game," with creditors using a variety of forms of harassment
and subterfuge in attempts to collect.[20]

CONSUMERS IN TROUBLE

Focusing on "consumers in trouble," Caplovitz (1974) lists loss of income, voluntary overextension (overspending), and creditor deception as
the three major reasons that consumers default in their debts. He also notes
that some debtors compound their situations by refusing to pay for
nonfunctioning or repossessed items. When other methods fail, creditors
may take debtors to court. While many debtors may make arrangements
to pay their debts prior to courtroom encounters, a great many cases that
actually go to court are uncontested. Thus over 90% of the debtors taken
to court in Caplovitz's study lost court decisions by failing to appear.
Creditors winning these settlements may use legally sanctioned collection
methods such as garnishment of salary and seizing the debtor's property.

Caplovitz's findings are largely substantiated by Siporin's (1967) analysis of "bankrupt debtors." Siporin adds a valuable time-process dimension in discussing the "careers of bankruptcies." He notes that loss of income and overextension of indebtedness are central to the process, but also indicates that a series of unexpected and accidental events may put even financially well-managed families into extensive debt.

When debts are seen as more consequential, personal bankruptcy becomes a more noteworthy option. Regardless of whether the bankruptcy petition is initiated by the debtor (usually) or creditors, a court-granted bankruptcy status results in a discharge of "dischargeable debts" on the condition that nonexempted goods be sold to pay creditors.[21] Nondischargeable debts would normally include such things as alimony, government taxes, mortgages, and liens. Exemptions of personal belongings are designed to ensure that bankrupt individuals are able to provide for themselves and their families. As Stanley and Girth (1971) indicate, however, any goods available for liquidation are most often purchased by the bankrupt individuals themselves (or by families and friends). Once a petition for bankruptcy is filed, the petitioner's income is exempt from creditors and, in the months it takes to process the case, the person may have earned (or be able to borrow) enough to purchase his own goods. Definitions of *dischargeable debts* and *exemptions* reflect local court rulings, and creditors may challenge court definitions of dischargeable debts. Evaluations of personal possessions will vary with the trustee handling the case, but typically little money is generated for the creditors in personal bankruptcy cases.

As an alternative to bankruptcy, arrangements may be made to allow debtors to pay creditors under court supervision. If creditors consent, the debtor may be allowed to pay off his debts over a longer period of time and/or pay a smaller percentage of his total debts to his creditors. Under this arrangement, a portion of the debtor's salary is taken for these payments, but other properties normally remain intact. Creditors would stand to benefit further from this arrangement than through straight bankruptcy hearings, but this plan requires the cooperation of all the parties involved.

In Perspective

In some ways, the customers may have become more choosey, more outspoken, but they're basically the same. We talk about consumers more now than we did years ago, and you see a lot more in the news, but things haven't really changed. Like years ago, people didn't just go and buy everything. They shopped around, they compared prices, tried out several stores sometimes, not so different from what they do now. And now, we do have more varieties offered to the customer, so they have become more choosey [stationery].

Troublesome customers are generally neglected in discussions of marketing and sales, but it is apparent that these "disruptive elements" are exceedingly important for understanding marketing as an ongoing social activity. While few people seem to anticipate this aspect of saleswork, it has important implications for vendors' day-to-day experiences and effectiveness. Dependent on the goodwill of the targets whose disruptions they are attempting to regulate, salespeople are concerned that actions taken to remedy these situations not offend prospective purchasers.[22] In a sense then, this material on disruptions provides yet a further indication of the extent to which diplomacy emerges as a significant feature in the sales setting.

A diplomatic role is not, however, an easy one to sustain on a consistent basis. Insofar as troublesome customers are seen to interfere with their effectiveness or threaten their personal integrity, salespeople tend to become indignant with those who violate their existing notions of order (i.e., their situational morality). A few of these expectations are explicitly defined (e.g., return policies, credit charges, dress codes, cash only), but other behaviors upsetting vendors represent "trust violations" (e.g., rudeness, carelessness, taking advantage of the store) in a more general sense. The resulting indignation and frustration becomes intensified when salespeople realize that they have little control over these "culprits." Not only are they unable to "restore justice," but their effectiveness vis-à-vis other prospects may be sharply disrupted by these "inconsiderates."

Since sales may be lost when salespeople allow their frustration to spill over onto the next customer, a calm disposition is generally beneficial in reference to troublesome customers as well. Salespeople are not always successful at this, but it denotes another aspect of the self-reflectivity that sales situations entail.

You can't let one customer affect how you approach the next one. That's something you learn over the years. You can't let a nasty or difficult person get to you where you start to take it out on the next person, that's bad for business [commercial— office supplies].

You have to be patient, much more than I ever thought you would have to be. They're rude, ignorant, just not aware of what's going on, messy, sloppy! . . . You have to have patience, and no matter how they're treating you, you have to be patient [men's clothing].

Prus (1983a) delineates four major ways by which people attempt to manage trouble. These involve "doing nothing," altering their own behavior, realigning the "offender's" behavior, and soliciting third-party assistance. As is evident from the preceding discussion, vendors frequently do nothing. They sometimes attempt to realign the target's behavior but typically do so in ways that represent "softer" versions of actions than those they privately desire. Vendors will sometimes call in the police (more likely in cases involving theft) or take troublesome customers to court, but these options are generally implemented as Emerson's (1981) "last resorts." Perhaps more noteworthy than attempts to involve third parties are alterations of the vendors' own situations through "preventative strategies." These practices need not be directed toward any particular person, but we find vendors adjusting their marketing practices and habits in attempts to reduce customer involvements in troublesome situations. While vendors may save money in the process, they may also avoid situations that may be embarrassing to any shoppers designated as offenders.

Although not denoting a unique situation, the sales setting draws our attention to the roles that discretion and diplomacy may play in the management of trouble. Since vendors rely on people who typically have other options for both their immediate commitments and their long-term affiliations, we find vendors exercising extensive discretion in their attempts to minimize disruptive exchanges. The vendor-buyer situation is somewhat parallel to that of union organizers and their prospects (Karsh et al., 1953), doctors and patients (Roth, 1962), teachers and students (Hargreaves et al., 1975; Martin, 1975; Stebbins, 1975), clergymen and their parishioners (Prus, 1976), and parole officers and their clients (Prus and Stratton, 1976; Spencer, 1983), but the openness of buyer-seller encounters makes these much more akin to relationships involving neighbors, friends, and dating couples wherein one party may be more desirous of continuing the relationship than the other. More fundamentally, it raises the question of how disruptions are handled when the regulators are dependent on the continued goodwill of the disruptors.

Troublesome customers, we don't have enough time to cover all that. There are a lot of nice people, but a lot of difficult people too. . . . Part of the problem is that people generally think that car dealers are a bunch of crooks. I don't think you can be and stay with this business for any length of time, but that's an image a lot of people still have. The customers walk in the door thinking they are going to get screwed. . . . In part, you have to watch you don't get sarcastic back with them or let their skepticism wear you away. . . . But being on the defensive, they're more aggressive when they come into the shop and if you're not careful in how you handle this, you can easily lose a sale. . . . If you get a few of these, one after the other, it's easy to get a little upset with them when they take that attitude. And then, you maybe win an argument with them, but you've lost a sale [auto].

Notes

1. Additionally, beyond immediate attempts to cope with disruptions, repeated instances of particular forms of trouble may result in new operating practices, some of which would be aptly described as approximating "last resorts" (Emerson, 1981).

2. Emerson and Messinger (1977) and Prus (1978) both provide generic statements on reactions to trouble in interpersonal settings. For other instances of informal control, see Roth's (1962) discussion of doctors treating tuberculosis patients; Hargreaves et al.'s (1975) portrayal of "deviance in the classroom"; Prus and Irini's (1988) depiction of the management of trouble by hookers, strippers, bar staff, and desk clerks; Emerson et al.'s (1983), Miller's (1983), and Warren's (1983) statements on the micropolitics of trouble in psychiatric settings. It should also be noted that much deviance is handled informally in formal control settings; see Bittner (967), Black and Reiss (1970), and Rubinstein (1973).

3. Readers are referred to Goffman (1956) for a most interesting statement on the nature of deference and demeanor.

4. As Durkheim (1950) postulated, deviance seems inevitable. Those customers who are the "least perfect" tend to be thought of as troublesome, regardless of the overall norms in effect at the time.

5. From this perspective, no act is inherently deviant or normal. *Deviance* and *normality* are definitions attributed to targets by audiences. See Becker (1963) and Prus (1983a).

6. As readers realize, vendors may impose time limits on "satisfaction guaranteed" policies. After specified times, or "reasonable" notions of time and wear, customers may find themselves subject to other policies.

7. For two other accounts of complaint management in retail settings, readers are referred to Greenberg (1980) and Karikas and Rosenwasser (1980).

8. Since complaints represent "accounts" of situations, Lyman and Scott's (1970) discussion of the contingencies affecting credibility is quite relevant here.

9. Similar tendencies are noted by Karikas and Rosenwasser (1980) in their study of department store complaint management. People recognized as "regulars" (personally or through store credit card usage) tend to be treated better overall.

10. As Karikas and Rosenwasser (1980) note, businesses also appear to benefit little from most complaints. Staff people typically try to avoid and otherwise discourage this sort of feedback. Managers seldom keep systematic records on whether complaints pertain to products, suppliers, services, or "chronic complainers."

11. Eaton (1980) provides a valuable statement on the history, functions, interests, and operations of the Better Business Bureau by examining the operations of a particular bureau. Extensive similarity will be noted to the agency discussed herein.

12. These frequencies should be tempered by the relative frequency of consumer contact with vendors, the costs and complexity of the product involved, and so on.

13. While concerned about shoplifting, it is apparent that employees (especially managers), as occupants of positions of trust, have more opportunities to steal than do their customers. Employees are also less likely to be prosecuted when caught. Cressey (1953), Horning (1970), and Prus and Irini (1988) discuss contingencies affecting employee theft, while Zweigman (1977) considers responses to employee theft by those in retail settings. Henry (1978) provides a valuable ethnographic account of the pilfering and "fiddling" of goods and services by employees in a wide variety of occupational contexts.

14. Cameron (1964) provides a valuable statement on vendor responses to consumer theft.

15. As Rock (1973: 47) notes, the pressure of competition forces many creditors to accept many marginal candidates (i.e., the acceptance of poor candidates may be a requisite for survival for some businesses). Also see Caplovitz's (1973) discussion of the merchants of Harlem, and Greenberg's (1980) portrayal of a ghetto business.

16. This distinction comes from Lemert (1972: 99-134). Naive check forgers usually provide sufficient personal identification on which they can be traced. It seems that these people eventually intend to pay for their purchases but find themselves temporarily short of funds. Professionals assume false identities and plan to not pay. See Kline and Montague's (1977) depiction of professional "paperhangers." As with card and dice hustlers (Prus and Sharper, 1977), the more successful check forgers generally operate in "kiting rings" (groups).

17. It should also be appreciated that absolute advantages diminish as the acceptance of credit cards becomes more widespread among vendors.

18. Carrying charges may approximate bank rates, but as Caplovitz (1963, 1974), and Greenberg (1980) indicate, these are sometimes much greater (resulting in greatly extended and increased debt).

19. Another marketing option, especially with large purchases, is to urge purchasers to obtain financing through banks and finance companies. This is typically arranged through standardized contracts the vendor has with the financier. In the process, vendors may receive commissions for their services, reduce direct credit risks, and avoid animosities that may arise in difficult collections.

20. Caplovitz (1963, 1973, 1974), Tyson (1966), Rock (1973), and Greenberg (1980) offer depictions of collection strategies. Rock provides a particularly insightful sociological statement on the activities of collection agents.

21. Readers are referred to Stanley and Girth (1971) for a more complete discussion of personal bankruptcy cases.

22. Hotel security guards express similar concerns in reference to their guests. Thus attempts are made to deal with trouble in this setting as expediently and politely as possible (Irini and Prus, 1982).

Chapter 7
DEVELOPING LOYALTY

There is good traffic in this mall and we do get a lot of new people coming in, but the regulars are so important to you. Some are much more regular than others, but the regulars keep you going. You need that! You build your business around them. The new people, you want to treat them well too, though, turn them into regulars if you can [men's clothing].

What is customer loyalty? What forms does it assume? How does loyalty differ from repeat patronage? How do vendors promote repeat patronage? What sorts of limitations do vendors encounter in their efforts to build customer loyalty?

While vendors are very concerned with acquiring new customers, a repeat clientele is vital to the well-being of most businesses. Thus the development and maintenance of repeat patronage is fundamental to a more complete notion of the recruitment process.[1] For if one considers recruitment as an ongoing process, then vendor concerns with maintaining repeat patronage (continuity) and deterring departure (disinvolvement) become central to the broader notions of buyer involvement.[2]

The terms *loyalty* and *repeat patronage* are often used interchangeably. However, they are not synonymous for analytical purposes. Loyalty represents only one dimension of repeat patronage. People may continue to do business with particular vendors on many bases (e.g., convenience, exclusives) other than as a consequence of "preference." In this respect, all aspects of vendor marketing programs (including stock available, initial recruitment practices, presentations, modes of obtaining commitments, and so on) may affect repeat purchasing behavior. While much vendor activity is oriented toward first-time shoppers and immediate purchases, we ask what vendors do to promote continuity more generally and loyalty more specifically. Following a discussion of the relevance of repeat customers to vendors, attention is given to styles and basis of repeat patronage, vendor attempts to encourage repeat patronage, and vendor concerns with losing and revitalizing patronage.

Repeat Patronage

With the possible exceptions of high-traffic tourist areas, one-time only products, and scams,[3] repeat customers may be seen as the "backbone" of all businesses. However, the actual proportions of regulars (repeat customers) to first-timers will vary considerably by the areas in which businesses are located, the products involved, the length of time businesses have been in operation, the relative emphasis placed on obtaining new customers, and the concern vendors have in maintaining their existing clientele.

Repeat customers may be seen to benefit businesses in several respects. Existing patrons tend to make multiple purchases, broaden the base of their own purchases over time, and direct others to these vendors.

The regular clientele, you have to have that. And then if they get to liking you as a salesman, you can really ring up the bill with them! So it's good that way too [men's clothing].

The repeat clientele is extremely important to us. We have people who go back over 20 years and we have gotten a lot of business over the years of generations of families. There are some who wouldn't have anybody else but us decorate their homes for them. That is the kind of rapport you want to establish with your clientele, and that is something that we try to emphasize with our staff, the value of long-term service, so we want to handle people very considerately and as carefully as we can because our objective is not to sell as many items to as many people as we can, but rather to build up a clientele through extremely good and careful service. . . . We don't have a high traffic flow and we encourage the staff to treat everyone who comes in here very well, and regardless of whether it is a big purchaser or a small purchaser, to treat them as considerately as they can. And also, you don't know, but today's small customer might be someone who comes by another day to buy a fair bit from you. You want to build customers' loyalty. So someone making a $200 purchase may be more important to you in the long run than someone who comes in and makes a $6,000 purchase, because if that person who is making that big purchase really doesn't care where they are spending their money, they may not come back. Whereas if you treat the person well, then even if it is a small purchase they are making right now, they'll be thinking better of you when next they are in buying something else. But that is something that is difficult to get across to the staff and you want them to put that much commitment into their job and have that much in the store [furniture].

At another level, the very presence of customers in the store denotes another contribution of repeat customers. While the presence of any customer seems to define businesses as safer or more interesting places in which to shop, repeat customers are especially beneficial in this regard. Not only do they appear more often, they also tend to stay longer than do other prospects.

The regulars save the job from being so boring because you have someone that you know who will come in and talk to you about things that you're interested in. Often in that situation, you can also do things while you're working. They don't expect you to stop everything. But if you're standing there, everything ready to go, and no one there, sometimes that keeps people away. Because I've noticed when people come in, they come in droves. One comes, and then 50 come in for an ice cream cone. So to have these people come in, it's an advantage to the store [candy].

Beyond these more general benefits accruing to businesses, individual salespeople typically prefer a regular clientele. Not only is any stage fright salespeople experience likely to be diminished, salespeople also see repeat customers as people satisfied with their products and service, whose preferences are more predictable and with whom they can establish more personal relationships.

We've got people who will come in every week. We have some who will come in once a month and such, and I still think of them as regulars. But you do get some who will come in every Saturday and some of them will buy and buy! But the big thing is being friendly, where you treat them really nicely even if they're not buying. That way they feel much more relaxed when they come in the store. . . . And it's nice for you, it makes you feel good too to have these people come in to see you, even if they're not buying at the time. And they'll bring you coffees and things. Makes a nicer atmosphere for you. And regardless of whether they're going to buy or not, you know that when they come in, here's someone who is going to be friendly to you because you do get some who are not friendly. So it gives you a nice feeling. And also, when they come in you know that their chances of buying are better than 50-50, better than the other people coming to the shop. And you'll joke around with them, and you'll have a good time too [women's clothing].

We have a lot of one-time customers and tourists, but we also have a lot of repeat customers. The repeat customers are generally people who've been satisfied with you in the past, so they're generally more pleasant, easier to deal with. . . . You try to get to know them, be a little more personal. If we recognize someone, you try to make that known to them, make them feel a little more comfortable. It's nice for them to know that you remember them [luggage].

Clearly, salespeople have different levels of opportunities to recognize regulars. Salespeople who work in busier and/or self-serve stores, work fewer hours, and sell products with longer life spans are less likely to recognize repeat customers than are others. However, even in these settings, one finds some recognition of a regular clientele.

You'll have your regular customers, even your daily customers in a larger department store like this. Some come in and it takes them an hour to go around and talk to all the employees. So you do get to know some of the customers and become friends with some of them. But since you're not really selling to people, providing service like you do in the specialty shops, you spend a lot more of your time running around the department, filling shelves, taking inventory, straightening displays, tidying up after the shoppers, things like that, directing people to the aisles where the children's toys are, the washrooms, the household glue, things like that. And then, with all the people coming through here in a day, you really don't have the time to get to know many of them. And with the size of the staff we have here and all the different shifts and the people coming and going, switching departments and all, the customer doesn't have that much of an opportunity to get to know you either. But you do get some who'll spend the afternoon here, maybe end up just buying something small or having a coffee with their friends or someone that they know that they met here. . . . You'll also get to meet the people who work in the other shops around here. They're around more. They see you here and you see them there, so you get to know them after a bit. Also, some of the other people who work in the area, you just see them a lot more, get to know them that way [discount department store].

You'll get your repeats after a period of years, where if they [manufacturers] develop more in the way of new features, then some of the people will come back and get the updated models [appliances].

Loyalty to Whom?

The question of loyalty to whom? indicates some of the bases on which buyers may affiliate themselves with particular vendors. Although customers may be seen to develop loyalties to particular companies as well as individual salespeople, repeat patronage may also reflect default patronage, and staff purchases.

COMPANY LOYALTIES

Company loyalties may be defined by preferred patronage of particular marketing entities (e.g., certain stores, chains, franchises). Salespeople who have worked in a number of branches of the same store seem more sensitive to company-based loyalty, but it is also an advantage commonly touted by those promoting franchises.

We have a definite clientele, repeat customers. You get to know them. They're more like friends. This is something I have found to be true of this chain generally. I've worked in four different branches. In all, the regular customers are very important. . . . We emphasize giving the customers full attention, so we may get more regular customers than some other places. . . . My personal philosophy is very consistent with the store, to emphasize the advising part of sales rather than the pressure selling. Emphasizing customer satisfaction, keeping people happy, keeping them coming back. Then you find that they become friends and some of them you will socialize with on the outside [women's clothing].

You have the franchise working for you. The shared publicity, the name, the image, the familiarity. . . . You're not an unknown. People buy from you with more confidence, you're part of a bigger network of services and resources [franchisor—appliances].

PERSONAL REGULARS

In addition to, or in lieu of, company loyalties, salespeople may develop "their own followings." By no means so limited, these personal regulars are especially valuable to commission salespeople.

The only way a salesman can be successful is to have your own clientele. Regardless of whether it's clothes or cosmetics, car sales, whatever it is. You have to follow up on your people, keep track of them, cater to them [cosmetics].

Your regular clientele is one of the most valuable things the car salesman can have. Unfortunately, a lot of salesmen don't seem to realize that. Don't ask me why, but they will sell a car, and they see the person drive off and that's it! Instead of keeping in touch with those people. Because your repeat business is one of the most valuable things you can have in that car business. And you can take people with you if you want to go to another dealership. A lot of the customers will follow you. So it's a big mistake for a salesman not to follow up on the customers, and a lot of them don't. . . . The longer you're in the business, the better it gets. After five years, it really gets to be good! You'll get certain repeats in your first year, the one-year car buyers. Then you'll get the two-year car buyers, and three. And now, the average is closer to four years before most people trade in. . . . And some families are good for five or six cars over a period of time, they might buy a number of cars over a few years, so it's valuable in that way. You want to treat them properly [auto].

DEFAULT PATRONAGE

Not all patronage reflects desires to deal with particular vendors (companies or salespeople). Some repeat purchasing activity clearly assumes a default dimension. As Jarvis and Wilcox (1977) note, repeat patronage is not synonymous with "true vendor loyalty." Many purchasing activities reflect one or more of the following elements: convenience, lack of awareness of alternatives, inability to find alternatives, preexisting bonds (e.g., family, long standing friends), and unwillingness to disrupt existing routines. These notions are also evidenced in salespeople's own buying practices.

_____ , I don't like that [grocery] store. Some of the clerks are rude when you're getting some of the "sales" items or when you bring in coupons that they say they honor from other stores. . . . But I keep going back to that store and I really begrudge giving them my money, but it's so much closer to my home than any of the other stores that I keep shopping there [department store].

We deal with _____ and _____ , but only because they carry some lines we want and they're convenient. We don't feel any loyalty to them and if we can find what we want some place else, we'll probably switch. Right now we're looking around, see if we can find someone we like dealing with more [jewelry].

STAFF REGULARS

Featuring a wider range of end-user products, retail outlets often have yet another significant source of repeat patronage. Although often overlooked, consideration should also be given to staff who "shop at home." And while they tend to be more aware of the merchandise in their own stores, salespeople are also frequently given discounts (e.g., 5-30%) to encourage them to patronize their own workplace.[4] These discounts may or may not be valid on "sales" items (varying store policies) and may also vary with the particular products involved. Stores may make proportionately less on these purchases individually, but staff purchases do contribute to the overall well-being of the store. Not only may the staff serve as models for some merchandise (i.e., part of the display case), but if the store carries a wide selection of goods, a great deal of salespeople's salaries may be spent in that location. When staff are part timers and/or when a second income is available for family support, salespeople may spend amounts exceeding their salaries in the stores in which they work.[5]

By giving the employees the discount, they encourage a lot of shopping by their own employees. They don't lose anything on it that way, because it pretty well all comes back to them in some cases, like me [department store].

We got a 5% discount at [store A], 5% at [store B], and 15% at [store C]. And with the 5% discount at [A], they wouldn't even give you the 5% off at the time. They would wait until you had spent $100, and then you wouldn't even get the $5 in cash but in a gift certificate! . . . You get people spending more money than what they're making at the store if someone else was working in the family. Oh yeah! . . . And they'll buy all sorts of things during the week while they're working there, like out on their lunch or after work. You'll have some who will get off at six and spend an hour shopping, so it's usually seven before they're leaving for home. And you can stock up on "specials" and all that way too [discount department store].

Developing and Maintaining Customer Loyalty

Having considered some variations in styles of patronage noted by vendors, attention now turns to the ways in which vendors attempt to cultivate long-term relationships with customers.[6] Many elements fostering initial purchasing contact (e.g., products, media promotions, displays, and so on) may remain relevant to continuity, but once buyers have done business with particular vendors, other considerations may become more central in accounting for buyer loyalty. The career contingency model (Chapter 1) suggests that the following five elements are central to people's continuity in situations: (1) acquiring perspectives compatible with particular involvements, (2) developing identities consistent with particular involvements, (3) attaining competence in the activities particular involvements entail, (4) making commitments to particular involvements, and (5) participating in relationships supportive of those involvements.

Mindful of the ensuing discussion, some further qualifications pertaining to retail versus other levels of trade may be in order. Hence, while a great many parallels exist, some relative overall differences may be noted. Potentially significant here are the proportionate numbers of clientele individual businesses are likely to have and the proportionate dollar value of exchanges that individual customers contribute to a business's overall base of trade. In general terms, this means that vendors in other areas of trade (versus retail) should be better able to identify and track their customers than can retailers (higher customer volumes). Likewise, vendors in other areas of trade tend to attribute greater importance to keeping the "average customer," since the average customer controls a greater proportion of the incoming business).[7]

PROMOTING PERSPECTIVES

Perspectives represent frameworks within which people's experiences are interpreted and thus suggest guidelines for action. But they also have important implications for people's continuity in situations. One element important to people's continuity in particular settings is the development of perspectives compatible with those of the other participants in the setting.[8] Once accepted, these interpretative frames provide participants with an orientational affinity with the other participants, a shared worldview setting them apart from others. As Simmons (1969) advises, care should be taken not to overly homogenize perspectives among participants in groups. Nevertheless, shared symbolic systems represent consequential dimensions not only to internal-external notions of community, but also for the ways in which people subsequently develop and pursue lines of action.

While vendors make some attempts to promote perspectives conducive to sustained customer involvements, vendors' "perspective work" seems more limited, more diffuse, and more situated than that we commonly associate with religious or political conversion (see Hoffer, 1951; Lofland and Stark, 1965; Klapp, 1969; Prus, 1976). Even when vendors promote particular types of life-styles (e.g., disco, western, liberated, wholesome), they do so more to gain access to prospects than to promote long-term involvements in any particular style. Each life-style seems to be (relatively) willingly discarded by vendors as they envision their prospects seeking out new sources of meaning. Vendors are much more reactively ("Are neon hula hoops in? We'll use those to sell _____ .") than ideologically oriented in their dealings with customers. They are much more concerned with providing the paraphernalia for change than with trying to change people's beliefs. This is not to imply that vendors themselves do not have their own operating philosophies. Beyond realizing that they need to make money to exist as vendors, one finds a wide range of styles by which vendors may elect to operate. Consider, for example, long-term versus short-run profit orientations, stocking "hot items" versus staples, specialization versus diversification, full service versus self-serve, centralized versus chain operations. Where these "philosophies" are made public, customers can act toward vendors on these bases.[9]

In a more general sense, vendors may be seen to invoke a sense of perspective by the images they project. Like others involved in recruiting targets, vendors may try to build on existing prospect interests in a wide variety of ways. For example, one finds involvement appeals highlighting anticipated prospect concerns with success, safety, financial solvency, entertainment, respect, and so forth. By emphasizing their relevance, uniqueness, quality, popularity, and such, vendors may be able to generate some company or product mystique. In this way, they may promote loyalty beyond that associated with the purchase of the physical objects involved in the exchange. These images also help distinguish vendors from their competitors. Vendors are ultimately dependent on their prospects for confirmation of any images they may wish to promote, but it is in this realm that one finds the clearest instances of buyer directed perspectives.

Some vendors have developed promotions and programs catering to company images (e.g., "the _____ look," "a _____ girl"). Others may approximate perspectives in their slogans and advertising themes. In these ways, they endeavor to project an aura around themselves and their products.

> That's why your name or your label is so valuable. It's what people associate with it. A certain quality, style, a price-range. . . . If you're buying somebody out, that's something you definitely want to consider, what the label is worth to you. If it's a name that people have a lot of respect for, it could be worth as much as the buildings and the stock and all over the years. You have a more marketable commodity [manufacture—clothing].

These images need not be extensive or well articulated to be effective. To the extent that buyers attend to these images and define them in positive terms, vendors may foster continuity via perspectives. Vendors sometimes explicitly use the media to promote these long-term messages, but most media presentations tend to either be focused on new prospects or reflect more diffuse, general appeals.

Vendors may also promote viewpoints or operating philosophies consistent with purchases of their products in presentations or in their attempts to quell buyer resistances. Thus they may emphasize their warranties, service, name brands carried, and the like. However, these themes are seldom explicitly directed to achieving loyalty, but to promote or confirm the purchases at hand. Thus, to the extent any life-style conversion occurs, it primarily reflects buyer assessments of the company, its personnel, and its products through media promotions, displays, presentations, pricing, service, and favorable experiences more generally. And while new prospects may be bombarded with justifications for purchases, repeat customers are generally assumed to have accepted the wisdom of buying from this particular company. In all, loyalty themes (via perspectives) are much less in evidence than might be expected, given the relative importance vendors attribute to a repeat clientele.

FOSTERING IDENTIFICATION

Referring to the extent to which people define themselves as participants in particular settings and have others identify them in these manners, identification represents another important base of buyer loyalty. Interestingly, vendors exhibit relatively little concern about identifying buyers as users of their products. Much like the promotion of perspectives, many instances of "identity work" on the part of vendors tend to be vague and diffuse rather than explicit and focused in nature.

Nevertheless, many businesses have found ways to generate vendor identification. Most commonly, this involves vendors putting their names prominently on products (or related packaging) sold to customers.

When we sell a suit or jacket, a coat, we make sure we give them one of our hangers. We want that to hit them each time they wear something from that hanger. Help keep us in mind, just hanging around [laughs]. It's a good quality hanger, and they appreciate it, usually. A lot of places are too cheap to do that [men's clothing].

Identification is sometimes explicitly pursued by giving customers specialty advertising items that display the vendor's name (and other messages).

I like things that people will use that have the company's name on it. It's sort of, "Hey, remember us? We've treated you well. We gave you this ruler, mug, hat, whatever." And when they go places with these things, or people visit them, other people notice that too, "You must deal with so and so." So you get it both ways [promotions—agency].

Some other identity work is more inadvertent, for everything that customers associate with particular vendors may serve to generate customer identification with the businesses involved. Thus each advertisement, piece of letterhead, vendor identifiable receipt, vendor charge card, and so forth may contribute to customer identification with particular businesses.

FACILITATING ACTIVITIES

A third theme affecting continuity in situations is people's participation in the focal activities in those settings (i.e., that those activities be found acceptable, manageable, worthwhile, enjoyable, and so on by the participants). And since most business exchanges revolve around (images of) product applications, the activity dimension becomes an especially central theme affecting continuity in buyer-vendor relations.[10]

There are three major ways in which vendors may facilitate prospects' activities. First, they may make it easier for their customers to buy their products (e.g., selection, financing). Second, they may make it easier for buyers to use their products (simplified operations, easy care, convenient repairs). And third, since people seldom buy products for the product's sake, vendors may show how their products can support the activities and ensuing outcomes buyers desire (e.g., make better cakes, save money, achieve greater efficiency). Although vendors seldom delineate these three aspects of purchases, they often describe service in ways that reflect these concerns.

Vendors discussing service may mean anything from prompt attention, accurate order taking, careful deliveries, friendliness, more complete presentations, sharing product knowledge, facilitating decisions, and arranging financing, to accepting returns or providing assistance quite unrelated to purchases. Generally referencing "good service" when asked about their methods for developing and maintaining customer loyalty, vendors typically assume that all such efforts will generate long-term benefits.

Service is a really key concern with us, and the way that I look at it is if you are providing a service today, you are actually investing in the future. And some days, you might spend 80% of your time providing that service, essentially investing in that future. Some businesses just don't see it that way, and what they want is the immediate sale today and they lose out on the long-term customers. And that is one of the reasons I have salary plus commission, because I realize that I am requiring my staff to invest in the future as well as any commission they might make from particular sales. It is also an investment for them in the future because if they stay around me for five years, they are going to get their regulars and they will be making money on the service that they are providing today [furniture].

I stand behind things. I try to deal in my store with my customers the same way I do in my life. Do unto others as you would have them do unto you, and if I'm buying something, whether it's a piece of luggage or a bag of potatoes from [store], if I get home and find that half the potatoes are rotten, then I just feel that they're going to want to know that. And I'm going to take them back and he's going to say, "Here's a new bag of potatoes. We don't want you to have those." Or if somebody buys a chain from me and they get home and it breaks, or they buy a diamond ring and the diamond falls out a week later or a month later, I want them to know and feel confident that when they come in and hand that to me, I'm not going to say, "Well, that's the breaks." I'm going to say, "Oh my goodness, I feel really bad that that happened. That shouldn't have happened because our quality is better than that. You leave it with me and I'll make it right for you." . . . Satisfaction is guaranteed. Now in so many places they'll have signs up: you buy it, it's yours. No refunds, no exchanges, no nothing. They don't want to look at you. All they want is the money in the till, and when that's in there, they don't care what you do from there, just don't come back. I don't feel that way. I want that person to come back into my store [jewelry].

As the following extracts suggest, however, additional service may reflect "recognized regular status" as opposed to attempts to develop new regular customers.

Now say you bought your car from another dealership, maybe because of price. If you bring your car here, you won't get treated very well. You'll get poorer service, and little things that our customers wouldn't get charged for, you will charge the person who bought his car elsewhere for that. But that's true for all the dealerships, because our customers have had problems with other dealerships when they've had to go there for repairs. You could get charged for everything that might be covered under warranty claims. . . . You don't treat the other people as good as your own customers [auto].

Compared to families, businesses are more limited in budgets, concepts, ideas of what they can or can't do. But there is a lot more money in turnover in factories, especially with bigger factories. . . . Once you're in there, it's really nice, as long as you're giving them good service and products. And with them, they'll do this wing this year and this other part the next year, so it's good that way. Lots of good-sized jobs. . . . But with them, whenever they call you, you pack your bag and away you go. Drop whatever else you're doing and go! Give them good service [manufacture—industrial].

OBTAINING ONGOING INVESTMENTS

Investments refer to the sorts of commitments people make in conjunction with particular lines of action. Especially noteworthy in shaping future action are investments that are more extensive and less retrievable.

While many purchases are isolated events, some vendors attempt to generate repeat patronage by creating situations that involve ongoing commitments on the part of buyers. Thus, by offering follow-up service, implementing long-term billing systems, and selling goods entailing more exclusive components,[11] vendors may build a regular clientele by creating ongoing buyer dependencies.[12]

It's like these video games. The cartridges are not interchangeable across systems, at least the major originals. There are some copies of systems that are compatible. Basically though, if you want this game, you have to have this system because _____'s and _____'s systems are not compatible with these cartridges [department store].

These collections [sets] are good that way. Hopefully, people will get one as a gift or because they like it. Then it's "Have you thought of starting a collection?" "No, I haven't." "Well, it would add a lot of value to your purchases. It would make it more of a collector's item." A number of the manufacturers have come out with that, figurines, plates, things of that nature. . . . Really, it's like collecting bubblegum cards. Good that way [giftware].

Likewise, vendors may attempt to build commitments by offering incentives for repeat patronage.

> Trading stamps have their ups and down in use, but they're good because they keep people coming back. Anything like that though, sets of glasses, towels, games, all these things can help build traffic [groceries].

> We have a preferred customer card and the way that it works is that after they buy so many items of a certain type, the next one they can get free. That way you tend to draw them into the store for the first several purchases and it is also a very good way of building customer loyalty [women's clothing].

BUILDING RELATIONSHIPS

The fifth element affecting people's continuity in situations reflects the relationships these people establish with others in those settings. Buyer-seller relationships are significantly affected by the other aspects of continuity (e.g., compatible perspectives, pertinent identities, activity competency, and commitments) previously discussed. Additionally, long-term relationships are sometimes explicitly pursued by vendors as they attempt to generate trust, indicate personal signification, provide entertainment, exercise diplomacy, and maintain contact with prospects.

Generating Trust

As indicated in our earlier discussion of trust, the perception that the vendor is acting in the best interest of the buyer has important implications for long-term buyer-seller relations as well as for people's immediate purchases. In conjunction with this, salespeople generally posit that trust is an important element in developing customer loyalty. Somewhat ironically, however, most of their trust-inducing activity is oriented toward specific purchases (e.g., attempts to portray product reliability, overcome skepticism at times of sales) rather than long-term involvements. Nevertheless, some carryover seems inevitable. Vendors who are seen to project a greater sense of vendor integrity, product performance, and concerns with minimizing customer risk in the short-term are apt to benefit over the long haul as well. Thus vendors foster long-term purchasing relationships in their attempts to match goods (and services) with customer interests (see also Bigus, 1972, and Kinsey, 1985).

The most successful way of having repeat customers is to have a successful campaign for them. And if it works, they're going to be back. . . . Also you treat them well. And you have to realize that his clients come first. So if you go in there and he's busy with a customer, you try to be aware of his situation, his problems. You have to be very sensitive to what his problems are. Treat him well. Do the best campaign you possibly can. . . . One of the most important things when you're selling anything is that you have to be honest. If you're not honest, it will backfire. Customers just will not be repeat customers if you're throwing them a line and it doesn't work. So rather than build someone's expectations: "You're going to get thousands of people into your store and all you have to do is buy two commercials!" You're going to kill yourself in the long run! Your reputation will be nothing. You've got to be legitimate. You've got to be honest, "Your budget cannot afford a big campaign at this time. What is your busiest time of the year? Let's put all that money into advertising at that particular time. This way, you might get a few people in, but not enough really to warrant the advertising money you're spending." If you're honest with them, and you've done your research properly so you know who you're targeting for and when to hit them, they will be repeat customers. And as they repeat and the business grows, then they've got a little more money because it's usually a percentage of sales that they're spending on advertising, you've got a little more money to work with, which means they have a little more money again. And the whole cycle keeps going [promotions—radio].

Indicating Personal Signification

In a manner somewhat akin to providing service, many vendors indicate that they encourage loyalty by taking more personalized interest in their customers.[13] Recollections of buyers' names represent a means of developing bonds within buyer-seller relationships. Likewise, salespeople may reference other bits of information pertaining to earlier encounters (e.g., specific purchases, product applications) thereby indicating that buyers are more consequential than the purchases they represent.

You try to remember the customer. Try to say, "Oh hi! Nice to see you again!" It's always nice to be recognized. If you can remember their name and say, "Hi Mary!" or "Hi Mrs. Jones!" I've had people's eyes just light up when they'll come in to pick up a repair and I'll say, "Oh hi Mr. Jones! I'll go get your watch for you." They're astounded! They'll say, "You remembered my name!" or "You knew what it was!" That really means a lot to a customer, and that's the type of loyalty that you build up and they think, "Gee, if I have something that's broken again or if I need a gift, I'm going to go see [me] at [store], because she knows me and I get personalized shopping when I go there." So that's one way of drumming it up and it's a very important way [jewelry].

In addition (or as an alternative) to recollections of names and/or other aspects of earlier encounters, vendors may also promote definitions of loyalty by taking greater interest in their prospects' situations and plans for the future.

> You give the best service that you know how. Make sure that all their garments are fitted well, that they are the way they are supposed to be. You try to get things that look good on them. And then you try to be as pleasant as you can be. Call them by their name, remember their size, remember what you sold them last time. Make them feel important! If you can make people feel important, they are going to come back. Everybody likes to feel important [men's clothing]!

Providing Entertainment

Although often overlooked, entertainment denotes another area of relationships worthy of attention. Thus some vendors anticipate that relationships will be strengthened when prospects find their purchasing activities more diversified and interesting. To this end, salespeople may feature ranges of interactional styles, subactivities, and displays to entertain their customers.

> We don't have any formal program for developing regulars. And there are more reliable companies out there these days. So you stress service. You go out of your way to help your customers. It's service with a capital S. . . . Now, we'll take people out to lunch and all. But you realize that it may have more effect on a smaller buyer. The purchasing agents in larger companies, they're always getting free lunches. So there, you may be better to concentrate on someone who doesn't get that sort of treatment that much. . . . The free lunch won't sell your products, but it will help keep the lines open. They're more likely to give you a chance [manufacture— industrial].

> With a contest, a draw, anything like that, it adds a little interest to your store. It makes shopping a little more fun. It's a game, a chance to win [hardware].

Exercising Diplomacy

Diplomacy is seldom specifically mentioned in reference to vendor attempts to develop loyal customers, but it is quite apparent from vendor discussions of troublesome customers that salespeople feel the ways in which disruptions are handled can have consequential effects for repeat patronage.[14]

Generally speaking, merchants endeavor to handle disruptions with tact, lest they offend prospective buyers or other witnesses. Thus, regardless of whether they are trying to discourage careless shopping, deal with returns or late payments, or "cool out" (Goffman, 1952) those with complaints, we find that vendors' treatment of these troublesome episodes is constrained by their concerns with both immediate sales and long-term relationships.

> Nobody likes returns, but we will take pretty well anything back if it comes down to it. You cut down on a lot of hassles that way. Some people will take advantage of you, but overall we encourage the staff to be as pleasant as possible to the customers. . . . Even with something like appliances, if you can't satisfy them you might end up taking it to the basement and sell it as "reconditioned." You will lose on some things, but we try to think long-term there [department store].

Maintaining Contact

This discussion has so far assumed encounters largely initiated by the patrons involved. Attention now shifts to the role vendors sometimes play in actively pursuing contact with existing patrons. Continued contacts not only buttress definitions (identities) of existing buyers as "one of ours," and of prospective customers as "someone we want to be one of ours," but also provide opportunities for expanded (or renewed) involvements. Regardless of purpose, vendor-initiated contacts usually assume media or more personal outreach (telephone/direct calls) formats.

Overall, vendors do not seem especially attentive to this dimension of media programs. However, since media promotions seem more likely to be noticed by existing customers (selective attention—increased sensitivity to logos, products, and so on) than new customers, these have the effect of sustaining contact with current and former customers.

When more explicit attempts are made to sustain contact through the media, this is often done by developing mailing lists.

> We do some mailings to our card customers, announcing specials not advertised in the other media. So that's a little extra for them [department store].

Albeit less common than mailings, the telephone may also be used to sustain contact with patrons.

> We would book the lessons one day after another, as much as possible. That way they were less likely to forget what they learned the day before. It was good for keeping their enthusiasm too. If for some reason they couldn't make it, you would call them up: "Did you do your homework?" There was that constant contact, you

would follow up on them, keep track of them, and keep them coming back [dance studio].

If you can build up your pool or regulars, and with them, you try to keep them happy. You service them, you call them up, even if it's just for a personal hello. You keep up with them, make them feel important. You get back to them: "Hi, John. Hope you liked your ad. I was very pleased with the way it came out!" And if it's a new customer, send them a few extra copies so that they can show it around, make them feel important that way [promotions—magazine].

The most effective but also the most costly method of sustaining contact is through direct personal follow-ups. As a result, this tends to be a relatively infrequent occurrence with all but the more costly and technical purchases.

After we've sold the appliances, we'll go out and make sure that everything is installed correctly. A lot of people are surprised to see us do that, but it's something they really seem to appreciate. So it's not just the selling of the item that we're involved in, but the extras, the follow-ups. . . . The department stores used to do a lot more of that, but they don't do that so much. They've pretty well lost that. It's fallen by the wayside. . . . The car people used to do more of that too. Maybe part of it is that the products, the appliances and the cars have gotten so sophisticated and commonplace that they figure the people don't need that anymore [appliances].

If you have someone who is your customer, it's good to visit and service them a lot. Make sure that they're not having any problems with the machines they've got from you. You use the in you have with the machine they have, to give them information about new machines [manufacture—office equipment].

Losing Customers

To me, customer loyalty comes, very simply, from getting the job done for the client. If you get the job done for the client, you're going to have client loyalty. If you are not getting the job done for the client, then you're not going to have a client, therefore, no loyalty. This has to do with the ongoing process of communicating with the client. It's one thing to communicate with the client to the point where he will use your media. It's another thing to communicate with the client so that the constant evolution that happens within his company or her company and the marketplace evolution, as it relates to that business, is constantly kept on the front burner in terms of attention, and gets reflected in the presentations made to the consuming public. Where that slips, then we can lose a client. We can lose a client for lots of reasons, but if it's our fault, that's where we've done it [promotions—TV].

Clearly, vendors do not want to lose customers. But just as vendors appear less concerned overall with developing a repeat clientele than with obtaining new customers, so do they seem less concerned about how customers are lost than how they are kept. This attitude partly reflects the generally conceded inability to "please all of the people" and the natural attrition resulting from changes in the situations of their patrons. More fundamentally, however, with the exception of noticeably disgruntled patrons, vendors often lack an awareness of customer activities.[15] Thus, while vendors realize that some (former) patrons will be lost to competing businesses, both abrupt and gradual shifts may escape timely notice.

I think we had a larger group of regulars before. Now, it seems that more of our customers are shopping for bargains. They're more likely to buy [elsewhere] on that basis [shoes].

Your customers are somewhat unpredictable. It's hard to keep track of them. Some of them you may see only every few months, less often maybe. It's the ones you see more often that you might miss, and you might only think of them when something new arrives that they might like. And they can go on holidays or something, and so if you don't see them for a while, a longer while, it doesn't mean you've lost them [mixed clothing].

REVITALIZING PATRONAGE

Although it may partially reflect their inability to determine when they have lost customers, vendors generally direct minimal attention toward the goal of reclaiming former customers. The major exceptions represent vital or larger accounts, more frequently of concern to non-retail traders. Former patrons may attend to media messages and may be called upon (although usually with decreasing frequency) by agents in the field. However, as long as promising prospects appear on the horizon, it is they who will likely be primary targets of marketing programs.

We mail to everyone on our list. We try to make our mailing attractive, so we try to come out with some new things; something to make it more exciting. So if someone's been dormant, hopefully, we can bring them back into it [hobby].

There, you have to make a decision. Do you want to go after the ones you may have lost or do you want to put that money into advertising that appeals more to everyone. Some companies will do both, but most, and we do the same, will go for a more general promotion. We try to beef up our image generally [men's clothing].

In Perspective

That's why it is important to get someone who's happy, because they'll tell their friends and they'll tell their friends and so on and so on. And that's the way it goes. It does. It means a lot! And it's nice for you too when they come back. Because you get to be, well not quite friends, because you still have to remember that you're still serving them, but you get more personal [department store].

Examining vendor concerns and practices affecting repeat patronage, this chapter summarizes a number of themes developed in greater detail throughout this monograph. While vendors generally seem much less concerned about cultivating loyalty than they are with most other aspects of marketing, it is abundantly clear that they recognize their dependency on repeat customers. Regular customers bring money into the business, but they also provide predictability, security, and enjoyment for those involved in sales.[16]

Vendors place much greater emphasis on preparing for customer contact (Prus, 1989) and generating sales (this volume) than on developing loyalty. Even troublesome customers (perhaps as a consequence of their impinging presence) receive more attention than do many regulars. To be sure, vendors generally express keen interest in "providing service," but this effort is much less well articulated in design (and in effect) than are most other marketing endeavors. Overall, those involved in other than retail trade evidence greater concern over maintaining the "average customer" than do those operating as retailers. In all realms of trade, however, the emphasis on loyalty work is very uneven and appears less extensively developed than one might expect.

In a broader sense, the inability of vendors to generate customer loyalty more extensively also very much reflects (1) the dependencies of vendors on their customers, (2) the problematics of internal coordination, and (3) the competitive context in which vendors find themselves.

From the vendors' perspective the role of the clientele is critical. It
is the customers who ultimately determine the viability of any particular
marketing practice and the eventual success any business venture experiences. And, as "minded beings," people lack the predictability of other
physical entities. This has central consequence for any quick fix solutions to loyalty. Not only are vendors dealing with continuously shifting
sets of clientele and "targets" at widely ranging points in their careers
(e.g., new prospects, former customers), they are also dealing with
targets who may assume strikingly different interpretations of the "same
situations," alter their interpretations dramatically over time, deliberately withhold information from vendors or otherwise mislead them,
and attend unevenly to the new and existing competitors vendors face
(e.g., as in comparison shopping). Further, vendors are dealing with
targets who are not only differentially (dis)trusting of vendors, but who
can also view vendors as targets for their pursuits (i.e., working vendors
for their best deals, possibly playing vendors off against another). In
short, vendors not only face multiple and shifting interpretations on the
part of their customers, they also operate within settings characterized
by potential doubt and insincerity.

Internal coordination denotes a second set of relationship work dilemmas that vendors encounter. All relationship work at an interpersonal level is complex, but front-line salespeople are in situations
of notably high dependency. Occasionally vendors will have products
so "hot" that buyers will tolerate very disquieting encounters in order
to obtain these goods. Typically, however, vendors are dependent on the
preferences of prospective buyers and their willingness to invest in
those vendors' products. Although vendor practices are more accurately
cast against those of other vendors rather than some ideal, it should be
noted that it is not easy to instruct people on relationship work. Likewise, it is not easy to pursue relationship work intensively over time.
Not all salespeople appreciate the value of repeat customers or their
own roles in pursuing long-term purchasing relationships. But even
those who explicitly take these positions tend to find it difficult to
maintain intensity in settings in which the results of their efforts are
distant and obscure at best, and that are characterized by widely shifting
assortments of prospective buyers (e.g., shopping styles, expressed
dispositions). Salespeople can be hired and retained on the basis of
interpersonal skills, and relationship work can be explicitly encouraged
by others and the salespeople themselves (as self-reflective entities),

but loyalty-inducing behavior is difficult to sustain even when this is a primary objective.

The role of competition should likewise not be overlooked in the production of loyalty. In addition to competitors' attempts to invoke buyer disenchantment with existing sources (and serve as their replacements), competitors tend to imitate one another. Imitation seems especially likely when attempts to invoke repeat patronage rely on more impersonal practices. Thus vendors may emphasize exclusive components, media promotions, and more extensively customer-oriented warranties, for instance. However, most quick-fix policies and practices are of limited value in that the more easily particular vendors can incorporate these into their routines, the more readily their competitors can do likewise. Thus one notes the commonplace "copies" (tradition and faddishness) of warranties, media promotions, games and contests, coupons, "sales," and the like. These practices may benefit initiators in the short-term and may result in some long-term customer gains. But as more competitors copy "good ideas," their relative usefulness as devices for achieving repeat patronage effectively diminishes. Taken together, these three elements (customer dependency, internal coordination, competitive contexts) indicate some of the most prominent practical limitations vendors encounter in their attempts to generate repeat patronage.

In many ways, vendor-buyer relationships seem parallel to those of dating couples as well as those of clergy and their congregations. Among dating couples, great attention is often paid to preparations, approaches, and dates (deals), but the continuity of the relationship remains problematic and may assume a secondary quality to one or more of the parties involved. In a manner somewhat akin to those ministering unto congregations (Prus, 1976), vendors also are apt to find themselves involved in multiple, simultaneous relationships with their customers; these relationships reflecting a variety of levels and modes of involvement.

They're all at different stages. New customers, old ones, people who've been dealing with you for years. Some who have left and are just coming back. Some you may be losing right now, like this other account I was just telling you about. I don't know how that one will work out. I've got my fingers crossed, but who knows? And then you're trying to set up appointments with new people, and you can't tell who will work out there. . . . Another thing is that you can't tell who will grow or when, or who you will have problems with next. Although, with some, you know you're walking on thin ice [manufacture—industrial].

Like dating couples and the clergy, vendors also find themselves caught up in a wide range of day-to-day activities that may detract from their "relationship work." Thus matters pertaining to other aspects of business (e.g., obtaining stock, staffing, managing disruptions) may significantly obscure (or otherwise divert) vendors from concerns with developing loyalty.

If we envision purchasing encounters as representing instances of voluntary association, as is implied by the parallels drawn to dating couples and religious recruitment, then the material presented herein seems highly relevant to relationship processes in a wide variety of other settings. Thus we may consider the ways in which people promote continuity of others in political parties, educational programs, and volunteer settings, as well as sports and recreational pursuits, for instance.

Notes

1. If one were to examine buyer loyalty from customer viewpoints, it would seem best to do so in "career" terms (see Chapter 1). In that case, we would be concerned with the experiences of the buyer in reference to initial involvements, continuities, disinvolvements, and reinvolvements with regards to particular products (companies, vendors).

2. The sociological literature on loyalty is rather sparse, but of relevance are Bigus's (1972) portrayal of milkmen's attempts to cultivate loyal customers, Hayes-Bautista's (1976) and Kasteller et al.'s (1976) discussions of "doctor shopping," Prus's (1976) analysis of clergy attempts to maintain a loyal congregation, Prus and Irini's (1988) depiction of "regulars" in bar settings, and Adler and Adler's (1983) study of drug dealing.

3. Even illicit operations may develop a repeat clientele. Thus, for instance, con artists and other hustlers may "work" particular targets multiple times (see Sutherland, 1937; Maurer, 1940; and Prus and Sharper, 1977).

4. Donovan (1929: 44) indicates that the practice of offering staff discounts as a means of encouraging their patronage was well established by that time. Readers are referred to Prus and Irini's (1988) discussion of staff regulars in bar settings for some interesting staff patronage parallels.

5. Some purchasing by staff (and that of some families and friends) reflects a sense of loyalty to "those who have been good enough to give the person a job." It is also worth noting that as salespeople shop more extensively at their employers' business or attract other people to the store, their salaries may be effectively reclaimed without recourse to other customers.

6. While our emphasis is broader, somewhat parallel inquiries have been made by Bigus (1972) and Kinsey (1985). Bigus introduced the concept of "cultivating relationships" in his study of milkmen and their customers. He notes that milkmen used several tactics explicitly designed to develop steady customers. These include personalizing services, making special (pricing) deals, using trust-inducing practices, nurturing pseudofriendships, and creating obligations. Kinsey (1985) recasts Bigus's notions somewhat in his discussion of the ways in which congressional aids attempt to consolidate themselves with others they see as influential to their careers. In addition to attempts to become known by achieving greater visibility, these people endeavored to enhance their positions by playing by the rules (avoiding trust violations), building obligations, doing fence-mending (cooling out offended parties) activity, and avoiding risky situations.

7. We should also note that in overall contrast to consumers, buyers in trade (including retailers purchasing products for resale) more explicitly anticipate long-term (i.e., partners-in-trade) relations with particular suppliers. This further encourages continuity in buyer-supplier relations at the "trade" level.

8. The relevance of each of these five elements (perspectives, identities, activities, commitments, and relationships) is illustrated in the earlier referenced work on career contingencies.

9. Matters of perspective and conversion typically assume much greater relevance and sharper direction in reference to company employees. It is they who are more apt to be exposed explicitly to corporate philosophies.

10. Much of Bigus's (1972) and Kinsey's (1985) discussions of cultivating relationships falls under the heading of facilitating activities.

11. Weigand (1980) uses the term *buying in* to refer to this latter (monopolistic) phenomenon, providing illustrations with cameras, razors, radios, public utilities, air traffic control systems, and franchises.

12. This theme is also addressed by Bigus (1972) and Kinsey (1985).

13. Bigus (1972) refers to this as "pseudo-friendship." While many encounters have a fleeting quality (also see Davis, 1959; Henslin, 1968; Wiseman, 1979), it should not be assumed that they are devoid of genuine interest or that both elements cannot occur within the same encounters.

14. Kinsey (1985) terms this practice "fence mending" in his study of congressional aides.

15. Similar inabilities to keep track of their clientele are noted among clergymen attempting to maintain their congregations (Prus, 1976).

16. Some attention was given to buyer perspectives and practices, as well as other aspects of buyer-seller relationships in Chapter 4 of *Pursuing Customers* (Prus, 1989), but we are again reminded of the desirability (and eventual necessity) of obtaining more material on the ways in which buyers envision and shape the relationships they have with vendors.

Chapter8
HOLDING "SALES"

You have to watch your inventory because as long as it's sitting there as stock it's not earning you any money. When I was with _____ , and interest rates were a lot lower (e.g., 5-10%), we figured that if the stock sat around for a year, even if we sold it at the regular price, you would be losing money [overhead] on it. . . . So your "sales" would be good to get your money back, reinvest it in something that would move better. Turns of stock are very important. If you can get $100,000 from $25,000 in stock, you're getting four turns on your merchandise. But if you get $150,000 in sales and still only $25,000 in stock, you're getting six turns. Much more profitable! . . . You guess that a particular item is going to sell, and if it doesn't, you have to get rid of it. Get your money out of it, as much as you can, and buy merchandise that will sell [department store].

What forms do "sales" assume? What sorts of items are featured? How do these price reductions fit into vendors' overall marketing schemes? Are they good for business? What problems do they generate? What are the practical limitations of holding "sales?"

Few marketing techniques generate more immediate "action" for stores than "sales" and yet few endeavors arouse more distrust and animosity on the parts of patrons and vendors. While these events can be seen to dramatize vendor-customer interaction, they also highlight central features of marketing activity. This chapter considers vendor concerns and strategies in reference to price reductions, locating these within the broader contexts of marketing activity and "respectability" (images associated with "sales").

The most common feature "sales" share is that they are alleged price reductions. Beyond this, each "special" is open to a variety of interpretations. Any business may hold a "sale" for any number of reasons, and

234

the specific items featured on any occasion may likewise reflect diverse reasoning. This is not to suggest that every "sale" involves chicanery on the part of the vendors, only that the when, what, and how of bargains is a multifaceted phenomenon. It is little wonder that consumers often find these alleged price cuts bewildering experiences. The vendors themselves are often uncertain about what to put on special and at what price. Further, denoting "cheaper goods," "sales" are also subject to some "stigmatization" (Goffman, 1963). While far from uniform, the disrespectability (products, staff, store, and patrons) associated with these promotions is an element which tends to make vendor-customer relations even more precarious than usual.

When one examines price reductions from the perspectives of the vendors (and their agents), it becomes apparent that not only do "sales" represent social activities to be planned and negotiated through to their conclusion with shoppers, but that vendors have concern as well for their aftermath (e.g., customer loyalty, store image). Accordingly, while we will be delineating aspects of "sales," it is important to view these components within the larger set of marketing processes in which vendors find themselves. And although one may speak of individual "sales" events as having "careers" (planning, implementation, cleaning up, and so on), each "sale" represents only one of multiple activities that affect (and reflect) the overall career (development, continuity, and demise) of the business entity featuring the "sale." Consumers often envision "sales" in reference to specific purchases, but their significance is much greater to the vendors. "Sales" denote consequential processes within a larger system of exchanges which together define the essence of identifiable businesses. To this end, attention will be given to "sales" with respect to a means of "creating action," the problems of dealing with shoppers seeking bargains, and the dilemmas price reductions pose for vendors. Together, these elements define basic vendor perspectives on the bargain and indicate vendor strategies designed to increase prospect commitments within the competitive context of the marketplace.

Creating Action

Whereas merchants may endeavor to attract customers in many ways (e.g., advertisements, acquiring "hot" items, and holding contests), one of the quickest and easiest ways of attracting customers is by holding "sales." Attracting customers is a critical aspect of "creating action,"[1] but the prime purpose of the "sale" is to promote "stock turns." If "sales" are to be more adequately understood, it is important that this be done within this fundamental notion of marketing. The following discussions of occasions, generating excitement, attracting crowds, clearing stock, and "(non)sales" consider contingencies affecting decisions to have "sales" and indicate some of the ways in which "sales" are structured and used to promote greater turns of stock.

"SALES" OCCASIONS

Since vendors may put merchandise on "sale" whenever they wish, "sales" occasions (e.g., Father's Day, Thanksgiving, and so on) assume some of the qualities of window dressing. This is not, however, to suggest that occasions are insignificant! First, occasions tend to legitimate these marketing endeavors as merchants keep up with the spirit of the occasion. Additionally, these events can be used to focus (e.g., spring specials, back-to-school sales) and justify expenditures as vendors emphasize the relevant ("We've got something for _____.") and practical ("We'll help you save money, too!") nature of the products they feature.

> What we have on "sale" depends on the occasions, so on Father's Day, we'll have some men's jewelry on "sale." The same with Valentine's, things like that. . . . It's important for our store, to keep the business going, to attract customers to the store [jewelry].

Clearly, occasions are not without significance. But from the vendor's perspective, the other elements characterizing "sales" (e.g., selecting merchandise, increased staffing, promoting additional shopping) are much more consistent than might first seem. Thus, more in the tradition of Simmel (1950), matters of content will be noted where relevant, but the emphasis will be on the forms (and processes) that "sales" assume.

GENERATING EXCITEMENT

Regardless of the occasion, "sales" can be used to generate excitement. Although most shoppers seem to realize that you don't get something for nothing,[2] "sales" may be seen to represent opportunities for shrewd shoppers to acquire bigger prizes with limited resources.[3] Thus media advertisements and display signs announcing "sales" suggest that something exceptional is happening.

> People melt when they see a "sales" sign. You can sell anything if you put a "sales" tag on it. I'm of that opinion. I've watched people. . . . People are really bad that way. And if you work at _____ or _____ , and people will come through your register on "sale" day, and they'll have junk. And all they've done is go from one bargain table to another and throw it on their buggy. And it's just junk! And they can't refuse the price. It's ridiculous! People will buy anything, they really will! . . . It's like something mystical happens when they see a "sales" sign, and they'll buy. . . . People are really affected by "sales" signs [discount department store].

Representing opportunities to acquire valued objects at significantly reduced prices, "sales" arouse interest. Anticipating that others may want the same objects appears to intensify interest, suggesting that the object is indeed worthy of possession (and sacrifice). To be able to save money in the process may further justify the purchase. Buyers thus are likely to experience a sense of freedom from their usual cautions about spending,[4] and having saved on one item may feel more entitled to purchase other items. "Sales" shoppers also tend to experience closure,[5] a perceived urgency to act ("Can I afford not to buy?"). This sense of urgency is promoted by the time limits and the potential savings characterizing "sales," and may be accentuated considerably by the perception of more buyers than desirable items available. "Sales" shoppers seem generally cognizant that "sales" purchases represent greater than usual risk, but like gamblers at the racetrack (Lesieur, 1977), who assume particularistic competence in their abilities to "pick winners," many shoppers find themselves willing to take risks in their attempts to get ahead. In the process, they sometimes find themselves more involved in these pursuits than they had anticipated. Generally speaking, the degree of excitement "sales" generate seems affected by the presale valuing of items, perceptions of greater potential savings, shorter time limits in which to respond, and an apparent excess of shoppers over desired items.

> I've seen some wild "sidewalk sales," especially if the thing has been well promoted. Say you have a flashing light for 15 minutes, you'll just get swamped with these people trying to get whatever it is that is on special for

15 minutes, so if it's promoted well, there can be also excitement in the mall [shoes].

Our _____ day is like your once-a-month Christmas. It's a big day, every month. A real rush, usually a Monday [discount department store].

Vendors engaged in field sales may also use "specials" (as "door openers") in attempts to obtain the attention of their prospects.

Your "sales" are nice because it makes the machine a little more attractive, and also it gives you a reason for approaching an existing customer about one of the machines. It's sort of a special event that way.... We'll have a "special" on different lines, almost constantly. Of course, with the commission, you only get it on the total of your sales, on the net, so you won't quite make as much there [commercial—office equipment].

Dealing with Slow Times

Recognizing that "sales" attract crowds, a central objective in having a "sale" is to build traffic. A "store-opening sale" may be valuable in providing initial community profile and prospective regular customers, but established businesses may also use "sales" for these same objectives (as well as to promote greater patronage on the part of existing and past patrons). Thus one common way of attempting to deal with slow times is to have a "sale." In general, "sales" events seem to be better attended when the savings are purported to be greater (e.g., 50% off versus 10%), when more items in a store are "sale" priced, and when more stores in the area are on "sale." Denoting activity, "sales" may also be a means of boosting the morale of a staff weary of rearranging unruffled merchandise.

The "sales" are good for bringing in business. Like we'll do well with the "sidewalk sales," for instance. So you do well in the items you want to clear. But because of all the people, once you get them out, they'll buy other things than what you have on "sale." ... You do get different customers for your "sales," much more of an assortment.... The "sales" create more work for you. You have to rearrange things more often, and you have a greater volume of merchandise to handle and then there's inventory before and after the "sale," so "sales" are more work in those ways, but you don't mind if you're cleaning up after you've done well. It's good for the staff. There's more activity. It picks you up [stationery]!

Should slow times persist longer than merchants consider viable, they may feel more acutely pressured (closure) into having "sales." Under these conditions one is apt to find more dramatic reductions.

It usually gets to the point with department stores, that regardless of the product, at some point they will crucify the price. How it gets there is like this. The manager is under pressure to produce, so he goes to each department head and asks them what they've got for the manager's "sale." And so they've got this and this. "Well, wasn't that the same price as before? And we've still got this left? Put it on for less. Take $50 off." "But that'll kill the margin. That's below any retailer." "I don't care. I want a 'sale' that's going to move things." So then he runs that "sale," for that store, and the price goes way down. They're not making money on those items, but he doesn't care. He's looking at the overall sales totals, and if it works out okay, fine. He got them the action they wanted [appliances].

If you're short on your cash flow, a "sale" is the fastest way of raising money. And there, depending on your situation, you may put your merchandise on at prices pretty close to your own costs. Hopefully, you wouldn't have to go below that. But depending on how desperate you are, you might need all the turnaround you can get. If you have to come up with money by a certain time, what choice do you have [giftware]?

Promoting Browsing

Beyond attempts to attract customers to their businesses, merchants may also use "sales" to encourage greater volumes of sales from the same body of customers. Thus, in addition to promoting multiple purchases of the same items (e.g., 2/$1.99), "sales" items may also be used to promote the purchases of other items. Shoppers may find it frustrating to have to search more extensively throughout the store to find "sales" merchandise, but these display practices are generally intended to promote exposure of other merchandise. While browsing is likely to generate sales in all settings, it is especially valuable in self-serve stores.

We have "sales" every week, but we will have a major "sale" every two weeks. We have our loss leaders, and then what we try to do is to hide the loss leaders throughout the store, to give more exposure to our regular items, get people to buy those too. Like we've had potato chips in the pharmacy, bread in ladies' wear. It's just wild sometimes! We don't even try to connect up the items. It drives the customers crazy, but whatever department is having a slower time, you might stick some of these things there. It's not always that bad, but you want to provide exposure for these other things [discount department store].

Facilitating Suggestive Selling

Stores featuring more service may also extend "specials" into additional purchases. Although all vendors may attempt to entice customers through displays, direct personal contact with the customer intensifies the negotiable aspect of buying. One may note the greater difficulty staff have in establishing rapport with "sales" shoppers, but suggestive selling can be a powerful marketing tool even in this context. Regardless of whether vendors are selling up (moving the customer to a better line) or are engaged in multiple selling (promoting multiple purchases of one item and/or purchases of multiple items; also second selling, add-on selling),[6] once customers have opened their minds to the possibility of initial purchases, they seem more amenable to subsequent purchases.

A large, rushed crowd of shoppers seems most desirable in self-serve stores, but salespeople relying on suggestive selling tend to prefer a slower, steadier stream of customers, providing greater opportunities for them to establish trust relationships with their patrons.

> There's three reasons you have a "sale." First, you want to get rid of the goods. Then you want to sell your store, get it better known. The third is to sell something else, to sell the other goods in the store, your second selling or add-on sales. [mixed clothing].

USING LOSS LEADERS

Sometimes, when "sales" seem more dramatic and pertain to items in season they are described as *loss leaders*. The term *loss leader* generally refers to the practice of selling (seemingly popular) goods at prices that appear to be below cost. And as Haring (1935) notes, popular name brands (representing standardized indications of quality) typically represent the most powerful loss leaders.[7] The implication is that the dramatic savings would generate traffic and thus result in the sales of other items. A merchant's other items may be sold at higher prices to offset the costs engendered by the loss leaders, but this would be a generally misleading inference.[8] While vendors may take smaller margins (losses occasionally) on some items in attempts to build crowds, many seeming loss leaders are items that merchants have obtained as "specials" from their suppliers.[9] Under these conditions, a regular margin (sometimes more) may still result in a dramatic overall price reduction.

> If you want merchandise for a "sale," you can approach the manufacturers and ask them for extra [clearance] merchandise, so they can can give you a good price on these lines [appliances].

> In the spring and fall we have our largest promotions, but the different companies [suppliers] may run "specials" any time of the year. The promotions are often used to get the customers to try some new colors or a new product [department store].

Second, if the "sales" items create a crowd, the extra volume in overall sales can offset any costs the loss leaders may entail for the vendor (assuming regular markups on the other products). Thus much more important than any costs of the loss leaders (and the money invested in media advertising, and so on), is the ability of "sales" items to attract more shoppers. Then, depending on the merchandising practices of the vendors (e.g., self-serve/personal service), they can attempt to put the "specials" to work to promote other purchases.

BOGUS BARGAINS

Although trust and honesty seem problematic in all relationships, and represent elements that cast notes of disrespectability on sales endeavors in more routine settings, opportunities for trust violations are increased in "sales" settings. Realizing that some shoppers see "sales" as opportunities to get shrewd buys, vendors may take advantage of these eager prospects. If one excludes deliberate bait-and-switch routines and highly misleading claims (all of which are more difficult to enforce than to legislate against), other, more "innocuous" forms of business can still reduce the bargain to a nonbargain.

> There are a lot of things you can do and not lose anything. You can move the merchandise to the center aisles. Some people think they're going to save on everything there. If you're having trouble moving something, just stick it out there. . . . You can put different colored tags on it, bigger tags, brighter colors. . . . You can also reduce the price by a few cents, make it more palatable. Now it's only $2.97 instead of the regular $3.00. Just take the old tag off, put a bright yellow tag on it, something like that. . . . You can put two

together: "Special, 2 for $6.95!" instead of $3.50 each. Big savings there! . . .
Sometimes if something's not moving well, you can raise the price and put it
on "special." Put it in the center aisle, big sign on it: "Limit 2 per customer."
They don't really know what's a good price. They just see the "sales" signs
[discount department store].

We will get lower lines for some of our promotions. We call them "promotions" or "specials," not "sales." . . . We'll do that with name brands if we
can, or even our own [store] brand. We'll still get our regular margins, but it
looks like more of a deal. That holds for appliances, shoes, clothes, whatever
[department store].

Appreciating the pulling power of "sales," some vendors have explicitly organized their operations around the theme of "conspicuous
cheapness."[10] Thus some merchants may strive for bargain basement
appearances on a consistent basis by using "no-name," "warehouse,"
"salvage," "bare bones" operations, "shabby settings," or names, slogans, or advertisements suggesting bargains, discounts and the like.

They run the range. Some deal on high volume, and if you can get your
volumes up, you can come down a little on your prices. Some pick up ends
of lines and discontinued lines, or old stock from suppliers, anything they can,
really. So their prices can be better, they should be a lot better than they are
sometimes. But they usually won't carry a very full line or a regular line. And
then you get places that look like you should be getting a real bargain because
the place looks scuffy or all run down, merchandise all piled up or dumped
in bins, discount signs all over. A tacky setting. But if you shop around, you'll
see that it often just looks like a bargain at the time. And some merchants will
do all of those things, so the customer has to be really watchful to get the best
deal. And it may not be in a place that looks the part. It could be. There are
some genuine deals to be had. But it may not be. : . . Factory outlets, the same
sort of thing. Some offer good deals, some take you for all they can. You have
to know your stores, how they merchandise, and you have to know your
products [discount department store].

CLEARING UNWANTED STOCK

So far, we have been discussing "sales" largely in reference to
achieving greater turns of regular stock. In conjunction with this,
"sales" may also be used to eliminate products whose "time" is near or
past.[11] The merchandise may be seasonal or have a shorter shelf life,
but subject to shifts in fashion, or otherwise be found to be moving too

slowly. The goods may also be damaged, or the selection remaining be too incomplete to feature as a main line.

Seasonal Clearances

Although vendors could keep calendar-dated merchandise with longer shelf lives for another year, they would have to cover the storage and handling costs as well as lose access to (or be forced to pay interest on) those funds. By selling these items on "sale," they may lose some of their potential market in these items next year, but in the process are able to reinvest their money in stock more immediately relevant (e.g., four stock turns are better than one). Next year, these vendors can order more factory fresh merchandise (with the latest improvements and/or changes in fashion).

> Basically, the way you work it is if you can sell the bulk of the merchandise at the full price, and then say you have to put the rest on for half, well you're really not losing. You're getting back what you paid on the "sale" items and made on the regular prices [department store].

Slow Movers

Although not necessarily seasonal, items that have not moved quickly (compared to other stock) threaten to become dated (shelf life, fashion) and are also prime candidates for clearances. They have become the "bad buys," and now represent financial liabilities to the merchant. While vendors may move their merchandise around within their stores (and chains may move their "tombstones" from one store to another) trying to achieve greater exposure for these products in the process, the "sale" remains a viable option.

> With the slow movers, you're in a bit of a dilemma. How long do you wait before you put it on "sale?" If you mark it down too soon, you'll lose money. If you wait too long, you may lose more. You just never really know for sure. Sometimes you can judge by your volume and how it's been moving compared to other things, but even then, how much of a markdown will it take [appliances]?

> Some things just don't sell well. There's nothing wrong with them. Same materials, same price, same company, and yet one style sells and the other style sits. You can try moving them around to different locations and they still don't sell. So put them on "sale," try to get rid of them that way [women's clothing].

Damaged Goods

Damaged goods share many qualities with the slow moving merchandise. Broken, soiled, incomplete in some way, they are even further discredited. If the damages are more extensive across a product line, attempts may be made to return the merchandise to the supplier for credit (depending on their arrangements). If the damaged products reflect a range of merchandise from different suppliers, merchants may not consider it feasible to spend staff time and efforts in attempts to reclaim their investments. While it is apparent that references to damaged goods are a matter of degree and definition, a major option is to put these items on "sale."

> If it's a larger shipment that's defective, we send it back to the manufacturer. But many times it's a dent or scratch here, a leg that comes loose on a stand or chair, parts missing. We have sort of a clearance area at the front of the store and we'll put those things there. Reduce the price somewhat depending on what we think it'll take to move it, where someone doesn't mind the scratch or figures he can fix it himself [discount catalogue house].

"Sales" may be effective ways of disposing of damaged goods, but some vendors are also concerned that these items not reflect unfavorably on their overall images.

> We'd rather destroy our damaged goods than put them on "sale." We don't want that kind of image. We sell first lines, and we don't want anything to suggest otherwise [men's clothing].

Line Changes

"Sales" are sometimes designed to eliminate particular lines of merchandise (possibly as a consequence of switching suppliers or the merchandise carried). When merchants perceive greater product incompatibility, they generally become more eager to eliminate the unwanted lines as quickly as possible.

> If you've got some oddballs or a line from before, and we've changed suppliers a few times, we like to get rid of those as soon as possible. They detract from your other lines. And you would rather use that display space to promote your better lines. Same thing with your last year's models to some extent. You want to concentrate on your hotter, newer lines [appliances].

Dealing with "Sales" Shoppers

> Overall, its more of a different class of people who shop specials. But
> people—and all types of people and upper-class people—definitely get pushy
> and short-tempered, very grabby, during "sales." Like we'll have our stuff on
> clearance and it'll be junk. We're almost ready to throw it out! And they'll be
> grabbing all over each other, sometimes just flying through the merchandise
> [department store]!

Having considered elements affecting vendor decisions to hold
"sales," attention now shifts to their experiences with "sales" shoppers.
While immensely valuable for both cleaning out "sales" merchandise
and making additional purchases, "sales" shoppers are among the most
disliked categories of patrons vendors encounter. They can be seen to
epitomize troublesome customers in the retail setting. Collectively,
"sales" shoppers are seen as *cheap* (frugal and inclined to comparison
shop, as well as haggle on the "sales" merchandise), *aggressive* (demanding, complaining, returning goods), *distrusting* (distant, skeptical),[12] and *disrespectful* (demeaning of products, store, and staff).[13]
Vendors generally indicate that they find it very difficult to establish
rapport with "sales" shoppers, and find themselves feeling more uneasy
and uncertain about how to approach them.

> The "sales" customers are pickier than the regular customers. If something is
> on "sale," the people will look it over twice as well, to make sure that it isn't
> flawed. They think that if it's on "sale" that there's something wrong with it.
> Sometimes you get really frustrated with people like that. Something is
> half-price, and they're going over it with a fine-tooth comb, and they want
> something more off it. And the people paying the higher price don't even look
> it over that well. If it's on "sale," the people are pickier, they really are [shoes]!

> Our "sales" store had a very different clientele than our store a few blocks
> down the street, which did not carry the "sales" items on a regular basis.
> People who came into the "sales" store tended to be older, much more picky,
> harder to sell; they wanted to pay half the price and to get twice the value.
> They were very rough, more difficult to deal with, a lot more problems with
> returns than what you would get with the same merchandise in our other
> stores. . . . That type of person does get drawn into the other stores when
> you're having a sidewalk sale, a mall promotion, something like that. . . . The
> "sales" shoppers are messier, rougher. They're a little neater in neater stores,
> but they're messier than your general customers [mixed clothing].

While staff-shopper ("sales") relationships are not uniformly negative, their relationships appear generally consistent with the "spurious
interaction" Lemert (1962) describes in his analysis of paranoia. Not
knowing how much (if any) trust they may accurately place in a "sale"
(advertisements, products, store, staff), "sales" shoppers seem more
sensitive to notions of cheapness and disrespectability (without any
immediate cues from the staff). Attempting to achieve quality and value
in a "pile of leftovers," they are inclined to be skeptical and demanding,
but to maintain identity, they tend to be distant and distrusting of offers
of assistance and service. Finding themselves receiving less than desired attention in crowded settings and/or dealing with "gun shy"
vendors, they may also become more vocal in an attempt to represent
their rights to staff and management. If one assumes that the "sales"
shoppers are uncertain of the "games being played," these interactional
notions seem reasonable.[14] From the vendor's perspective, these styles
of shopping make the encounter more difficult and frustrating.

> "Sales" shoppers irritate me. They're shopping on "sale" and they still want
> a bargain. They want a lower price. And they're more likely to return the goods
> too. So they're more difficult. They try to dicker with the price, which is
> annoying because it's on "sale" anyways. And they start telling you how it's
> so much cheaper down the way in this and that store, and a lot of times, they'll
> be lying to you. They just want a bargain [department store].

> Messy shoppers can be a problem, especially if you have merchandise on
> "sale." And here I've noticed that you can have the same items, where they're
> on "sale" the next day, and you'll find that the customers now treat the items
> with less respect than they would have the day before. It can be the same rack
> in the same location in the store, and yet they're much rougher with the
> merchandise when you put them on 20% or 30% off. . . . And with the staff
> it's the same way, I have to get the girls to think that the "sales" items are just
> as important, just as valuable to the store as the other merchandise. Just
> because it's on "sale" doesn't mean that you can show less respect for the
> items or the customers who are buying the merchandise. And that's a problem
> too. Some of the "sales" customers are more difficult, more demanding. They
> want to know what's wrong with this and that, "How come it's put on sale?"
> "Bet you marked it up to mark it down!" So the "sales" customers are more
> frustrating for the staff, and after you meet a few difficult customers and
> you're busy, getting run off your feet, it is more frustrating. It's more difficult
> to maintain your composure [women's clothing].

Emergent Dilemmas

Although valuable for business, "sales" create notable dilemmas for vendors. "Sales" not only entail more work (and staff-time) than usual, but their success is problematic. Stores on "sale" may attract new customers (some of whom may return as repeat customers) and may become "better known" to shoppers, but by going on "sale" more frequently, stores may also experience a loss of prestige among existing patrons and in the community more generally. At the same time, however, vendors typically experience company (and/or self-imposed) pressures to produce greater cash flows. Thus, in attempting to be competitive, vendors may find themselves more involved in "sales" than they wish.

UNPREDICTABILITY

In addition to increased (and often more intense) encounters with shoppers, "sales" denote other forms of extra work for the vendors as they find themselves working extra hours, doing more display work, unpacking, inventory counts, and housecleaning activities.

> "Sales" create higher volumes in customers, and the more people in the shop, the messier things are going to get, and the less chance you have to straighten things out. And the messier they find the store in, the messier the store is going to be when they leave, so it's a self-perpetuating thing. It's more difficult to keep things orderly, just keeping the store clean. You have more customers hanging around after closing time, more problems with people wanting to use checks and slowing things down at the cash register. Just all the things associated with high volume [children's clothing].

As with other merchandising endeavors, vendors do not know if a given "sale" will be well attended, or even that the "sales" merchandise will sell and/or outsell the regular stock (assuming that was the intent). Further, should the staff on duty be insufficient to deal with the possible surges of shoppers, stores may lose business (on all merchandise) and risk offending customers wanting service. On the other hand, an overstaffed situation may result not only in boredom (and animosity if on commission), but also misplaced (and costly) overhead.

> With the "sales," you can be really, really busy, but the problem there is that you don't know how to predict how busy you will be. Sometimes you expect

to be not so busy and so you just have a few people there and you get run off your feet. Other times, you have a larger staff because you expect to do a lot of business, and there's nothing to do. So that's a big problem with the "sales." You don't know for sure when they'll take off and when they'll fizzle [shoes].

Given the greater congestion characterizing "sales," routine problems (e.g., returns, customer indecisiveness, personal checks) tend to become intensified at this time. Some other confusions, however, are more "sales"-specific, as customers find their desires to save frustrated.

A misprint in the advertisement—the "specials"—that can cause a lot of problems for you. Say where people come in wanting a piece of luggage for $9 instead of $59 or whatever it was. Or if there is a word missing or it's not explained quite right so that there's confusion, you can get a lot of disappointed or irate customers. A few of those, sometimes all through the day or week; that can be quite frustrating. It can spoil the whole "sale" for you [department store].

It is also difficult to tell how how profitable "sales" are on both a short-run and a long-term basis. Total sales figures can be especially misleading for a "sale." While more money may flow through the cash register, if the margin is smaller as with bona fide price reductions, the "sale" may represent little more than the reclaiming of former investments. Additionally, if shoppers are concentrating their buying more exclusively on "sales" merchandise in a particular line, other (competing) items may be passed over by the dollar-conscious shoppers.[15]

LOYALTY AND IMAGE CONCERNS

So far, we have been focusing on "sales" as marketing devices largely on their own. It is exceedingly important that "sales" be viewed within the more complete scheme of merchandising. And just as advertising, displays, and services can affect the likelihood of generating repeat customers and the sort of images the store achieves in the community, so can "sales." While vendors may anticipate (correctly and otherwise) the effects of "sales" on customer loyalty and vendor image, others have become aware of these elements (and some of their unexpected twists) only in retrospect.

Customer Loyalty

Beyond endeavors designed to bring money into the business and clear merchandise, "sales" may be used to attract new customers, reward existing customers, and entice former customers to return.[16] Those using "sales" in this way operate on the assumption that the customers will define the store as one in which to obtain good items at good prices. While regular customers are sometimes treated to advance showings (maximal selection, minimal congestion) of "sales," it is the busier "sales" that tend to define the store as one in which to find better bargains. However, the very congestion characterizing these "sales" results in lowered levels of service and fewer opportunities for vendors to cultivate relationships with these shoppers.

> We have "specials" all year long. We try to be seasonal, but something going on as much of the time as possible. We will have major seasonal clearances twice a year, get room for the new merchandise coming in the store and getting a change of colors. . . . We'll get some people who ask when our things are going on "sale," and if we know, we'll tell them, because they're probably people who wouldn't buy at the regular prices, but this way at least they will help us clear out the season's merchandise. Sometimes these people will become "sales" regulars, you see them every "sale." [luggage].

> You get everybody during the "sale," but you can't spend as much time with the people then. Everybody wants attention, but during the "sale" you can't give the regulars the same attention as usual. They usually realize that, so some won't bother coming in during "sales." . . . The "sales" are where people often get frustrated and annoyed and mad, because they're not getting the service they think they should get. But you can't do much about that because you don't know all that much in advance when exactly it is going to be busy. If they were in retail themselves they would understand your situation a lot better, but they don't see it that way [women's clothing].

Under these circumstances, offers of similar quality at slightly lower prices may effectively attract many of the "sales" shoppers elsewhere.

Image Losses

Although "sales" (through advertising and/or increased patronage) contribute to a store's prominence in the community, the longer and more extensively a store is on "sale," the greater it's likelihood of being defined as a "discount" and/or "second-rate" store.[17] And just as one's merchandise, decor, and location can serve as cues by which store images may be defined, so may the shoppers that others associate with particular businesses shape their images.[18]

> Because we have so many things on "sale" so much of the time, we've become essentially a discount jewelry store. We're trying to get out of that, but that's what happened with us. We're trying to get into some more expensive merchandise, but we're having difficulties there. You need a certain clientele, and if they're not there, you can have problems. We've tried that with some of our merchandise, but the regular customers, they'll say, "We'll wait until you put them on 'sale.'" We've had things on "sale" for so long, that people just get used to that [jewelry].

> It hasn't been like that always, but now people expect everyone to be on "sale," and now everybody is on "sale." . . . If you constantly have "sales" signs up at times when most other stores aren't, you would get to be known as a discount store, like _____ and _____ . People expect them to have something on "sale." [shoes]

BEING COMPETITIVE

In spite of some instances of artificial competition (e.g., a number of closely situated outlets owned by the same company, but operating out of different "fronts") and some misleading ploys, "sales" also reflect marketplace competition. Like other marketing practices, "sales" are subject to variable popularity among vendors over time. However, one finds that many stores are on "sale" more often and more extensively than they would like. While higher levels of skepticism and distrust are associated with "sales," these events seem to have become an institutionalized element of retail merchandising, and few businesses seem able and/or willing to eliminate them from their repertoire. Not unlike customers feeling the pressure of buying limited goods in the midst of a seeming surplus of shoppers, retailers feel the pressure of selling goods in the midst of a seeming surplus of competition. In both instances, the "chase" (Lesieur, 1977) is intensified as each witnesses one's competitors pursue these options.

> This year our sidewalk sale was the first week in July. It seems to be getting earlier and earlier. Some of the [summer] things you'll be able to get in June. But you want to be able to make room for your winter things, because some of our winter stock started coming in the end of May, so your storage areas

get really jammed as it is. Then too, if the competition is having a "sale," you
don't want to be left out [children's clothing].

If your competitors put something on "sale," that's one of your staples, say
like running shoes in the spring, then you really get concerned about it. And
you have to make a decision and you have to make it quickly, whether you're
going to go on "sale" as well. . . . And with your regular merchandise, it's
harder, because you have so much money you can spend on markdowns in a
month. So you have to make a decision, if you take a markdown on this, you
can get yourself in a lot of shit. Now as long as you come out looking like a
hero, saleswise, they don't care if you mark down or not, but if you blow it!
But you have to watch the competition [shoes].

Vendors may use "sales" to create action and attempt to gain a larger
piece of the consumer dollar, but customers emerge as willing participants in this undertaking.

They keep marking it down, and people keep waiting for you to mark it
down. . . . You'll have people in the store and someone will come in and say,
"How much is that?" You say, "$49.95." And they say, "When's it going on
sale?" And I'm taking it out of the carton, out of the bag, and the creases
haven't even fallen out of it, and they're asking when am I putting it on "sale."
And it's frustrating, so you say, "Well, I don't know. Give it three weeks."
Sure enough, they'll come back in three weeks [men's clothing].

The ones that come out for all the "sales" tend to be a little less well-to-do.
They just wait until they hit the "sales" and then they buy everything in sight
that's on "sale," whether they need it or not. You'll also get some well-to-do
people hitting the "sales," but they buy differently, more selectively. . . .
People are always looking for a deal, and they think that everything is going
on "sale." "I really like it, but when is it going on sale?" . . . And in this day
and age, you might as well ask because everything goes on "sale" eventually.
In one day, the prices can change quite a bit, 20%, 50% when it goes on "sale,"
so that can be quite a difference to the person who's making the purchase
[jewelry].

There are many other ways of creating action than having "sales,"
such as holding draws and contests, giving demonstrations, providing
clinics, offering courtesy services, and "gifting" (giving premium/
specialty items to) regular shoppers. And there seems no clear evidence
that these other options are less productive (or more costly) than
"sales." Further, while any promotional activity is likely to generate

some skepticism on the part of shoppers, and may affect the images shoppers have of particular businesses, these other options may more successfully avoid the stigma associated with "sales." In contrast to many of these alternatives, however, "sales" are quicker and easier to implement, and in addition to targeting specific merchandise for reduction, "sales" tend to suggest more immediate payoffs. As a result of (1) desiring more instantaneous cash flows, (2) wishing to move specific merchandise, and (3) perceiving shoppers to be especially price-conscious, vendors may find themselves "closed" into "sales" as a routine merchandising practice. Thus, much like Lemert's (1972) "secondary deviants," once stores acquire reputations as "sales" stores and (in attempts to be competitive) develop their routines more extensively around "sales," it becomes increasingly difficult for them to do business in other ways.[19] Thus, in addition to providing insight into aspects of risk taking and disrespectability, an analysis of "sales" also sheds light on the emergence and maintenance of identities and relationships in a competitive context.

In Perspective

"Sales" may seem more exciting and relevant to most shoppers than many other aspects of doing business, but these events are best seen within the more general context of marketing activity. Involving elements such as recruitment, closure, deception, distrust, disrespectability, and gaming behavior, and denoting an apex at which a number of fundamental aspects of marketing (e.g., purchasing, pricing, recruitment, customer encounters, enthusiasm, and competition) merge, "sales" are pivotal for the fuller understanding of a great many marketing endeavors. Finally, while "sales" suggest quick-fix solutions to many marketing problems, it is worth noting that these events themselves may generate many other dilemmas. Particularly noteworthy in this latter regard are the unpredictability "sales" entail relative to stock carried, pricing decisions, and staffing arrangements; the added difficulties "sales" pose for staff-customer encounters; the potential image losses "sales" imply; and the tendency for "sales" to become more widely integrated into merchandising practices (on an individual or broader basis) and shaping the subsequent decisions and activities of those thusly involved.

Notes

1. Readers may refer to Goffman (1967: 149-270) for a most interesting statement on "where the action is."

2. Readers should recognize that qualities attributed to shoppers in this paper represent my own observations and those of the vendors (who in addition to observing shoppers are also consumers in their own right) interviewed. Thus, although these attributions also correspond with those of Donovan (1929: 65), this material on "sales" shoppers should be considered more tentative.

3. It is worth noting that vendors have long realized (see Haring, 1935: 27) that they may generate more purchasing activity of goods generally by more extensively discounting only some items (e.g., 20% off) than by reducing the costs of all items overall by some relative dollar amount (e.g., a 1% discount on all items carried).

4. See Matza (1964, 1969), Prus (1978), and Prus and Irini (1988) for discussions and applications of the concept of "drift."

5. Lemert (1953), Prus (1978), and Prus and Irini (1988) provide more extensive discussions of closure as this pertains to involvements in bogus checks, violence, and deviant subcultures.

6. While the sales staff are often encouraged to sell customers up to better lines (more profitable sales, assuming the same percentage markup), "bait and switch" legislation has made this activity a little more awkward when "sales" merchandise is involved.

7. While suppliers may themselves initiate "sales," they do not appreciate merchants independently using their lines as loss leaders. A much feared result is that when vendors cut the price of the supplier's products, other vendors (and these very same vendors who cut the prices) will seek lower prices on subsequent orders. The rationale these merchants provide is that if they are to continue carrying this supplier's lines, they need these price cuts to maintain acceptable margins in the face of increasingly intense competition.

8. Haring (1935) wavers on this point. On page 14, he alleges that the leader is sold at a loss; while on page 140, he contends that leaders (generally denoting supplier specials) in practice bring merchants full margins. Other than clearance sales (discussed later), it appears that losses are most apt to be incurred when vendors are engaged in predatory pricing (attempts to rapidly eliminate the competition) or in (the sometimes related) price wars.

9. These "specials" may be items suppliers wish to introduce to the market, but may also represent ends of lines, overstock, and seconds. Some "specials" also reflect supplier desperation. As with the merchants to whom they sell, suppliers may also need cash to pay their bills, deal with unexpected shortfalls, costly expansions, and the like. Although the public sees much less of this backstage area of merchandising, the activities of the suppliers are strikingly parallel with those of the retail merchants. Some supplier "specials" will be tagged as such by the supplier, but others may be passed on entirely at the discretion of the merchants involved (they may prefer a higher margin to a "sales" item). Additionally, not unlike shoppers who wish to create their own "sales" by dickering, vendors may approach suppliers with requests for better priced merchandise for regular or "sales" stock.

10. This term was suggested to me by Dorothy Counts. The inference, as with Veblen's (1953) notion of "conspicuous consumption," is that image sells.

11. It is with these products that merchants are most likely to cut margins dramatically (ergo, loss leaders, albeit somewhat by default).

12. While also concentrating primarily on vendor perspectives, Haring's (1935) statement indicates that customer skepticism is not an especially recent phenomenon. It is also worth noting, however, that "sales" purchases may involve some suspension of trust-related concerns as shoppers more ardently pursue bargains.

13. One implication is that stores promoting more consistent self-definitions as discount outlets are more apt to encounter difficult customers.

14. See Lyman and Scott (1970) for an insightful discussion of games and paranoia.

15. Some vendors view "sales" as clearly representing self-defeating modes of merchandising. Not only do "sales" promote price-oriented comparison shopping, they also create expectations that products will go on "sale" if only buyers will wait long enough.

16. For other discussions of vendors attempting to cultivate repeat patronage, see Bigus's (1972) discussion of milkmen and their customers and Prus and Irini's (1988: 192-204) depiction of bar staff and their customers.

17. Particularly striking in examining vendor concerns with store images are the seeming parallels of reputations of businesses with those of individuals. Thus the "labeling" literature is most relevant with respect to vendors' attempts to negotiate favorable images in the community. See Prus (1975a, 1975b) and Cullen and Cullen (1978) for reviews of this literature.

18. Similar tendencies to type establishments by the clientele they keep were also noted in the bar setting (Prus and Irini, 1988).

19. Haring's (1935) discussion of retail price cutting remains one of the best discussions on "sales" available. While providing a historical testimony to the generalizability of the present material, it also suggests a fadishness to the prominence of particular marketing techniques (including "sales") from that time to the present.

Chapter 9
MAINTAINING ENTHUSIASM

Maintaining enthusiasm, that's one of the real keys to this business. You can't let any problems or disappointments show or affect you when you're dealing with the next customer. You have to be prepared to spend time with the customer and be pleasant, keep your spirits up. If you don't, you won't be in this business long. It's just that important [women's clothing]!

Of what significance is enthusiasm for the sales process? What sorts of things make it difficult for salespeople to be as enthusiastic as they might like? How do salespeople try to maintain enthusiasm? What role do other people play in enhancing or diminishing the enthusiasm salespeople experience?

Enthusiasm as a Social Process

Despite vendors' attempts to refine their marketing programs and to shape the directions the purchasing decisions of their customers assume, vendors are subject to considerable shifts in their own perspectives in both long-term and short-run time frames. Although often described as being "up" (versus being "down"), enthusiasm generally entails some optimism, confidence, and a readiness to act. It denotes a sense of intensity and application in the short run; dedication and continuity over the long term. In what follows, attention is given to the elements serving to diminish enthusiasm in the sales setting as well as to those promoting enthusiasm in both immediate and more enduring senses.

One may speak of some people as generally more enthusiastic about saleswork than others, but it is most important to recognize that *enthu-*

siasm is social process and needs to be examined as such.[1] Enthusiasm is very much affected by the support (or lack of support) others provide in reference to sales activities over time. While salespeople are expected to be enthusiastic about their products, they have the task of maintaining their enthusiasm in the face of frequent rejection, difficult customers, and inactivity.

Losing Enthusiasm

In order to gain a fuller appreciation of the problems of generating and sustaining enthusiasm, it is important to consider when and how people's sense of enthusiasm is likely to diminish. When salespeople were asked about the sorts of things that made it difficult for them to be as enthusiastic about their work as they might like, the following themes emerged: the wearing aspects of saleswork, the pressures salespeople feel to sell more products, the unpredictability of sales, slow times and personal slumps, unpleasantries and distractions, and the disrespectability often associated with sales work. Not everyone views these elements in the same way, but taken together they provide valuable insight into the sales arena.

WEARYING WORK

Sales work may seem easy to many outsiders, but it can be a physically as well as a mentally demanding activity. People working in stores do not have to contend with the travel of those in field sales, but their work can be as difficult. In addition to stocking and maintaining attractive displays, they are expected to appear "on" and be effective should prospects appear.

> People perceive salespeople to have jobs that are not really that difficult, but I've worked in some other places, in a warehouse and a railroad, but the physically most demanding job was being in sales. And people just can't understand it! You're just wiped out at the end of a day, and people just don't understand that it can be a tough job, mentally, physically, whatever, it is. . . . They don't think that you really do anything. . . . They think that you don't really work. Even hours in management, you're putting in between 50 and 60 hours a week, constantly, and officially you're not getting paid for more than your regular hours. The same is true of your staff. They're putting in more

than their 40 hours, but that's all they're getting paid for. And you work hard. If you're not in the front selling, you could be in the back moving your stock around, so you've got physical labor as well as the mental work of selling on the floor [shoes].

PRESSURE TO PERFORM

People on direct commission generally experience the most pressure to sell and are most apt to become disappointed when sales are low. However, salespeople in other settings may also experience similar pressures as they attempt to attain acceptable levels of sales.

In sales, they always want to know if you couldn't have done better, made more sales, squeezed more out of people who came by. In reality, the most frustrating thing is that thing haunting you: "Have you done enough?" There is always that pressure on you, to sell, and to sell more. You might feel a little concerned about the customer, whether they can afford it and all, while they're there, but after, you think, "Well I've sold this much today. Could I have done better? Couldn't I have pushed her a little harder?" You sort of feel guilty if you aren't selling enough [cosmetics].

Success generates enthusiasm, but it also provides a measure of performance against which subsequent performance can be measured. When repeat customers are accumulated, it helps salespeople realize rising expectations. Nevertheless, and somewhat ironically, earlier "tastes of success" may also provide standards by which subsequent efforts are defined as disappointing.

You expect after a good week, that things will get better next week, next month, whatever. You feel that you're better and that since you've been getting more regulars, you should be selling more. So when that doesn't happen, you're disappointed. That's why having a real good stretch is not so good. You just can't keep getting better, and you get let down [women's clothing].

UNPREDICTABILITY OF SALES

While in part reflecting the rather precarious relationship of success to effort in the sales setting, the uneven occurrence of sales is another element makes it difficult to sustain enthusiasm. This is especially true

with larger ticket items since salespeople may go for extended periods
of time without any sales.

It's bust and boom in real estate. All these ups and downs. It gets hairy! People
might go for months without a sale, and then, bang, bang, bang! Three in a
row. A lot can't take it. You have a lot of pressure on you that way. . . . If you
have a husband or wife that is working as well, things are a lot better because
then you have that other income to fill the gaps. But if you're trying to do it
all yourself, it can be murder! You develop a living style and then, can you
support it? You have a high turnover in real estate, because of that pressure
[real estate].

Even when salespeople seem likely to make some sales each day, the
unpredictability of purchases is still bothersome as they find themselves
haphazardly shifting between boredom, time-filling activity, and "action." Thus sales work generally entails considerable switching back
and forth from intense interaction to inactivity. This is further com-
pounded by the expectation of appearing ready for the next encounter.

Sales is not so routine. You know where you're going to be all day, but you
don't know what you're going to sell or not sell, or who or how many are
coming in. . . . You can have your day planned out, say where you plan to get
other things done in the store—there's more than just the selling—and never
get around to it. You also have to be careful not to ignore your customers if
you're taking inventory or marking prices, whatever, because that's the most
important part of your job. And that's something that a lot of the salespeople
fall prey to. You'll have something to do and you set out to do that and you
tend to ignore or resent the customers, and sometimes that really shows. You
have to put the customers first and let the other things ride until you have time
for them [men's clothing].

SLOW TIMES

While the unpredictability of prospects' appearances and purchases
can make saleswork a frustrating and wearying experience, a sustained
lack of sales is especially difficult to manage. Slow times assume three
basic forms: seasonal slows, slow days, and individual slumps.

Seasonal Slows

Slow times in businesses can vary greatly with the products being
sold, and once recognized they can be dealt with more readily (e.g.,

vacation times, reduced staff). Nevertheless, slow times can reduce
overall enthusiasm for those on duty.

> January, February, March, and April, all those months are extremely slow. So
> there you find things to do. You rearrange the store about ten times, have a
> lot of coffee, smoke a lot of cigarettes, be foolish. That's how you get by. The
> people are not there. It's not busy. . . . You can't make the people come in!
> You can put your ads in the paper, display your items the best way you can,
> but you can't take it personally. If there are people in the center, I can sell. If
> they're not there, there's nothing I can do about it. . . . You'll set your goals
> accordingly, so that you might only expect to do half or less of the business
> you might do at other times [shoes].

Slow Days

While slow days may coincide with seasonal slows, any quiet period
can affect general enthusiasm.

> The boredom, that can really get to you. You've seen what it's been like the
> last couple of hours, and right now we're working on a markdown, but if we
> didn't have that to do, we did everything else on Tuesday. I don't know what
> we'd do. You just get talked out. You're with each other four or five days, and
> you really run out of things to say. You look at one another, and maybe light
> up a cigarette. It's tiring! You're standing here on a soft carpet, looking out
> into a vast no-man's land, waiting for a camel on the horizon, and it doesn't
> come. What do you do? A lot of managers go down to the bar for dinner, and
> it's not a solid dinner [men's clothing].

When salespeople are working on a commission basis, slow times
tend to generate additional pressures as well as personal animosities
among the staff.

> You'll get times where you have the customers and there's not enough
> salesmen to look after them, and then you'll get times where the salesmen are
> pretty well fighting with one another to get a chance to look after someone
> who comes in [auto].

> When it gets slow, she [manager] will send you to the back. That way she can
> get the customers for herself, get the commission [3%] herself [shoes].

Slow times are of special concern to store managers. In addition to
dealing with their own lack of activity, they are also concerned about
the ways in which their staff handle these situations.

You have to keep them from knowing that you're depressed. You want to be able to do a good job when the customer does come in. So you try to keep your staff up. . . . The slower you are, the less enthusiasm you have when a customer does come in. It's strange how that works, you should be glad to see them, but for some reason the slower it gets, the less you feel like trying [shoes].

Personal Slumps

Seasonal slows and slow days can rapidly diminish staff enthusiasm, but a lack of individual success is even more difficult for salespeople to handle. In addition to other pressures (commission, job security), they generally have to deal with these failures on a more solitary basis.

A sale is such an elating thing! All right!!! Nice people! I like them and they like me. But if you go for a few weeks and nothing, it's difficult! There, you keep talking to yourself. Keep yourself up, telling yourself that they're not rejecting you. It's only the product that they're not so keen on. You try to keep active, doing something, making some progress in some area [insurance].

It should also be noted that notions of slumps vary considerably.

You do get discouraged sometimes. And sometimes it's hard to be nice to people. You're working for nothing for the whole month, so you get very discouraged sometimes [furniture].

If I have a couple of bad calls, first thing, I'll get off the road. Because even if you persevered, if you start off badly, the whole day is likely to turn out poorly [manufacture—industrial].

UNPLEASANTRIES AND DISTRACTIONS

Incidents involving troublesome customers were discussed at length (Chapter 6), but it is also apparent that these occurrences can dampen vendor enthusiasm.

You see people in a different light when you're selling. I've found that I've gotten down on people a lot more since I've started selling. You see people not always in a good light. You're around people all the time, all day. . . . You'll see women who drag young children, babies around the store when they're crying. And some are mean and grouchy to you, and others, they look down on you. They won't talk to you. . . . Every day you will get some difficult people. Some customers are going to be not too pleasant to deal with.

Usually you can just brush it off, but sometimes you let it get to you, as I sometimes do. And then I'll be taking longer breaks or spending more time in the ladies' room, trying to get over it. But some days are worse than usual. . . . I get home some days and I'm just feeling miserable, really depressed, from some of the customers you have. You just feel like quitting, where you say, "What's the use? What am I doing this for?" And you have some days that are really bad that way. Or you'll see a mother stuffing things in a child's coat, trying to steal something. I just think, "How can you do this to a child?" . . . If you could separate yourself completely from the people, not pay any attention to what they're doing or how they're treating you, not letting it bother you, then you could handle the job a little easier [discount department store].

Some other unpleasantries emerge from within, and reflect managerial policies and practices.

What I find depressing about sales is not the customers but the management. They do not reward you for your efforts. You get paid the same salary regardless of how much you're putting into the job. And I put a good bit into the job. I do a lot of things that other staff people don't do, and you don't get rewarded for it. That's what I find depressing about the job. . . . The customers will get on you for the higher prices, things like that, and that can be annoying, but my main gripe's with the company [candy].

If you screw up, the way they [management] handle it can affect you for the day. Say you go in and the guy starts yelling at you, it'll affect your whole day. You might have gone in in good spirits and now you really don't feel like approaching your customers. . . . But you have to keep yourself up too, try not to let things like that bother you [manufacture—industrial].

As well, a number of elements external to the sales situation affect the general levels of enthusiasm with which salespeople approach customers. These spillovers or inabilities to subjugate distractions (and moods) to the tasks at hand can also affect vendor enthusiasm and success.

There are times when you can really sell. You can't seem to miss! And then there are other times when you can't seem to do anything right. There are times when you just can't seem to connect and you ask yourself, "What am I doing wrong?" And "What image am I portraying?" "Am I projecting that my feet hurt, or that I'm tired, or whatever?" You can be doing this and not even realize that you're doing it. Sometimes the other people in the store will tell you that you're looking glum or whatever, so that helps because you are projecting these images to the customer and you may not even realize that you're doing it. But when you get really involved in your work, it's funny. You forget about your feet hurting or your problems. You just forget about all these other things and concentrate on your customers. . . . You may have to really fight your moods because sometimes you'll be feeling a little down or something is bothering you and you really don't want to be bothered with people, so you may have to fight these moods where you pretty well have to force yourself to go and approach the customer. Or if you've gotten angry about something, you tend to stand back, you'll be thinking, "I really don't want to approach her." And when that happens, you've got to fight it. You've always got to be fighting yourself and your attitudes to sell the way you want to sell, because you'll be thinking, "Let someone else take care of them." So you've got to be fighting yourself to keep that willingness to approach people [women's clothing].

DISRESPECTABLE WORK

Despite its legitimacy, a great many salespeople perceive others to define their work as disrespectable.[2] Concerns with "stigma" (Goffman, 1963) are likely to be episodic rather than constant, even when acutely felt. Nevertheless, this general viewpoint promotes vendor sensitivity to obstacles (especially troublesome customers) encountered on a day-to-day basis in their sales situations.

The extracts following provide a sense of the discomfiture some salespeople experience in disclosing their occupations to others.[3]

When people ask me what I do, you can make it sound bigger or more important. But sales is not a profession and you don't make much money at it [retail sales], so you don't get a lot of prestige for telling people what you do. If I say that I used to teach school, that helps because then they think that you must be a little bright [appliances].

I don't know what it is exactly, but I don't really like telling people what I do for a living. I don't know whether I am ashamed of working in sales or just what it is exactly. "So what do you do?" "Nothing exciting." I don't know, but you kind of get the impression that sales is an underrated job. . . . But it is hard to say just how much of it is me and how much of it is other people acting a certain way towards me. . . . But I do know it has been a major disappointment to my mother because she always thought that I should make something better out of myself. So they are disappointed. They want better things from me than to be in sales. We have had some talks about that and I

know they are quite upset about me being in sales and that they e〉
things of me and how I am not living up to my potential. Thing
[jewelry].

This sense of disrespectability seems to have several origins. From
salespeople's standpoints, it reflects the notion that other people view
sales work as easy, nonproductive, deceptive, aggressive, and selfish.
There is the recognition that some people consider saleswork respectable and even glamorous, but a more general perception is that outsiders
do not see salespeople as doing productive, challenging, honest work
entailing service to others.

You get that a lot, "Boy, I wish I had your job! Then I would get paid for doing
nothing!" . . . They have that image of the salesman. They think you come in
here and just stand here, put your mind "on sleep" and just stand here. . . .
And you're under pressure to make sales, make your budgets. If you don't
make budget, they [head office] want to know why, so the pressure is there.
You have to get the next customer or someone else will get him. And you
never know when there is a shopper coming by, working for the company,
testing you out. Maybe go back and give a bad report on you [men's clothing].

Although many salespeople feel that saleswork is generally discredited, the stigma associated with saleswork appears to be offset when
more prestige is attributed to the company's clientele, the products
being sold, the company involved, and the position of the individual
involved therein.

A lot of times when I tell people that I work at _____ , they'll say, "Oh,
couldn't you get anything better?" There is that stigma attached to sales work,
and then if you're working in a discount department store, you probably get
even more of that. . . . It's a lower-class store, it caters to a lower-class
clientele. It's a lower quality of merchandise overall. We're towards the
bottom of the totem pole. Most of the department stores are above us in
standing, in their clientele [discount department store].

You know it exists, and even as a manager you get some of that, but not as
much. It's more: "Oh, the manager! You must be more important, know more."
Sort of, "You must be different from them!" [men's clothing]

Sustaining Enthusiasm

So far, a number of contingencies people perceive as diminishing their sense of enthusiasm have been outlined. The focus now shifts to people's attempts to achieve higher levels of enthusiasm, and to the encouragements they receive from others as well as the limitations they encounter in this regard. Of particular relevance here are making sales, helping yourself, family support, company support, co-worker relations, and external networks.

MAKING SALES

While those able to maintain higher levels of enthusiasm tend to sell more, sales success generates enthusiasm. Salespeople will sometimes complain about extremely busy times, but in general, a flow of purchasing customers (enabling vendors to fulfill their roles) appears the single most effective element affecting enthusiasm.

> If things are selling, it's a whole different situation. You can joke with the customers, relax more maybe. Everybody's happier, easier to get along with [department store].

> If things are selling good, you feel good. That's what I like best about sales [luggage].

Favorite and Exciting Sales

As might be expected, there is considerable overlap among favorite and exciting sales. Larger and/or more extensive sales more readily generate excitement, as does a greater sense of challenge.

> You always feel good after a good sale, say where a person comes in to buy a sports jacket or just a pair of slacks, and you end up selling him slacks, sports jacket, sweater, shirt, and tie. . . . It just comes so easily! And the salesman hasn't been pushing and yet he's made a good sale. Or other times you'll have a difficult time on a single item where you'd had to really work with the person, and you'll spend a lot of time with the person, and he's tried on everything in the store, and you've had to convince him all the way. And you go to the back and you think, "I thought I was never going to sell this guy!" Then for the next person, you're up a little because you were sure half-way through that you weren't going to get the sale [men's clothing].

In "big ticket" situations, almost any sale can result in acutely higher levels of enthusiasm for the vendors involved.

> If you get that sale, that contract, there isn't another thing in the world that gives you that same sense of thrill, accomplishment! You have that interrelationship between two people and when you come out on top, there isn't a better feeling in the world than having done that [manufacture—industrial].

Also noteworthy as favorite sales are those in which vendors find customers to be especially congenial and are able to serve in more complete advisory capacities. In these respects, salespeople's sense of excitement tends to reflect the enthusiasm they attribute to their prospects.

> The kinds of sales that I like is where you have worked with the person, and you have fitted them and taken care of them and they are happy when they walk out the door. They're pleased with the merchandise and what you do for them. . . . The other kind of exciting sale is the big sale where someone comes in and makes an extraordinary large purchase. It does so much for you to do a big sale [women's clothing]!

Situational Advantages

Success in sales reflects enthusiasm and effort, but clearly it is easier for people to be both more enthusiastic and more successful when they represent more established companies or carry "hotter lines."

> When you're selling, it depends on your importance to the market, how they treat you. When I was selling with this last company, in the early years, you were just another rep. Later, as the company grew and was better recognized, they were almost jumping at your products, and if you introduced a new product, people would be very keen on it, so there you get treated a lot differently when you are in that situation [manufacture—appliances].

As well, people who have been able to develop or tap into previously established larger pools of repeat customers are apt to find themselves considerably advantaged over others.

> If you've got a better territory, that'll help you sell more. If you make more calls, the more calls you make, the more sales you make. And you have to be a bit creative. You have to be more aware of what all applies to paper handling,

there are so many options and you try to adapt to each situation, so that can help too [manufacture—office equipment].

Since it is easier to maintain enthusiasm when products are selling well, it is particularly important to ask how salespeople maintain enthusiasm in the absence of sales. It is here that concerns with helping yourself, family support, and company support become more central to salespeople's sense of enthusiasm.

HELPING YOURSELF

Given people's capacities for self-reflectivity, many vendors attempt to generate and sustain enthusiasm on their own. To this end, they may set goals for themselves, strive for "positive thinking," and otherwise plan for greater success.

> I set a goal for myself everyday, for total sales. . . . I keep track of my sales, write down all my sales as I go along, on a separate piece of paper, so I know exactly how well I'm doing. And you will have some idea of what the other people on your shift are doing, so you'll try to keep up with them. . . . But with some things, like the larger purchases, one or two of these can really make the difference between a poor day and a good day for you [shoes].

> In this job, if I don't keep myself up, nobody else will do it. My wind up comes from books. I read a lot of books on motivational thinking and such. That's the only way I can keep my own enthusiasm up to where it should be. . . . That and also the enthusiasm of seeing someone come in and they're all excited about the job they did on something. But the customers also mirror what you show them [hobby].

Likewise, salespeople may turn to "the odds" or otherwise define their efforts in larger contexts. In these ways, they may minimize the significance of immediate obstacles.[4]

> When you hit a slump and you've been through slumps before, it's a matter of putting it in perspective. You talk to yourself, "You've done it before, right? Put on the old charm and try again." There though, how long can you keep trying to start yourself up before the battery goes dead? You know you should keep going, but you can't. You reach a point where you just don't want to [insurance].

It's very easy to get down. It's like a very emotional roller coaster. It really is! I've never encountered anything like it before. . . . It's incredible to watch when you've been through it a few times and it feels like it's going to strike again. And it doesn't have any relation to whether you're working or not. There are times when you just have difficulty getting up and going to the open houses. It's easy to lapse into not doing those things. And there are days when you're just sailing. When you're hot, you're hot! That is how it is. . . . It can be really slow at times and then all of a sudden, in a couple of days, you can't believe how things are working out. And before that it didn't seem to matter what you did, you couldn't make a sale. And it's very difficult to keep yourself up. After a while you start to realize that you have to go with the flow. But it's a very emotional roller coaster kind of existence. . . . It can cause a lot of stress in a family. I know it has in ours [real estate].

Since enthusiasm is difficult to sustain on a solitary basis for extended periods of time,[5] other support systems assume considerable significance.

FAMILY SUPPORT

Somewhat ironically, the relationship between family relationships and success in sales has a precarious quality. When salespeople have family members to whom they are accountable, the responses of these others can very significantly affect the individual's sense of enthusiasm. As the following extracts suggest, the tolerances of one's spouse can be critical.

The wives think, "Why don't you get a regular job, nine to five and get a pay check every Friday?" like in industry. And usually that comes when you're not making the money. It's frustrating enough without having the pressures at home [real estate].

It makes a difference. Lavonne's a big help. You can get down on yourself in sales quite easily. But if you've got that support at home, you can talk about things, joke about it more. It's not so hard to get yourself going to face the next customer [wholesale—giftware].

Further, as people strive for success in the business world, they typically organize their lives more fully around sales.[6] These practices are likely to result in more successful sales careers, but they may interfere with existing family relationships.

When you have a down day, you bring it home with you because there's no
one else to talk to. And who's going to listen to you but your wife, so it's hard
on the women and it's hard on the children. Other times you'll come home
and, "Let's do something! Let's go! Let's get moving!" You don't want to
settle down. It's like having a high, and you can't think of anything better
that you could be doing! And I had a great day! Made some great sales.
"Wowee!" . . . And the next day you come in and your wife expects you to be
somewhat the same and you're there like a sore bear. . . . Then they figure
that you're a psychotic or something, and after, they start to realize that when
you walk in the door you're going to be one of two things. It is tough on them,
because you do bring it home [manufacture—industrial].

Most of the women who have worked [their way] up in the company have
family problems. The hours are long and you have to work Saturdays and
evenings, and that causes problems. It is pretty rough on the family. . . . A lot
of women don't stay in retail very long. They just can't take it! If you take it
seriously, it's more than just a job. And if you want to move up, it's more
demanding, and you may have to move around a fair bit [women's clothing].

COMPANY SUPPORT

In broader terms, whatever companies do to facilitate sales (ordering
goods, pricing, promotions, and so on) may be seen as beneficial in
generating enthusiasm. Managerial support may also take a variety of
other forms. This would include sales and motivational meetings; feedback, goals and incentive programs; and recreational outings for work
groups. Managers are by no means equally concerned about these
options, but all may affect employee enthusiasm.

Sales and Motivational Meetings

Sales meetings may be used variously as training sessions; occasions
for discussing policies, practices, and problems; teamwork and planning sessions; motivational forums; and accountability devices to promote daily effort.

We have meetings every few weeks where we'll discuss our sales, what we
can do to improve our sales, what we want to promote, what we want to put
on "sale." I try to get the whole staff involved in that. I want them to feel that
it's their store, where they get to give their advice on things and help make
the decisions [jewelry].

We try to get everybody together once a week or so. Usually on a Friday, but Mondays may be a little better in some ways. It's a chance to go over their calls, see what problems they've run into. Talk about product features, closes, things like that. . . . Fridays are better for reviewing the week's events, but Mondays are better motivationally. Your weekends get in the way, especially if things have been going well. They're distracting. So with your Monday sessions, you try to get everyone back on track. Get their motors running. You hate to take that time at either end of the week, but we want to leave ourselves that hour or two together someplace most every week [manufacture—office equipment].

Recognizing that salespeople encounter periods of lows, companies may explicitly hold motivational meetings for their employees. These meetings may involve other aspects of marketing such as developing sales techniques and increasing product knowledge, and they may be led by company personnel or outsiders, but a central task is that of promoting enthusiasm.

I think that there are highs and lows in any sales and generally speaking, when you're making more sales, more income, you tend to be high. And when you're high, you've got to hit a low. You can't stay high all the time. . . . One of the benefits of a large corporation like this is that we have sales meetings several times a year, have motivational speakers. You want to keep the motivations going, the momentum. Sometimes you lose track of it, what you really came into this industry for. And it's very disappointing when you've worked very hard, and you'll work 9:00 to 9:00 for a few days with a particular couple and they might then end up buying a house privately that they saw an ad on. Meanwhile you might spend two or three full days and lose out, gain nothing on it whatsoever, so it can be very disappointing [real estate].

This business is hills and valleys. It's easy to get depressed in this business. It's "When you're hot, you're hot!" And it's enthusiasm, where something good happens, when you're more enthusiastic with the next customer, the sales seem easier, you've got yourself up. That's really important. . . . Most of my meetings with the staff are motivational meetings. I don't believe in shit sessions. My guys, I like to give them a charge, tell them a joke, give them some product information, tell them that we're number one, get them pumped up, where they're enthusiastic when they go out to meet the customer [auto].

In addition to group sessions, managers may provide salespeople with other motivators.

At _____ , we have all kinds of material, tapes, brochures. The tapes are made by the successful people in the organization, so [you get] their material on prospecting, your presentations, rejections, and all [insurance].

As the following material suggests, however, the success of many motivational messages may be nullified by the limited applicability of group enthusiasm to the solitary daily activity sales work generally entails.

People react differently to these [motivational] sessions. For some, they come out and they're gung ho, and, "These are just terrific!" I don't find them all that much help. But I think I'm more of a self-starter. I think of it as an intrusion on my day. I don't like giving up two and a half hours Monday morning when I could be talking to clients and working on campaigns. I find them a pain! Unfortunately, I have no choice. I have to go to them. I also find that complaining about things that didn't go right the week before is very counterproductive at the beginning of the week. . . . I don't find them very motivational at all [promotions—radio].

You can have a motivational seminar and have those people so jacked up by the time you're finished, they think they can go out and sell the world. But when they get out there, they find that it's different. You've got your own feelings to contend with. . . . When you approach somebody and they're negative to you, it's a hurt feeling, a degrading feeling, and your self-image drops. And it's hard for an individual to carry on. . . . That's why there are so many people lined up by the wayside. And this is why. They can't stand the negativity that they're running into, and the uncertainty, this sort of thing. That's what makes it so hard [mixed sales]!

Likewise, as recurrent events, the relative gains of motivational sessions may dissipate with frequency.

Staff meetings are a problem for me. First, you have problems getting the staff together at one time. They come in on different shifts. And then I talk to my staff a lot. Just during the day, telling them how to do things, what's coming in, what they might just have done wrong. So when it comes to a meeting, I don't have all that much to say. And yet head office wants to know what happened at that meeting, what topics were covered, things like that. And with me and my staff, we find it's just a rehash. I'm not telling them anything different. I'm telling them things all day [women's clothing].

Feedback, Goals, and Incentive Programs

In attempts to prompt individual accomplishment, some businesses provide feedback on staff performances, set explicit sales targets, and feature a variety of other incentive programs.

Since sales work has uneven outcomes even with consistent efforts, it is difficult for salespeople to tell how successful they are in the absence of some standards. Those on commission may have minimum levels of sales that they consider sufficient, but some measure of accomplishment seems of interest to salespeople in all settings. Thus, while some salespeople keep fairly accurate track of their sales, regularized feedback on performance may generate a greater sense of intensity for others.

> Some people keep close track of their sales. I don't. So for me it's helpful at the end of the day or the week to see what I've done [sales figures provided by the company]. It's the sense of accomplishment, I suppose, but I just want to know how well I'm doing too [shoes].

> I am very concerned about my sales totals. I won't steal customers from other staff, but I am concerned about getting my sales up higher. I'm the kind of person who likes to impress, and I want to impress my sales manager. I want to see that I can improve. I realize that you can only improve so much, given the volume of customers you have, but I like to improve, to keep getting better sales totals. Then we get feedback from our department, so that way you know where your sales are. Like it's a personal challenge to try to improve my sales totals [department store].

Somewhat mindful of these performance definitions, many companies set specific goals for their salespeople.

> If they set reasonable quotas for you, it is something to try for. And we have all these little bonuses. So much for the month, the quarter, the year. It makes it more of a game. But if it's set too high, eventually you realize that you can't get it. Then it loses some of its effect. It becomes sort of a measure of failure then [manufacture—industrial].

> We're very conscious of sales totals. We have them broken down day-by-day. They [head office] want to see us beat every day over last year. But I think more on a month-by-month basis. Day by day, anything can happen. You put too much pressure on yourself and your staff that way [women's clothing].

As some of the preceding quotes imply, an emphasis on sales totals and targets seems to work best when sales are being made. This does not always happen. Thus, in addition to regular salaries, commissions, bonuses, and the like (see Prus 1989: Chapter 3), companies may also introduce a variety of incentives (and contests) to foster sales effort. These promotions may be used to generate activity on any number of levels (e.g., get new leads, introduce new products, move odd stock, overcome slow seasons), but as "extras" providing contrasts with daily routines, these events tend to arouse added interest on the part of sales staff.

Some promotions involve cash awards, but those featuring other items seem to more readily lend themselves to a variety of themes. It should be noted, however, that while more costly and colorful items seem to generate more interest, winnings are generally enhanced by the recognition they are seen to denote.

We have internal contests because you have to keep the people excited, motivated. Sometimes these are individual competitions, sometimes team events where you divide the staff into a couple of teams and introduce some incentives that way. . . . We will also increase commissions on certain cars that are not moving so well otherwise, to get the staff more involved in showing this particular line of automobiles or trucks, whatever, or maybe a night out for the wife and family if you sell one of these. Things like that. . . . Whoever makes the first sale of the day gets a new pair of shoes, any little thing. Not very expensive, but motivational [auto].

We have regional competitions across the country and in the area, and then we have competitions within the office on listings, sales, various things of that nature. People like to be recognized and that's the reason for the contests, to give people that recognition [real estate].

Beyond internal promotions directed at a business's immediate employees, some promotions are initiated by the suppliers with whom businesses deal.

The suppliers had some contests so that whoever sold the most jeans of a certain brand might get some prize. Some records, a watch, things like that [mixed clothing].

That's how I own this watch. A deal from _____ . They had a contest last month, based on volume. Sell so much _____ and you win it [variety].

While some promotions are in-house creations, others are developed by people in the premiums and incentives business. The statement following is especially valuable for indicating the scope of incentive programs.

Basically, I set up an incentive program involving travel for their people. So you go to the people in the company and tell them that if you sell so much, meet this quota that your company has established, you will be rewarded by getting this holiday. I supply the holiday end of it and I set up the actual incentives, what is going to make them get out and sell. . . . So I go in and design an incentive program for each company. . . . It depends on the product line for the company, what they're selling, the size of their sales staff, their budget, and how much sales they need. Like, is the market down? If so, we may go in with a very strong incentive program to get their people moving. If they're in a very strong position, you can go in with a much milder program. They don't need a big hype. The basic thing is that whatever they're paying for the package, their profit margin results should be much greater than that. . . . If they expect 50 people to travel, and then we set up an incentive program, we are hopefully going to achieve a hundred winners instead of 50. And there, if the number of winners is twice what they expected, their profits should also be twice as high as they expected. . . . Normally, everyone has highs and lows in their fiscal year. Oftentimes a 12-week program is best because in three months you can accomplish enough and it's not so long that people will get bored. What you try to instill in them is some idea of a quota, but you make it a lot more fun and a lot more visible. What you're trying to do with a holiday is make it more tangible. So the first week, when we launch the program, we send every single person a box with a whole set of logo-designed materials. Maybe a travel bag, sunglasses, some coins from the country. A whole box of items related to the trip, so when they open the box, it really hits them in the face, gets them to experience these things. But it's basically a reminder that if they go out and really sell they will get to use all these things in five months or whatever. And you can get poster calendars for them to mark their sales along the way. And then, within thirty days, if we haven't achieved a certain level with profit, and you work that out with the company at that time, we rework the program. But usually it's successful, and at that point we'll be giving out "fast start" prizes, things again related to travel or the destination. So instead of waiting until the very end to give them any satisfaction or results on how they're doing, you give them a fast start prize early. And obviously, we have our contacts to buy these things at a minimal cost instead of retail. And often we put out or use their newsletter announcing these winners. And all of a sudden people start talking, and you might go into the sales meeting with slides or another box of incentives for them. Keep the trip fresh on their minds. You want them to think about it

274   MAKING SALES

constantly. So we'll do things too, like send postcards to the wives from the hotel, "Hope to see you here at such and such a time." Get them interested in the trip too. And if you can get the people at home behind them, the results are often better. So when I say it's a hype program, this is what I'm talking about. . . . [Afterwards] we also do things like when they're there on one of the last days and everyone is looking happy, well-tanned, and all, we'll take their group picture. Blow it up and send it to everyone who didn't make it, who lost, and say, "Hope to see you here next year." If that doesn't get them moving, nothing will. And then on the next sales meeting, we get everyone to bring in their photos. It's not like giving someone a cash award where they put it into the bank and the effects are not seen. With a travel incentive program, we get everyone to bring in their photographs, give them little prizes, a bottle of rum, whatever, and you keep them talking about the trip for sometime after. You keep the memories, the talk, the chatter going as a result for months after. And if it works out, it can be a regular, annual kind of thing. Sometimes you'll get companies who, when they're coming back, will announce where the next year's trip is going to be [promotions—travel].

As the quotes following imply, however, contests and other awards are subject to multiple and shifting interpretations. Recipients and others may view these events with much more ambiguity (and negativity) than organizers anticipate.

These contests are funny things. They can really get people going, but they can generate a lot of resentments too. Sometimes, like with the "salesman of the month" kind of thing, it's kind of embarrassing to win it. It's good in the eyes of management, but you can get a lot of razzing from the people you work with. It's like getting all these stars in grade school. You'd be better to just get the top commission and leave the award for somebody else. It's a barrier, a "teacher's pet" sort of thing. . . . It's good for some. They really like that. But it creates animosity and resentment. And top sales, it doesn't mean that you're any better or that you've actually worked harder or had a tougher territory. So what's it really worth [manufacture—computers]?

You know what people sometimes do with these things. They load up their orders so they'll fall more on this or that time period. If they know a contest is coming up, they might be a couple days slow in submitting orders or load somebody up on extra products. So you can play games with them [company] that way too. . . . A few good sized orders, one way or the other, can make quite a difference [manufacture—industrial].

Company Sponsored Gatherings

Somewhat as an alternative to individual incentives, some companies try to encourage workplace enthusiasm by organizing group events such as picnics, parties, and other recreational outings. As "off time" occasions, these assemblies tend to foster relaxation, camaraderie, and fuller awareness of one's work-related associates.

> We don't get much of that here. But at [a large chain specialty store] we had a lot of group events. Picnics, baseball games, parties. It was a better place to work at that way, for sure. It was more like a family that way. You get to know everybody and all [shoes].

> These staff parties are good. If you're working with people day in, day out, it's easy for them to get under your skin. This way, you see them in a different light. It's a more relaxed atmosphere. It keeps the hard feelings from building up so much [men's clothing].

Despite some seemingly clear advantages to these gatherings, it should be noted that any problems emerging in these settings may very well spill over into the work setting.

> These company picnics and all, they're funny things. They can be good for morale and making friends and all, but they can also create a lot of problems if something gets out of hand. So we've gone through periods where we did have these things and periods where we didn't, depending on how we thought they would work out. But there again, you just can't predict it. You'll have people who get along well and then, boom, something happens and they may never get back to where they were before. And that can hurt the company because if their sales are falling off because of that or the service is suffering because of that, it comes back on us [manufacture—industrial].

CO-WORKER RELATIONS

While sometimes distracting and otherwise disruptive of salespeople's enthusiasm, people's co-workers represent another significant source of support.

> If you're working alone, it can be really difficult. Like with Jack, I'm really not alone because we're always working our strategies together, talking about proposals, and that really helps. But if you're on your own, like LaMar, it's more difficult. And it doesn't take long for time to go by and you wonder, "What have I been

doing?" And in this business, you're paid by how much business you bring in. . . .
You get to the point where you say, "If I see so many people, I'm going to do
business with so many." So all you have to do is plan to see your ten or so
people. . . . You have to look at it like, "Well, if I miss this sale, it doesn't matter,
because you're going to do business with the next ones." So there's comfort in the
averages. You have to go out and get the names, but you know that if you do this
and this and this, you're going to get the names. And if you get names, you're going
to get so many appointments, put on so many presentations, and make so many
sales [investments].

Salespeople are a different breed of people. Their life-styles are different. They
have all your ups and downs. . . . I'm like a social worker here. They get excited.
They get depressed. They can be very moody! You have to help them. You have
to support them, and put up with all their highs and lows [sales agency receptionist].

It is with respect to people's co-workers that the concept of *fitting in*
becomes so central to enthusiasm. Fitting in refers to an individual's
sense of comfort with and acceptance by others in a setting. It has
central implications for short-run and long-term continuity in the sales
arena. Although some people are hired as a consequence of preexisting
contacts (friends, relatives) and are generally advantaged by having
others to assist them in dealing with their setting, the extent to which
all newcomers feel comfortable with and accepted by others is problematic.[7] But people feeling more comfortable with their workmates are
apt to find sales work more enjoyable and more central to their lives.

I like the people I work with. That is one of the big reasons I'm still there.
And it's not that you're just friends within the store, because you'll do a lot
of things with the same people on the weekends and all. . . . When you first
start, you feel like an outsider and that's something that I guess sort of stops
me from leaving here to go to work in another store, because you know what
you've got here, and you see with the new people coming in, they have some
difficulty fitting in, and that's sort of how it would be if you went some place
new. You would be the outsider again [discount department store].

There's usually one guy who's such a "yes man" that if the boss stops short,
they collide. Now some bosses like that, but it's not good for the employee.
That happens in every situation, though, not just sales. . . . When the new
person comes in, usually everyone gives him his chance. But if the boss builds
him up, "Hey, he's a super guy!" really it's a reflection on the other guys and
they're thinking, "Are you saying we're not super, fellow?" If the manager
says, "We've got another super guy to fit in with our super team!" that's a

little different. But if the manager comes in and talks this guy up, the rest of you are thinking, "Hey, what's the matter with us?" So if he comes in in that situation, he's got a strike against him. The people are going to be a little icy towards him. If they then find out that the guy likes to go out for a drink, to carouse around, that he's not a yes man to the boss, that he's going to be one of us, well, then it's different. They're more likely to accept him. . . . It's almost like a club, an exclusive club. It's easy to get into, but you've got to be one of the guys to get into it. You don't have to be antimanagement, but you've got to be considerate of the other guys. If you start defending the manager or the company when everyone else feels it is a wrong move or situation, then you're going to get some static. Now we probably all do it on occasion, but if you're doing it more consistently, they're going to start avoiding you. Like if the guys go out drinking after a sales meeting, he's the guy who's left behind. Not a good feeling! But when you're out drinking, after a few drinks your tongue gets a little more fluid, and you're liable to say things. And if he's the yes man, or always accepting everything the company does without questioning, you're afraid of him saying something to the boss. So you can't socialize with that one individual, and usually they don't get any further ahead than you. And if the management is smart, they wouldn't promote that person, because once they move up higher, the people in management should wonder if they can trust a person like that. Does the manager want someone like that as a peer [manufacture—industrial].

Polite relationships may do little directly to promote continuity, but animosities developing within businesses tend to result in reduced efficiencies and departures.

If you have two people on the floor that are not getting along, you've got a problem! The work doesn't always get done, they're too busy fighting over who's going to do what [shoes].

A conflict in the store, that's not good for anyone. It makes working here more difficult for everyone. And you're supposed to be up when the customers come around, so that becomes tougher too. . . . Usually if it gets bad, someone leaves. There are other jobs [women's clothing].

Concerns about maintaining viable working relationships may also result in the terminations of otherwise productive salespeople.

I've had to let hundreds of salespeople go, literally hundreds. Now at this particular dealership it's not really that much of a problem, because the people are so stable. Like most have been here for eight or ten years. But at some of

the other places I managed, where you don't have the stability and where you
don't have the selection of people we get here, I would say that only about
two of five people worked out. Then through the years, things happen with
salespeople. Some become disturbers and cause more aggravation than what
they're worth. Like even a grand master salesman, a guy who was the top
salesman in the place, I had to fire him. He was just causing more trouble than
his sales were worth to the place. The biggest and best salesman in the place!
But I guess it was the right decision because after, sales picked up and
everyone else seemed happier [auto].

EXTERNAL BUSINESS NETWORKS

Another element affecting people's sense of enthusiasm revolves
around the relationships these people have with others in the business
world. These networks not only represent general friendships, but also
denote work-related support in the form of sales practices and performance. As a result, these networks may have considerable impact on
people's continuity in sales. In developing this discussion, attention will
be given to networks reflecting neighboring businesses, field contacts,
and clubs and associations. Although each contact source will be discussed separately, there are often overlapping interests among the
people involved in these associations. For instance, people from neighboring businesses or clubs may represent opportunities for alternative
employment and recreational pursuits as well as signifying sales-related
contacts and sources of encouragement.

Neighboring Businesses

People working in nearby businesses tend to have greater opportunities for interpersonal contact. While this is especially evident
among those in fixed locations, other neighboring arrangements (e.g.,
trade shows) also lend themselves to these sorts of contacts.

Fixed locations. Salespeople working in stores often become acquainted with those in neighboring businesses over time. This seems
more true for those in smaller businesses as opposed to people working
in department stores, wherein people in other departments may remain
relative strangers. However, any mutually involving activities (such as
shopping in neighboring stores or eating in common settings) promotes
association as does the mere frequency of people's paths crossing by
virtue of their common territories.

Mostly you'll associate with the people in the stores right around you. That seems pretty well true for all the malls in which I've worked. . . . The other way to get to know the sales people is to drop into the local bar. In some of the malls, you can get to meet everyone in the local bar [men's clothing].

It's nice to deal with people in the same complex as yourself. You can't comparison shop as much, but it helps build a good working relationship with these other people. You get to know them better and it's good for business all around. . . . It can be a problem though, if you don't like their selection or if you think their prices are way out of line [appliances].

Shows and exhibitions. Although the vendors involved in trade shows and other exhibits may be in one another's territories only for short periods of time, one notices similar tendencies for these people to associate with their neighbors. Certain neighbors may be preferred over others, but these contacts represent opportunities to exchange information about other shows, assess the present show, and make sales-related as well as more personal contacts.[8]

It's like a little group and you get to know one another a fair bit and see what the other people are doing. . . . We have had the same spots in the different shows for a number of years, so that way you do get to know the people around you quite well because often they are going for a number of years too [wholesale—giftware].

When I come to the [trade] show, it is like old times week because, although I have changed lines, a lot of my old friends are here. They're people I have worked with, some are competitors and there are a lot of old customers here too, so in the evening it will be just great because you will be socializing with all these people. You're saying, "Hello, how are you?" It's nice in that regard. . . . A big part of the show is the socializing. They are all staying at the same hotel and so you have these opportunities to get together, and the public relations aspect of it. If the client is one who likes to drink, then you are more likely to go drinking. If he likes strip joints, then you go to a strip joint. You might suggest that if you've heard from someone else that he likes them: "Let's go to _____ ." And he sort of says, "Well, it might be okay. Why not?" And he acts surprised that someone might ask him. He would like to go, but he can't come out and say that. In some ways, you would hope that it wouldn't be part of the business, but it is. It really is! And you have to get along with the people. You have to relate to them, and if they like you, then they're more likely to do business with you [manufacture—industrial].

Trade shows are also salesmen's conventions, where they pick up chicks, find lost lovers, make deals for broadening their own lines, where they pick up scuttlebutt. You could do a study just on trade shows [manufacture—giftware].

Field Contacts

Not unlike those working in neighboring stores or vendors occupying neighboring booths at shows, those involved in field sales work also find themselves in contact with other businesspeople.[9] On some occasions, these contacts are one-time encounters (as when two salesmen embark in conversation at a hotel in which they both are guests). Other times, as agents calling on the same basic sets of clientele, they may find their encounters more frequent.

> If you're in the field for any length of time, you do get to know the other reps, your competitors. And it's good, too. You find out more about their companies and what morale is like there. And later, it may be a job offer if these people move up and if they like you or one of their people leaves. So it's good to be friendly to everyone, including the competition [manufacture—industrial].

> We're competing, but there's a lot of intercompany socializing going on. And quite often the reps—when they're on the road they arrange to be in town with certain other reps—to get together. You would get that gypsy feeling otherwise, because the only people you would get to meet would be clients. . . . There's really no secrets, and in fact at these trade shows we quite openly go from one booth to another to pick up information on what everyone else has. Most everyone is quite open, although you do get the odd company which has super aggressive, unfriendly reps [publisher—books].

Clubs and Associations

Salespeople generally have access to a number of clubs and associations. Some groups are product-oriented (e.g., clothing, graphics), while others have more general themes such as "industrial," "retail," "sales and advertising," "community business and fellowship clubs," and the like. Product-oriented organizations provide opportunities to share experiences with those involved in similar endeavors and discuss problems and other concerns specific to their industry. Organizations involving members of more diverse backgrounds are apt to emphasize the local or regional aspects of their association. While one finds the sharing of experiences, dilemmas, strategies, and such here, there is a greater likelihood of cross-purchasing (and referral activity) in these settings than in product-focused associations.

Members of business clubs have some advantages over others. Not only may they become acquainted with more prospects in this manner, but they also have a chance to meet them under generally pleasant circumstances. It should be noted that business clubs provide back regions for members to discuss (joke, assess experiences, gripe) about business and their customers as well as affording an atmosphere in which sales activity is a most acceptable endeavor. . . . When people in related but different businesses assemble, they will frequently suggest third parties the other person should contact. Club members are more apt to do business between themselves, but these gatherings also allow people in related industries to tap into these other prospects. It is also worth noting that those in attendance are provided with career opportunities more generally. They are often in excellent positions to learn of and/or be recruited into openings at one another's businesses [notes].

One of the reasons we've gotten involved with some of the community clubs and such is because of the contacts they offer. It's maybe a selfish motive, but we were also hoping to learn more about the business community and how people do business more generally. They [clubs] are opportunities to make yourself known to people in the community who could be of great assistance to us in promoting our name, and there does tend to be a loyalty among people in these organizations. . . . And with ourselves, it's the same. We would rather go to someone who's a member of _____ , for instance, regardless of what he was charging. Although price is a factor, if there's only a few dollars difference, you would sooner give that person the business. So there's the old clique forming. . . . So at this point in time, we're joining groups and associations, not for what we can put into it, but for what we can get out of it. I think that's a recognized thing, and it's one of the things that they use to attract new members. Their hope is that as you develop you will be able to put something back into the group. . . . So these groups are valuable contacts, very definitely. And not only that, it forms part of a support group that you find lacking when you start as a small businessman going into business for yourself. You're filled with enough doubts and reservations about doing business, and it gives you the opportunity to socialize with people who do have a lot in common with you and it gives you a sounding board, although they may not be in the same business. Most businesses all have a basic foundation and they all pretty well operate on the same rules. So it does give you an opportunity to get a sounding board and to find out if what you're doing isn't working. And there's also the emotional support that it gives you more than anything else. . . . If business is poor, and you go to a meeting and everyone is moaning and groaning, you realize that it's not just you. And you realize that you're not going poorly because you're you, but everyone's in the same situation and you expect that things have got to start looking up. . . . It does help you a lot, being part of that clique. Your banker will recognize the effort you are putting in to making the business grow and is more likely to be understanding of you, because your banker is likely to be a member of the same organization. Also, these organizations tend to promote a variety of community things which you then become affiliated with, and your name then becomes known through these things.... I've never been a joiner. I've always tried to stay away from this sort of thing, being in a position where I feel obligated to perform certain duties and I don't know if I will get conned into doing something I really don't feel like doing, but I can only see it helping us right now. It may not be a good thing for us to remain in these organizations later on, once we are more established and feel more comfortable in the community, but for the time being it seems good for us [appliances].

In addition to the other ways in which these organizations may affect members' careers, many also offer programs designed to promote enthusiasm on the part of their members. Thus many community and/or merchandising associations frequently feature motivational speakers for members and other interested parties.

Generally speaking, motivational speakers begin with a few jokes, often localizing these to the gathering [product or community] and follow with their messages. While the overt value of most messages is unclear [one hears relatively little of the analysis of marketing activity] most in attendance find these sessions interesting, if not beneficial. Beyond the specifics of any message, speakers generate impact in a variety of ways. First, most businesspeople appreciate entertaining performances. While definitions vary, smooth, colorful, witty, and lively presentations seem to fare better. Secondly, speakers focusing on concerns mutual to the audience and able to provide new or more explicit perspectives for the listeners to consider tend to achieve stronger definitions of interest and worth. Third, speakers able to elicit audience involvement, thereby indicating greater acceptance of the speaker by others, tend to be rated more highly [notes].

Careers in Sales

While we have been considering enthusiasm largely on a situated, immediate basis, some references to long-term participation have been inevitable. Albeit brief, the ensuing discussion sheds further light on this more enduring feature of sales work.

The career contingency model (introduced in Chapter 1) suggests that five components are central to continuity. These are perspectives, identities, activities, commitments, and relationships. Applied to people's involvements in sales, we would expect salespeople to continue to work in sales (and stay with particular companies) to the extent that they develop perspectives conducive to saleswork (more specifically con-

gruent with their present company's mode of sales), achieve self identities and social reputations as salespeople (especially an identity as a
_____ representative), attain competence and interest in sales activities (particularly with the tasks at hand), make commitments to a sales
life-style (more specifically organizing one's life around this company's sales program), and establish relationships supportive of one's
sales involvements (more specifically with regards to this company).
Expressed another way, the very elements that enable people to be
successful in sales serve to mitigate against departure.

It does appear, however, that it is much easier for people to disentan-
gle themselves from particular sales situations than to disengage themselves from sales work more completely. Thus one encounters a considerable amount of mobility of salespeople across companies and product
areas. While each position entails a certain amount of product knowledge, the recognition that sales skills are somewhat generic, combined
with perceived opportunities and/or existing dissatisfactions, makes
mobility more attractive. One finds long-term employment in many
cases, but it should not be assumed that the following instances are
atypical.

> I've been in sales for 14 years. Five years with [department store], a year with [shoe
> manufacturer], then with [bookstore] for three years, and now five years in our own
> gift store. It's kind of a coincidence, how one thing leads to another, but I've never
> really been out of it for any length of time. . . . It was just something that happened.
> I started out in business administration and sort of got into retailing from there. But
> now I'm thinking in terms of long-term commitments with three stores, long-term
> leases [giftware].

> When you're in sales, the easiest thing to do is to stay in sales. So even if you
> change companies or products, you'll still likely end up in sales. . . . You get known
> and, of course, that's where your experience is, in sales. If you're in sales, you can
> get a job almost anyplace. And that makes it easier because everybody needs
> somebody to promote their products. . . . Your sales experience is your ticket. You
> feel comfortable in sales. It doesn't matter so much what you're selling, within
> reason. That should be immaterial. You're a salesman [manufacture—industrial].

Further, while the turnover in sales is high, it is worth noting that not
only the successful remain.

> You are largely on your own, timewise, so you could slack off. And some who
> stayed were people like that, who weren't doing well. You had the two types who

stayed, those who did really well and those who were always just getting by. And part of the reason that they could stay is that so many people left, either to improve themselves or because the whole thing got to them. So there was such a constant turnover of people leaving that there were people who just sort of hung on. They had some experience and made some sales, made quota some months and not others. One reason that they got by was because of the turnover rate. They couldn't find replacements that would last. . . . These were people who just found that it was comfortable to stay at that level [manufacture—office equipment].

Interacting with a great many other businesspeople, salespeople also find themselves in excellent positions to learn of openings in other businesses.

You see a lot of people switching around in the mall. A lot go from store to store in the mall. It happens a lot! You hear that this one has an opening, and you think this might be easier or that the pay is better, and so they try the other place [men's clothing].

It's interesting because each company you deal with, they're somewhat different. And if you're interested they'll tell you more about their businesses, show you how they make their products, tell you about the problems in their industries, and what they're up against in dealing with their competition. And the amount of job offers I've got are incredible! And it's not that I'm looking for another job right now, but if I am ever looking for another job, I know of a number of companies not related to travel that would find me a spot in sales or marketing, something like that. And you're dealing with companies all across North America, and large and small businesses, so really a variety. . . . It's great because it never gets boring. It's always different people and different products, and they're all selling something, but every one is different. Really fascinating [promotions—travel]!

In Perspective

One of the problems is that you can try 100% one day and sell a lot, but you can try 100% another day and not be able to sell. So it's not just a matter of what you put into it [women's clothing].

Although it may be tempting to divide the world into go getters and deadbeats, the material presented herein attests to the situated nature of enthusiasm as expressed by salespeople. Rather than signifying a fixed individual quality, enthusiasm denotes a social process. Enthusiasm may be greatly diminished or enhanced depending on the situations in which people find themselves and the ways in which others act towards them. As a social phenomenon, enthusiasm can not be reduced to "personalities" or individual efforts. Vendors can plan and act for success, but enthusiasm very much reflects the interchanges those in sales have with their associates.

Perhaps now, better understanding the elements affecting enthusiasm, we would not want readily to dismiss adages such as, "When you're hot, you're hot! And when you're not, you're not!" At the same time, however, we would want to be sensitive to the long-term features of enthusiasm as well as it's situated nature. Further, in addition to elements affecting enthusiasm within particular company contexts, we would also wish to consider the broader interactional contexts (family, friends, business associates) in which people find themselves and the shifting opportunities these contacts represent.

Before moving into the last chapter, it may be instructive to conclude this discussion by considering the practical limitations of company-induced enthusiasm. Insofar as enthusiasm seems contingent on the shifting and uncertain interactions salespeople have with others, it seems likely that companies will have difficulty achieving quick-fixes of an enduring nature. Given people's capacities for self-reflectivity and ongoing assessments of managerial practices, we not only find varying appreciations of any management practices from one salesperson to another but also over time as salespeople reconsider the situations in which they find themselves. Company support programs (i.e., motivational meetings, incentive programs, and recreational gatherings) are all subject to ongoing sets of interpretations at both individual and group levels. Any managerial attempt to generate enthusiasm is apt to be defined differently by each person experiencing the situation. As well, these endeavors are subject to variations in assessments by the same individuals and groups over time. While some managerial practices lend themselves to generally higher levels of dedication, we would also want to keep in mind the very precarious nature of saleswork. In addition to the very direct dependencies of salespeople on their customers for affirmations of their work, salespeople also seem vulnerable to spillovers from interactions with family, friends, co-workers, and management, and the opportunities for workplace comparisons and mobility that routine contacts with outsiders provide.

Notes

1. Despite the seeming centrality of notions such as motivation, intensity, momentum, and the like for the ongoing performance of activities, sociologists have given little attention to this aspect of "role." Some pioneering work on this topic has been done by Adler and Adler (1978) and Zurcher (1982). Although not explicitly addressing enthusiasm, Goffman's (1967: 88-153) concept of "role distance" is also relevant in a more general sense.

2. It may be the case that many people tend to (de)value their own activities relative to some ideal. In a prior study (Prus and Irini, 1988), we encountered a lot of hookers and strippers who located themselves at the "bottom of the barrel" in reference to respectability. The bar staff (waitresses, waiters, and managers) made parallel statements. It is interesting therefore to find a lot of salespeople making similar claims about themselves.

3. See Prus (1982) for a more complete statement on the problematics of honesty and disclosure in everyday life.

4. These contextualized definitions of performance may be central in accounting for individualized differences in motivation. However, as the overall chapter indicates, these definitions are highly amenable to the social contexts in which people find themselves.

5. For indications of the process of sustaining involvements on an individual as opposed to group basis, see Ray's (1961) portrayal of heroin users' attempts to "go straight;" Lemert's (1972) discussion of systematic (but isolated) check forgers; Lesieur's (1977) study of gamblers; Prus and Sharper's (1977) depiction of card and dice hustlers; and Prus and Irini's (1988) statement on those involved in the hotel community.

6. Similar observations are made by Donovan (1929: 124). Albeit in deviance contexts, Lemert (1962, 1972), Prus and Sharper (1977), and Prus and Irini (1988) provide indications of the extent to which "people's self and other identities" and "attempts to be successful" make it difficult for persons to later disengage themselves from those very same activities.

7. Donovan (1929) reports similar observations in her study of department store saleswomen. Strikingly parallel experiences can be found among the police (Skolnick, 1966; Rubinstein, 1973), hustlers (Prus and Sharper, 1977), people in the hotel community (Prus and Irini, 1988), and workers in rehabilitation settings (Hall, 1983).

8. See Prus (1989: Chapter 8) for an extended analysis of trade shows as a marketing format.

9. For a fuller discussion of field sales work and the elements affecting enthusiasm among those involved in this mode of sales, see Prus (1989: Chapter 7).

Chapter 10
IN PERSPECTIVE

> In sales, you see people at their worst when you're trying to sell them something. They're the most cynical. They want to establish dominance in the situation. There's the feeling that if you let the salesman get the upper hand in the situation that you're going to buy something you don't want. They're also parting with their money. I think we all have a little of the miser in us, and I'm not different from anyone else that way. . . . They put on a different kind of front [mixed clothing].

In concluding this volume, I am keenly reminded that this book has two interrelated thrusts. The first task was that of providing an ethnographic analysis of sales activity. The second objective was that of depicting influence work as interpersonal accomplishment. The major subheadings, *Ethnographic Reflections* and *Influence as Interpersonal Accomplishment* reflect these dual pursuits. In addition, however, a discussion of buyer behavior has been inserted. Insofar as all examinations of influence imply corresponding behavior on the part of the targets of influence endeavors, this material has been dealt with implicitly throughout the monograph. Thus, although it may appear to disrupt the flow somewhat, a more explicit consideration of buyers as targets is helpful in understanding vendors as tacticians.

Ethnographic Reflections

This volume on sales behavior is best seen within the context of a larger study of vendor activity, which also encompassed vendor preparations for customer encounters (Prus, 1989). When I embarked on this project, I didn't know how it would fare. Styllianoss Irini and I had completed a study of the hotel community (Prus and Irini, 1988) and as we finished that project, I was struck by the extent to which we had studied a number of businesses. Not all of these pursuits are considered respectable or legal, but we had effectively tapped into aspects of the entertainment, liquor, and hospitality industries at a retail level. Off-hand, I wasn't able to recall much that sociologists or psychologists had written on marketplace exchanges, and while I was puzzled by this, I also realized that a rather extensive marketing and business literature existed. Surely, I thought, these people would have examined the ways in which business was being conducted. My preliminary probes into these sets of literature and discussions with colleagues suggested that not much attention had been given to the ways in which marketplace exchanges were conducted. Even later, as I was well into the project, I expected (with some trepidation) to find numerous studies of this sort, but such was not to be the case. I encountered many textbooklike definitions of the marketplace, a great deal of advice on how to do business, and an immense amount of research directed at uncovering the causes of buying behavior and selling success, but remarkably little on how these activities were actually accomplished by the people involved.

In approaching the study of the marketplace, I found myself some-what tentative. Not only did I expect to find that the study I was in the process of doing had already been done, but I also was unsure of the parameters and terms of reference characterizing this arena. Another source of hesitation in studying the marketplace was that it appeared too forbidding for a sociologist or a social psychologist to pursue. There was the suggestion that it would be a valuable site in which to study persuasion and compliance processes. But the marketplace also seemed a realm of life characterized by much aura, formality and finality, an arena that on the surface appeared to be driven by principles of economics and accounting.

Orientationally, I approached this project as a symbolic interaction-ist. I wanted to examine the world as it was experienced by the partic-ipants—to uncover vendors' perspectives and interpretations of the world in which they operated, and to examine the ways in which they deal with other people in both negotiated and relational terms. Further, it was to be a study of process, an examination of the ways in which people went about their activities. I knew too, that I would rely heavily on extended, open-ended interviews and ongoing observations (and situated commentary) with those involved. I hadn't planned to use trade shows as a source of data, nor had I anticipated my subsequent involvements in a craft (leather and weaving) enterprise at the start. However, both of these involvements proved invaluable, generating much more data and insight than I could have expected. Likewise, although my initial focus was on retailers, I soon found myself talking with their suppliers and the people involved in supplying products to those in manufacture, as well as people involved in the promotions business. As I encountered these people and their practices, the project developed and took its eventual shape.

Readers familiar with the study of the hotel community (Prus and Irini, 1988) will recognize a great many conceptual parallels. Although we hadn't articulated the social production of action as precisely in that statement as I did herein, that study served as a major conceptual frame for the present project. Most fundamentally in that study, and even more explicitly in the present inquiry, was a focus on activity as a means of learning about people's life-worlds. I didn't realize how complex the business world was (with all of its variants), nor was I able to fathom the thoroughly and fundamentally social essence of the marketplace(!), but my plan was to obtain as detailed an account as possible of all the activities that vendors did in the course of their conducting their enterprises.

I was there to learn, to observe, inquire, and probe, to reflect upon and accumulate understandings and a detailed stock of knowledge of vendor practices and dilemmas, and continue to do this on an ongoing basis. While individual interviews and other forms of assistance varied considerably in their depth and overall value to the study, the participation of those involved in marketing and sales was central to this project. As I often observed, "I need all the help I can get." And I asked the participants to provide me with as much detail as they possibly could, combining this with rather relentless probing ("How's that?" "Can you tell me more about that?" "Had you thought of doing anything else?" "What happened there?"). I envisioned this as a major education and I tried to be the best student they could possibly have. By gaining intimate familiarity with their worlds, I hoped to be able to indicate to others in a piece-by-piece fashion just what vendors experienced as they went about assembling the various activities that constituted their inputs into the marketplace.

The focus on activities became a most viable analytical tool. Not only does it enable one to access the social production of human behavior on a here and now basis, but it is in reference to doing activities that aspects of the past and anticipations of the future assume much relevance. As well, it is in the formulation of action that people's perspectives, identities, negotiations, relationships, and commitments are interlinked. Instances of action are by no means equally dramatic, creative, or consequential. Some may be boring, repetitive, or taken for granted. However, it is only by examining the ongoing production of action (in all its forms) that we can appreciate the ways in which people accomplish their behaviors.

Other researchers might have arranged the activities around which the study has been organized in somewhat different orders (or with different emphases or breaks in the sequence of activities). Indeed, as I reworked the manuscript I moved the materials around trying to find a frame that seemed to best capture and communicate the essence of vendor activities for the reader. In part the problem stems from the recognition that while some things happen in general patterns of sequences, any number of things may happen at once and in a number of rather different sequences.

In writing this conclusion, I entertained the idea of trying to summarize the ethnographic themes of the research, but deemed this unfeasible. Thus, while one may view the outline (of the chapters) as a summary statement of the processes (and subprocesses) that seemed most central to this study, anyone seeking to summarize the ethnographic content in textbook form inevitably destroys the rich, contextual, and processual features of human interchange. An ethnography is intended to enhance one's stock of knowledge regarding human conduct in a specific setting; to provide a fuller appreciation of a particular life-style by examining instances of human behavior in detail, as these unfold. One attempts to follow as many processes as can be managed, realizing that one can never be totally exhaustive and that any attempt to comprehend and communicate these insights to others will likewise be incomplete. Thus, rather than attempt to distill the ethnographic material contained herein into this or that many points, I invite the reader to use the processes outlined as "keys" with which to pursue particular passageways into the text—to use these as entry points for examining the ways in which sellers attempt to produce trust, neutralize resistance, or foster loyalty, for instance. Providing windows into the worlds of those engaged in marketing and sales activity, this study enables readers to become intimately familiar with the lifeworlds of those involved in the marketplace.

I hope, however, that readers will not stop here. While each chapter suggests many additional areas for substantive inquiry in the marketplace, we would be much shortchanged were we to overlook the generic implications of this study. By elaborating on their practices in such detail, those in sales have done us a major service by providing us with some of the best material available for considering the ways in which influence work is accomplished. And using the vendor material as a reference point, I will discuss the processes basic to persuasion in point form. Before doing so, however, I would like to consider the roles that buyers as targets of influence play in this process.

Buyers and Other Targets

Although I have comparatively little material on which to draw in discussing the behavior of buyers and other targets of persuasion,[1] it is important to consider the situations of buyers and other targets before attending to the persuasion practices of vendors and other tacticians. Every theory of marketing (and sales) behavior implies a theory of buying behavior (and vice versa), just as every model of influence implies a model of being influenced (and vice versa). I tried to incorporate this notion into the framing of the project (see Chapter 1) and the presentation of the vendor material throughout, but it is essential that we make this point here as well, as we try to elaborate on what we've learned about influence as interpersonal accomplishment. This statement on buyer behavior (and by implication, other targets) is necessarily more tentative.[2] Nevertheless, these understandings of target behaviors are vital in more fully defining the background against which vendors and other tacticians may be seen to operate. With these caveats and concerns in mind, attention is drawn to the *interactive* (temporal and situated features of involvements), *symbolic* (images and audiences), and *performance* (shopping as situated accomplishment) aspects of target behavior.

TEMPORAL AND SITUATED FEATURES OF INVOLVEMENT

In what follows, a *situated* view of purchasing is more explicitly incorporated into the career contingency model (outlined in Chapter 1). This model addresses people's initial involvements, continuities, disinvolvements, and reinvolvements in particular situations. The *temporal* dimension of the career contingency model considers people's involvements in particular kinds of situations over time. But, it loses some of the immediacy of the "here and now" aspects of people's experiences which, when taken in series, constitute these very same careers.

In contrast to the temporal or historical dimension, the situated theme addresses the ongoing formulation of action. The task is that of detailing the processes by which people work out or accomplish their behavior in particular instances. The temporal dimension enables us to trace patterns of involvement over time, but we should not forget that these themes build on people's activities in the here and now, albeit at this, that, and other points in time. The two dimensions are complementary, but some conceptual refocusing is entailed as one shifts back and forth from the temporal features of involvements to the more situated or episodic nature of participation in specific settings.

Since situated behavior takes place within the context of people's ongoing experiences, the temporal dimension helps us understand each more situated instance of purchasing activity. While concentrated on the here and now, a viable situated approach would be sensitive to both people's past experiences and their anticipation of the future. Ergo, the ensuing consideration of images and audiences, and shopping as situated accomplishment.

IMAGES AND AUDIENCES

In contrast to those who would reduce the marketplace to matters of supply and demand or dollars for goods, this study indicates that the marketplace is thoroughly and fundamentally a social arena. It is not merely rich in images. It could not exist without images! Every single feature of the marketplace that we can identify has a symbolic essence (true by definition), but it is only as people act toward these various features (images) of the marketplace that the marketplace takes on a dynamic, "objectified" (Schutz, 1971) quality.

I am not denying any physical referents people may associate with symbols. However, the significance of these physical referents derives from the (symbolic) applications of human behavior to these items both as intersubjective acknowledgments and at more personalized reflective levels. In the first instance, while people may individually attribute any variety of valuings to particular items, the significance of objects for exchange depends on the willingness of other people to acknowledge these items as worthy of possession (i.e., being willing to offer other items [symbols] in exchange [Simmel, 1978]). It is only as the parties to an exchange work out a settlement that the value of an item becomes objectified—and although each exchange may suggest a pattern for future trade, these objectifications are best seen as problematic relative to subsequent trade. Implied in the notion of objectification (via intersubjective consensus [and negotiation]), the concept of symbolic significance has a more individualized relevance as well. Insofar as people incorporate objects into their activities (i.e., relative to their past experiences, present circumstances, or anticipations of the future), their images (and valuings) of these objects can change dramatically. For example, before answering the question: "Would you rather have 500 pounds of cork or 500 pounds of gold?" you might well consider your circumstances (e.g., "Am I heading towards a bank, or am I shipwrecked at sea?"). The meanings we attach to objects reflects both our estimates of the meanings that others attach to those objects and our own sense (past experiences, immediate circumstances, and anticipations) of situations.

While rather truncated, the following discussions of people's images and concerns regarding objects to be purchased, objects offered in exchange, vendors being dealt with, and witnessing audiences, indicate the centrality of images in purchasing situations.

Objects to be Purchased

Although people may attribute various physical properties (e.g., bulk, weight, elasticity) to the goods being considered for purchase, people engaged in trade are most basically exchanging symbols. For instance, in buying an automobile, people may obtain 1,500 or 5,000 pounds of metal, plastic, glass, rubber, and whatnot in the process, but they are (variously) buying images of transportation, style, prestige, fuel efficiency, adventure, romance, safety, and so on. And a century ago, people appear to have bought horses with somewhat parallel sets of concerns.

But just as we have largely replaced the horse with the automobile, anyone delivering these images in other forms may be able radically to affect the purchase of automobiles.

When people purchase objects, it is vital not only to ask what these objects mean to the people making these purchases, but to be sensitive as well to the variable meanings that the same people may attach to the same objects at particular points in time (i.e., individuals may simultaneously attribute multiple meanings to the same object at one time or over any time frames to which researchers may attend). Thus, for example, while someone may have mixed feelings about having made a particular purchase, the same person may later decide that this was a good buy, a bad buy, or may continue to view the purchase with mixed definitions on the same or other grounds.

Objects Offered in Exchange

Insofar as buyers are preparing to trade some of their possessions to sellers, we should also ask about the meanings they attach to the (symbols) they offer in exchange for the seller's goods. Do buyers see themselves as "sacrificing their hard earned (symbols)," or as "having (symbols) to burn," or are they concerned about "stretching out their (symbols) as far as they will go," or "getting a good deal on their (symbols)?" It is important to ask about the sorts of images people attach to their expenditures (as well as their purchases). Also, do the meanings of contemplated expenditures change over time ("I'll get it now, while I'm loaded with [symbols]!"). What reservations do they have about parting with their (symbols)? And, of course, what role do other people play in the process (e.g., "A fool and his/her [symbols] are soon parted!" or, as your friend says, "Hey, its only [symbols]! Go for it!")?

Images of Vendors

Although buyers sometimes purchase items regardless of, or in spite of, the particular vendors involved, buyers may significantly attend to the images they associate with particular vendors. These images range from perceptions of store location, decor, and (specific) product displays to definitions of service, warranties, return policies, and the interpersonal styles of the sellers working therein. Further, customer interpretations of the same "features" can vary immensely. A display seen as "strikingly attractive" by some shoppers may be seen as "dull" or "tacky" by others. Likewise, vendors attending to customers in identical manners may be seen variously as inattentive, providing good service, or "hovering" by different customers or even the same sets of customers over different time frames (e.g., when engaging in recreational versus focused shopping). While subject to diverse interpretations and relevancies, images of vendors (e.g., retailers, manufacturers) can readily affect buyers' overall willingness to invest in the "objects" at hand.

Attending to Audiences

The concept of audience draws our attention to the people (salespeople, co-shoppers, witnesses) present in the immediate purchasing setting, the recipients of contemplated purchases, specific others thought likely to pass judgments on one's purchases, and the relevance of the "generalized other" in purchasing situations. Purchasers need not take all of these audiences into account, but to the extent that they do, their images of these other people can be quite consequential in shaping their eventual purchasing decisions.

First, we ask to what extent buyers attend to the presence of other people in immediate purchasing situations, seeing whether buyers take these others into account in formulating their purchasing activities. Elements of trust and skepticism attributed to these others (especially vendors and companions) would seem particularly relevant here, as would any concerns they may have regarding the ways in which these other people see them (e.g., "Will I look cheap if . . . ?"). The emphasis, here, is on buyer interpretations of the inputs or images of these people, and on the ways in which buyers deals with these situations (e.g., invoking distance or seeking advice).

Concerns with intended recipients of purchases are often highly apparent when purchasing items for others ("Well, I don't know if she'd really like that." "I'm not sure if that'll fit him."), but these sorts of "recipient images" would also encompass items purchased for oneself ("Is it really me?" "Would I get enough wear out of it?"). Here, buyers may be concerned about matching images of objects for purchase with their images of prospective recipients of those purchases.[3] Thus, even when fully confident in the products and vendors in the situation, people may waver over, postpone, or decline particular purchases when they have reservations about those (self or others) for whom these purchases are intended or concerns with the perceived "goodness of fit" between the goods and the prospective recipients.

Beyond concerns with the recipients of particular purchases or others in the immediate purchasing setting, buyers may also attend to other people's definitions (images) of their purchases. The items in question may be purchased for oneself or others, but buyers may make decisions mindful of the acceptability of these items to specific people (e.g., friends, spouses, and other "local critics") other than those for whom they were intended.

Addressing the expectations of the more vaguely or collectively defined other, Mead's (1934) concept of the "generalized other" represents another source of definitions (images) to which prospective buyers may attend. Buyers appear differentially attuned to concerns with the generalized other ("What would they think?") both in terms of individual operating styles and from one realm of product purchase to another. Nevertheless, whether one is discussing clothing, holiday plans, or computers, buyers attuned to images about "being somebody" in the world of others may opt for purchases quite different from those they would have selected otherwise.

SHOPPING AS SITUATED ACCOMPLISHMENT

If one envisions shopping as an activity to be performed in manners comparable to other activities, then we may begin to ask how people go about "doing" shopping. At a more general level, the following processes seem basic to this activity.

- making (preliminary) plans
- getting prepared
- managing stage fright (reservations, if any)
- developing competence (stock of knowledge, tactics, applications)
- coordinating events with others (team members and others)
- dealing with obstacles, resistances, distractions
- conveying images of competence (displaying ability, composure)
- encountering competition
- making ongoing assessments and adjustments (Prus, 1987: 278)

Although I can do little more than sketch out these processes, it should be noted that people may approach individual shopping episodes with considerable variations along these lines. Planning may be extensive or minimal, preparations may vary greatly in scope, and concerns with one's receptivity by others (stage fright) are highly variable. The mastery of product knowledge and applications is also problematic both in its scope and people's concerns therein, over time. Likewise, shopping expeditions (and vendor encounters) may assume a variety of forms. People may or may not go shopping with their associates, and may or may not be able to work things out with the vendors involved. Similarly, buyers may or may not be concerned with the images they generate while shopping, and they may react quite differently on any given occasion to any competition they may encounter from other shoppers (e.g., at "sales"). Regardless of whether or not purchases have been made, shoppers may assess or reassess their circumstances and their own activities as well as the activities of those they have encountered, possibly with the anticipation of becoming more knowledgeable shoppers in the future.

If we focus on these activities a little more, we see that shoppers may pursue cooperation from those with whom they contemplate dealing, face the prospects of making (or avoiding) commitments, and experience relationships with the vendors that they encounter. Briefly consider the following.

Although salespeople are often envisioned as the people involved in pursuing cooperation from buyers, buyers may also assume roles as tacticians (with vendors representing targets for their enterprises). Where buyers have interests in securing particular objects at lower prices or perceive other obstacles en route to obtaining the deals they wish, they may (in manners that parallel vendor pursuits) engage in more promotional activity. Thus one may witness more planning and role-taking activity on the part of buyers, as well as attempts to generate trust on the part of the vendors involved, neutralize vendor resistance, and make various concessions toward vendors to encourage vendors to deal with them.

The notion of making (or reserving) commitments is especially central to shopping or purchasing activity. Commitments not only denote decision points, but imply some corresponding (re)shuffling of one's behaviors and other items of this or that (symbolic) significance. While vendors may envision buyers as elusive targets, we would want to attend to the options that buyers recognize in this or that purchasing situation, along with their sense of existing commitments, and their abilities to hedge their bets in various ways.

The concept of experiencing relationships draws our attention to the bonds and affectations that buyers may develop with vendors. Overall, buyers (especially consumers) appear much less concerned about becoming repeat customers than do vendors express concern about developing repeat patronage. But that should not divert our attention from the sense of loyalty that some buyers develop in reference to particular vendors or the situated features of buyer-seller relationships. Buyers' satisfaction or dissatisfaction with previous encounters may greatly enhance or deter subsequent exchanges with particular vendors, but buyers also appear concerned about managing levels of intimacy (openness) and distancing in dealing with sellers more generally.

BUYER BEHAVIOR IN CONTEXT

Albeit at a very rudimentary level, the preceding discussion alerts us to the reflective and interpersonally mediated processes by which people go about constructing or assembling their purchasing behaviors. In addition to addressing the temporal nature of people's participation in particular situations, we need to attend more fully to the situated aspects of people's participation in specific settings; to examine the ways in which buyers (and other purported targets) endeavor to accomplish their immediate undertakings. Further, people's images (or symbolizations) are not superficial or inconsequential for their purchasing activities. These images appear to be of paramount importance for sustained examinations of buyer behavior.

Exchanges in the marketplace may be somewhat more explicit and more fleeting than those in other realms of our lives, but similar processes of influence and involvement seem in evidence across settings.[4] Thus we may ask to what extent targets in other settings also operate in reference to images and audiences, how they experience temporal and situated notions of involvement, and how they accomplish their activities amidst the influence efforts of others. The critical message for analysts of the pursuits of vendors and other tacticians is that we not ignore the symbolic, interactive or enterprising activities of targets; that we attend to targets' abilities to act back on those trying to influence them.

As implied in this discussion of buyer behavior, there is no substitute for data grounded in people's lived experiences. To this end, this statement very much represents an invitation for others to embark on ethnographic research on buyer behavior and to extend our knowledge of the processes by which these targets (and tacticians!) accomplish their activities in a world that they jointly shape with others.

Influence as Interpersonal Accomplishment

Mindful of the preceding discussion of buyers and other targets of influence, this section of the conclusion focuses on the practices of those endeavoring to influence others in various ways. Following a baseline review of the ways in which influence processes have been depicted in the literature, attention will be directed to a statement on influence that is grounded in the study of vendors' persuasion practices.

INFLUENCE PROCESSES IN THE LITERATURE

Despite the centrality of the influence process for people's lived experiences, the social sciences literature has surprisingly little to offer concerning the ways in which people actively shape the experiences of others. Even social psychology, which assumes the study of interpersonal influence at its core,[5] is of much less help than one might expect on the surface. The social psychologists in both sociology and psychology have largely neglected the study of the ways in which persuasion (and resistance) is accomplished in practice. This is not to imply that the topic of influence has been overlooked by social psychologists. However, instead of directly attending to the what and how of human interchange, social psychologists in both disciplines have focused heavily on factors (individual attributes and background characteristics) thought to "cause" people to act in particular ways.[6]

This neglect of influence as interpersonal accomplishment is strikingly evident when one examines the *Journal of Personality and Social Psychology* (sponsored by the American Psychological Association) and the *Social Psychological Quarterly* (sponsored by the American Sociological Association).[7] Ironically, the methodological statements in these journals depict extensive "influence work" on the part of the researchers. But while the researchers assume that they are able to affect the behaviors of others (typically through experimental manipulations), they generally have overlooked the interpersonal processes characterizing influence work on the part of other people.[8] Despite a great proliferation of theories and an even greater amount of research activity, this literature provides very little insight into the ways in which people directly shape one another's behaviors.[9]

In contrast to those whose work is typified by the *Journal of Personality and Social Psychology* and the *Social Psychology Quarterly*, the "interpretive" social psychologists (mostly in sociology) are immensely more attuned to the negotiable essence of human experience. However, despite the value of their work for an interactive conceptualization of social order (and their immediate epistemological relevance for this statement), only minimal attention has been given directly to "influence as interpersonal accomplishment" by the major theorists in this tradition.[10] While clearly recognizing the multiperspectival and reflective nature of human association, as well as its ongoing negotiable essence, much of the actual accomplishment of interpersonal influence has been taken for granted.[11]

Still, some of the clearest illustrations of influence as a social process come from the interpretive (interactionist) literature. This includes studies of union organizers and their targets (Karsh et al., 1953), cab drivers and their fares (Davis, 1959), doctors and patients (Roth, 1962; Glaser and Strauss, 1964; Emerson, 1970), instructor-student encounters (Hargreaves et al., 1975; Martin, 1975; Haas and Shaffir, 1977), disputes (Emerson and Messinger, 1977; Prus, 1978), control agent-citizen encounters (Bittner, 1967; Emerson, 1969; Davis, 1983, Darrough, 1984; Peyrot, 1985), confidence games (Sutherland, 1937; Maurer, 1940; Blumberg, 1967; Prus and Sharper, 1977), and situated involvements in deviance (Shaw, 1930; Becker, 1963; Lofland, 1966; Lesieur, 1977; Prus, 1983b; Adler, 1985; Sanders, 1988). This literature provides exceedingly powerful evidence of persuasion as an interactive process, but it is characterized by much diversity of emphasis. Generating much insight into people's lived experiences, this is a probing, revealing body of research that, when taken collectively, sensitizes us to a wide variety of influence processes. To date, however, these research thrusts have been too limited, too uneven, and too fragmented to be melded into a detailed, unified theory of the influence process.

INFLUENCE IN PROCESS

As implied in the preceding discussion of buyer behavior and the (rather terse) review of the literature on interpersonal influence processes, we have a great deal to learn about the ways in which people influence (and resist) one another on a day-to-day basis.

In what follows, 10 subprocesses germane to persuasion in practice will be examined. This listing rather closely reflects the central themes of this monograph represented by the chapter headings. However, it was developed at a later stage in the analysis and allows us to attend to a fuller vision of the influence process than that which I had developed earlier, in the course of organizing the chapters for the volume. These processes are as follows:

- formulating (preliminary) plans
- role-taking (inferring/uncovering the perspectives of the other)
- promoting interest in one's objectives
- generating trust
- proposing specific lines of action
- encountering resistance
- neutralizing obstacles
- seeking and making concessions
- confirming agreements
- assessing "failures" and recasting plans (Prus, 1987: 278-279)

These processes are presented in a particular order, but tacticians may invoke a number of these processes somewhat simultaneously as well as in highly diverse and uneven sequences. Since the discussion of each of these subprocesses is necessarily abbreviated, references will be made to particular chapters (or parts thereof) that address these processes so that readers might more clearly envision the activities under consideration. Because it also addresses a number of these processes, materials in the companion volume *Pursuing Customers* (Prus, 1989) will also be referenced in developing this statement.

Readers will note some shifting back and forth between vendor endeavors and the practical limitations these tacticians encounter in their attempts to realize the activities at hand. Ultimately, salespeople are dependent on their targets, not only for "reasonable" interpretations of their efforts, but also for their cooperation throughout the encounter. Additionally, while their targets have capacities to assume "evasive action," they become even more elusive in that they may also alter their interests and frames of reference in very short time spans both on an individual (reflective) basis and through association with others.

Some shifting between influence endeavors directed toward generalized versus particularized targets will also be apparent. Like tacticians involved in recruiting people in many other contexts (e.g., religious movements, unions, political parties, volunteer organizations), those involved in sales develop messages and practices designed to appeal to the generalized other. However, in the process of pursuing commitments in interpersonal encounters, salespeople (like many other tacticians) also deal with people on a one to one basis. And it is here that the emphasis on particularized forms of influence is most striking.

Finally, although the analysis is very much grounded in vendor endeavors, I have attempted to illustrate the more generic features of influence implied by the vendor role. To this end, I very much encourage the reader to assess the viability of these processes relative to any and all instances of influence discernable in other settings.

Formulating (Preliminary) Plans

Denoting vendor preparations in anticipation of customer contact, the companion volume (Prus, 1989) is almost entirely a study of planning as social accomplishment. However, the plans (e.g., regarding goods ordered, prices set, promotional messages developed) depicted therein are very much directed toward the generalized other (Mead, 1934). Many of the activities discussed in the present volume also reflect anticipations of the generalized other, but they are more situated and individualized in their overall thrusts. Thus the material on "getting scripted" (chap. 2) attests to planning at a general level, as do some of the practices vendors implement with respect to approaching customers and developing interest (chap. 2), generating trust (chap. 3), neutralizing resistance, (chap. 4), obtaining commitments (chap. 5), dealing with troublesome customers (chap. 6), developing loyalty (chap. 7), and holding "sales" (chap. 8). Nevertheless, since each encounter has to be worked out anew by the people involved, these preparations often recede into the background as people engaged in interpersonal selling find themselves formulating plans on the spot. Some interchanges nicely fit into vendors' preexisting schemes, but others introduce con-

siderable ambiguity and extensive (re)adjustments. Under these circumstances, planning becomes more tentative, short term, context-specific,
and reactive.

These two notions of planning are very much interrelated as vendors
have their earlier preparations on which to build or to which to adjust
as specific encounters take place. So long as buyers seem accepting of
vendors' initial plans (implied or explicit), the selling process can be
greatly facilitated. However, any question, challenge, hesitation, or
uncertainty, may generate some "ad hocing" (Garfinkel, 1967) on the
part of the vendors involved. Under these conditions, a central task for
the tacticians becomes that of tapping into the more particularized
symbolic significances of their prospects. It is in reference to dealings
with specific others that one becomes most attentive to strategy as a
situated process and to the very fundamental consequence of the following processes which further depict the more tentative, reactive
nature of planning involved in the pursuit of target commitments.

Role Taking

Mead (1934) uses the term, *role taking,* to refer to the practice of
people attempting to ascertain the viewpoint of the other. As was the
case with tacticians formulating their preliminary plans, those involved
in sales exhibit wide variations in the extent to which they endeavor to
take the role of the other in reference to their own general operating
styles, encounters with particular people, and attempts to deal with
particular situations. While concern with the viewpoint of the other was
most explicitly considered in reference to qualification work (chap. 2),
vendors may also engage in role taking as they formulate plans directed
toward the generalized other as well as in their ongoing adjustments to
situations involving specific others.

Role taking is often taken for granted when customers' activities
closely correspond to vendors' expectations. And, using their knowledge of the generalized other, vendors may be able to implement any
number of practices that customers may find acceptable with a minimum of active role taking on anyone's part. However, should either
interactant encounter ambiguity, confusion, or define themselves as
more dependent on the actions of the other, we would expect to find
greater concern directed toward taking the role of the other. More
focused role taking could enable tacticians to uncover targets' more
individualized symbolic significances as well as attend to any shifts

these prospects may make in their interpretations. In this respect, it could foster vendor abilities to make adjustments considered more viable by their prospects. At the same time, however, we would want to be sensitive to substantial variations in tacticians' interests in pursuing this information as well as in their abilities to elicit information from people in general. On a case-by-case basis, both the accuracy and depth of information is problematic. Beyond matters of time or potentially distracting third parties, those engaging in role-taking activity are fundamentally constrained by the willingness of their targets to co-operate with them. The situation becomes even more challenging from the tacticians' point of view when one recognizes that role taking is relevant across the range of processes subsumed by the concept of persuasion, and that customers or other targets may shift their defini-tions of situation and selves in relatively short time frames. Viewed thusly, role taking can not only affect other aspects of people's interac-tions, but it also warrants much attention as an ongoing social process.

Promoting Interest in One's Objectives

A third process basic to people's persuasion practices involves at-tempts to draw attention to, and generate interest in, one's pursuits on the part of others. In some cases, targets will have developed precontact preferences for particular products (e.g., buyers engaged in seekership) or may see themselves as having little choice but to pursue particular lines of action (i.e., closure). Where target preferences or definitions of closure coincide with the lines of action tacticians are endeavoring to promote, commitment may be made somewhat regardless of the tacticians' efforts. In other cases, however, people's involvements in situations may very much reflect tacticians' abilities to (re)define the significance of particular lines of activity for the targets at hand.

A number of promotional practices pitched at the generalized other were detailed in *Pursing Customers* (Prus, 1989), via considerations of price-setting activity (chap. 5), media promotions (chap. 6), field sales campaign (chap. 7), and showrooms and exhibits (chap. 8). Focusing on "sales," Chapter 8 of the present volume also depicts promotions oriented toward the generalized other.

The matter of developing interest at an interpersonal level was most explicitly pursued in Chapter 2 of the present volume, but surfaces throughout in examinations of the processes by which people generate trust, neutralize resistance, pursue commitments, hold "sales," and develop loyalty. In each of these discussions, we witness salespeople's attempts to define or redefine the symbolic meanings that people attribute to the objects that vendors wish to promote. As with "ad hoced" planning and focused role taking, the situated features of the production of interest become strikingly evident as salespeople attempt to adjust to specific others on a here-and-now basis.

The present study indicates that tacticians may attempt to develop interest in the objects they feature by encouraging prospect participation, defining product significance, and arousing discontent with people's present situations. In all cases, developing interest is a matter of image work; of generating, focusing, and elaborating on images; and attempting to indicate the relative goodness of fit of these images with those deemed desirable by the prospect at hand. These attempts to develop interest on the part of others imply capacities for self-reflectivity on the part of targets. However, insofar as targets define themselves as having particular interests (seekership) or pressing obligations (closure) beyond those promoted herein, tacticians may have considerable difficulty refocusing target interests that do not correspond to their own. Further, these same reflective abilities enable targets to recontextualize incoming information (and question tactician interests). Tactician enterprises can be significantly neutralized in the process, as targets distance themselves accordingly.

Generating Trust

Trust (chap. 3) was defined relative to people's perceptions that others would act in their best interests. Viewing the promotion of trust as a preventative tactic intended to instill buyer confidence in purchasing situations, vendors were seen to employ three major thrusts in fostering trust. Portrayals of trust centered on exhibiting vendor integrity, product performance and minimized buyer risks.

Although salespeople are differentially attentive to, and concerned with, these three dimensions of trust, we would also want to recognize that buyers are also apt to be unevenly concerned about these three aspects of trust. As well, they may interpret vendor efforts in ways other than they were intended. Noteworthy too, are buyer tendencies to forgo or suspend considerations of trust when they consider purchases to be more inconsequential, face time pressures, or perceive a lack of viable alternatives. Other instances of confidence work may be rendered ineffective when buyers are able to postpone purchasing decisions or become more extensively involved in comparison shopping. While trust may become less consequential in these situations, this should not discourage us from attending to the great many instances in which the development of trust may be pivotal not only for buyers making immediate purchases but also for development of long-term loyalty.

In addition to Chapter 4, which may be seen to deal with vendor attempts to (re)establish trust on a more "remedial" basis by neutralizing resistances, and Chapter 5, in which vendors try explicitly to pursue commitments from people who may or may not trust them, other aspects of trust (or conversely skepticism, and distancing) are evident in Chapter 7 ("Developing Loyalty") and Chapter 8 ("Holding 'Sales' "). The relationship of trust and repeat patronage is certainly a most important one and appears to reflect ongoing adjustments and assessments on the part of both buyers and vendors. Interpretations of "sales" are likewise worth examining in reference to trust. In part, the inference is that where buyers establish higher levels of confidence in the vendor's integrity and in the products being featured, price reductions may engender a heightened sense of trust. However, should buyers lack information or already be skeptical of vendors or their products, price reductions may serve to intensify skepticism and subsequent distancing.

When one asks about the more general implications of vendor's trust-inducing practices relative to other settings, the following is implied. Agents can endeavor to foster trust on the part of targets by establishing their own integrity as insiders of sorts relative to their targets, by providing evidence that the "objects" (products, concepts, information) they are promoting are viable and will meet target expectations, and minimizing the risks these lines of action entail. However, despite the progress they may make with people overall, tacticians are in every case dependent on target interpretations for their eventual effectiveness. Likewise, confidence work may be nullified when targets consider the commitments entailed to have little consequence, lack sufficient time to consider the alternatives, deem themselves to have no viable options, or define themselves as being in situations in which they can readily avoid commitments of the sort entailed in the encounter at hand. Here as well, however, we should not be diverted from the importance of the production of trust for both immediate commitments by targets and their long-term involvements.

Proposing Specific Lines of Action

While customers often "self-select" items (especially evident in self-serve stores or in the use of vending machines), salespeople may also attempt to steer, guide, or otherwise encourage people to pursue particular items or to make their selections at particular points in time. Some of this "directional" or "focusing" activity is accomplished as vendors promote buyer interest in particular products. This is an objective that vendors may pursue at both generalized and more personalized, interactive levels.

Though oriented toward the generalized other, much focusing may be noted in discussions of media, field and showroom promotions (Prus, 1989: chaps. 6, 7, 8, respectively). As part of their attempts to develop interest in certain types of products, vendors produce a great many messages that direct prospects to purchase particular brands or features (typically more exclusive) of objects.

When we shift to an interpersonal level (the present volume) of promotional activity, we find this theme most sharply addressed in examinations of the ways in which products are presented (chap. 2), suggestive selling (chap. 3), and closing activity (chap. 5). In each of these discussions, we see vendors attempting to lead or encourage customers to pursue specific lines of action, at particular points in time.

As with the other processes subsumed by notions of influence, we are mindful of the dependency of salespeople on the cooperation of the customers in their attempts to generate direction. As well, it is vital that we recognize buyer abilities to assume initiative in proposing particular lines of action (which may or may not correspond to those preferred by the vendors) as appropriate for the vendor in the situation. This (focusing) feature of association was not investigated as fully as would have been desirable. Nevertheless, it raises some promising directions for subsequent inquiry both in the marketplace and in other settings.

Encountering Resistance

Vendor experiences with buyer resistances were examined most explicitly in Chapter 4, but buyers' capacities for resistance were implied throughout the analysis. Target capacities for resistance affect tacticians' plans at more general levels as well as necessitating adjustments as actual encounters develop.

When we examine vendors' marketing practices (Prus, 1989), we find that vendors are more or less continuously adjusting the offerings they pitch at the generalized other in attempts to minimize buyer resistance. Thus the dilemmas vendors experience in preparing for customer contact not only reflect their anticipations of future buyer assessments (and reservations), but very much represent reactive adjustments which are mindful of the resistances encountered in dealings with customers to date. This is evident in discussions of promotional practices (media, field, and displays), as well as in considerations of establishing marketing structures (e.g., chains, franchises), doing management (e.g., training, staff selection), purchasing goods for resale, and pricing practices.

/The realm of interpersonal selling also reflects generalized adjustments that vendors have made mindful of earlier customer resistances. Thus, for instance, scripts (chap. 2) may become more selective in content over time or attempts may be made to generate trust more completely (chap. 3) in order that certain types of resistance encountered in the past may be averted in the present. However, on a case by case level, adjustments are much more focused, customized, and immediate in the realm of interpersonal selling. The resistances salespeople encounter are contingent on customer assessments (images) of both background preparations and the information buyers glean from interpersonal encounters to that point. Additionally, insofar as customers enter encounters with greatly varying stocks of product knowledge, anticipated applications, definitions of and access to mediums of exchange, skepticism, and interpersonal styles, as well as preconceived images of the vendors at hand and images (and anticipations) of the competition, vendors may have considerable difficulty anticipating and discerning the reservations they encounter on a case-by-case basis. Not only do customers' viewpoints (and ongoing interpretations) transcend the definitions that vendors attempting to deal with these customers are able to develop, but vendors are dealing with entities reflectively able to act back on them. ╱

The most common categories of resistance encountered by the tacticians in this study reflect skepticism regarding the tactician (vendor), the object (product) being featured, or the intended recipient (target or others); people's existing relationships with outsiders (affiliations with competitors), the commitments (prices) involvements entail, and the options available (comparison shopping). However, as analysts, it is vital that we realize that these typifications are not so readily applied by those encountering resistance on an instance by instance basis. Actual interchanges are often difficult to decipher (being rather nebulous in essence) and tactician definitions often assume a more tentative, ambiguous quality.

Given targets' abilities to conceal information and to reveal selectively (and misrepresent) their situations, as well as their abilities to shift frames of reference and attend unevenly to this or that aspect of a situation over time, tacticians are unlikely to be cognizant of all of the reservations that their targets may have. Further, even when targets have openly conveyed reservations to them, tacticians do not know how long these issues will be of relevance to targets or how important they are relative to the commitments at hand.

On the surface, many potential resistances would seemingly be averted by more extensive presentations or more sustained trust-producing activity on the part of tacticians, but we cannot assume that targets will fully attend to these messages or interpret these in the manners intended. As a result, resistances may be more commonly encountered than tacticians may expect, based on their inputs in particular cases. And, in practice, unless tacticians work at uncovering reservations (i.e., engage in more qualification work—more probing and other role-taking activities), they are apt to be relatively disadvantaged in dealing with these concerns.

Neutralizing Obstacles

Should tacticians uncover or infer target resistance, they may embark on some remedial work lest targets disengage themselves from these encounters or otherwise refuse to make the commitments tacticians desire. As illustrated by the material on salespeople, tacticians able to define target reservations more precisely may be very selective in the ways in which they address particular prospects. Thus, for instance, salespeople may implement one set of strategies for dealing with price resistances, but attempt to invoke other sets of images to neutralize buyer concerns with existing loyalties or product-directed skepticism. When they have been unable to ascertain the base of the resistance, tacticians may assume more of a shotgun approach, hoping that they will be able to neutralize prospect concerns (while also hoping that they do not create other problems for themselves by raising issues not previously of concern to the targets).

Although salespeople often develop specific counters to the more common resistances signified by skepticism, price, existing loyalties, and comparison shopping, one may delineate three general methods (affirmations, role taking, making concessions) of neutralizing resistance that transcend these and other realms of resistance vendors encounter. In their attempts to affirm the desirability of their promotions, tacticians commonly challenge unwanted definitions, make qualified acknowledgments, generate favorable comparison points, explain limitations, overlook objections, and refocus prospect directions. Each of these affirmation tactics seems fairly generic or transsituational in essence, such that we might expect to see these practices invoked by tacticians in any number of other settings in which target resistance is encountered. The second basic strategy, that of role taking, encompasses the practices of being attentive, inquiring into expressed concerns and locating limits. While targets sometimes "talk themselves out of particular reservations" in discussing these more openly, the information gained in this way may be used to pinpoint target concerns and enable tacticians either to pursue some of the earlier mentioned affirmation tactics or to redefine the situation by proposing concessions (see next section) of various sorts. As well, beyond enabling tacticians to relate more intensively with their targets throughout their encounters, this display of tactician interest in their targets may also serve to nullify resistance by encouraging a greater sense of trust on the part of these targets.

Presumably, vendors and other people more actively engaged in persuasion work would develop relatively greater skills in neutralizing target resistance with experience. But the applicability of these insights appears rather uneven on a case-by-case basis. In addition to the ambiguities tacticians experience in deciphering target reservations and their abilities to recall and implement particular tactics on an immediate, situated basis, their own sense of the appropriateness (rigor, and timing) of their pursuits seems central to the manner in which they deal with these reservations.

Further, as implied in the next section on people seeking and making concessions, it is important to appreciate targets' ongoing accumulations of knowledge, both as sources of resistance and as agents of pursuit as they move from one encounter to the next. Tacticians may acquire greater levels of skill in pursuing cooperation over time, but so may their targets; with each encounter providing potentially greater insight into subsequent ones for all of the parties involved.

Seeking and Making Concessions

Discussions of concessions assume their most explicit forms in Chapters 4 ("Neutralizing Resistance") and 5 ("Obtaining Commitments"), wherein we find vendors entertaining focused compromises of various sorts in attempts to maintain buyer interests and consolidate commitments. However, it is worth noting that vendor compromises typically begin much earlier in the process. Thus a great number of the adjustments vendors make in preparation of customer contact (e.g., product lines carried, pricing changes, promotional practices) reflect concessions made in anticipation of encounters with the generalized other. From the buyers' viewpoint, these often appear as "givens" (Brand X, $4.99 a pound) and may similarly escape the attention of some analysts. As evident in *Pursuing Customers,* though, these concessions often represent matters of considerable ambiguity and risk taking on the part of vendors who try to balance out their concerns with their perceived sense of buyer willingness to enter into trade agreements with them.

Somewhat similar notions may be noted in vendor presentations or trust producing endeavors in the present volume, when vendors stipulate the commitments (goods offered, prices, warrantees, and so on) they are prepared to make to the people dealing with them. Thus a noteworthy difference between buyers and sellers in the study reflects the practices of vendors stating many of their concessions "up front" so to speak, with the buyers holding their concessions in abeyance. This is by convention only, and it could be readily reversed by a seller who says, "Make me an offer," or by a buyer who says, "I have this to offer you, what can you do for me along these lines?"[12] Parties to an exchange need not assume equal initiative in proposing exchanges or in defining the concessions each is willing to make at the outset, but an exchange implies concessions on the part of each.

The objects desired by the other party may represent major or inconsequential accommodations from the trader's point of view, but further compromises also emerge as quick fixes of sorts. Thus, beyond one's initial proposals, subsequent accommodations may be made to resolve any of a great many concerns targets may have. And some tacticians may become so reliant on the strategy of making concessions that they may often forego other tactics seemingly readily available to them.

However, tacticians making more concessions in attempts to reach agreements with prospects often encounter tactical dilemmas that those using affirmation techniques are better able to avoid. First, the objectives that tacticians achieve in the end may be so heavily compromised that they are of minimal or even negative worth. Second, tacticians may have made concessions that lock them into undesired, long-term, or costly commitments. Third, the accommodations made may establish interactional styles with particular targets that tacticians may find frustrating or costly to continue over time. Fourth, others learning of these arrangements may pressure these tacticians for similar types of deals.

Confirming Agreements

Although a great deal of emphasis is sometimes placed on closing the sale, and the well-being of particular businesses and the careers of individual salespeople are contingent on establishing a greater proportion of purchasing agreements, the closing or completion of sales is in many respects anticlimactic. Some sales hinge on "strong closes," but in a great many other cases, the close merely signifies a mutually acknowledged agreement between the two parties. There are some instances in which buyers are surprised to realize that they have committed themselves to particular purchases or that the commitments they have made are not the ones they thought they had anticipated, but on most occasions buyers make commitments that appear mindful of vendor preparations and interactions.

Commitments represent decision points for people, and the pressure of making decisions is often the greatest when people experience more uncertainty regarding future circumstances or attempt to assess the relative merits of situations that do not lend themselves to easy comparison. This is often accompanied by the recognition that items expended in pursuit of one object may threaten one's ability to obtain other objects one might wish to possess.

The commitments implied may vary greatly in prominence or duration, for instance, but these commitment decisions also signify that for practical purposes an exchange has been completed. It means that these traders may go on with other aspects of their lives. Anticipating that they have other situations with which to deal, people often expect that they will be able to complete exchanges within certain time frames. And just as customers will attend to purchasing activity in more leisurely fashions on certain occasions, but feel rushed at other times, so do salespeople develop definitions of appropriate amounts of time to spend with the customers they encounter. It might also be noted that the same sorts of concerns appear to hold for people pursuing other kinds of commitments (e.g., funds for charities, religious conversions, marriage) within limited time frames. It is in these circumstances that closure becomes more prominent and that targets (citizens, prospects, and potential spouses) are apt to feel more pressure.

Seven closing techniques were delineated in Chapter 5. By casting these in more abstract terms, their general applicability becomes more apparent. People may use more than one of these tactics in any given encounter on a more or less simultaneous basis. Likewise, they may be invoked in sequences of various sorts as tacticians try to strike agreements with others. These strategies are as follows: asking for commitments, presuming commitments, justifying commitments, indicating pressing limitations, providing options, putting the onus on the target, and getting others to help convince targets to make the commitments desired.

As indicated in the discussion of vendors' attempts to close deals involving multiple buyers, the task of consolidating commitments becomes more complicated when agents deal with targets within groups. Under these conditions, tacticians are not only apt to encounter more mixed receptions at the outset, but are also apt to experience more and more diverse resistances as well as have greater difficulty uncovering and neutralizing target reservations. The situation becomes even more precarious for the tacticians in that it may not be easy for them to sort out preexisting relationships between the targets, or decide when, how, and to what extent to concentrate on particular members of the group, as they endeavor to shape the direction of the ensuing interactions. These complexities or ambiguities may result in greater "slippage" in tacticians' abilities to pinpoint and resolve the reservations experienced within the target group. In addition to the other means by which tacticians may endeavor to strike agreements in one on one situations, some salespeople have developed strategies geared specifically to groups of targets. If we abstract these tactics somewhat, they appear applicable to the pursuit of cooperation in other group settings. Noteworthy in this regard are the practices of soliciting favorable definitions of the objects being promoted from within the group, pitching to those thought more influential, pursuing group consensus, blending in with the group, discrediting disruptors, and creating two-person encounters.

The agreements struck may involve people signing contracts, making pledges, shaking hands, nodding heads, or making any other mutual acknowledgments. And at times, people may presume agreements until explicitly challenged by others. However, while exchanges become "objectified" by virtue of their underlying agreements, it is essential to recognize that these agreements are rooted in the symbolic interchanges between people. Thus it is these processes rather than the end products that should be of central consequence to students of social behavior.

Assessing "Failures" and Recasting Plans

Should targets follow tacticians' cues as intended and make the appropriate gestures and commitments along the way, then this last subprocess may be circumvented. However, this often does not happen, and this point alerts us to two other aspects of persuasion processes experienced by tacticians.

On a more immediate or situated basis, tacticians unable to obtain desired commitments from prospects or make other headways at particular points in time may recast their plans and pursue the very same targets immediately or at later points in time. Here, tacticians may build on all of the information gleaned in earlier interchanges, but can also go through any and all the preceding processes in an attempt to obtain agreements desired from their targets. Depending on tactician persistence and target tolerances, this interchange may be stretched out indefinitely. Only limited attention was given to when and how tacticians define targets as lost causes or otherwise not worth pursuing further, or to how salespeople recast their plans at this or that point in their encounters, but these notions are important in appreciating the ongoing adjustments that influence work entails. And this takes us back to the earlier discussed processes in this list. Far from being circular, however, we note the reflective and interactive nature of persuasion work as it takes place in actual instances.

It is also instructive to consider notions of accomplishment and pursuit as these pertain to people's more general involvements as tacticians in particular enterprises. This second sense of performance is implied by expressions such as, "You can't win them all!" or "Win some, lose some." On some occasions, tacticians will attain desired commitments with very little effort on their part, but at other times find that their successes are minimal despite seemingly high levels of preparation, interpersonal skill, and effort. Although their overall success is affected by each particular case they encounter, tacticians typically find that influence work is rampant with failure and unpredictability on an individual level.

While Chapters 2 to 5 depict the more situated aspects of selling activity, Chapters 6 to 9 alert us to a great many senses of failure (and obstacles to success) and salespeople's adjustments to these. These chapters also provide a greater sense of the context in which these situated encounters are developed and sustained.

Focusing on interchanges with troublesome customers, Chapter 6 highlights some of the more frustrating, disappointing, and distracting aspects of saleswork. On an instance-by-instance basis, most of the problems discussed herein may appear petty or inconsequential. But to the extent that these episodes divert vendors' attention from other activities (e.g., making sales, developing loyal customers), they assume a significance far beyond the inconvenience or unpleasantries they connote in any given case. From the seller's point of view it is not only a matter of exercising diplomacy lest customers be lost in either the immediate situation or the long-term, but it is also a matter of transcending these situations with sufficient composure to concentrate on other aspects of the persuasion process involving these same or other prospects. While the material presented on troublesome customers is very much oriented toward the retail sector, somewhat parallel concerns are noted in the trade sector (Prus, 1989: chap. 4) and seem likely to evidence themselves in most realms of people work.

Chapter 7 ("Developing Loyalty") denotes an attempt on the part of tacticians to establish hedges against failure by generating a more predictable and readily satisfiable clientele. From the vendors' viewpoint, the development of a large, stable clientele would facilitate all aspects of the persuasion process from formulating (preliminary) plans to confirming agreements and (even) assessing failures and recasting plans. The inference is that with a more reliable clientele, the vendors involved could concentrate on "fine-tuning" their marketing programs (and sales pitches). Ironically, however, while a repeat clientele is seen as constituting the core of most successful businesses, existing customers are typically given much less attention than one might assume, given their purported significance to the vendors involved. One may well ask to what extent the regulars in other enterprises are also taken for granted or relatively overlooked as tacticians in these other settings also find themselves engaged in the tasks of pursuing commitments from new prospects or handling disruptive cases within. In other settings, as well, we may be mindful of the problems tacticians have in tracking their current members as well as in dealing with a plurality of targets at very different stages in their careers (as participants) in those settings. In all of these instances, perceptions or anticipations of failure become noteworthy sources of concern leading to possible (and sometimes dramatic) adjustments in tacticians' plans at both generalized and particularized levels.

The "sales" phenomenon also has interesting implications for notions of failure and often represents a form of adjustive planning in itself. While some vendors explicitly and consistently use "sales" or discount themes in their promotions, "sales" also represent common ways of attempting to deal with a variety of failures vendors have encountered. Thus, as events designed to invoke action (and stock turns), "sales" may be used as a means of eliminating slowly moving stock or dated merchandise, compensating for ineffective media promotions, or overcoming seemingly inept influence work by salespeople. The anticipation is that by making greater concessions (via price reductions, bonus merchandise, and the like), and creating collective (potentially competing) interests and excitement,[13] sellers will more readily be able to strike bargains with prospective buyers. Even here, however, we are reminded of the precarious nature of influence work. These quick fixes often result in other problems for vendors, most notably more skeptical and difficult customers, greater image losses, decreased buyer loyalty, and increased pressures on the part of buyers to make more concessions in the future. Hence, even in this realm of (seeming) quick fixes, one witnesses targets and tacticians attending to various other features of the persuasion process and to subsequent assessments of performance and ongoing adjustments.

Addressing enthusiasm as a social process which entails both long-term and short-run dimensions, Chapter 9 also speaks to the matter of assessing failure and recasting plans in a rather central sense. Although enthusiasm is often relegated to the subjective or the epiphenomenal, it is pivotal to the ways in which people present themselves to others and pursue their roles as tacticians. This material is far from exhaustive, but demonstrates the reflective and intersubjective nature of people's sense of enthusiasm.

The first and most obvious affirmation of people's roles in sales comes about when customers make purchases. So long as sellers are achieving or surpassing the bottom-line expectations set by themselves or others, there is an objectified sense of achievement. Although people may become disenchanted with saleswork on a number of bases (e.g., wearying work, unpleasant exchanges, disrespectability), enthusiasm becomes more of a problem when sales are not being made at a level one expects. It is here, in the absence of these affirmations, that the question how tacticians maintain intensity of effort in the short run or continuity in the long term assumes such central significance. It is here as well that we move from a highly situated to a more temporal notion of enthusiasm even in the short run. Hence, while salespeople may derive some enthusiasm from interacting with some customers even when no sales are made, typically they are looking toward the future (e.g., getting warmed up or in the mood). This same future orientation is reflected in association with their experiences with family members and friends, company support programs, co-worker relations, and others involved in promotional activity. Definitions of enthusiasm often reflect people's past experiences. However, in the absence of immediate success, they build heavily on images or projections of the future. Viewed in these manners, enthusiasm has vital implications for the extent to which tacticians are willing to pursue the same targets over extended periods of time, or to continue to promote the same set of interests to yet other targets.

Influence as Interaction

While social scientists often address notions of influence, persuasion, or power in highly abstract terms and imbue these concepts with considerable mystique or aura, this grounded study of persuasion practices points to the necessity of examining influence as a matter of reflective (symbolic) interaction and a generic feature of human association.

Taken together, these 10 points imply a theory of influence that is not only interactive at its core, but is also fundamentally steeped in reflectivity. It is a view of persuasion which builds thoroughly on people's images, interpretations, anticipations, and ongoing adjustments. It recognizes the multiple viewpoints, varying stocks of knowledge, and diverse interests with which people may enter encounters. However, it also acknowledges people's abilities to shift conceptual frames, to accumulate and assess (and reassess) information, and to redefine their interests in the process of interacting with others. It portrays human activity as intersubjective in its base and incorporates notions of temporality, not only by virtue of its attention to process but also by acknowledging people's abilities to invoke images of the past and anticipations of the future into their emergent, interactive, constructions of the present.

As well, it recognizes the mutuality or interchangeability of the roles of target and tactician. Although we have focused heavily on the role of the vendor as tactician, consideration has also been given to the vendor as a target of buyer pursuits. Noteworthy too are notions of influence directed at the generalized versus the specific other, and the ways in which messages pitched to people at one of these levels may have implications for influence work at the other level. We also witness short-run and long-term aspects of influence work. In addition to various preparations and adjustments that tacticians may make in attempts to appeal to, and shape the behaviors of, specific others, we become appreciative of the necessity of attending to the relationships that people have to one another over time and to the implications of these images of one another for subsequent exchanges.

HUMAN BEHAVIOR AS INTERPERSONAL ACCOMPLISHMENT

Although this study draws attention to the marketplace as an arena deserving much more attention on the part of social scientists, and as a realm of inquiry from which we may be able to acquire much insight about social behavior more generally, it also raises some very fundamental questions about the ways in which social scientists have approached the study of human behavior.

By no means is this statement the first that addresses the necessity of examining human behavior as lived experience,[14] or the lack of recognition given to the ways in which human activity is accomplished.[15] Further, while this statement (along with its companion volume, Prus, 1989) provides a sustained empirical challenge to those who would reduce human behavior to a search for factors purported to cause people to act in this or that way, or be subject to these or those outcomes, it is best seen within the context of an extremely valuable literature on ethnographic research that originated at the University of Chicago (i.e., Chicago-style interactionism) in the early 1900s. The issues raised here, however, are very basic to anyone who purports to study human behavior and center on the prevailing practices of those doing research in the social sciences.

Attending to the lived experiences of people involved in marketing and sales, this project has transcended the boundaries of several disciplines, including marketing, consumer behavior, management, psychology, economics, anthropology, and sociology. I cannot claim expertise in all of these disciplines, but I have grappled with issues germane to each and have searched rather intensively across these disciplines for materials depicting the lived experiences of people accomplishing marketing and sales activities or those activities that may be viewed as parallel in processual terms. Based on my own observations and those of others who have surveyed their own disciplines,[16] I cannot help but conclude that the social sciences as a whole have not attended to the lived experiences of people as their primary subject matter.

While claiming to be scientific, empirical, and the like, and churning out mountains of quantitative data, mainstream social science tells us very little about the ways in which people *acquire perspectives* (e.g. receive, interpret, resolve, and promote worldviews and emergent definitions), *establish identities* (i.e., assign and promote as well as assess and resist definitions of self and others), *become involved in situations* (i.e., initial involvements, continuities, disinvolvements, reinvolvements), *do activities* (i.e., perform activities, do persuasion work, develop, maintain, promote and resist organizational principles, and make commitments), or *develop relationships* (i.e., prepare for encounters, approach and assess others, develop understandings, juggle multiple relationships, sever and renew bonds with others). And if mainstream social science has not been concerned about studying the ways in which people make sense of the world, develop identities and reputations in a community of others, get in and out of situations, accomplish their activities, or develop bonds and a sense of community in conjunction with others, then it doesn't appear to have contributed much to our understanding of human lived experiences.

Some will likely take exception to the explicit (and implicit) criticisms this statement makes of the study of human behavior as it is presently practiced by mainstream (quantitative, positivist) social scientists. And I would readily acknowledge that there are unlimited ways in which to approach the study of any phenomenon, including the study of human behavior. However, I would contend that any approach that ignores people's fundamental involvements in reflective interaction fails to achieve intimate familiarity with its subject matter. In these respects, the key distinction is not between the (rather arbitrary) disciplinary boundaries people have created within the social (and applied social) sciences, but between those students of human behavior who recognize the interpretive, interactive foundations of human behavior at the core of their conceptual frames and methodological procedures and those who would reduce the production of human behavior to a series of (dehumanized) factors.

It matters not whether one studies marketplaces, schoolyards, families, governments, prisons, churches, workplaces, or recreational arenas, human existence is known only through human experiences. As symbol-using creatures, we can reflect on the past and act in manners that are mindful of the future. We can create traditions and histories, and do analysis of any object of our awareness, including our own behaviors. And we can pass many aspects of our reflective enterprises on to others through physical artifacts, and written and audio-visual records, as well as through direct verbal (or other symbolic) communications. But in all cases, we do so with a sense of immediacy or nowness. And it is precisely in their neglect of the ongoing production of human action, that the social sciences have been so remiss. Hence, while it is hoped that this study will be seen as making contributions to an understanding of the marketplace activity, and that it will generate a greater appreciation of influence as a matter of interpersonal accomplishment, the further hope is that this statement will encourage the study of human behavior as it is accomplished by people living, thinking, and interacting in the here and now, regardless of the setting or the social processes under consideration.

Notes

1. The lack of sustained research on buying behavior has haunted me throughout the project. In addition to some data I was able to gather on people buying merchandise for resale or for manufacture (Prus, 1989: chap. 4) and buying promotional (media) materials (Prus, 1989: chap. 6), I have also embarked on a study of consumer behavior. While a considerable amount of the data for that project has been collected, I have not yet had an opportunity systematically to analyze that material. However, I have benefited from the present study in another respect. Insofar as those involved in the marketplace as sellers also have extensive and ongoing involvements as consumers (as does the author and others he has been able to observe), the insights gained through these multiple role occupancies were especially valuable in framing the present discussion of buyer behavior.

2. Some noteworthy material on consumption as situated activity can be found in Ray's (1961) analysis in "Abstinence Cycles and Heroin Users," Roth's (1962) depiction

of "The Treatment of Tuberculosis as a Bargaining Process," Becker's (1963) discussion of "Becoming a Marijuana User," Lesieur's (1977) account of "The Chase" (gambling involvements), Prus's (1983b) consideration of "Drinking as Activity," and Sander's (1988) portrayal of "Becoming and Being Tatooed."

3. One's ability to be an "object unto oneself" (Mead, 1934) does not imply that one will continually self-monitor or apply all incoming information to oneself. Like other aspects of situations to which people may attend, their images of self are subject to uneven consideration. It means, however, that people's images of self can be rather consequential for their eventual purchasing commitments (e.g., "It looked like a nice jacket in the window, but I didn't like the way it looked on me.").

4. On an overall basis, one may argue that influence work is more sustained, explicit, and institutionalized in sales settings than in other contexts, but even this point may be debated when one considers the efforts of union organizers (Karsh et al., 1953) or those involved in religious prosletyzing (Lofland, 1966) or the pursuits of various hustlers (Prus and Sharper, 1977; Prus and Irini, 1988). I say this mindful, as well, of the great lack of research on influence (and resistance) work in settings such as workplaces, playgrounds, and homes.

5. As implied in Gordon Allport's now classic statement, the study of interpersonal influence is the hallmark of social psychology.

> With few exceptions, social psychologists regard their discipline as an attempt to understand and explain how the thought, feeling, and behavior of individuals are influenced by the actual, imagined or implied presence of other human beings [Allport, 1965: 5].

Perhaps the field of social psychology might be better depicted as the study of interpersonal relations, but inescapably at base is the notion that people influence one another's behavior.

6. Given all the conceptual variants (and cross-derivatives) evident in this literature, it is exceedingly difficult to accurately summarize these developments. In the main, however, the factors that social psychologists have attempted to relate to interpersonal influence reflect personality typifications, motivational forces (e.g., self interest, rational calculations), attitudinal dispositions, cognitive (in)consistencies, attributional tendencies (also stereotyping, person perception, attraction), and background characteristics (e.g., age, gender, social class). For some recent valuable statements of this literature, see Tedeschi (1972), Burgoon and Bettinghaus (1980), Berger (1985), Seibold et al. (1985), and Howard et al. (1986). A very comprehensive statement, the Seibold et al. review, is exceptionally valuable in synthesizing this sprawling literature. Together, these summary statements provide further testimony to the inattention given to influence as a matter of interpersonal endeavor.

7. A somewhat related set of observations is made by Carlson (1984) who in examining past issues of the *Journal of Personality and Social Research* pointedly asks, "What's Social about Social Psychology? Where's the Person in Personality Research?" However, it is Garfinkel (1967), Blumer (1969), Harré and Secord (1972), Giddens (1976), and Gergen (1982, 1985) who most forcefully draw our attention to the neglect of interpretive (and socially constructed) processes in the social science literature.

8. In this respect, Garfinkel's (1967: 66-75) depictions of the "psychological dope" and the "cultural dope" in referring, respectively, to the psychologists' and the soci-

ologists' "person on the street" are quite apropos. One finds little recognition of people as minded, reflective, interacting, enterprising entities in what passes as mainstream social psychology. In this regard, things have not improved significantly over the past 20 years.

9. On the surface, the material rooted in statements on the basis of power (French and Raven, 1959) or in exchange theory (Homans, 1958; Thibaut and Kelly, 1959; Blau, 1964; Burgess and Huston, 1979) might seem most relevant to the study of influence practices. However, typifications of the French and Raven genre (see Marwell and Schmidt, 1977; Clark and Delia, 1976; Falbo and Peplau, 1980; Rule et al., 1985; Seibold et al., 1985: 560-583; Howard et al., 1986) are highly reductionist in nature and gloss over the ways in which people do influence work. The emphasis is on coding underlying (power) dimensions of interpersonal tactics and correlating these with other variables rather than showing when and how people actually manage their interchanges with others.

Exchange theory is vulnerable to similar criticisms, as is its more comparative focused extension, "equity theory" (Walster et al., 1973; Walster and Walster, 1978). These theories assume psychological hedonism in conjunction with a rationalistic calculus. Blau adds a functionalist dimension to his model, while equity theorists more closely approximate models of cognitive consistency. However, as noted in Chapter 1 (note 15), "exchange (et al.) theorists" do not attend to the ways in which exchanges take place(!).

10. I include herein, Simmel (1950), Mead (1934), Blumer (1969), Goffman (1959, 1961, 1963, 1967, 1971), Schutz (1971), Berger and Luckmann (1966), and Garfinkel (1967).

11. Considerable hope for an interactionist statement on influence was generated by Strauss' (1978) volume on negotiation. However, although highly instrumental in drawing attention to the "negotiated order of organizational life" (see Hall and Spencer-Hall, 1982; Kleinman, 1982; Maines, 1982; Strauss, 1982), this work extensively emphasizes "negotiation contexts" (properties entering into the course of negotiation) rather than negotiation as a process shaped by the participants. This point receives further elaboration from Couch (1979), who in reviewing this monograph also provides a general commentary on the lack of overall attention given to negotiation processes by sociologists. Two other interactionist depictions of politics and power (Hall, 1972; Luckenbill, 1979) are likewise applicable in a general sense, but they also tend to overlook more direct instances of influence.

12. This latter practice is more common among those in "the trade." In addition to seeking bids from vendors on specific types of items, these buyers may request that particular types of objects be produced within particular price ranges.

13. The closest parallels I've noted to "sales" in other settings would include such things as political campaigns, religious rallies, morals crusades, and membership drives more generally. These events also seem to be characterized by increased concessions by tacticians, and by attempts to generate collectively displayed interests, as well as a sense of urgency and excitement. These events may also be subject to tactician dilemmas regarding skepticism, image losses, and an unstable clientele.

14. See Ermarth's (1978) portrayal of the works of Wilhelm Dilthy (1833-1911).

15. Blumer's (1969) work is especially relevant here, but also see Garfinkel, 1967; Harré and Secord, 1972; Giddens, 1976; and Gergen, 1982, 1985.

16. In reviewing the literature on management, Henry Mintzberg (1973) concluded that one could spend a couple of hundred hours reading this literature and come away not knowing how management is done. In a somewhat similar vein, Bagozzi (1979), Enis

(1979), and Lutz (1979), in a set of addresses to the American Marketing Association, noted that marketers have spent a great deal of time developing models and giving advice, but they have given minimal consideration to the actualities of marketplace activities, interactions, and the relationship emerging therein. This critique is further pursued by Anderson (1983, 1986) in reference to recent developments in the philosophy of science. Drawing upon several in-house critiques (especially those of Leontief and McCloskey) of economics, Kuttner (1985) argues that this discipline has become excessively preoccupied with hypothetical, mathematical metaphors and models. Economics, these scholars contend, should not be envisioned as a science. It does not build on observation or data derived from the actual practice of economic life. An earlier collection of articles (Bell and Kristol, 1981) draws further attention to the "crises" in economics. Psychology has also been the site of some devastating internal assessment. Kock's (1981) discussion of the (psychologists') "syndrome of ameaningful thinking" represents a very striking critique of mainstream practices in this discipline, as do Elms's (1975) examination of the "crises in social psychology" and Rae Carlson's (1984) questions: "What's Social about Social Psychology? Where's the Person in Personality Research?" However, the most systematic, extensive, and devastating critiques are those developed by Harré and Secord (1972) and Gergen (1982, 1985). Mainstream sociology fares rather poorly in these respects as well. Thus Blumer's (1969) highly cogent debunking of the theoretical foundations and methodological practices of mainstream sociology and psychology has been reinforced by more phenomenologically oriented scholars (e.g., Berger and Luckmann, 1966; Garfinkel, 1967; Schutz, 1971; and Giddens, 1976), as well as by the research of Kuhn (1962) and those working in the "strong program in the sociology of science" (see Bloor, 1976, 1983; Barnes, 1977, 1982).

REFERENCES

Adler, Patricia (1985) Wheeling and Dealing. New York: Columbia University Press.

Adler, Patricia and Peter Adler (1983) "Relationships between dealers: the social organization of illicit drug transactions." Sociology and Social Research 67: 260-278.

Adler, Patricia and Peter Adler (1984) The Social Dynamics of Financial Markets. Greenwich, CT: JAI.

Adler, Peter (1981) Momentum. Beverly Hills, CA: Sage.

Adler, Peter and Patricia Adler (1978) "The role of momentum in sport." Urban Life 7: 153-176.

Allport, Gordon (1964) "The historical background of modern social psychology," pp. 3-56 in Gardner Lindzey (ed.) Handbook of Social Psychology. Reading, MA: Addison-Wesley.

Anderson, Paul (1983) "Marketing, scientific progress, and scientific method." Journal of Marketing 47 (4): 18-31.

Anderson, Paul (1986) "On method in consumer research: a critical relativist position." Journal of Consumer Research 13: 155-173.

Angrist, Shirley (1955) "Real estate salesmen." Ph.D. dissertation, McGill University, Montreal.

Angrist, Shirley (1984) "Selling real estate: reflections and persuasion," pp. 132-145 in Audrey Wipper (ed.) The Sociology of Work in Canada. Toronto: Carleton Library.

Bagozzi, Richard (1979) "Opening statement," pp. 6-10 in O. C. Ferrel, S. W. Brown, and C. W. Lane Jr. (eds.) Conceptual and Theoretical Statements in Marketing: Proceedings of the American Marketing Association Conference. Chicago: American Marketing Association.

Bain, Robert K. (1959) "The process of professionalization: life-insurance sales." Ph.D. dissertation, University of Chicago.

Barber, Bernard (1983) The Logic and Limits of Trust. New Brunswick, NJ: Rutgers University Press.

Barnes, Barry (1977) T. S. Kuhn and Social Science. London: Macmillan.

Barnes, Barry (1982). T. S. Kuhn and Social Science. London: Macmillan.

Becker, Howard S. (1963) Outsiders. New York: Free Press.

Becker, Howard S. (1982) Art Worlds. Berkeley, California: University of California Press.

Bell, Daniel and Irving Kristol (1981) The Crises in Economic Theory. New York: Basic Books.

Berger, Charles (1985) "Social power and interpersonal communication," pp. 439-499 in Mark Knapp and Gerald Miller (eds.) Handbook of Interpersonal Communication. Beverly Hills, CA: Sage.

Berger, Peter and Thomas Luckmann (1966) The Social Construction of Reality. New York: Anchor.

Bigus, Odis (1972) "The milkman and his customers." Urban Life and Culture 1: 131-165.

Bittner, Egon (1965) "The concept of organization." Social Research 32: 230-255.

Bittner, Egon (1967) "The police on skid row: a study of peace-keeping." American Sociological Review (32): 699-715.

Black, Donald J. and Albert J. Reiss (1970) "Police control of juveniles." American Sociological Review (35): 63-77.

Blau, Peter (1964) Exchange and Power in Social Life. New York: John Wiley.

Bloor, David (1976) Knowledge and Social Imagery. London: Routledge and Kegan Paul.

Bloor, David (1983) Wittgenstein: A Social Theory of Knowledge. New York: Columbia University Press.

Blumberg, Abraham (1967) "The practice of law as a confidence game: organizational cooptation of a profession." Law and Society Review 1: 15-39.

Blumer, Herbert (1969) Symbolic Interactionism. Englewood Cliffs, NJ: Prentice-Hall.

Bogdan, Robert (1972) "Learning to sell door to door: teaching as persuasion." American Behavioral Scientist 16: 55-65.

Bogdan, Robert and Steven Taylor (1975) Introduction to Qualitative Research Methods. New York: John Wiley.

Bohannan, Paul and George Dalton (1962) Markets in Africa. Chicago: Northwestern University Press.

Bonoma, Thomas V. and Gerald Zaltman (1978) "Introduction," pp. 1-30 in Thomas V. Bonoma and Gerald Zaltman (eds.) Organizational Buying Behavior. Chicago: American Merchandise Association.

Borden, Neil (1964) "The concept of marketing mix." Journal of Advertising Research 4 (2): 2-7.

Brookfield, H. C. (1969) Pacific Market-Places. Canberra: Australian National University Press.

Browne, Joy (1973) The Used-Car Game: The Sociology of the Bargain. Lexington, MA: Lexington Books.

Burgess, Robert L. and Ted L. Huston (1979) Social Exchange in Developing Relationships. New York: Academic Press.

Burgoon, Michael and Erwin Bettinghaus (1980) "Persuasive message strategies," pp. 141-169 in Michael Roloff and Gerald Miller (eds.) Persuasion: New Directions in Theory and Research. Beverly Hills, CA: Sage.

Cameron, Mary O. (1964) The Booster and the Snitch: Department Store Shoplifting. New York: Free Press.

Caplovitz, David (1963) The Poor Pay More. New York: Free Press.

Caplovitz, David (1973) Merchants of Harlem. Beverly Hills, CA: Sage.

Caplovitz, David (1974) Consumers in Trouble. New York: Free Press.

Caplovitz, David (1979) Making Ends Meet: How Families Cope with Recession and Inflation. Beverly Hills, CA: Sage.

Carey, James (1968) The College Drug Scene. Englewood Cliffs, NJ: Prentice-Hall.

Carlson, Rae (1984) "What's Social about Social Psychology? Where's the Person in Personality Research?" Journal of Personality and Social Research 47: 1304-1309.

Cavan, Sherri (1972) "The class structure of hippie culture." Urban Life 1: 211-237.

Clark, Robert E. and Larry J. Halford (1978) "Going . . . going . . . gone: preliminary observations on 'deals' at auctions." Urban Life 7: 285-307.

Clark, Ruth Ann and Jessie Delia (1976) "The development of functional persuasive skills in childhood and early adolescence." Child Development 47: 1008-1014.

Clinard, Marshall B. (1969) The Black Market: A Study of White Collar Crime. New York: Holt, Rinehart and Winston.

Clinard, Marshall B. and Peter C. Yeager (1980) Corporate Crime. New York: Free Press.

Comte, Auguste (1968). Cours de Philosophie Positive. Paris: Editions Anthropolos Paris. (Original work published 1830-1842)

Couch, Carl J. (1979) "Anselm Strauss . . . negotiations: varieties, contexts, processes, and social order." Symbolic Interaction 2: 159-163.

Cressey, Donald (1932) The Taxi-Dance Hall. Chicago: University of Chicago Press.

Cressey, Donald (1953) Other People's Money. New York: Free Press.

Cullen, Francis T. and John B. Cullen (1978) Towards a Paradigm of Labeling Theory. Lincoln: University of Nebraska Series (no. 58).

Darden, Donna, William Darden, and G. E. Keiser (1981) "The marketing of legal services." Journal of Marketing 45 (Spring): 122-134

Darrough, William (1984) "In the best interests of the child: negotiating parental cooperation for probation placement." Urban Life 13: 123-154.

Davis, Fred (1959) "The cab driver and his fare." American Journal of Sociology 65: 158-165.

Davis, Philip (1983) "Restoring the semblance of order: police strategies in the domestic disturbance." Symbolic Interaction 6: 261-278.

Ditton, James (1977) Part-Time Crime: An Ethnography of Fiddling and Pilferage. London: Macmillan.

Ditz, Gerhard (1967) "Status problems of the salesman." Michigan State University Business Topics 15 (1): 68-80.

Donovan, Frances R. (1929) The saleslady. Chicago: University of Chicago Press.

Durkheim, Emile (1950) Rules of the Sociological Method (George Catlin, ed.). Glencoe, IL: Free Press. (Original work published 1895)

Durkheim, Emile (1951) Suicide. New York: Free Press. (Original work published 1897)

Eaton, Marian (1980) "The Better Business Bureau: the voice of the people in the marketplace," pp. 233-281 in Laura Nader (ed.) No Access to the Law. New York: Academic Press.

Edgerton, Robert (1967) The Cloak of Competence: Stigma in the Lives of the Mentally Retarded. Berkeley, CA: University of California Press.

Elms, Alan (1975) "The crises of confidence in social psychology." American Psychologist 30: 967-976.

Emerson, Joan (1970) "Behavior in private places: sustaining definitions of reality in gynecological examinations," pp. 74-97 in H. P. Dreitzel (ed.) Recent Sociology No. 2. New York: Macmillan.

Emerson, Robert M. (1969) Judging Juveniles. Chicago: Aldine.

Emerson, Robert M. (1981) "On last resorts." American Journal of Sociology 87: 1-22.

Emerson, Robert M. and Sheldon L. Messinger (1977) "The micro-politics of trouble." Social Problems 25: 121-134.

Emerson, Robert M., Burke Rochford Jr., and Linda Shaw (1983) "The micro-politics of trouble in a psychiatric board and care facility." Urban Life 12: 349-367.

Enis, Ben M. (1979) "Opening statement," pp. 1-3 in O. C. Ferrel, S. W. Brown, and C. W. Lane Jr. (eds.) Conceptual and Theoretical Statements in Marketing. Proceedings of the American Marketing Association Conference. Chicago: American Marketing Association.

Ermarth, Michael (1978) Wilhelm Dilthey: The Critique of Historical Reason. Chicago: University of Chicago.

Evans, Franklin B. (1963) "Selling as a dyadic relationship: a new approach." American Behavioral Scientist 6: 76-79.

Falbo, Toni and Letita Anne Peplau (1980) "Power strategies in intimate relationships." Journal of Personality and Social Psychology 38: 618-628.

Farberman, Harvey A. (1975) "A criminogenic market structure: the automobile industry." Sociological Quarterly (16): 438-457.

Festinger, Leon (1957) A Theory of Cognitive Dissonance. Evanston, IL: Row, Peterson.

Fields, Allen B. (1984) "Slinging weed: the social organization of streetcorner marijuana sales." Urban Life 13: 247-270.

Foxall, G. R. (1974) "Sociology and the study of consumer behavior." American Journal of Economics and Sociology 33: 127-135.

French, Cecil L. (1958) "The interrelationship of norms, social structure and productivity in a competitive retail sales group." Ph.D. dissertation, Washington University, St. Louis.

French, Cecil L. (1960) "Correlates of success in retail selling." American Journal of Sociology 66: 128-134.

French, J. R. P., Jr. and Bethram H. Raven (1959) "The basis of social power," pp. 118-149 in D. Cartwright (ed.) Studies in Social Psychology. Ann Arbor: University of Michigan Press.

Frisby, David (1984) Georg Simmel. New York: Tavistock.

Garfinkel, Harold (1956) "Conditions of successful degradation ceremonies." American Journal of Sociology 61: 420-424.

Garfinkel, Harold (1963) "A conception of, and experiment with, 'trust' as a condition of stable, concerted actions," pp. 187-238 in O. J. Harvey (ed.) Motivation and Social Interaction. New York: Ronald Press.

Garfinkel, Harold (1967) Studies in Ethnomethodology. Englewood Cliffs, NJ: Prentice-Hall.

Gergen, Kenneth (1982) Toward Transformation in Social Knowledge. New York: Springer-Verlag.

Gergen, Kenneth (1985) "The social constructionist movement in modern psychology." American Psychologist 40: 266-275.

Giddens, Anthony (1976) New Rules of Sociological Method. New York: Basic Books.

Gilderbloom, John I. (1985) "Social factors affecting landlords in the determination of rent." Urban Life 14: 155-179.

Glaser, Barney (1972) The patsy and the subcontractor: a study of the expert-layman relationship. Mill Valley, CA: Sociology Press.

Glaser, Barney and Anselm Strauss (1964) "Awareness contexts and social interaction." American Sociological Review 29: 669-679.

Glaser, Barney and Anselm Strauss (1967) The Discovery of Grounded Theory: Strategies for Qualitative Research. Chicago: Aldine.

Glick, Ira O. (1957) "A social psychological study of futures marketing." Ph.D. dissertation, University of Chicago.

Glock, C. Y. and F. M. Nicosa (1964) "Uses of sociology in studying 'consumption' behavior." Journal of Marketing 28: 51-54.

Goffman, Erving (1952) "Cooling out the mark." Psychiatry 15: 451-463.

Goffman, Erving (1956) "The nature of deference and demeanor." American Anthropologist 58: 473-502.

Goffman, Erving (1959) Presentation of Self in Everyday Life. New York: Anchor.

Goffman, Erving (1961) Asylums. New York: Anchor.

Goffman, Erving (1963) Stigma. Englewood Cliffs, NJ: Prentice-Hall.

Goffman, Erving (1967) Interaction Ritual. New York: Anchor.

Goffman, Erving (1971) Relations in Public. New York: Harper.

Greenberg, David (1980) "Easy terms, hard times: complaint handling in the ghetto," pp. 379-415 in Laura Nader (ed.) No Access to the Law. New York: Academic Press.

Gross, Alfred (1959) Salesmanship. New York: Ronald.

Haas, Jack and William Shaffir (1977) "The professionalization of medical students: developing competence and a cloak of competence." Symbolic Interaction 1: 71-88.

Hall, Ian (1983) "Playing for keeps: the careers of front-line workers for handicapped persons." Master's thesis, University of Waterloo, Ontario.

Hall, Peter (1972) "A symbolic interactionist analysis of politics," pp. 35-76 in Andrew Effrat (ed.) Perspectives in Political Sociology. Indianapolis: Bobbs-Merrill.

Hall, Peter and Dee Ann Spencer-Hall (1982) "The social conditions of negotiated order." Urban Life 11: 328-349.

Hargreaves, D. H., S. K. Hester, and F. J. Mellor (1975) Deviance in the Classroom. London: Routledge and Kegan Paul.

Hammersley, Martyn and Paul Atkinson (1983) Ethnography: Principles in Practice. New York: Methuen.

Haring, Albert (1935) Retail Price-Cutting and Its Control by Manufacturers. New York: Arno Press.

Harré, Rom and Paul Secord (1972) The Explanation of Social Behavior. Oxford: Basil Blackwell.

Hayes-Bautista, David (1976) "Termination of the patient-doctor practitioner relationship." Journal of Health and Social Behavior 17: 12-21.

Henry, Stuart (1978) The Hidden Economy: The Context and Control of Borderline Crime. Oxford: Martin Robertson.

Henslin, James (1968) "Trust and the cab driver," pp. 138-155 in Marcello Truzzi (ed.) Sociology and Everyday Life. Englewood Cliffs, NJ: Prentice-Hall.

Hewitt, John P. and Randall Stokes (1975) "Disclaimers." American Sociological Review 40: 1-11.

Hindelang, Michael (1971) "Bookies and bookmaking: a descriptive analysis." Crime and Delinquency 17: 245-255.

Hoffer, Eric (1951) The True Believer. New York: Harper & Row.

Homans, George C. (1958) "Social behavior as exchange." American Journal of Sociology 63: 597-606.

Hong, Lawrence, William Darrough, and Robert Duff (1975) "The sensuous rip-off: consumer fraud turns blue." Urban Life and Culture 3: 464-470.

Horning, Paul (1970) "Blue collar theft," pp. 46-64 in Erwin Smigel and H. Lawrence Ross (eds.) Crimes Against Bureaucracy. New York: Van Nostrand.

House, J. D. (1977) Contemporary Entrepreneurs: The Sociology of Residential Real Estate Agents. Westport, CT: Greenwood Press.

Howard, Judith, Philip Blumstein, and Pepper Schwartz (1986) "Sex, power, and influence tactics in intimate relationships." Journal of Personality and Social Psychology 51: 102-109.

Howton, F. William and Bernard Rosenberg (1965) "The salesman: ideology and self-imagery in prototypic occupations." Social Research 32: 277-298.

Hughes, Everett (1979) The Growth of an Institution: The Chicago Real Estate Board. New York: Adorno Press. (Original work published 1931)

Hyman, H. H. (1960) "Reflections on reference groups." Public Opinion Quarterly 24: 383-396.

Irini, Styllianoss and Robert Prus (1982) "Doing security work: keeping order in the hotel setting." Canadian Journal of Criminology 24: 61-82.

Jacobs, Jerry (1979) " 'Burp seltzer? I never use it': an in-depth look at market research," pp. 133-142 in H. Schwartz and J. Jacobs (eds.) Qualitative Sociology.

Jacobs, Jerry (1984) The Mall: The Attempted Escape from Everyday Life. Prospect Heights, IL: Waveland Press.

Jarvis, Lance P. and James B. Wilcox (1977) "True vendor loyalty or simply repeat purchase behavior?" Industrial Marketing Management 6: 9-14.

Johnson, John (1975) Doing Field Research. New York: Free Press.

Kaiser, Susan (1985) The Social Psychology of Clothing. New York: Macmillan.

Karsh, Bernard, Joel Seidman, and D. M. Lilienthal (1953) "The union organizer and his tactics." American Journal of Sociology 59: 113-122.

Karikas, Angel and Rena Rosenwasser (1980) "Department store complaint management," pp. 283-316 in Laura Nader (ed.) No Access to the Law. New York: Academic Press.

Kasteler, Josephene, R. Kane, D. M. Olsen, and C. Thetford (1976) "Issues underlying prevalence of 'doctor-shopping' behavior." Journal of Health and Social Behavior 17: 328-339.

Katovich, Michael and Ron L. Diamond (1986) "Selling time: situated transactions in a noninstitutional environment." Sociological Quarterly 27: 253-271.

Kinsey, Barry (1985) "Congressional staff: the cultivation and maintenance of personal networks in an insecure work environment." Urban Life 13: 395-422.

Klapp, Orrin (1962) Heroes, Villains, and Fools. Englewood Cliffs, NJ: Prentice-Hall.

Klapp, Orrin (1964) Symbolic Leaders: Public Dramas and Public Men. New York: Irvington.

Klapp, Orrin (1969) Collective Search for Identity. New York: Holt, Rinehart and Winston.

Klapp, Orrin (1971) Social Types: Process, Structure and Ethos. San Diego: Aegis.

Klein, John and Arthur Montague (1977) Check Forgers. Lexington, MA: Lexington Books.

Kleinman, Sherryl (1982) "Actor's conflicting theories of negotiation: the case of a holistic health center." Urban Life 11: 312-327.

Klockars, Carl B. (1975) The Professional Fence. New York: Free Press.

Kock, Sigmund (1981) "The nature and limits of psychological knowledge. American Psychologist 36: 257-269.

Kreisberg, Louis (1956) "Occupational controls among steel distributors." American Journal of Sociology 61: 203-212.

Kuhn, Thomas S. (1962) The Structure of Scientific Revolutions. Chicago: University of Chicago Press.

Kuttner, Robert (1985) "The poverty of economics." Atlantic Monthly: February: 74-84.

LaBarre, Weston (1947) "The cultural basis of emotions and gestures." Journal of Personality 16: 49-68.

Lazarsfeld, Paul (1959) "Reflections on business." American Journal of Sociology 65: 1-31.

Lemert, Edwin (1953) "An isolation and closure theory of naive check forgery." The Journal of Criminal Law, Criminology and Police Science 44: 296-307.

Lemert, Edwin (1962) "Paranoia and the dynamics of exclusion." Sociometry 25: 2-25.

Lemert, Edwin (1972) Human Deviance, Social Problems and Social Control. Englewood Cliffs, NJ: Prentice-Hall. (Original work published 1967)

Leonard, William N. and Marvin G. Weber (1970) "Automakers and dealers: a study of criminogenic market forces." Law and Society Review 4: 407-424.

Lesieur, Henry (1977) The Chase. New York: Anchor.

Levine, Donald (1971) George Simmel: On Individuality and Social Forms. Chicago: University of Chicago Press.

Levine, Edward M. (1972) "Chicago's art world: the influence of status interests on its social and distribution systems. Urban Life and Culture 1: 293-322.

Levy, Sidney J. (1978) Marketplace Behavior. Chicago: American Marketing Association.

Lewis, David T. and Andrew J. Weigert (1985a) "Social atomism, holism, and trust." Sociological Quarterly 26: 455-471.

Lewis, David T. and Andrew J. Weigert (1985b) "The social reality of trust." Social Forces 63: 967-985.

Lilly, Robert and Richard Ball (1979) "Bidding and betting: the definitions of a good race horse and a closed community." Presented at the Mid-South Sociological Association meetings.

Lofland, John (1966) Doomsday Cult. Englewood Cliffs, NJ: Prentice-Hall.

Lofland, John and Lyn Lofland (1984) Analyzing Social Settings. Belmont, CA: Wadsworth.

Lofland, John and Rodney Stark (1965) "Becoming a world saver: a theory of conversion to a deviant perspective." American Sociological Review 30: 862-875.

Lombard, George F. (1955) Behavior in a Selling Group. Boston: Harvard University Press.

Luckenbill, David F. (1979) "Power: a conceptual framework." Symbolic Interaction 2: 97-114.

Luckenbill, David F. (1984) "Dynamics of the deviant sale." Deviant Behavior 5: 337-353.

Luhmann, Niklas (1980) Trust and Power. New York: John Wiley.

Lutz, Richard J. (1979) "Opening statement," pp. 3-6 in O. C. Ferrel, S. W. Brown, and C. W. Lane Jr. (eds.) Conceptual and Theoretical Statements in Marketing. Proceedings of the American Marketing Association Conference. Chicago: American Marketing Association.

Lyman, Stanford M. and Marvin B. Scott (1970) A Sociology of the Absurd. New York: Appleton-Century-Crofts.

Macaulay, Stewart (1963) "Non-contractual relations in business: a preliminary study." American Sociological Review 28: 55-67.

MacAndrew, C. and R. B. Edgerton (1969) Drunken Comportment. Chicago: Aldine.

McCall, Michal M. (1977) "Art without a market: creating artistic value in a provincial art world." Symbolic Interaction 1: 32-43.

MacLean, Annie M. (1899) "Two weeks in department stores." American Journal of Sociology 4: 721-741.

Maines, David (1982) "In search of mesostructure." Urban Life 11: 267-279.

Maisel, Robert (1974) "The flea market as an action scene." Urban Life and Culture 2: 488-505.

Maisel, Roberta (1986) "The antique trade." Master's thesis, University of California, Berkeley.

Malinowski, Bronislaw (1987) The Sexual Life of Savages in North Western Melanasia. New York: Methuen. (Original work published 1929)

Maslow, A. H. (1954) Motivation and Personality. New York: Harper.

Martin, Wilfred (1975) "Teacher-pupil interactions: a negotiation perspective." Canadian Review of Sociology and Anthropology 12: 529-540.

Marwell, G. and D. R. Schmidt (1967) "Dimensions of compliance-gaining behavior." Sociometry 30: 350-364.

Matza, David (1964) Delinquency and Drift. New York: John Wiley.

Matza, David (1969) Becoming Deviant. Englewood Cliffs, NJ: Prentice-Hall.

Maurer, David (1940) The Big Con. Indianapolis: Bobbs-Merrill.

Mead, George H. (1934) Mind, Self and Society. Chicago: University of Chicago Press.

Mead, Margaret (1950) Sex and Temperament. New York: Mentor.

Merton, Robert K. (1957) Social Structure and Social Theory. New York: Free Press.

Mill, John S. (1986) A System of Logic. Charlottsville, VA: Ibis. (Original work published 1843)

Miller, Gale (1983) "Holding clients responsible: the micro-politics of trouble in a work incentive program." Social Problems: 31: 139-151.

Miller, Stephen J. (1964) "The social base of sales behavior." Social Problems 2: 15-24.

Mintzberg, Henry (1973) The Nature of Organizational Work. New York: Harper & Row.

Nicosa, Francesco M. and Robert N. Mayer (1976) "Toward a sociology of consumption." Journal of Consumer Research 3 (September): 65-75.

Olmstead, A. D. (1986) "What will you give me? Buying and selling at public auctions." Presented at the conference, Ethnographic Research: an Interactionist/Interpretative Inquiry. Waterloo, Ontario.

Peven, Dorothy (1968) "The use of religious revival techniques to indoctrinate personnel: the home-party organizations." Sociological Quarterly 9: 97-106.

Peyrot, Mark (1985) "Coerced voluntarism: the micropolitics of drug treatment." Urban Life 13: 343-366.

Phillips, L. W. and L. W. Stern (1977) "Limit pricing theory as a basis for anti-merger policy." Journal of Marketing 41: 91-97.

Pinch, Trevor and Colin Clark (1986) "The hard sell: patter merchandising and the strategic (re)production and local management of economic reasoning in the sales routine of market pitchers." Sociology 20: 169-191.

Pope, Daniel (1983) The Making of Modern Advertising. New York: Basic Books.

Prus, Robert (1975a) "Labeling theory: a reconceptualization and a propositional statement on typing." Sociological Focus 8: 79-96.

Prus, Robert (1975b) "Resisting designations: an extension of attribution theory into a negotiated context." Sociological Inquiry 45: 3-14.

Prus, Robert (1976) "Religious recruitment and the management of dissonance: a sociological perspective." Sociological Inquiry 46: 127-134.

Prus, Robert (1978) "From barrooms to bedrooms: towards a theory of interpersonal violence," pp. 51-73 in M. A. B. Gammon (ed.) Violence in Canada. Toronto: Methuen.

Prus, Robert (1983a) "Deviance as community activity: putting 'labeling theory' in perspective," pp. 108-145 in Thomas Fleming and Livy Visano (eds.) Deviant Designations. Toronto: Butterworth.

Prus, Robert (1983b) "Drinking as activity: an interactionist analysis." Journal of Studies on Alcohol 44 (3): 460-475.

Prus, Robert (1987) "Generic social processes: maximizing conceptual development in ethnographic research." Journal of Contemporary Ethnography 16: 250-293.

Prus, Robert (1989) Pursuing Customers: An Ethnography of Marketing Activities. Newbury Park, CA: Sage.

Prus, Robert and Augie Fleras (1987) "Corporate site location as social process: towards an interactionist analysis of industry location activity." Presented at the Canadian Sociology and Anthropology Association meetings, Hamilton, Ontario.

Prus, Robert and Wendy Frisby (1989) "Persuasion as practical accomplishment: tactical maneuverings at home party plans." In Helena Znanecki Lopata (ed.) Current Research on Occupations and Professions. Greenwich, CT: Jai.

Prus, Robert and Styllianoss Irini (1988) Hookers, Rounders, and Desk Clerks: The Social Organization of the Hotel Community. Salem, WI: Sheffield. (Original work published 1980)

Prus, Robert and C. R. D. Sharper (1977) Road Hustler: The Career Contingencies of Professional Card and Dice Hustlers. Lexington, MA: Lexington Books.

Prus, Robert and John Stratton (1976) "Parole revocation related decision making: private typings and official designations." Federal Probation 40: 48-53.

Quinney, Richard (1963) "Occupational structure and criminal behavior: prescription violation by retail pharmacists." Social Problems 11: 179-185.

Ralph, Jack (1950) "Junk business and the junk peddler." Master's thesis, University of Chicago.

Rasmussen, Paul and Laurence Kuhn (1967) "The new masseuse: play for pay." Urban Life 5: 271-292.

Ray, Marsh B. (1961) "Abstinence cycles and heroin addicts." Social Problems 9: 132-140.

Reingen, Peter H. and Arch G. Woodside (1981) Buyer-Seller Interactions. Chicago: American Marketing Association.

Rock, Paul (1973) Making People Pay. London: Routledge and Kegan Paul.

Ross, H. Lawrence (1970) Settled Out of Court. Chicago: Aldine.

Roth, Julius (1962) "The treatment of tuberculosis as a bargaining process," pp. 575-588 in A. Rose (ed.) Human Behavior and Social Process. Boston: Houghton-Mifflin.

Roth, Julius (1965) "Who's complaining? The inhibitions of the dissatisfied customer." Transaction 2 (5): 12-16.

Roth, Paul (1987) Meaning and Methods in the Social Sciences. Ithaca, NY: Cornell University Press.

Rubinstein, Jonathon (1973) City Police. New York: Ballantine.

Rule, Brendan Gail, Gay Bisanz, and Melinda Kohn (1985) "Anatomy of a persuasion schema: targets, goals, and strategies." Journal of Personality and Social Psychology 48: 1127-1140.

Sanders, Clint (1985) "Tattoo consumption: risk and regret in the purchase of a socially marginal service," pp. 17-22 in E. Hirshman and M. Holbrook (eds.) Advances in Consumer Research.

Sanders, Clint (1988) "Marks of mischief: the process of becoming and experience of being a tatooed person." Journal of Contemporary Ethnography 16: 395-432.

Sanders, William [ed.] (1976) Sociologist as Detective. New York: Praeger.

Schudson, Michael (1984) Advertising: The Uneasy Persuasion. New York: Basic Books.

Schutz, Alfred (1971) Collected Papers I: The Problem of Social Reality. The Hague: Martinus Nijhoff.

Seibold, David, James Cantrill, and Renee Meyers (1985) "Communication and interpersonal influence," pp. 551-611 in Mark Knapp and Gerald Miller (eds.) Handbook of Interpersonal Communication. Beverly Hills, CA: Sage.

Shaw, Clifford (1930) The Jack-Roller. Chicago: University of Chicago Press.

Shaffir, William, Robert Stebbins and Alan Turowitz (1980) Fieldwork Experience. New York: St. Martins.

Shibutani, Tamotsu (1961) Society and Personality. Englewood Cliffs, NJ: Prentice-Hall.

Simmel, Georg (1900) "A chapter in the philosophy of money." American Journal of Sociology 5: 577-603.

Simmel, Georg (1950) The Sociology of Georg Simmel (Kurt Wolff, ed. and trans.). New York: Macmillan.

Simmel, Georg (1978) The Philosophy of Money (Tom Bottomore and David Frisby, trans.). London: Routledge and Kegan Paul. (Original work published 1900)

Simmons, J. L. (1969) Deviants. Berkeley, California: Glendessary press.

Siporin, Max (1967) "Bankrupt debtors and their families." Social Work 12: 51-62.

Sklar, Fred (1973) "Franchises, independence, and action: a study in the sociology of entrepreneurship." Ph.D. dissertation, University of California, Davis.

Sklar, Fred (1977) "Franchises and independence: interorganizational power relations in a contractual context." Urban Life 6: 33-52.

Skolnick, Jerome (1966) Justice Without Trial. New York: John Wiley.

Smith, Charles W. (1981) The Mind of the Market: A Study of Stock Market Philosophies, Their Uses, and Their Implications. Totowa, NJ: Rowman and Littlefield.

Smith, Charles W. (1986) "The auction: a sociological process!?!" Presented at the conference, Ethnographic Research: an Interactionist/Interpretative Inquiry, Waterloo, Ontario.

Smith, Robert H. T. (1978) Periodic Markets, Hawkers, and Traders in Africa, Asia, and Latin America. Vancouver: Centre for Transportation Studies.

Sofer, Cyril (1965) "Buying and selling: a study in the sociology of distribution." Sociological Review 13: 183-209.

Spencer, Jack (1983) "Accounts, attitudes, and solutions: probation officer-defendant negotiations of subjective orientations." Social Problems 30: 570-581.

Stanley, D. T. and Marjorie Girth (1971) Bankruptcy: Problems, Process, Reform. Washington, DC: Brookings Institution.

Stebbins, Robert (1975) Teachers and Meanings. Leiden: Brill.

Stets-Kealey, Jan (1984) "Selling as an act of control." Presented at the North Central Sociological Association meetings.

Stone, Gregory P. (1954) "City shoppers and urban identification: observations of the social psychology of city life." American Journal of Sociology 60: 36-45.

Strauss, Anselm (1978) Negotiations: Variations, Contexts, Process and Social Order. San Francisco: Jossey-Bass.

Strauss, Anselm (1982) "Interorganizational negotiation." Urban Life 11: 350-356.

Strauss, George (1962) "Tactics of lateral relationship: the purchasing agents." Administrative Science Quarterly 7: 161-186.

Strauss, George (1964) "Work-flow frictions, interfunctional rivalry, and professionalism: a case study of purchasing agents." Human Organization 23: 137-149.

Strodtbeck, Fred and Marvin Sussman (1956) "Of time, the city, and the one-year guarantee: the relations between watch owners and repairers." American Journal of Sociology 61: 602-609.

Sutherland, Edwin (1937) The Professional Thief. Chicago: University of Chicago Press.

Sutherland, Edwin (1949) White Collar Crime. New York: Dryden.

Swan, John (1986) "Trust building by medical salespeople." Presented at the conference, Ethnographic Research: An Interactionist Inquiry, Waterloo, Ontario.

Tedeschi, James T. (1972) The Social Influence Process. Chicago: Aldine.

Thibaut, John W. and Harold H. Kelly (1959) The Social Psychology of Groups. New York: John Wiley.

Tucker, W. T. (1964) The Social Context of Economic Behavior. New York: Holt, Rinehart and Winston.

Tyson, Eugene (1966) Tested Collection Methods and Procedures. New York: McGraw-Hill.

Valdez, Alvaredo (1984) "Chicano used car dealers." Urban Life 13: 229-246.

Veblen, Thorstein (1953) The Theory of the Leisure Class. New York: Mentor. (Original work published 1899)

Velarde, Albert J. and Mark Warlick (1973) "Massage parlors: the sensuality business." Society 11: 63-74.

Wallendorf, Melanie (1978) "Social roles in a marketing context." American Behavioral Scientist 21: 571-582.

Walsh, Marilyn E. (1977) The Fence. Westport, CT: Greenwood Press.

Walster, Elaine, E. Berscheid, and G. W. Walster (1973) "New directions in equity research." Journal of Personality and Social Psychology 25: 151-171.

Walster, Elaine and G. W. Walster (1978) Equity: Theory and Research. Boston: Allyn-Bacon.

Warner, W. L. and P. S. Lunt (1941) The Social Life of a Modern Community. New Haven, CT: Yale University Press.

Warner, W. L., M. Meeker, and K. Eels (1949) Social Class in America: A Manual of Procedures for the Measurement of Social Status. Chicago: Science Research Associates.

Warren, Carol A. B. (1983) "The politics of trouble in an adolescent psychiatric hospital." Urban Life 12: 327-348.

Wasson, Chester and David McConaughy (1968) Buying Behavior and Marketing Decisions. New York: Appleton-Century-Crofts.

Weber, Max (1947) The Theory of Social and Economic Organization (A. M. Henderson and Talcott Parsons, trans.), New York: Free Press.

Winch, Peter (1958) The Idea of Social Science. New York: Humanities.

Weigand, Robert E. (1980) " 'Buying in' to market control." Harvard Business Review 58 (November-December): 141-149.

Wiseman, Jacqueline (1979) "Close encounters of the quasi-primary kind: sociability in a second-hand clothing store." Urban Life 8: 23-51.

Zakuta, Leo (1970) "On filthy lucre," pp. 260-270 in Tamotsu Shibutani (ed.) Human Nature and Collective Behavior: Papers in Honor of Herbert Blumer. Englewood Cliffs, NJ: Prentice-Hall.

Zurcher, Louis (1982) "The staging of emotion: a dramaturgical analysis." Symbolic Interaction 5: 1-22.

Zweigman, Arthur (1977) "The decision to report employee thieves: a study of designating discretion." Master's thesis, University of Windsor, Windsor, Ontario.

ABOUT THE AUTHOR

Viewing humans as living, thinking, interacting beings, Robert Prus (a sociologist at the University of Waterloo) has been extensively involved in developing a social science attuned to people's lived experiences. He has examined a number of social worlds, finding that an intimate understanding of each realm of human enterprise helps to better understand people's interchanges in other settings.

Following some graduate school work on revocation decision making by parole officers, Dr. Prus embarked on a study of the recruitment practices of clergymen. The insights gained from these inquiries were to lay some of the foundations for the present study, as was an examination of the careers and pursuits of some confidence operators (*Road Hustler,* Prus and Sharper, 1977). The conceptual materials developed in this study, along with the tutelage in fieldwork technique provided by C. R. D. Sharper, readily lent themselves to a detailed investigation of the careers, activities, and entanglements of the people whose lives intersect in the bar/hotel community (*Hookers, Rounders and Desk Clerks,* Prus and Irini, 1988). It was from this study that much of the substantive and conceptual impetus for the present inquiry into the marketplace developed.

The present volume is one of two books generated by a larger study of marketing and sales activity. *Pursuing Customers* concentrates on vendor preparations and the pursuit of customer contact, while *Making Sales* is very much a study of influence as interpersonal accomplishment. Dr. Prus hopes to extend the knowledge of both the marketplace and the interpretive analysis of social action by incorporating insights and concepts developed from the present study into ongoing research on consumer behavior and the corporate site-selection process.